BASIC Stamp Syntax and Reference Manual
Version 2.2

Warranty

Parallax Inc. warrants its products against defects in materials and workmanship for a period of 90 days from receipt of product. If you discover a defect, Parallax Inc. will, at its option, repair or replace the merchandise, or refund the purchase price. Before returning the product to Parallax, call for a Return Merchandise Authorization (RMA) number. Write the RMA number on the outside of the box used to return the merchandise to Parallax. Please enclose the following along with the returned merchandise: your name, telephone number, shipping address, and a description of the problem. Parallax will return your product or its replacement using the same shipping method used to ship the product to Parallax.

14-Day Money-Back Guarantee

If, within 14 days of having received your product, you find that it does not suit your needs, you may return it for a full refund. Parallax Inc. will refund the purchase price of the product, excluding shipping/handling costs. This guarantee is void if the product has been altered or damaged. See the Warranty section above for instructions on returning a product to Parallax.

Copyrights and Trademarks

This documentation is copyright 1994-2005 by Parallax Inc. By downloading or obtaining a printed copy of this documentation or software you agree that it is to be used exclusively with Parallax products. Any other uses are not permitted and may represent a violation of Parallax copyrights, legally punishable according to Federal copyright or intellectual property laws. Any duplication of this documentation for commercial uses is expressly prohibited by Parallax Inc. Duplication for educational use is permitted, subject to the following Conditions of Duplication: Parallax Inc. grants the user a conditional right to download, duplicate, and distribute this text without Parallax's permission. This right is based on the following conditions: the text, or any portion thereof, may not be duplicated for commercial use; it may be duplicated only for educational purposes when used solely in conjunction with Parallax products, and the user may recover from the student only the cost of duplication.

This text is available in printed format from Parallax Inc. Because we print the text in volume, the consumer price is often less than typical retail duplication charges.

BASIC Stamp, Stamps in Class, Board of Education, Boe-Bot, Todder, SumoBot, and SX-Key are registered trademarks of Parallax, Inc. If you decide to use registered trademarks of Parallax Inc. on your web page or in printed material, you must state that "(registered trademark) is a registered trademark of Parallax Inc." upon the first appearance of the trademark name in each printed document or web page. HomeWork Board, Parallax, and the Parallax logo are trademarks of Parallax Inc. If you decide to use trademarks of Parallax Inc. on your web page or in printed material, you must state that "(trademark) is a trademark of Parallax Inc.", "upon the first appearance of the trademark name in each printed document or web page. Other brand and product names are trademarks or registered trademarks of their respective holders.

ISBN #1-928982-32-8

Errata

While great effort is made to assure the accuracy of our texts, errors may still exist. If you find an error, please let us know by sending an email to editor@parallax.com. We continually strive to improve all of our educational materials and documentation, and frequently revise our texts. Occasionally, an errata sheet with a list of known errors and corrections for a given text will be posted to our web site, www.parallax.com. Please check the individual product page's free downloads for an errata file.

Disclaimer of Liability

Parallax Inc. is not responsible for special, incidental, or consequential damages resulting from any breach of warranty, or under any legal theory, including lost profits, downtime, goodwill, damage to or replacement of equipment or property, or any costs of recovering, reprogramming, or reproducing any data stored in or used with Parallax products. Parallax Inc. is also not responsible for any personal damage, including that to life and health, resulting from use of any of our products. You take full responsibility for your BASIC Stamp application, no matter how life-threatening it may be.

Access Parallax via Internet

We maintain very a active web site for your convenience. These may be used to obtain software, communicate with members of Parallax, and communicate with other customers. Access information is shown below:

Web:	http://www.parallax.com
General e-mail:	info@parallax.com
Tech. e-mail:	support@parallax.com

Internet BASIC Stamp Discussion List

We maintain active web-based discussion forums for people interested in Parallax products. These lists are accessible from www.parallax.com via the Support → Discussion Forums menu. These are the forums that we operate from our web site:

- <u>BASIC Stamps</u> – This list is widely utilized by engineers, hobbyists and students who share their BASIC Stamp projects and ask questions.
- <u>Stamps in Class®</u> – Created for educators and students, subscribers discuss the use of the Stamps in Class curriculum in their courses. The list provides an opportunity for both students and educators to ask questions and get answers.
- <u>Parallax Educators</u> –Exclusively for educators and those who contribute to the development of Stamps in Class. Parallax created this group to obtain feedback on our curricula and to provide a forum for educators to develop and obtain Teacher's Guides.
- <u>Translators</u> – The purpose of this list is to provide a conduit between Parallax and those who translate our documentation to languages other than English. Parallax provides editable Word documents to our translating partners and attempts to time the translations to coordinate with our publications.
- <u>Robotics</u> – Designed exclusively for Parallax robots, this forum is intended to be an open dialogue for a robotics enthusiasts. Topics include assembly, source code, expansion, and manual updates. The Boe-Bot®, Toddler®, SumoBot®, HexCrawler and QuadCrawler robots are discussed here.
- <u>SX Microcontrollers and SX-Key</u> – Discussion of programming the SX microcontroller with Parallax assembly language SX – Key® tools and 3rd party BASIC and C compilers.
- <u>Javelin Stamp</u> – Discussion of application and design using the Javelin Stamp, a Parallax module that is programmed using a subset of Sun Microsystems' Java® programming language.

Supported Hardware, Firmware and Software

This manual is valid with the following software and firmware versions:

BASIC Stamp Model	Firmware	Windows Interface
BASIC Stamp 1	1.4	2.2
BASIC Stamp 2	1.0	2.2
BASIC Stamp 2e	1.1	2.2
BASIC Stamp 2sx	1.1	2.2
BASIC Stamp 2p	1.4	2.2
BASIC Stamp 2pe	1.1	2.2
BASIC Stamp 2px	1.0	2.2

The information herein will usually apply to newer versions but may not apply to older versions. New software can be obtained free on web site (www.parallax.com). If you have any questions about what you need to upgrade your product, please contact Parallax.

Credits

Authorship and Editorial Review Team: Jeff Martin, Jon Williams, Ken Gracey, Aristides Alvarez, and Stephanie Lindsay; Cover Art: Jen Jacobs; Technical Graphics, Rich Allred; with many thanks to everyone at Parallax Inc.

Contents

Contents

Contents

Contents

Thank you for purchasing a Parallax BASIC Stamp® microcontroller module. We have done our best to produce several full-featured, easy to use development systems for BASIC Stamp microcontrollers. Depending on the Starter Kit you purchased, your BASIC Stamp model, development board and other contents will vary.

This manual is written for the latest available BASIC Stamp modules and software as of February 2005. As the product-line evolves, new information may become available. It is always recommended to visit the Parallax web site, www.parallax.com, for the latest information.

This manual is intended to be a complete reference manual to the architecture and command structure of the various BASIC Stamp models. This manual is not meant to teach BASIC programming or electrical design; though a person can learn a lot by paying close attention to the details in this book.

If you have never programmed in the BASIC language or are unfamiliar with electronics, it would be best to locate one or more of the books listed on the following page for assistance. All are available, either to order or to download, from www.parallax.com.

Books available in Adobe's PDF format are published for free download on the Parallax web site or on the CD-ROM which ships with our different Starter Kits. Books available in print may be purchased directly from Parallax or other distributors.

In addition, there are hundreds of great examples available on the Parallax CD and web site (www.parallax.com). Also, Nuts & Volts Magazine (www.nutsvolts.com / 1-800-783-4624) is a national electronic hobbyist's magazine that features monthly articles featuring BASIC Stamp applications. This is an excellent resource for beginners and experts alike!

Preface

Book	Part #	Author and Publisher	Availability	
			PDF	In Print
What's a Microcontroller?	28123	Andy Lindsay; Parallax Inc.; ISBN 1-928982-02-6	Yes	Yes
Robotics with the Boe-Bot	28125	Andy Lindsay; Parallax Inc.; ISBN 1-928982-03-4	Yes	Yes
IR Remote for the Boe-Bot	70016	Andy Lindsay; Parallax Inc.; ISBN 1-928982-31-X	Yes	Yes
Basic Analog and Digital	28129	Andy Lindsay; Parallax Inc.; ISBN 1-928982-04-2	Yes	Yes
Applied Sensors	28127	Tracy Allen, PhD.; Parallax Inc.; ISBN 1-928982-21-2	Yes	Yes
Understanding Signals	28119 (With Full Kit)	Doug Pientak; Parallax Inc.; ISBN 1-928982-23-9	Yes	Yes
Industrial Control	27341	Marty Hebel / Will Devenport; Parallax Inc.; ISBN 1-928982-08-5	Yes	Yes
Elements of Digital Logic	70008	John Barrowman; Parallax Inc.; ISBN 1-928982-20-4	Yes	Yes
The Microcontroller Application Cookbook Volumes 1 and 2	Vol. 1&2: 28113 Vol. 2: 28112	Matt Gilliland; Woodglen Press; ISBN 0-616-11552-7 and 0-972-01590-6	No	Yes
Al's "World Famous" Stamp Project of the Month Anthology	70013	Al Williams; Parallax Inc.; ISBN 1-928982-25-5	Portions	Yes
The Nuts and Volts of BASIC Stamps Volumes 1, 2, 3, 4, and 5	Vol. 4: 70010 Vol. 5: 70015	Jon Williams, Scott Edwards and Lon Glazner; Parallax, Inc.; ISBN 1-928982-10-7, 1-928982-11-5, 1-928982-17-4, 1-928982-24-7 and 1-928982-30-1	Yes (all)	Yes (Vol 4 and Vol 5)
StampWorks	27220	Jon Williams; Parallax, Inc.; ISBN 1-928982-07-7	Yes	Yes
Stamp 2 Communication and Control Projects	70004	Thomas Petruzzellis; McGraw-Hill; ISBN 0-071411-97-6	No	Yes
Programming and Customizing the BASIC Stamp Computer	27956	Scott Edwards; McGraw-Hill; ISBN 0-071371-92-3	No	Yes
BASIC Stamp 2p	70001	Claus Kuehnel and Klaus Zahnert; Parallax, Inc.; ISBN 1-928982-19-0	Yes	No

Welcome to the wonderful world of BASIC Stamp® microntrollers. BASIC Stamp microcontrollers have been in use by engineers and hobbyists since we first introduced them in 1992. As of November 2004, Parallax customers have put well over three million BASIC Stamp modules into use. Over this 12-year period, the BASIC Stamp line of controllers has evolved into six models and many physical package types, explained below.

General Operation Theory

BASIC Stamp modules are microcontrollers (tiny computers) that are designed for use in a wide array of applications. Many projects that require an embedded system with some level of intelligence can use a BASIC Stamp module as the controller.

Each BASIC Stamp comes with a BASIC Interpreter chip, internal memory (RAM and EEPROM), a 5-volt regulator, a number of general-purpose I/O pins (TTL-level, 0-5 volts), and a set of built-in commands for math and I/O pin operations. BASIC Stamp modules are capable of running a few thousand instructions per second and are programmed with a simplified, but customized form of the BASIC programming language, called PBASIC.

PBASIC Language

We developed PBASIC specifically for the BASIC Stamp as a simple, easy to learn language that is also well suited for this architecture, and highly optimized for embedded control. It includes many of the instructions featured in other forms of BASIC (GOTO, FOR...NEXT, IF...THEN...ELSE) as well as some specialized instructions (SERIN, PWM, BUTTON, COUNT and DTMFOUT). This manual includes an extensive section devoted to each of the available instructions.

Hardware

At the time of this writing, there are currently seven models of the BASIC Stamp; the BS1, BS2, BS2e, BS2sx, BS2p, BS2pe, and the BS2px. The tables below are provided to easily compare their specifications, followed by diagrams that detail the various package types of these modules. Schematics for the SIP/DIP packages of all models can be found in Appendix D.

Introduction to the BASIC Stamp

BASIC Stamp Model Comparison Table

Products	BS1	BS2	BS2e
Environment	0° - 70° C (32° - 158° F) **	0° - 70° C (32° - 158° F) **	0° - 70° C (32° - 158° F) **
Microcontroller	Microchip PIC16C56a	Microchip PIC16C57c	Ubicom SX28AC
Processor Speed	4 MHz	20 MHz	20 MHz
Program Execution Speed	~2,000 instructions/sec.	~4,000 instructions/sec	~4,000 instructions/sec
RAM Size	16 Bytes (2 I/O, 14 Variable)	32 Bytes (6 I/O, 26 Variable)	32 Bytes (6 I/O, 26 Variable)
Scratch PadRam	N/A	N/A	64 Bytes
EEPROM (Program) Size	256 Bytes, ~80 instructions	2K Bytes, ~500 instructions	8 x 2K Bytes, ~4,000 inst
Number of I/O Pins	8	16 + 2 Dedicated Serial	16 + 2 Dedicated Serial
Voltage Requirements	5 - 15 vdc	5 - 15 vdc	5 - 12 vdc
Current Draw@ 5 volts	1 mA Run, 25 µA Sleep	3 mA Run, 50 µA Sleep	25 mA Run, 200 µA Sleep
Source/Sink Current per I/O	20 mA / 25 mA	20 mA / 25 mA	30 mA / 30 mA
Source/Sink Current per unit	40 mA / 50 mA	40 mA / 50 mA per 8 I/O pins	60 mA / 60 mA per 8 I/O pins
PBASIC Commands*	32	42	45
PC Interface	Serial (w/BS1 Serial Adapter)	Serial (9600 baud)	Serial (9600 baud)
Windows Text Editor Version	Stampw.exe (v2.1 and up)	Stampw.exe (v1.04 and up)	Stampw.exe (v1.096 and up)

* PBASIC Command count totals include PBASIC 2.5 commands on all BS2 models.
** See below for industrial rated module information.

Industrial-Rated BASIC Stamp Modules

Some BASIC Stamp models come in Industrial-rated versions, with an environmental temperature tolerance range of -40°C to +85°C . Contact the Parallax Sales Team directly for the latest information regarding industrial-rated product availability and specifications.

BS2sx	BS2p24	BS2p40	BS2pe	BS2px
0° - 70° C (32° - 158° F) **	0° - 70° C (32° - 158° F) **	0° - 70° C (32° - 158° F) **	0° - 70° C (32° - 158° F) **	0° - 70° C (32° - 158° F) **
Ubicom SX28AC	Ubicom SX48AC	Ubicom SX48AC	Ubicom SX48AC	Ubicom SX48AC
50 MHz	20 MHz Turbo	20 MHz Turbo	8 MHz Turbo	32 MHz Turbo
~10,000 instructions/sec.	~12,000 instructions/sec.	~12,000 instructions/sec.	~6000 instructions/sec.	~19,000 instructions/sec.
32 Bytes (6 I/O, 26 Variable)	38 Bytes (12 I/O, 26 Variable)	38 Bytes (12 I/O, 26 Variable)	38 Bytes (12 I/O, 26 Variable)	38 Bytes (12 I/O, 26 Variable)
64 Bytes	128 Bytes	128 Bytes	128 Bytes	128 Bytes
8 x 2K Bytes, ~4,000 inst.	8 x 2K Bytes, ~4,000 inst.	8 x 2K Bytes, ~4,000 inst.	16 x 2K Bytes (16 K for source)	8 x 2K Bytes, ~4,000 inst.
16 + 2 Dedicated Serial	16 + 2 Dedicated Serial	32 + 2 Dedicated Serial	16 + 2 Dedicated Serial	16 + 2 Dedicated Serial
5 - 12 vdc	5 - 12 vdc	5 - 12 vdc	5 - 12 vdc	5 - 12 vdc
60 mA Run, 500 µA Sleep	40 mA Run, 350 µA Sleep	40 mA Run, 350 µA Sleep	15 mA Run, 150 µA Sleep	55 mA Run, 450 µA Sleep
30 mA / 30 mA	30 mA / 30 mA	30 mA / 30 mA	30 mA / 30 mA	30 mA / 30 mA
60 mA / 60 mA per 8 I/O pins	60 mA / 60 mA per 8 I/O pins	60 mA /60 mA per 8 I/O pins	60 mA / 60 mA per 8 I/O pins	60 mA / 60 mA per 8 I/O pins
45	61	61	61	63
Serial (9600 baud)	Serial (9600 baud)	Serial (9600 baud)	Serial (9600 baud)	Serial (19200 baud)
Stampw.exe (v1.091 and up)	Stampw.exe (v1.1 and up)	Stampw.exe (v1.1 and up)	Stampw.exe (v1.33 and up)	Stampw.exe (v2.2 and up)

Phone: (916) 624-8333
Toll free in the US or Canada: 1-888-512-1024
Email: sales@parallax.com

BASIC Stamp 1

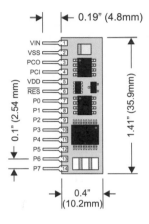

Figure 1.1: BASIC Stamp 1 (Rev B) (Stock# BS1-IC).

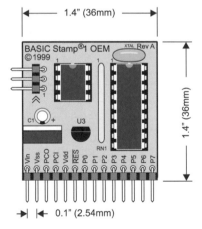

Figure 1.2: BASIC Stamp 1 OEM (Rev. A) (Stock# 27295).

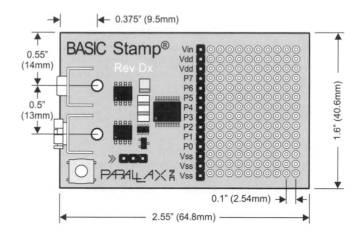

Figure 1.3: BASIC Stamp 1 (Rev Dx) (Stock# 27100).

The BASIC Stamp 1 is available several physical packages. The BS1-IC (Figure 1.1) uses surface mount components to fit in a small 14-pin SIP package. The preassembled BASIC Stamp 1 OEM (Figure 1.2) features an easier-to-trace layout meant to aid customers who wish to integrate the BASIC Stamp 1 circuit directly into their design (as a lower-cost solution). The BASIC Stamp 1 Rev. Dx (simply called the Rev. Dx), see Figure 1.3, includes a prototyping area suitable for soldering electronic components. These three packages are functionally equivalent, except that the Rev. Dx does not have an available reset pin.

In addition to the packages shown, there are prototyping boards available that feature a surface mounted BS1 and programming cable connector. Please check www.parallax.com → Products → Development Boards for product descriptions.

Pin	Name	Description
1	VIN	Unregulated power in: accepts 5.5 - 15 VDC (6-40 VDC on BS1-IC rev. b), which is then internally regulated to 5 volts. May be left unconnected if 5 volts is applied to the VDD (+5V) pin.
2	VSS	System ground: connects to BS1 Serial Adapter ground for programming.
3	PCO	PC Out: 4800 baud serial output (TTL level) to PC.
4	PCI	PC In: 4800 baud serial input (TTL level) from PC.
5	VDD	5-volt DC input/output: (Also called +5V) if an unregulated voltage is applied to the VIN pin, then this pin will output 5 volts. If no voltage is applied to the VIN pin, then a regulated voltage between 4.5V and 5.5V should be applied to this pin.
6	RES	Reset input/output: goes low when power supply is less than approximately 4.2 volts, causing the BASIC Stamp to reset. Can be driven low to force a reset. This pin is internally pulled high and may be left disconnected if not needed. Do not drive high.
7-14	P0-P7	General-purpose I/O pins: each can sink 25 mA and source 20 mA. However, the total of all pins should not exceed 50 mA (sink) and 40 mA (source).

Table 1.1: BASIC Stamp 1 Pin Descriptions.

See the "BASIC Stamp Programming Connections" section on page 27 for more information on the required programming connections between the PC and the BASIC Stamp.

BASIC Stamp 2

Figure 1.4: BASIC Stamp 2 (Rev. G) (Stock# BS2-IC).

Figure 1.5: BASIC Stamp 2 OEM (Rev. A2) (Stock# 27290 assembled, or #27291 in kit form).

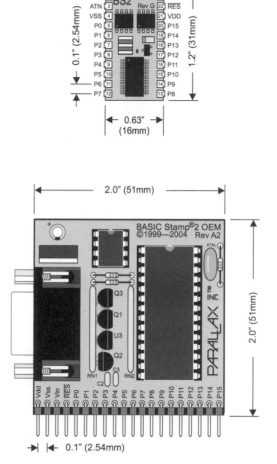

The BASIC Stamp 2 is available in several physical packages. The BS2-IC (Figure 1.4) uses surface mount components to fit in a small 24-pin DIP package. The BASIC Stamp 2 OEM (Figure 1.5) features an easier-to-trace layout meant to aid customers who wish to integrate the BASIC Stamp 2 circuit directly into their design (as a lower-cost solution). The BASIC

Introduction to the BASIC Stamp

Stamp 2 OEM is available in either an assembled form or a kit form. These three packages are functionally equivalent.

In addition to the dual-inline and OEM packages, there are prototyping boards available that feature a surface mounted BS2. Please check www.parallax.com → Products → Development Boards for product descriptions.

Pin	Name	Description
1	SOUT	Serial Out: connects to PC serial port RX pin (DB9 pin 2 / DB25 pin 3) for programming.
2	SIN	Serial In: connects to PC serial port TX pin (DB9 pin 3 / DB25 pin 2) for programming.
3	ATN	Attention: connects to PC serial port DTR pin (DB9 pin 4 / DB25 pin 20) for programming.
4	VSS	System ground: (same as pin 23) connects to PC serial port GND pin (DB9 pin 5 / DB25 pin 7) for programming.
5-20	P0-P15	General-purpose I/O pins: each can sink 25 mA and source 20 mA. However, the total of all pins should not exceed 50 mA (sink) and 40 mA (source) if using the internal 5-volt regulator. The total per 8-pin groups (P0 – P7 or P8 – 15) should not exceed 50 mA (sink) and 40 mA (source) if using an external 5-volt regulator.
21	VDD	5-volt DC input/output: if an unregulated voltage is applied to the VIN pin, then this pin will output 5 volts. If no voltage is applied to the VIN pin, then a regulated voltage between 4.5V and 5.5V should be applied to this pin.
22	RES	Reset input/output: goes low when power supply is less than approximately 4.2 volts, causing the BASIC Stamp to reset. Can be driven low to force a reset. This pin is internally pulled high and may be left disconnected if not needed. Do not drive high.
23	VSS	System ground: (same as pin 4) connects to power supply's ground (GND) terminal.
24	VIN	Unregulated power in: accepts 5.5 - 15 VDC (6-40 VDC on BS2-IC Rev. e, f, and g), which is then internally regulated to 5 volts. Must be left unconnected if 5 volts is applied to the VDD (+5V) pin.

Table 1.2: BASIC Stamp 2 Pin Descriptions.

See the "BASIC Stamp Programming Connections" section on page 27 for more information on the required programming connections between the PC and the BASIC Stamp.

BASIC Stamp 2e

Figure 1.6: BASIC Stamp 2e (Rev. B) (Stock# BS2E-IC).

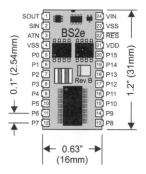

The BASIC Stamp 2e is available in the above 24-pin DIP package.

Table 1.3: BASIC Stamp 2e Pin Descriptions.

Pin	Name	Description
1	SOUT	Serial Out: connects to PC serial port RX pin (DB9 pin 2 / DB25 pin 3) for programming.
2	SIN	Serial In: connects to PC serial port TX pin (DB9 pin 3 / DB25 pin 2) for programming.
3	ATN	Attention: connects to PC serial port DTR pin (DB9 pin 4 / DB25 pin 20) for programming.
4	VSS	System ground: (same as pin 23) connects to PC serial port GND pin (DB9 pin 5 / DB25 pin 7) for programming.
5-20	P0-P15	General-purpose I/O pins: each can source and sink 30 mA. However, the total of all pins should not exceed 75 mA (source or sink) if using the internal 5-volt regulator. The total per 8-pin groups (P0 – P7 or P8 – 15) should not exceed 100 mA (source or sink) if using an external 5-volt regulator.
21	VDD	5-volt DC input/output: if an unregulated voltage is applied to the VIN pin, then this pin will output 5 volts. If no voltage is applied to the VIN pin, then a regulated voltage between 4.5V and 5.5V should be applied to this pin.
22	RES	Reset input/output: goes low when power supply is less than approximately 4.2 volts, causing the BASIC Stamp to reset. Can be driven low to force a reset. This pin is internally pulled high and may be left disconnected if not needed. Do not drive high.
23	VSS	System ground: (same as pin 4) connects to power supply's ground (GND) terminal.
24	VIN	Unregulated power in: accepts 5.5 - 12 VDC (7.5 recommended), which is then internally regulated to 5 volts. Must be left unconnected if 5 volts is applied to the VDD (+5V) pin.

See the "BASIC Stamp Programming Connections" section on page 27 for more information on the required programming connections between the PC and the BASIC Stamp.

BASIC Stamp 2sx

Figure 1.7: BASIC Stamp 2sx
(Rev. E) (Stock# BS2sx-IC)

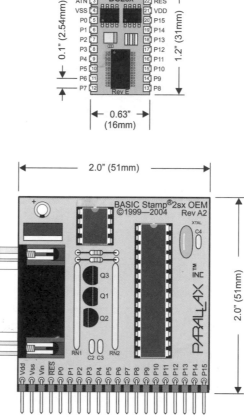

Figure 1.8: BASIC Stamp 2sx OEM
(Rev. A2) (Stock# 27294)

The BASIC Stamp 2sx is available in the above two physical packages. The BS2sx-IC (Figure 1.7) uses surface mount components to fit in a small 24-pin DIP package. The preassembled BASIC Stamp 2sx OEM (Figure 1.8) features an easier-to-trace layout meant to aid customers who wish to integrate the BASIC Stamp 2sx circuit directly into their design (as a lower-cost solution). The BASIC Stamp 2sx OEM is available in assembled form only.

Pin	Name	Description
1	SOUT	Serial Out: connects to PC serial port RX pin (DB9 pin 2 / DB25 pin 3) for programming.
2	SIN	Serial In: connects to PC serial port TX pin (DB9 pin 3 / DB25 pin 2) for programming.
3	ATN	Attention: connects to PC serial port DTR pin (DB9 pin 4 / DB25 pin 20) for programming.
4	VSS	System ground: (same as pin 23) connects to PC serial port GND pin (DB9 pin 5 / DB25 pin 7) for programming.
5-20	P0-P15	General-purpose I/O pins: each can source and sink 30 mA. However, the total of all pins should not exceed 75 mA (source or sink) if using the internal 5-volt regulator. The total per 8-pin groups (P0 – P7 or P8 – 15) should not exceed 100 mA (source or sink) if using an external 5-volt regulator.
21	VDD	5-volt DC input/output: if an unregulated voltage is applied to the VIN pin, then this pin will output 5 volts. If no voltage is applied to the VIN pin, then a regulated voltage between 4.5V and 5.5V should be applied to this pin.
22	RES	Reset input/output: goes low when power supply is less than approximately 4.2 volts, causing the BASIC Stamp to reset. Can be driven low to force a reset. This pin is internally pulled high and may be left disconnected if not needed. Do not drive high.
23	VSS	System ground: (same as pin 4) connects to power supply's ground (GND) terminal.
24	VIN	Unregulated power in: accepts 5.5 - 12 VDC (7.5 recommended), which is then internally regulated to 5 volts. Must be left unconnected if 5 volts is applied to the VDD (+5V) pin.

Table 1.4: BASIC Stamp 2sx Pin Descriptions

See the "BASIC Stamp Programming Connections" section on page 27 for more information on the required programming connections between the PC and the BASIC Stamp.

BASIC Stamp 2p

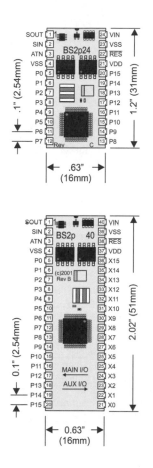

Figure 1.9: BASIC Stamp 2p24 (Rev. C) (Stock# BS2p24-IC)

This module is identical in function to the BS2p40-IC, except that it has 16 I/O pins.

Figure 1.10: BASIC Stamp 2p40 (Rev. B) (Stock# BS2p40-IC)

This module is identical in function to the BS2p24-IC, except that it has 32 I/O pins.

The BASIC Stamp 2p is available in the above two physical packages. Both packages use surface mount components to fit in a small package. The BS2p24-IC (Figure 1.9) is a 24-pin DIP package. The BS2p40-IC (Figure 1.10) is a 40-pin DIP package. Both packages are functionally equivalent accept that the BS2p40 has 32 I/O pins instead of 16.

Pin	Name	Description
1	SOUT	Serial Out: connects to PC serial port RX pin (DB9 pin 2 / DB25 pin 3) for programming.
2	SIN	Serial In: connects to PC serial port TX pin (DB9 pin 3 / DB25 pin 2) for programming.
3	ATN	Attention: connects to PC serial port DTR pin (DB9 pin 4 / DB25 pin 20) for programming.
4	VSS	System ground: (same as pin 23 on BS2p24, or pin 39 on BS2p40) connects to PC serial port GND pin (DB9 pin 5 / DB25 pin 7) for programming.
5-20	P0-P15	General-purpose I/O pins: each can source and sink 30 mA. However, the total of all pins (including X0-X15, if using the BS2p40) should not exceed 75 mA (source or sink) if using the internal 5-volt regulator. The total per 8-pin groups (P0 – P7, P8 – 15, X0 – X7 or X8 – X15) should not exceed 100 mA (source or sink) if using an external 5-volt regulator.
{21-36}	X0-X15	(BS2p40 Only!) Auxiliary Bank of General-purpose I/O pins: each can source and sink 30 mA. However, the total of all pins (including P0 – P15) should not exceed 75 mA (source or sink) if using the internal 5-volt regulator. The total per 8-pin groups (P0 – P7, P8 – 15, X0 – X7 or X8 – X15) should not exceed 100 mA (source or sink) if using an external 5-volt regulator.
21 {37}	VDD	5-volt DC input/output: if an unregulated voltage is applied to the VIN pin, then this pin will output 5 volts. If no voltage is applied to the VIN pin, then a regulated voltage between 4.5V and 5.5V should be applied to this pin.
22 {38}	RES	Reset input/output: goes low when power supply is less than approximately 4.2 volts, causing the BASIC Stamp to reset. Can be driven low to force a reset. This pin is internally pulled high and may be left disconnected if not needed. Do not drive high.
23 {39}	VSS	System ground: (same as pin 4) connects to power supply's ground (GND) terminal.
24 {40}	VIN	Unregulated power in: accepts 5.5 - 12 VDC (7.5 recommended), which is then internally regulated to 5 volts. Must be left unconnected if 5 volts is applied to the VDD (+5V) pin.

Table 1.5: BASIC Stamp 2p Pin Connections

See the "BASIC Stamp Programming Connections" section on page 27 for more information on the required programming connections between the PC and the BASIC Stamp.

Basic Stamp 2pe

Figure 1.11: BASIC Stamp 2pe
(Rev. B) (Stock# BS2pe-IC)

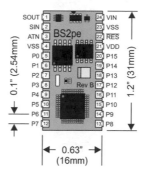

The BASIC Stamp 2pe is available in the above 24-pin DIP physical package.

Table 1.6: BASIC Stamp 2pe Pin Descriptions.

Pin	Name	Description
1	SOUT	Serial Out: connects to PC serial port RX pin (DB9 pin 2 / DB25 pin 3) for programming.
2	SIN	Serial In: connects to PC serial port TX pin (DB9 pin 3 / DB25 pin 2) for programming.
3	ATN	Attention: connects to PC serial port DTR pin (DB9 pin 4 / DB25 pin 20) for programming.
4	VSS	System ground: (same as pin 23), connects to PC serial port GND pin (DB9 pin 5 / DB25 pin 7) for programming.
5-20	P0-P15	General-purpose I/O pins: each can source and sink 30 mA. However, the total of all pins should not exceed 75 mA (source or sink) if using the internal 5-volt regulator. The total per 8-pin groups P0 – P7 or P8 – 15 should not exceed 100 mA (source or sink) if using an external 5-volt regulator.
21	VDD	5-volt DC input/output: if an unregulated voltage is applied to the VIN pin, then this pin will output 5 volts. If no voltage is applied to the VIN pin, then a regulated voltage between 4.5V and 5.5V should be applied to this pin.
22	RES	Reset input/output: goes low when power supply is less than approximately 4.2 volts, causing the BASIC Stamp to reset. Can be driven low to force a reset. This pin is internally pulled high and may be left disconnected if not needed. Do not drive high.
23	VSS	System ground: (same as pin 4) connects to power supply's ground (GND) terminal.
24	VIN	Unregulated power in: accepts 5.5 - 12 VDC (7.5 recommended), which is then internally regulated to 5 volts. Must be left unconnected if 5 volts is applied to the VDD (+5V) pin.

Introduction to the BASIC Stamp

See the "BASIC Stamp Programming Connections" section on page 27 for more information on the required programming connections between the PC and the BASIC Stamp.

Basic Stamp 2px

Figure 1.12: BASIC Stamp 2px (Rev. A) (Stock# BS2px-IC)

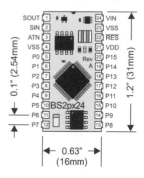

The BASIC Stamp 2px is available in the above 24-pin DIP physical package.

Table 1.7: BASIC Stamp 2px Pin Descriptions.

Pin	Name	Description
1	SOUT	Serial Out: connects to PC serial port RX pin (DB9 pin 2 / DB25 pin 3) for programming.
2	SIN	Serial In: connects to PC serial port TX pin (DB9 pin 3 / DB25 pin 2) for programming.
3	ATN	Attention: connects to PC serial port DTR pin (DB9 pin 4 / DB25 pin 20) for programming.
4	VSS	System ground: (same as pin 23), connects to PC serial port GND pin (DB9 pin 5 / DB25 pin 7) for programming.
5-20	P0-P15	General-purpose I/O pins: each can source and sink 30 mA. However, the total of all pins should not exceed 75 mA (source or sink) if using the internal 5-volt regulator. The total per 8-pin groups P0 – P7 or P8 – 15 should not exceed 100 mA (source or sink) if using an external 5-volt regulator.
21	VDD	5-volt DC input/output: if an unregulated voltage is applied to the VIN pin, then this pin will output 5 volts. If no voltage is applied to the VIN pin, then a regulated voltage between 4.5V and 5.5V should be applied to this pin.
22	RES	Reset input/output: goes low when power supply is less than approximately 4.2 volts, causing the BASIC Stamp to reset. Can be driven low to force a reset. This pin is internally pulled high and may be left disconnected if not needed. Do not drive high.
23	VSS	System ground: (same as pin 4) connects to power supply's ground (GND) terminal.
24	VIN	Unregulated power in: accepts 5.5 - 12 VDC (7.5 recommended), which is then internally regulated to 5 volts. Must be left unconnected if 5 volts is applied to the VDD (+5V) pin.

Introduction to the BASIC Stamp

See the "BASIC Stamp Programming Connections" section on page 27 for more information on the required programming connections between the PC and the BASIC Stamp.

Guidelines and Precautions

When using the BASIC Stamp, or any IC chip, please follow the guidelines below.

1. **Be alert to static sensitive devices and static-prone situations.**
    a. The BASIC Stamp, like other IC's, can be damaged by static discharge that commonly occurs touching grounded surfaces or other conductors. Environmental conditions (humidity changes, wind, static prone surfaces, etc) play a major role in the presence of random static charges. It is always recommended to use grounding straps and anti-static or static dissipative mats when handling devices like the BASIC Stamp. If the items above are not available, be sure to touch a grounded surface after you have approached the work area and before you handle static sensitive devices.
2. **Verify that all power is off before connecting/disconnecting.**
    a. If power is connected to the BASIC Stamp or any device it is connected to while inserting or removing it from a circuit, damage to the BASIC Stamp or circuit could result.
3. **Verify BASIC Stamp orientation before connection to development boards and other circuits.**
    a. Like other IC's, the BASIC Stamp should be inserted in a specific orientation in relation to the development board or circuit. Powering the circuit with an IC connected backwards will likely damage the IC and/or other components in the circuit. Most IC's have some form of a "pin 1 indicator" as do most IC sockets. This indicator usually takes the form of a dot, a half-circle, or the number 1 placed at or near pin 1 of the device.

        The BS1-IC has a "1" and a half-circle indicator on the backside of the module. Additionally, Figure 1.1 above indicates the pin numbering and labels.

        All BS2 series modules have a half-circle indicator on the topside of the module (see Figure 1.13). This indicates that pin number one is the first pin counterclockwise from the notch. The socket that accepts this 24-pin module also has a half-circle or notch on one end, indicating the correct orientation. See Figure 1.14 for other examples.

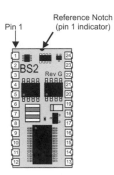

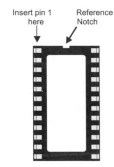

Figure 1.13: Pin 1 Indicators BS2-IC shown in the correct orientation in relation to a 24-pin socket.

Note: The Half-Circle indicator is also known as a Reference Notch

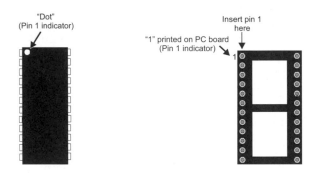

Figure 1.14: Additional Examples of Pin 1 Indicators (chip and socket shown in the correct orientation in relation to each other)

BASIC Stamp Programming Connections

We suggest using a Parallax development board and cable for programming BASIC Stamp modules. When these items are not available, you may create your own board by duplicating the following diagrams with your own circuits and cables.

Be very careful to follow these diagrams closely; it is quite common for programming problems with the BASIC Stamp to be a result of a poorly made custom cable or programming connections on your applications board. With the programming connections for all the BS2 models, it is possible to reverse a couple of wires and still get positive results using some of the "connection" tests our Tech. Support team tries and yet you still will not be able to communicate with the BASIC Stamp. It is vital that you check your connections with a meter and verify the pin numbering to avoid problems like this.

Figure 1.15: BS1 Programming Connections with BS1 Serial Adapter

Note: Though it is not shown, power must be connected to the BS1 to program it.

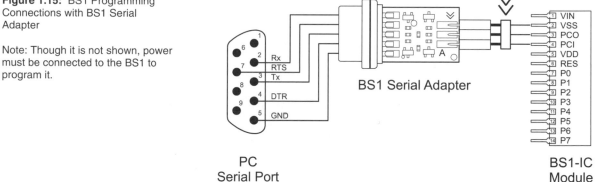

PC
Serial Port

BS1 Serial Adapter

BS1-IC
Module

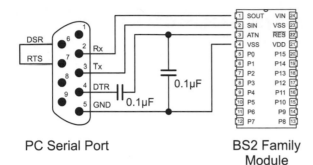

PC Serial Port

BS2 Family
Module

Figure 1.16: Programming and Run-time Communication Connections for all BS2 models.

Note: Though it is not shown, power must be connected to the BASIC Stamp to program it.

Also, the programming connections are the same for the BS2p40.

Quick Start Introduction

This chapter is a quick start guide to connecting the BASIC Stamp to the PC and programming it. Without even knowing how the BASIC Stamp functions, you should be able to complete the exercise below. This exercise assumes you have a BASIC Stamp and an appropriate development board. For the latest Parallax development board selection and documentation, go to www.parallax.com → Products → Development Boards. For a more detailed introduction to the BASIC Stamp Editor software, see Chapter 3.

Equipment Needed

- BASIC Stamp module
- Compatible carrier board and programming cable
- Power supply (wall mount or battery) rated for your carrier board
- PC running Windows® 2000/XP, with
  o Quantity of RAM recommended for the OS
  o 3 MB of hard drive space
  o CD-ROM drive or Internet access
  o Available port compatible with your carrier board and cable (serial or USB)

Connecting and Downloading

1) If the BASIC Stamp isn't already plugged into your development board, insert it into the socket. Refer to Figure 1.13 and Figure 1.14 on page 26 to make sure that you orient it correctly. For a complete listing of Parallax development boards for the various BASIC Stamp modules, go to www.parallax.com and look for Development Boards on the Products menu.

2) If you are using a Parallax development board, follow the directions that came with it to connect the board to the appropriate port in your computer. Figure 2.1 below shows the proper sequence for setting up with a BS1 and a BS1 Carrier Board. Figure 2.2 on page 31 shows the proper sequence to connect any BS2. Note: if you are using your own

development board or a breadboard, carefully follow the
Programming Connections guidelines on page 27 before proceeding.

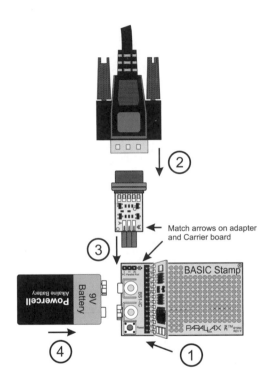

Match arrows on adapter
and Carrier board

Figure 2.1: BS1-IC, BS1 Carrier
Board, and BS1 Serial Adapter

1) Insert the BASIC Stamp module
into its socket, being careful to
orient it properly.

2) Connect the 9-pin female end of
the serial cable to an available serial
port on your computer, then attach
the male end to the BS1 Serial
Adapter, Note: you cannot us a null
modem cable.

3) Plug the BS1 Serial Adapter into
the programming header on the BS1
Carrier Board.

4) Plug a 9 volt battery into the 9
VDC battery clip.

Figure 2.2: BS2-IC and Board of Education

1) Insert the BASIC Stamp module into its socket, being careful to orient it properly.

2) Connect the 9-pin female end of the serial cable to an available serial port on your computer, and then connect the male end to the Board of Education. Note: you cannot use a null modem cable.

3) Plug in the 6-9 V 300mA center-positive power supply into the barrel jack.

OR

4) Plug a 9 volt battery into the 9 VDC battery clip.

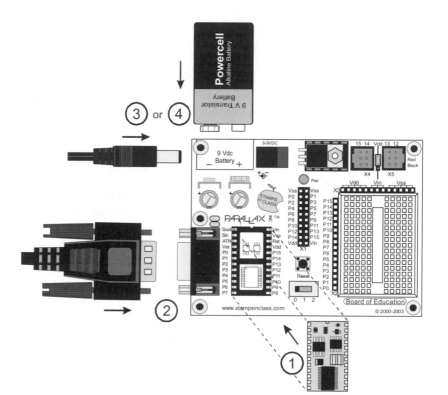

3) Install and run the BASIC Stamp Editor software.

    a) If using the Parallax CD, go to the Software → BASIC Stamp → Windows section to locate the latest version. Click the Install button and follow the prompts to install and run.

    b) If using the Parallax website, go to www.parallax.com → Downloads → Basic Stamp Software and look in the Software for Windows section for the latest version. Click the Download icon and follow the prompts to install and run.

    c) Test your PC's connection to the BASIC Stamp by selecting Run → Identify from the menu bar, as shown in Figure 2.3. If the BASIC Stamp module is not found, check your power and cable connections and retry.

Figure 2.3: Test your PC connection to the BASIC Stamp.

Select Run → Identify

Verify that the BASIC Stamp was detected on one of the COM ports.

4) Enter a $STAMP Directive into the Editor window by clicking on the toolbar icon for the BASIC Stamp module you are using. (Hold the cursor over the icons for flyover help labels.) The example below shows the Stamp Directive that would be inserted for the BS2.

```
' {$STAMP BS2}
```

5) Enter a $PBASIC Directive into the Editor window with the toolbar icon. For a BS1, you must use PBASIC 1.0. All BS2 series modules can use PBASIC 2.0 or 2.5. The command set differences between PBASIC 2.0 and 2.5 are covered in Chapter 5.

Figure 2.4: Entering the $STAMP and $PBASIC directives from the toolbar

The examples shown would be used for programming a BS2 module in PBASIC 2.5

Click on the icon that corresponds to your BASIC Stamp model to automatically place the $STAMP directive in your program.

Click on the icon for the PBASIC language version that is compatible with your BASIC Stamp model.

You should now see both a $STAMP directive and $PBASIC directive on your PC screen:

```
' {$STAMP BS2}
' {$PBASIC 2.5}
```

a) Note: These directives may be typed in from the keyboard, but failure to type this line properly may cause the editor to fail to recognize your BASIC Stamp during the next step.

6) Type the line DEBUG "Hello World!" below the compiler directives:

```
' {$STAMP BS2}
' {$PBASIC 2.5}
DEBUG "Hello World!"
```

7) Download this program into the BASIC Stamp. You may select Run → Run from the menu bar, press CTRL-R from the keyboard, or click on the Run ▶ icon on the toolbar.

Figure 2.5: To run your program, you may use the task bar menu or the Run icon.

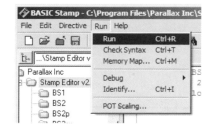

Selecting Run → Run

Using the Run toolbar icon

a) If the program is typed correctly, a progress bar window should appear (perhaps very briefly) showing the download progress. Then a Debug Terminal window should appear and display "Hello World!"

Figure 2.6: Debug Terminal displaying program output

b) If there is a syntax error in the program, the editor will highlight the text in question and display an error message. Review the error, fix the code and then try downloading again.

c) If the error reported a connection problem with the BASIC Stamp, make sure the first line of code indicates the proper module name and verify the programming cable connections, module orientation (in the socket) and that it is properly powered, then try downloading again.

8) Congratulations! You've just written and downloaded your first BASIC Stamp program! The "Hello World!" text that appeared on the screen was sent from the BASIC Stamp, back up the programming cable, to the PC.

Introducing the BASIC Stamp Editor

This section describes the BASIC Stamp Editor for Windows version 2.2. This software supports all 7 BASIC Stamp modules available as of February 2005, and all 3 versions of the PBASIC programming language, PBASIC 1.0, PBASIC 2.0, and PBASIC 2.5.

The Programming Environment

The BASIC Stamp Windows Editor, shown in Figure 3.1, was designed to be easy to use and mostly intuitive. Those that are familiar with standard Windows software should feel comfortable using the BASIC Stamp Windows Editor.

Figure 3.1: BASIC Stamp Windows Editor.

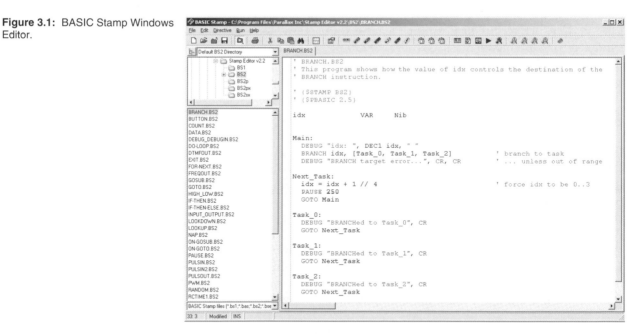

THE EDITOR WINDOW.

The editor window consists of the main edit pane with an integrated explorer panel to its left, as shown above.

THE MAIN EDIT PANE.

The main edit pane can be used to view and modify up to 16 different source code files at once. Each source code file that is loaded into the editor will have its own tab at the top of the page labeled with the name of the file, as seen in Figure 3.2. The full file path of the currently displayed source code appears in the title bar. Source code that has never been saved to disk will default to "Untitled#"; where # is an automatically generated number. A user can switch between source code files by simply pointing and clicking on a file's tab or by pressing Ctrl+Tab or Ctrl+Shift+Tab while the main edit pane is active.

Figure 3.2: Example Editor Tabs. Shown with 6 separate files open; Title Bar shows current code's file path.

The status of the active source code is indicated in the status bar below the main edit pane and integrated explorer panel. The status bar contains information such as cursor position, file save status, download status and syntax error/download messages. The example in Figure 3.3 indicates that the source code tokenized successfully.

Figure 3.3: Status Bar beneath the Main Edit Pane.

Each editor pane can be individually split into two views of the same source code. This can be done via the Split button on the toolbar, pressing Ctrl-L, or clicking and dragging the top or bottom border of the editor pane with the mouse.

SPLIT WINDOW VIEW.

Once split, the top and bottom edit controls allow viewing of different areas of the same source code; this can be handy when needing to keep variable declarations or a particular routine in view while modifying a related section of code elsewhere. Note that the Split button and Ctrl+L shortcut act like a toggle function, splitting or un-splitting the edit pane.

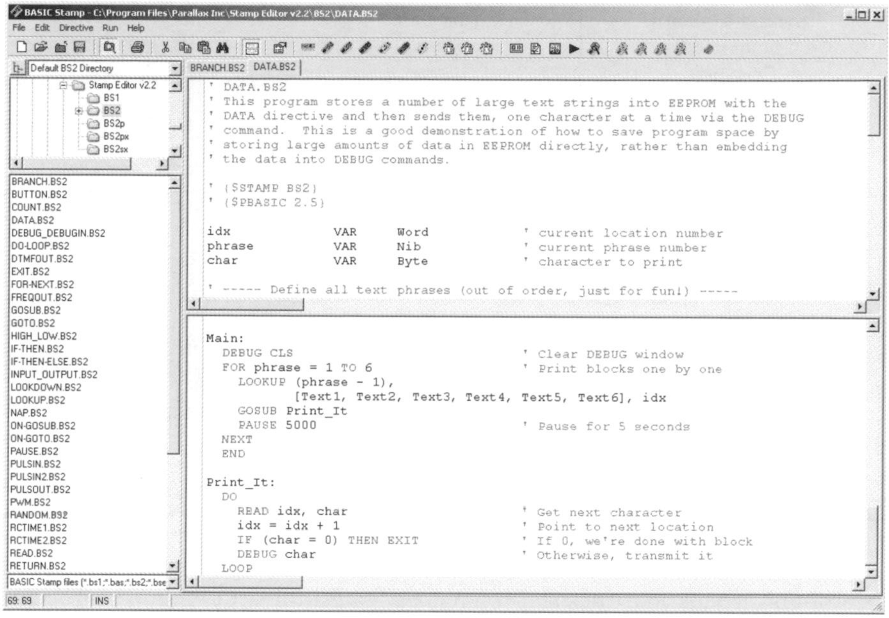

Figure 3.4: The Split Edit Pane Feature displaying the beginning and end of a long program at the same time.

SYNTAX HIGHLIGHTING.

NOTE: a complete list of reserved words can be found in Appendix B.

Within the edit pane, BASIC Stamp source code files are displayed with syntax highlighting. Syntax Highlighting applies designated colors and character case (upper, lower, capitalized) to reserved words in the PBASIC language . This happens automatically as you type. Table 3.1 shows the default syntax highlighting settings for each syntax element.

If you copy and paste a program into a blank edit pane, select Run → Syntax Check or click on the toolbar checkmark icon to activate the syntax highlighting in that file. The syntax highlighting settings can be changed or customized via the Preferences → Editor Appearance tab; for details see the Setting Preferences section which begins on page 55. Source code can be printed to paper with the active syntax highlighting (and in color if using a color printer).

Using the BASIC Stamp Editor

Syntax Element	Text Color	Character Case
Command	Blue	Upper Case
Comment	Green	No Change
Constant -Binary	Default	No Change
Constant - Decimal	Default	No Change
Constant - Hexadecimal	Default	No Change
Constant – Predefined	Purple	Upper case
Constant – String	Red	No Change
Operators	Default	Upper case
Declaration	Default	Upper Case
Directive, Conditional Compile	Gray(Bold)	Upper case
Directive, Editor	Teal (Bold)	Upper case
Directive, Target module	Teal (Bold)	Upper case
Input/Output Formatter	Navy	Upper case
Selection	White on Navy	No change
Search match	Lime on black	No change
Variable modifier	Default	Upper case
Variable – predefined	Purple	Upper case
Variable, type	Default	Capitalize

Table 3.1: Syntax Highlighting Defaults for the PBASIC Scheme.

NOTE: The default edit pane has a white background with black characters.

Automatic line numbers can be enabled or disabled via the "Show Line Numbers" checkbox on the Preferences → Editor Appearance tab. Line numbers, when enabled, appear in a gutter (the gray area on the left of the edit pane as shown in Figure 3.5). When printing, the line numbers may be included if desired.

AUTOMATIC LINE NUMBERING.

```
NAP.BS2 | PULSOUT.BS2 | PAUSE.BS2 |
    1 ' PAUSE.BS2
    2 ' This program demonstrates the PAUSE command's time delays. Once a second,
    3 ' the program will put the message, "Paused..." on the screen.
    4
①   5 ' {$STAMP BS2}
    6
    7 Main:
    8   DEBUG "Paused...", CR
②   9   PAUSE 1000
   10   GOTO Main
```

Figure 3.5: Automatic Line Numbering appears in the gutter to the left of the edit pane. Yellow Bookmarks are visible on lines 5 and 9.

Bookmarks can be enabled or disabled via the "Show Bookmarks" checkbox on the Preferences → Editor Appearance tab. The bookmarks appear in the gutter as small numbered icons, providing a way to mark lines or sections of code that you need to navigate to quickly or repeatedly. You can define up to nine bookmarks by clicking on the gutter where you want one placed, or by pressing Ctrl+B when the cursor is on the desired line. You can instantly navigate to any defined bookmark by pressing Ctrl+(#) (where # can be the 1 through 9 keys) or by selecting Go To

BOOKMARKS.

Bookmark from either the Edit menu or from the shortcut menu (right-click) in the edit pane.

EDITING YOUR CODE.

You can navigate through and edit your code in the edit pane with keyboard shortcuts, most of which will be familiar to Windows users.

Table 3.2: Keyboard Shortcuts for Editing and Navigation Functions.

Editing and Navigation Functions	
Shortcut Key	**Function**
Ctrl+A	Select all text in current source code
Ctrl+B	Set or clear bookmark on current source code line
Ctrl+(#)	Go to bookmark #, where # can be 1 through 9
Ctrl+C	Copy selected text to the clipboard
Ctrl+F	Find or replace text
Ctrl+L	Split or un-split edit pane
Ctrl+N	Insert line
Ctrl+V	Paste text from clipboard to selected area
Ctrl+X	Cut selected text to the clipboard
Ctrl+Y	Delete current line of code
Ctrl+Shift+Y	Delete from cursor to end of current line
Ctrl+Z	Undo last action (unlimited)
Ctrl+Shift+Z	Redo last action (unlimited)
Tab	Indent block (Inserts tab or space characters)
Shift+Tab	Outdent block (Deletes tab or space characters)
F3	Find text again
F4	Replace current found selection
Ctrl+F4	Perform replace and find next
Ctrl+Home	Jump to top of file
Ctrl+End	Jump to end of file
Ctrl+PageUp	Jump to top of screen
Ctrl+PageDown	Jump to bottom of screen
Ctrl+CursorUp	Move source view up one line without moving cursor
Ctrl+CursorDown	Move source view down one line without moving cursor
F5	Open Preferences window

Some editing functions, specifically Cut, Copy, Paste, and Find/Replace, can also be accessed from the edit pane's shortcut menu (by right-clicking in the edit pane).

THE FIND/REPLACE WINDOW.

The Find/Replace window allows you to set several search parameters. Match whole or partial words, match case, and match with wildcard options can be used singly or together. You can begin your search at the cursor or at the top or bottom of the selection or the entire file, and search in the forward (downward) or backward (upward) direction. You may replace a single instance of a given item or all instances at once. Recent

Using the BASIC Stamp Editor

Find and Replace items are saved in the Find: and Replace: field's drop-down lists.

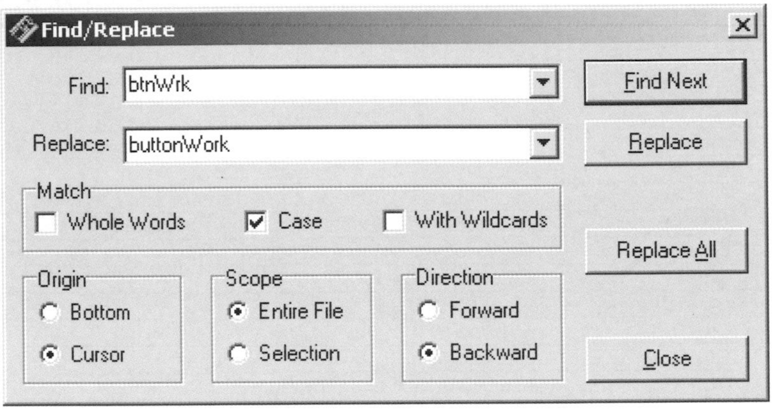

Figure 3.6: The Find/Replace Window.

The Find/Replace window will stay visible when using the Find Next and Replace options for quick and convenient source code editing. Using the Replace All function, however, will close the Find/Replace window and perform the designated find/replace operation.

The integrated explorer panel to the left of the main edit pane is divided in to four portions: the Recent, Directory, File and Filter lists. The upper portion is the Recent list, a drop-down list of default, favorite, and recently visited directories.

THE INTEGRATED EXPLORER PANEL.

If you select a directory from the Recent list drop down field, the integrated explorer will automatically navigate to that directory. The button to the left of the Recent list allows you to limit the Directory list display below it to only the directories that are in the Recent list. This makes it easy to find your commonly used source code directories among a large set of directories and local and network hard drives. The Recent list button behaves like a toggle switch: 1) selecting it switches to the "Show Recent folders only" mode, 2) selecting it again switches back to the "Show all folders" mode.

Figure 3.7: The Integrated Explorer Panel's Recent list (top), Directory list (middle), and File list (bottom).

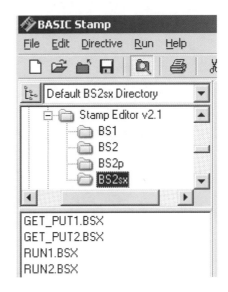

THE DIRECTORY LIST.

The Directory list, right below the Recent list, displays drives and directories in a hierarchical tree fashion. If a directory is selected, the Folders list displays the files in that directory.

THE FILE LIST.

The File list, below the Directory list, displays all the files in the selected directory that match the selected filter (from the Filter list at the bottom. see Figure 3.8). You can select one or more files from this list and double-click, or drag-and-drop them over the editor pane, to open those files.

OPEN FROM... AND SAVE TO... OPTIONS.

You may also open files with the Open From... option by selecting File → Open From, or by pressing Ctrl+Shift+O. This allows quick access to any directory for the default and favorite directories set within Preferences (see page 60) as well as any recently used directory. The Save To... option works similarly; select File → Save To or press Ctrl+Shift+S. These features can be very helpful if you organize your files in many different directories.

THE FILTERS LIST.

The Filter list at the bottom of the explorer panel (Figure 3.8), is a drop-down list of file extension filters to apply to the File list. It works just like the "Save as type:" field of a standard Open or Save dialog.

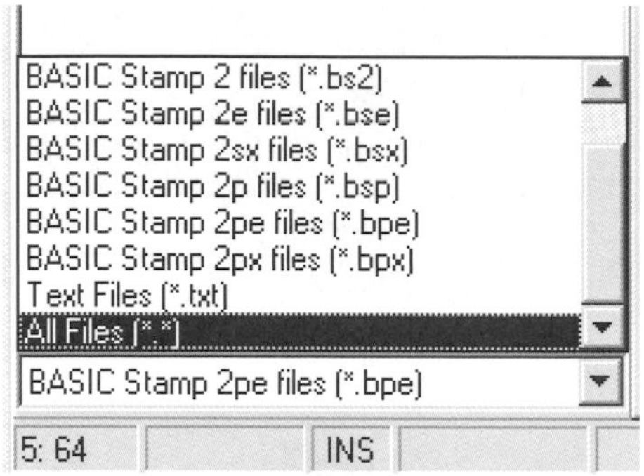

Using the BASIC Stamp Editor

Figure 3.8: The Filter List found at the bottom of the Integrated Explorer Panel.

The BASIC Stamp Editor automatically associates BASIC Stamp source code file types (.bs1, .bs2, .bse, .bsx, .bsp, .bpe, and .bpx) with itself. This feature can be configured through automatic prompts or through the Preferences → Files & Directories tab. Also, when using any Explorer-shell for file browsing, right-clicking on a BASIC Stamp source code file provides you with an Open With Stamp Editor option.

The integrated explorer panel can be resized via the vertical splitter bar that separates it and the edit pane. The Directory list and File list can be resized via the horizontal splitter bar that separates them. The integrated explorer can also be hidden or shown via the Explorer toolbar button, by pressing Ctrl+E, or by resizing it to zero width using the vertical splitter bar.

Table 3.3 lists keyboard shortcuts for several file functions.

File Functions	
Shortcut Key	**Function**
Ctrl+E	Show/hide explorer panel
Ctrl+L	Show/hide split view in edit pane
Ctrl+O	Open a source code file into edit pane
Ctrl+Shift+O	Open a source code file from a recent directory into edit pane
Ctrl+S	Save current source code file to its current location on disk
Ctrl+Shift+S	Save current source code file to a recent directory on disk
Ctrl+P	Print current source code
Ctrl+Tab	Switch to next open file page
Ctrl+Shift+Tab	Switch to previous open file page

Table 3.3: Keyboard Shortcuts for File Functions.

Compiler Directives

COMPILER DIRECTIVES.

The BASIC Stamp Editor supports all of the BASIC Stamp models, and all versions of the PBASIC programming language. Compiler directives must be placed in each program to indicate the desired BASIC Stamp model and language version. In addition, it is sometimes useful to target a given program to a particular communication port. The Directive menu contains options for setting the $STAMP, $PBASIC, and $PORT directives. Since the $STAMP and $PBASIC directives are used most often, they are most easily inserted or modified with the toolbar buttons, as shown in Figure 3.9.

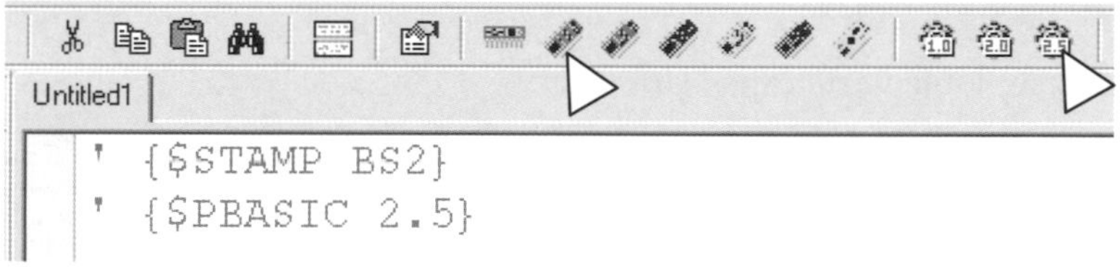

Figure 3.9: Toolbar icons make it easy to insert or modify $STAMP and $PBASIC directives directly in your program.

THE $STAMP DIRECTIVE.

A $STAMP directive is required in each PBASIC program. The editor determines which BASIC Stamp model to target for compiling and downloading based on this directive. Any code that is missing the $STAMP directive, but whose filename contains a known BASIC Stamp extension (.bs1, .bs2, .bse, .bsx, .bsp, .bpe, .bpx) will be recognized by that extension and an appropriate $STAMP directive will be added automatically when you run, tokenize, view the memory map or download the program. If there is no file extension present, an error message will prompt you to enter a $STAMP directive.

FORMAT OF THE $STAMP DIRECTIVE.

You may choose to manually type the $STAMP directive into the program from the keyboard. This line should be entered into your code on a line by itself, usually near the top. Note that the directive appears on a comment line, as indicated by the apostrophe (').

```
' {$STAMP BS1}      'This indicates to use a BASIC Stamp 1 module
' {$STAMP BS2}      'This indicates to use a BASIC Stamp 2 module
' {$STAMP BS2e}     'This indicates to use a BASIC Stamp 2e module
' {$STAMP BS2sx}    'This indicates to use a BASIC Stamp 2sx module
' {$STAMP BS2p}     'This indicates to use a BASIC Stamp 2p module
' {$STAMP BS2pe}    'This indicates to use a BASIC Stamp 2pe module
' {$STAMP BS2px}    'This indicates to use a BASIC Stamp 2px module
```

Using the BASIC Stamp Editor

If you choose to type the $STAMP directive, care must be taken, or it will not be recognized. The directive itself must be enclosed in curly braces, {...}, not parentheses (...) or square brackets [...]. There should not be any spaces between the dollar sign ($) and the word STAMP; however, the directive may contain additional spaces in certain other areas. For example:

EXTRA SPACES ARE ALLOWED IN CERTAIN AREAS.

```
'     {       $STAMP    BS2       }
```

-- or --

```
' {$STAMP      BS2}
```

-- and --

```
' {$STAMP  BS2    }
```

are all acceptable variations. However:

```
' {$    STAMP  BS2}
```

-- and --

```
' {$STAMPBS2}
```

are not acceptable and will be ignored. If one of the above two lines were entered into the source code, the editor would ignore it and, instead, rely on the extension of the filename to determine the appropriate model.

The $STAMP directive is read and acted upon by the BASIC Stamp Windows Editor any time a source code file is loaded, tokenized, downloaded (run) or viewed in the Memory Map.

In some cases you may wish to write a program that can run on multiple BASIC Stamp models. In this case, conditional compile directives can be employed that will cause the editor to determine which Basic Stamp model is detected, and then download only those program elements applicable to that model. Many of the demo programs in Chapter 5 use this technique. To read about conditional compilation, see the Advanced Compilation Techniques section which begins on page 68.

PROGRAMS FOR MULTIPLE BASIC STAMP MODELS – CONDITIONAL COMPILE.

The $PBASIC directive allows you to indicate which version of the PBASIC language to use. At the time of this printing, the options are 1.0, 2.0 and 2.5. If no $PBASIC directive is present in the program, version 1.0 is assumed for BS1 module source code, and version 2.0 is assumed for

THE $PBASIC DIRECTIVE.

any BS2 model source code. A $PBASIC directive is required to use version 2.5, which is compatible with all BS2 models.

PBASIC 2.5 has enhanced syntax options for several commands, as well as some additional commands not available in PBASIC 2.0. Table 3.4 shows the number of PBASIC commands that are available in each version of the PBASIC language, on each BASIC Stamp model. Details about the syntax differences among the three versions of PBASIC are denoted by icons in the margins of Chapters 4 and 5; also refer to Table 5.1 on page 124 and individual command syntax descriptions.

Table 3.4: Number of Available Commands for each BASIC Stamp Model with each version of the PBASIC language .

	BS1	BS2	BS2e	BS2sx	BS2p	BS2pe	BS2px
PBASIC 1.0	32	-	-	-	-	-	-
PBASIC 2.0	-	37	40	40	56	56	58
PBASIC 2.5	-	42	45	45	61	61	63

A categorical listing of all PBASIC commands is included at the beginning of Chapter 5, followed by detailed descriptions of each command in alphabetical order.

Note that the syntax-highlighting feature of the BASIC Stamp Editor will also adjust to the language version indicated by the $PBASIC directive. The best way to select the $PBASIC directive is to use the toolbar icons, as was shown in Figure 3.9. Like the $STAMP directive, you must use care if you choose to type it in by hand. The syntax is:

```
' {$PBASIC 1.0}    'Default when a BASIC Stamp 1 module is detected
' {$PBASIC 2.0}    'Default when any BASIC Stamp 2 module is detected
' {$PBASIC 2.5}    'Required for PBASIC 2.5 command set & enhanced syntax
```

If you try to run a program that contains command syntax specific to PBASIC 2.5 without including the corresponding compiler directive, you will probably get an error message. In this case, insert a $PBASIC 2.5 directive and try running the program again.

THE $PORT DIRECTIVE.

The optional $PORT directive allows you to indicate a specific PC communications port through which to download a program to a BASIC Stamp module. The syntax is as follows:

```
' {$PORT COM#}
```

where # is a valid port number. When any PBASIC program containing this directive is downloaded, all other ports will be ignored. This directive is especially convenient when using two of the same BASIC Stamp models (such as two BS2s) on two ports and you have two different PBASIC programs to download (one to each BS2). Without this directive, developing and downloading in this case would be a tedious task of always answering the "which BASIC Stamp?" prompt.

The $PORT directive can be automatically inserted or modified by selecting the appropriate port from the Directive → Port menu. The COM ports listed in the Directive → Port menu are automatically updated any time a change is made to the exiting computer hardware or to the available ports list. See the Setting Preferences section which begins on page 55 for more information.

Special Functions

The Identify function will identify which BASIC Stamp model, if any, is detected on any available communications port. This information is displayed in the Identification window (Figure 3.10), which can greatly aid in troubleshooting your connection to your BASIC Stamp module. Activate this function by selecting Run → Identify, by pressing Ctrl-I, or pressing F6.

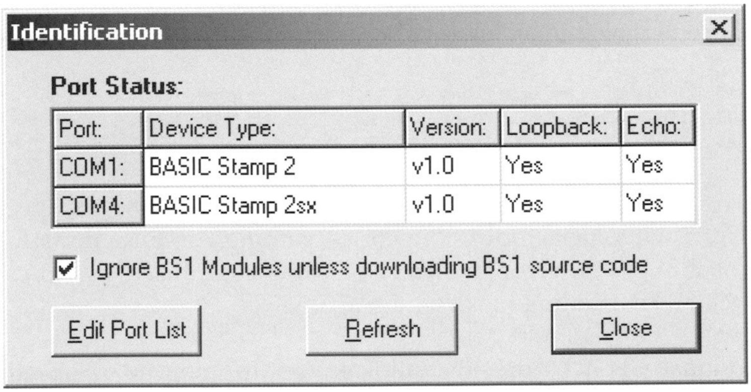

THE IDENTIFICATION FUNCTION.

Identification

Port Status:

Port:	Device Type:	Version:	Loopback:	Echo:
COM1:	BASIC Stamp 2	v1.0	Yes	Yes
COM4:	BASIC Stamp 2sx	v1.0	Yes	Yes

☑ Ignore BS1 Modules unless downloading BS1 source code

[Edit Port List]   [Refresh]   [Close]

Figure 3.10: The Identification Window.

The Port column shows the available ports (those that the BASIC Stamp Editor is trying to access). You can modify the available Port List by clicking on the Edit Port List button. Modifying this list only affects which ports the BASIC Stamp Editor tries to use; it does not affect which serial ports are installed on your computer. It is recommended that you delete all known modem ports and any problematic ports from this list.

The Device Type column shows the model of BASIC Stamp found on the respective port. For example, in Figure 3.10 above, the BASIC Stamp Editor found a BS2 on COM port 1 and a BS2sx on COM port 4.

The Version column displays the firmware version number of the BASIC Stamp module that was found.

The Loopback column indicates whether or not a loopback connection was found on the port. The loopback connection is created by BASIC Stamp development boards, such as the Board of Education, across serial port pins 6 and 7 (of a DB9). A "Yes" in this column is an indication that the serial port and serial cable are properly connected to a BASIC Stamp development board. Note that the Loopback column should always indicate "No" when using a BS1 Serial Adapter, regardless of whether or not the adapter is properly connected to a BASIC Stamp development board.

The Echo column indicates whether or not a communication echo was detected on the port's transmit and receive pins (pins 2 and 3). All BASIC Stamp 2 models create this echo naturally, even without power. BASIC Stamp 1 modules do not create this echo. A "Yes" in this column is an indication that the serial port and serial cable are properly connected to a BASIC Stamp 2 (or higher) module, and if using a BASIC Stamp development board, it's an indication that the module is properly connected to the development board.

For all BASIC Stamp 2 models, the Loopback and Echo columns are great for doing some simple connection diagnosis when using a serial port. For example, a Yes in both columns indicates the serial port and serial cable are properly connected and that the BASIC Stamp is properly inserted into its socket. See Table 3.5 below. Note that the Loopback column does not give reliable results when using a USB to serial adapter, or a USB-based development board. Usually this is not an error, and the Loopback status can simply be ignored.

Loopback	Echo	Interpretation
Yes	Yes	Serial port and serial cable properly connected. BASIC Stamp properly inserted into socket. If no BASIC Stamp is detected, it is probably because the BASIC Stamp is not connected to power. Other causes could be: 1) low battery, 2) Reset pin of BASIC Stamp is connected to Vdd (it should be left disconnected), 3) the BASIC Stamp is damaged or 4) there is some other type of communication error (software or hardware).
Yes	No	Serial port and serial cable properly connected to the development board. BASIC Stamp improperly inserted into socket (i.e.: inserted backwards or not inserted at all).
No	Yes	Serial port and serial cable may be improperly connected, or you may not be using a standard BASIC Stamp development board. The Echo indicates there may be a BASIC Stamp properly connected to the port (the Loopback is not required for successful connection) or there may be another device connected to the serial port.
No	No	Serial port and serial cable are not properly connected, or not connected at all, to the BASIC Stamp 2 (and higher) modules. Could also be an indication of a serial port hardware/software problem. When using a BS1 Serial Adapter, this Loopback and Echo is normal and expected.

Table 3.5: Using Loopback and Echo to troubleshoot your serial port (DB9) connection.

NOTE: When using a USB port, the Loopback column does not give reliable results. Usually this is not an error and the Loopback status can be ignored.

Selecting the "Ignore BS1 Modules unless downloading BS1 source code" checkbox at the bottom of the Identification window optimizes identification speed. All BS2 models can be identified very quickly. For BASIC Stamp 1 modules, the identification process can take as much as five seconds per communications port. Since the Identification function checks all available serial ports for any possible model of BASIC Stamp, the five-second timeout for BS1's can be very inconvenient, especially if you are not using a BS1.

SPEED UP IDENTIFICATION WITH THE "IGNORE BS1 MODULES" CHECKBOX.

When this checkbox is checked, the Identification function will not attempt to locate BS1 modules, and thus saves time. If, however, you are downloading BASIC Stamp 1 code, the Download function will attempt to locate BS1 modules regardless of the setting of this checkbox. This feature can also be found and modified via the Preferences → Editor Operation tab.

Like the Identification function, the Download function provides information to help guide you through the downloading process. After entering the desired source code in the editor window, you may run it in one of three ways: select Run → Run, press Ctrl+R on the keyboard, or click on the "▶" toolbar icon. This will tokenize and download the code

THE DOWNLOAD FUNCTION.

to the BASIC Stamp module (assuming the code is correct and the BASIC Stamp is properly connected). The Download Progress window looks similar to the Identify window with the exception of the additional Download Status progress bar, and the indicator LED by the port transmitting the data.

Figure 3.11: The Download Progress Window.

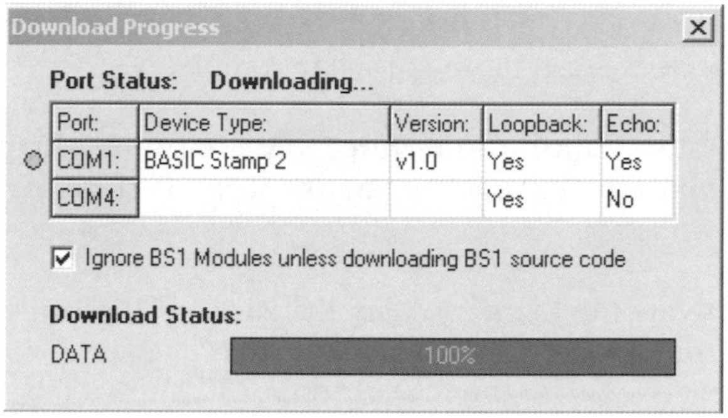

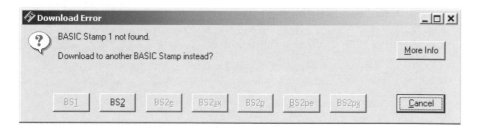

If any errors occur, such as communication failure or inability to detect a BASIC Stamp module, you will be prompted appropriately. One possible error occurs when the BASIC Stamp your PBASIC program is targeting does not appear to be connected to the PC (see Figure 3.12). This may be caused, for example, by opening up a BASIC Stamp 1 program (usually has a .bas or .bs1 extension) and trying to download it to a BASIC Stamp 2 module, instead.

Figure 3.12: A Download Error message.

When this happens, you'll be prompted to correct the situation, quickly done by clicking on the BS2 button (if you really intended to download to the BS2 in the first place). Keep in mind that programs written for one BASIC Stamp model may not function properly on a different BASIC Stamp model. Click on the More Info button for more detail. NOTE: If you select the BS2 button, as in this example, the editor will modify the

Using the BASIC Stamp Editor

$STAMP directive in the program, notify you of this change and what it means, and then will try to download to the BS2.

Another possibility is having two or more of the same BASIC Stamp model connected to the PC. In this case, the editor will prompt you for clarification as to which BASIC Stamp module you want to download to. In this case using a $PORT directive in your code will save you some tedium in repeatedly responding to such prompts.

MEMORY MAP FUNCTION.

The BASIC Stamp Editor also features a Memory Map that displays the layout of the current PBASIC program. Type Ctrl+M, or press F7, to activate this window.

When you activate the Memory Map, the editor will check your program for syntax errors and, if the program's syntax is okay, will present you with a color-coded map of the RAM and EEPROM. You'll be able to tell at a glance how much memory you have used and how much remains.

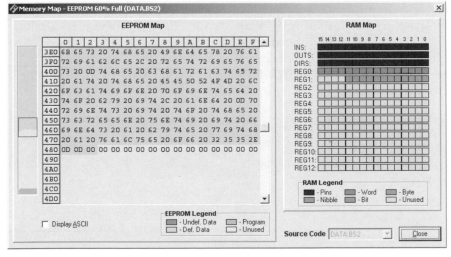

Figure 3.13: Memory Map for Demo Program DATA.bs2.

The Memory Map is divided into two sections, the RAM map and the EEPROM map. The RAM map shows how much of each register has been allotted to program variables. The RAM legend details how much is used by I/O Pins, Word, Byte, Nibble and Bit variables, and how much is unused.

THE RAM MAP.

THE EEPROM MAP.

The EEPROM map is shown in two scales. The main view is the detailed EEPROM map, which displays the data in hexadecimal format in each location. The condensed EEPROM map is the vertical region on the left that shows a small-scale view of the entire EEPROM; the red square over it corresponds to the scroll bar handle in the detailed EEPROM map and indicates the portion of the EEPROM that is currently visible in the detailed EEPROM map.

Checking the Display ASCII checkbox switches the detailed EEPROM display from hexadecimal to ASCII. In this program, the textual data can be read right off the EEPROM map when using this option.

Two important points to remember about this map are: 1) it only indicates how your program will be downloaded to the BASIC Stamp module; it does not "read" the BASIC Stamp memory, and 2) for all BS2 models, fixed variables like B3 and W1 and any aliases do not show up on the memory map as memory used. The editor ignores fixed variables when it arranges automatically allocated variables in memory. Remember, fixed and allocated variables can overlap.

THE DEBUG TERMINAL.

The Debug Terminal window provides a convenient display for data received from a BASIC Stamp during run-time, and also allows for the transmission of characters from the PC keyboard to the BASIC Stamp. The Debug Terminal is automatically opened and configured when a PBASIC program, containing a DEBUG command, is downloaded. You can manually open a Debug Terminal one of three ways: select Run → Debug → New, press Ctrl+D on the keyboard, or click on the Debug Terminal toolbar button. Up to four (4) Debug Terminals can be open at once (on four different ports) and all can be left open while editing and downloading source code.

Figure 3.14 below shows the demo program DEBUG_DEBUGIN.bs2 in the edit pane, and the Debug Terminal that opens when this program is run.

```
DEBUG_DEBUGIN.BS2
' DEBUG_DEBUGIN.BS2
' This program demonstrates the ability to accept user input from the
' Debug terminal, and to accept numeric entry in any valid format.

' {$STAMP BS2}
' {$PBASIC 2.5}

myNum            VAR        Word


Main:
  DO
    DEBUG CLS, "Enter a number: "
    DEBUGIN SNUM myNum

    DEBUG CRSRXY, 0, 2,
          SDEC ? myNum,
          SHEX ? myNum,
          SBIN ? myNum
    PAUSE 3000
  LOOP
  END
```

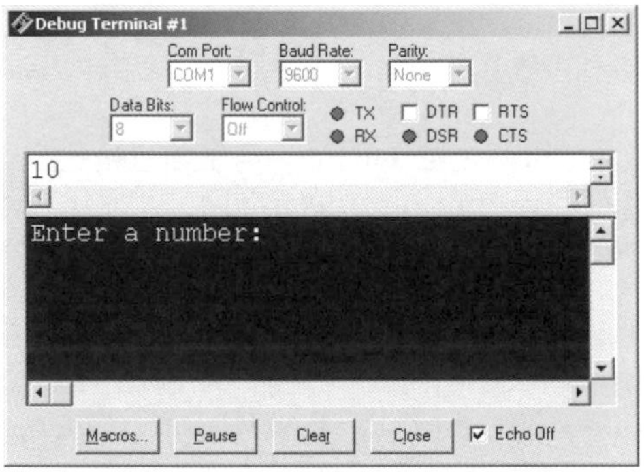

Figure 3.14: Demo program using the Debug Terminal

The text in the Debug Terminal's Receive pane (blue area) prompts the user to enter a number into the Transmit pane (white area) . After typing the number 10 and pressing Enter, the Receive pane displays the number in decimal, hexadecimal, and binary format as dictated by the program (Figure 3.15).

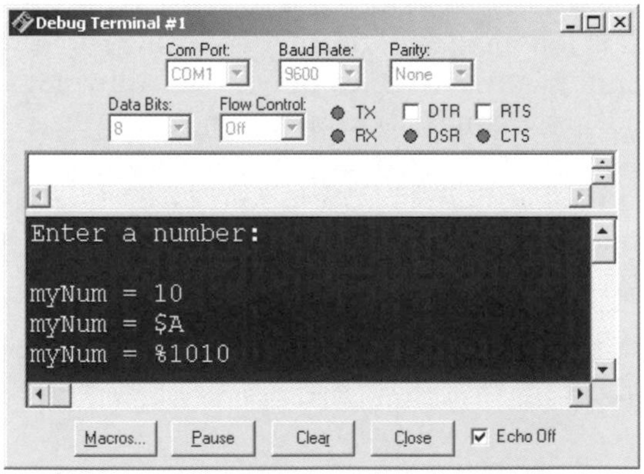

Figure 3.15: Debug Terminal output after entering a number.

The fields across the top of the Debug Terminal window allow configuration of the communication port settings. These fields will be automatically configured and disabled if the Debug Terminal was

PORT SETTINGS AND STATUS.

automatically opened by the editor, however, if manually opened, these fields will be enabled to allow manual configuration. The signal status LEDs turn bright green when activity on the indicated port line is detected. The signal checkboxes (DTR and RTS) can be selected to set or clear the respective output line on the port.

The Echo Off checkbox (bottom of window) causes the Receive pane to throw away the characters that arrive in the port's receive buffer immediately after transmitting characters from the transmit buffer. This produces a cleaner Receive pane display for interactive programs such as the example above. Keep in mind, however, that this feature does not verify that the character it throws away is actually a match to a character that was just transmitted (because data collisions on the port can cause echoed characters to be garbled). You should only use the Echo Off feature in situations where it is required, as it may result in a strange display in certain applications.

KEYBOARD SHORTCUTS FOR CODING FUNCTIONS.

There are keyboard shortcuts for several coding functions, some of which are unique to the BASIC Stamp Editor.

Table 3.6: Coding Function Keyboard Shortcuts.

Coding Functions	
Shortcut Key(s)	**Function**
Ctrl+J	Show code templates.
F6 or Ctrl+I	Identify BASIC Stamp firmware.
F7 or Ctrl+T	Perform a syntax check on the code and display any error messages.
F8 or Ctrl+M	Open Memory Map window.
F9 or Ctrl+R	Tokenize code, download to the BASIC Stamp and open Debug window if necessary.
F11 or Ctrl+D	Open a new Debug window.
F12	Switch to next window (Editor, Debug #1, Debug #2, Debug #3 or Debug #4)
Ctrl+1, Ctrl+2, Ctrl+3, Ctrl+4	Switch to Debug Terminal #1, Debug Terminal #2, etc. if that Terminal window is open.
Ctrl+`	Switch to Editor window.
ESC	Close current window.

HELP FILES.

The BASIC Stamp Editor includes searchable, indexed help files. Access Help by selecting Help → Contents or Help → Index. Context sensitive help (highlighting a word in the editor and pressing F1 key) is also supported. The help file can remain open in a separate window while using the BASIC Stamp Editor; simply press Alt+Tab to toggle back and forth between the editor and the Help window.

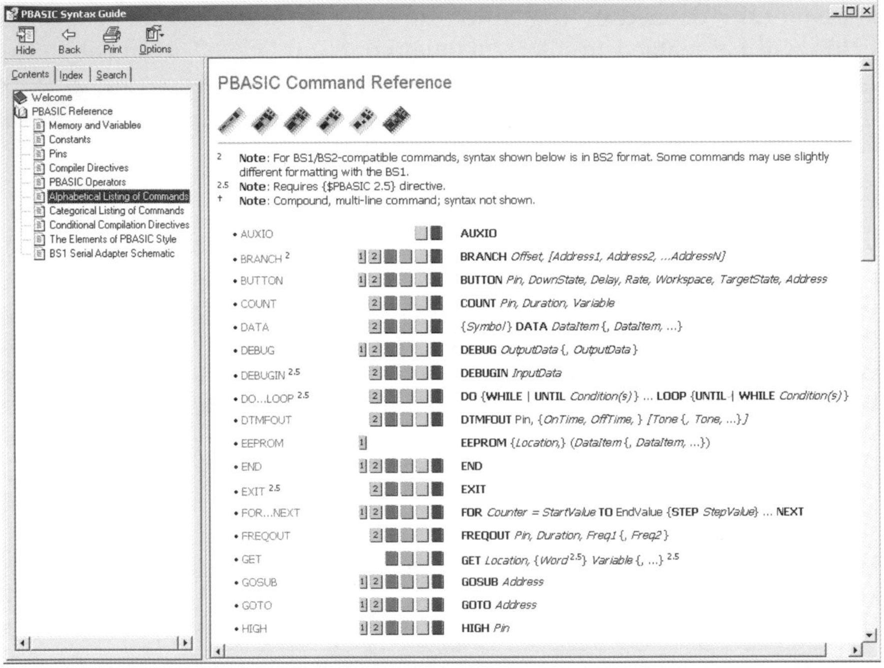

Using the BASIC Stamp Editor

Figure 3.16: The Help file contains the complete PBASIC syntax documentation.

The current help files contain the entire PBASIC syntax documentation. In addition, the example demo code programs that appear after most command descriptions in Chapter 5 are automatically placed in default directories during the BASIC Stamp Editor v2.2 installation. These programs can be accessed via hyperlinks within the help file.

NOTE: The BASIC Stamp Editor Help file requires Microsoft's HTML Help utility and Internet Explorer 4.0 or above (IE 6.0 recommended). The proper version of HTML Help is included with Windows 2000 and Windows XP. On other versions of Windows you may have to install or upgrade your HTML Help utility to properly view the Stamp Editor's on-line help. The HTML Help upgrade program (hhupd.exe) is included as part of the BASIC Stamp Editor setup program and the editor will automatically prompt you to run it if it determines you need to upgrade. You can download the latest version of Internet Explorer from Microsoft's web site at www.microsoft.com.

HELP FILES REQUIRE MICROSOFT'S HTML HELP UTILITY.

TIP OF THE DAY.

The Tip of the Day function displays a new message each time you run the BASIC Stamp Editor. There are many useful tips, and you may browse through them any time with the Next Tip and Previous Tip buttons. You may also use the Edit Tips option to change the contents of any tip. All tips are contained in a single file, named Stamp_Tips.txt, that is stored in the editor's installation directory, usually a path similar to C:\Program Files\Parallax Inc\Stamp Editor v2.2.

Figure 3.17: Tip of the Day #24.

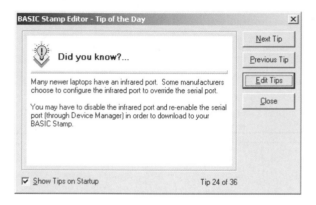

You can turn this feature off by unchecking the Show Tips on Startup box at the bottom of the window. To access it again, choose Help → Tip of the Day from the menu bar.

Setting Preferences

The BASIC Stamp Editor allows the user to set preferences for the appearance and operation of many aspects of the application. Select Edit → Preferences, press F5 or click on the Preferences toolbar button to open the Preferences window, where you will see these options organized under 6 tabs. Each tab has a Restore Defaults button in case you make a royal mess of things.

EDITOR APPEARANCE PREFERENCES.

Under the Editor Appearance tab (Figure 3.18), you can set the font size in the edit pane. The other text attributes, such as background and foreground color, character case, and bold, italic and underline, are controlled by the Syntax Highlighting scheme. There are 3 predefined schemes, and you may also create a custom scheme. Please note that the preferences are specific to the editor, and are not saved as part of any BASIC Stamp program that you may have open while setting preferences.

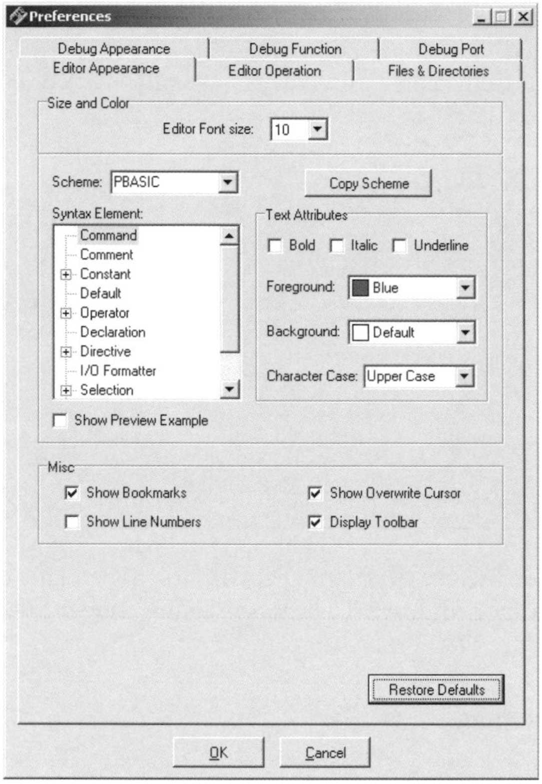

Figure 3.18: The Editor Appearance Tab under Edit → Preferences.

The default font size for the edit pane is 10 point, but there are 12 fixed options ranging from 8 to 40 point. The Editor Font size setting and all the other text attribute settings under this tab will not affect the text in the Debug Terminal.

The default scheme is the "PBASIC" scheme, with the syntax highlighting text attributes described above in Table 3.1. The "plain text" scheme is just that – the default foreground and background for all entered text, with no other attributes applied. The "simple" scheme is the same as the "plain text" scheme, except comments appear in green. Both the plain text and simple schemes use the PBASIC scheme defaults for selected text.

SYNTAX HIGHLIGHTING SCHEMES.

CUSTOMIZED SYNTAX HIGHLIGHTING.

To create a custom scheme, select a default scheme you wish to modify, and click on the Copy Scheme button. Then, select (highlight) an element within the Syntax Element list, and apply new Text Attributes with the checkboxes and drop-down menus to the right. As you try various text attributes and color combinations, the Show Preview Example checkbox lets you audition your custom scheme without closing the Preferences window.

The BASIC Stamp Editor supports one custom scheme at a time. It can be modified indefinitely, but it cannot be copied. If you again copy a default scheme, you will be asked to confirm that you wish to overwrite your current custom scheme.

Under this tab, you will also find checkboxes that allow you to show or hide bookmarks, line numbers, the overwrite cursor, and the toolbar.

EDITOR OPERATION PREFERENCES.

Under the Editor Operation tab (Figure 3.19), you may set preferences for automatic indentation and tab behavior.

AUTO INDENTING / UNINDENTING.

The Auto Indent on Enter option makes it easy to indent nested loops to make code easier to read. The Auto Unindent option enables quick reversal of an indented line by simply using the backspace key, provided that the cursor is to the left of the first character on the line.

TAB CHARACTER.

The editor lets you choose whether a tab character or spaces are inserted into source code whenever you press the Tab key. The default setting, insert space characters upon Tab key presses, is recommended because it enforces the intended formatting regardless of what editor you use to view the code later.

In addition to the actual character used for the Tab key, there are three behaviors of tabbing employed by the editor: Smart Tabs, Fixed Tabs and Fixed plus Smart Tabs.

TAB BEHAVIOR.

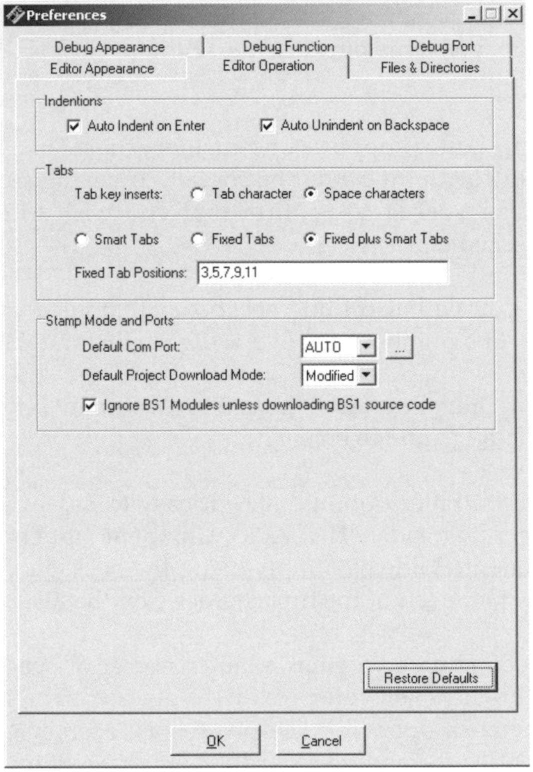

Figure 3.19: The Editor Operation Tab under Edit → Preferences.

Smart Tabs (Figure 3.20) cause the tab key to move the cursor to a position that is aligned with the nearest break between words in nearby lines above the current line. It has the effect of providing a somewhat intuitive, auto adjusting behavior based entirely on how you have aligned previous lines.

SMART TABS.

Fixed Tabs (Figure 3.21) cause the tab key to move the cursor to the position indicated by the Fixed Tab Positions field. If the position is already beyond the end of the Fixed Tab Positions list, it moves by a multiple of the distance between the last two positions in that list. For example, with Fixed Tabs set, the default Fixed Tab Positions list will

FIXED TABS.

make the Tab key move the cursor to positions, 3, 5, 7, 9 and 11, then afterwards, 13, 15, 17, 19, etc. (a multiple of two (11 – 9 = 2) after the last listed position.

FIXED PLUS SMART TABS.

The last option is a mixture of the first two, Fixed plus Smart Tabs (Figure 3.22); it is the default and recommended setting. Fixed plus Smart Tabs will cause the tab key to move the cursor to the position indicated by the Fixed Tab Positions field, or if the position is already beyond the end of that list, it reverts to Smart Tabs behavior. This setting, combined with a carefully configured Fixed Tab Positions field, allows for a fixed level of indenting on the left side of the source code (for executable code blocks), with very flexible indenting to the right of executable code (for comments that appear to the right of code). The default settings provide a quick, single-key method of indenting up to five (5) levels of executable code and easy alignment of multiple lines of comments to the right of that code.

Figure 3.20: Smart Tabs.

```
Main:
   DO
      DEBUG CLS, "Enter any number: "      ' prompt user to enter a number
      DEBUGIN SNUM myNum                    ' get number
```

Figure 3.21: Fixed Tabs.

```
Main:
   DO
      DEBUG CLS, "Enter any number: "      ' prompt user to enter a number
      DEBUGIN SNUM myNum                    ' get number

   3  5  7  9  11 13 15...
```

Figure 3.22: Fixed plus Smart Tabs.

```
Main:
   DO
      DEBUG CLS, "Enter any number: "      ' prompt user to enter a number
      DEBUGIN SNUM myNum                    ' get number

   3  5  7  9  11
```

The Fixed Tab Positions list is used to provide a list of desired fixed tab positions (used with Fixed Tabs or Fixed plus Smart Tabs options). The list can be a single number, or a list of comma separated numbers in ascending order. The allowable range is 2 to 512 and the list size is virtually unlimited. When multiple values are entered, the difference between the last two values will be used to set tab positions beyond the last position. For example, in the default list, the last two positions are 9 and 11; resulting in further tab positions of 13, 15, 17, etc. (multiples of 2 after the last specified position). Since source code is usually indented by multiples of two (2) spaces, the default list of 3, 5, 7, 9 and 11 is recommended.

THE FIXED TAB POSITIONS LIST.

The Default Com Port setting allows you to specify which COM port to download through. If you specify a specific port here, the Identification window will report that it is "ignoring" other known ports. This can be selectively overridden by placing a $PORT directive in the program. If this setting is left on "AUTO", the default, the editor will open and scan all known ports for the correct BASIC Stamp. The button to the right, labeled '...', opens the a window allowing the known port list to be edited. Modifying the known port list only affects which ports the BASIC Stamp Editor tries to use; it does not affect which serial ports are installed on your computer. It is recommended that you delete all known modem ports and any problematic ports from this list.

DEFAULT COM PORT.

For an explanation of the Default Project Download Modes, see Table 3.7 on page 70. This is part of a discussion on BASIC Stamp Projects in the Advanced Compilation Techniques beginning on page 68, below.

Selecting the "Ignore BS1 Modules unless downloading BS1 source code" checkbox optimizes identification speed by attempting to locate BS1 modules only if you are downloading BASIC Stamp 1 code. This feature can also be activated via the Identification or Download window.

Under the Files and Directories tab (Figure 3.23), you can set preferences for saving and accessing files, as well as automatically creating backup copies.

THE FILES AND DIRECTORIES TAB.

Figure 3.23: The Files and Directories Tab under Edit → Preferences.

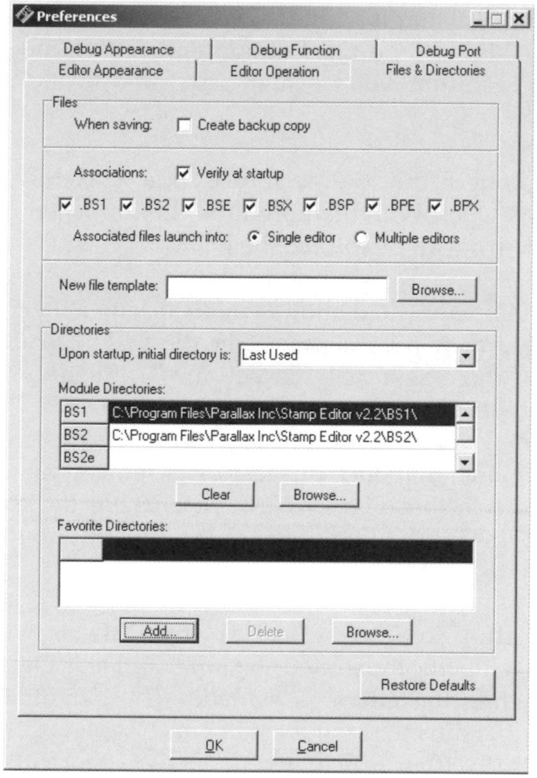

BACKUP COPY.

Check the "Create backup copy" option to cause the editor to automatically create a backup copy of any file that is being re-saved under the same name. The backup file will be stored in the same directory and named the same as the existing file, but with a .bak extension appended to the existing extension. For example, "test.bs2" becomes "test.bs2.bak" and then the new file called "test.bs2" is created from the source code being saved. Note: the .bak files will not appear in the integrated explorer's file window unless you change the Filter list to show All Files (*.*).

FILE ASSOCIATIONS.

BASIC Stamp source code file types (.bs1, .bs2, .bse, .bsx, .bsp, .bpe, .bpx) can be associated with the BASIC Stamp Editor. Check the "Verify at startup" option to have the editor verify the proper associations each time it is started. The "Associated files launch into" option changes the way Windows behaves when you open BASIC Stamp source code from any Explorer-shell. Choosing "Single Editor" causes all programs to open up into a single BASIC Stamp Editor, including an editor that is already running. The "Multiple Editors" option will cause a new BASIC Stamp Editor to open each time you open an associated BASIC Stamp file from any Explorer-shell.

Also, by associating BASIC Stamp source code with the editor, Windows will provide an "Open With Stamp Editor" option when right-clicking on that source code from any Explorer-shell.

OPEN WITH STAMP EDITOR OPTION.

The "New file template" field allows you to specify a file to load each time the File → New function is selected. The file will be loaded into the new edit page, but the name will be set to "Untitled#"; where # is an automatically generated number. This feature provides a convenient way to start every new source code project with a specified code template of your choosing. Note that once this feature is set, you may hold down the Shift key while selecting File → New, or clicking the New File toolbar button, to suppress the loading of the code template and thus end up with a blank edit page.

NEW FILE TEMPLATE FEATURE.

The "Upon startup, initial directory is" field affects what directory is initially selected in the integrated explorer and the Open and Save As dialog boxes when the editor is started. The default is "Last Used," meaning the initial directory will be that which was most recently used by the editor. If this setting is changed to "Set Via Shortcut" the editor will initially view the directory indicated by the "Start in" field of the Windows shortcut that launched the editor. The other options include the default module directories and favorite directories.

INITIAL DIRECTORY ON STARTUP.

The Module Directories list contains a list of module-specific directories that are called the "default module directories." Upon installation of the BASIC Stamp Editor software, the PBASIC source code examples in this text are copied to the installation folder and organized into appropriate subfolders. If the default installation folder is used during software installation, the source code files will be copied to a path similar to: C:\Program Files\Parallax Inc\Stamp Editor 2.2\BS1, BS2, BS2sx..., etc. The BASIC Stamp Editor automatically sets its default directories to point to these source code examples, making them immediately available via the File → Open From... and File → Save To... menus as well as the Recent list in the integrated explorer panel.

MODULE DIRECTORIES.

You may use the Clear and Browse... buttons under the Module Directories list to select new default directory locations for each model of BASIC Stamp. These new folders will then appear as options when you use the File → Open From... and File → Save To... menus as well as the Recent list in the integrated explorer panel.

Note that if you are upgrading from a previous version of the BASIC Stamp Editor and you have set your own default directories, they will not be replaced with the new source code example directories. Upon opening the editor, only default directory options that are blank will be redirected to the source code examples.

FAVORITE DIRECTORIES.

The Favorite Directories list allows you to add and delete folder locations that will appear as additional options in the File → Open From... and File → Save To... menus as well as the Recent list in the integrated explorer. It works in a similar way as the Module Directories list; however, you can set your own descriptive names for those folders.

DEBUG APPEARANCE PREFERENCES.

Under the Debug Appearance tab (Figure 3.24) you can set the color and size of the various Debug Terminal elements; settings apply to all the Debug Terminal windows at once. A Debug Terminal itself can be resized and/or moved by simply clicking and dragging the window; each window's size and position is remembered even after closing the editor.

THE CHOOSE... BUTTONS.

The Choose... buttons allow you to change the background and font color of both the Transmitter and Receiver panes, independently. The font size of both panes can be changed to one of 8 sizes: 6, 8, 10, 12, 14, 18, 24, and 36. The Debug Terminal font size is independent of the font size in the main editor window.

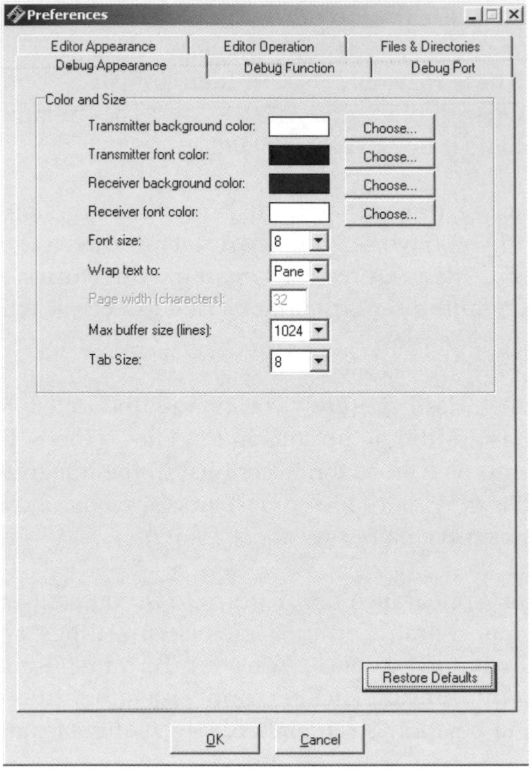

Figure 3.24: The Debug Appearance Tab under Edit → Preferences.

The "Wrap Text to" field gives two options, Pane and Page. Wrapping to Pane is the default, and causes text to wrap at the right edge of the Receiver pane, reflecting the current visible size that the user happens to have set for the Debug Terminal's window. Wrapping to Page, however, causes text to wrap at a specific line width, regardless of the user's current Debug Terminal window size. The "Page width (characters)" field is enabled when wrap mode is set to Page. The default page width is 32, characters and the range is 32 to 128. Note: wrapping to page can be handy to maintain formatting of formatted tabular information, but could lead to information being displayed off the edge of the Receive pane if the Debug Terminal is sized too small.

TEXT WRAPPING IN THE DEBUG TERMINAL.

The maximum Receive pane buffer size is defined in terms of lines. It can be set to any power of two between 256 and 8192; 1024 is the default. Data received by the Debug Terminal is maintained in this buffer for display on

MAXIMUM BUFFER SIZE.

the screen. If the default is used, for example, you could receive 1024 lines worth of text from a BASIC Stamp, and still be able to scroll back and view the first line that was received. Upon receiving the 1025th line of text, the first line of text is pushed out of the buffer and is lost for good, making the first visible line in the Receive pane actually be the 2nd line of text that was received. Larger buffer sizes consume more PC memory (256 * buffer_size * Number_of_Open_Debug_Terminals bytes), so it is best to set it only as high as you need it for your application.

The Tab size can be adjusted as well, anywhere from 3 to 16 character spaces. The default is 8. Keep in mind that most people don't change this value, so writing code that relies on a particular setting other than 8 may display improperly on other user's Debug Terminals.

DEBUG FUNCTION PREFERENCES.

Under the Debug Function tab (Figure 3.25), checkboxes allow enabling or disabling of special processing for 16 different control characters. The default is for all 16 control characters to be processed, but you may disable one or more of them if you are using the Debug Terminal to view data coming from a device other than a BASIC Stamp.

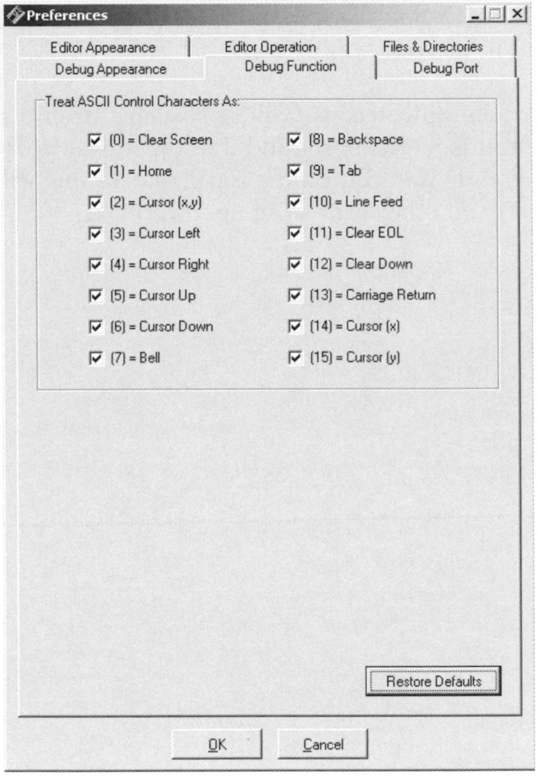

Figure 3.25: The Debug Function Tab under Edit → Preferences.

For example, a device that sends out a 0 to indicate something other than Clear Screen will cause unintentional clearing of the Receive pane; unchecking the checkbox for "(0) = Clear Screen" will prevent this from happening.

DEBUG PORT PREFERENCES.

Under the Debug Port tab (Figure 3.26), each of the four (4) Debug Terminal's default COM port settings may be configured separately. These settings are only used when the Debug Terminal is manually opened.

Figure 3.26: The Debug Port Tab under Edit → Preferences.

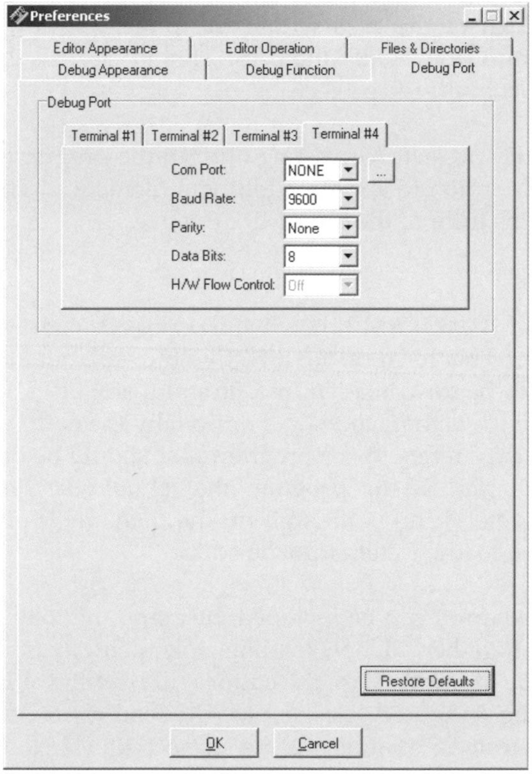

You may assign a specific COM port from the available drop-down list; this list can be changed by clicking on the (...) button to the right. Note that any Debug Terminals that are opened automatically after a PBASIC program is downloaded will always default to the COM port and settings used during download. If NONE is selected as the COM port, the manually opened Debug Terminal will not open any port upon startup, so you will have to manually select the desired COM port from the Debug Terminal window each and every time you open that Debug Terminal.

Using the BASIC Stamp Editor

Advanced Compilation Techniques

For BS2e, BS2sx, BS2p, BS2pe and BS2px modules, each editor page can be a separate project, or part of a single project. A project is a set of up to eight files that should all be downloaded to the BASIC Stamp for a single application. Each of the files within the project is downloaded into a separate "program slot". Only the BASIC Stamp 2e, 2sx, 2p, 2pe, and 2px modules support multi-file projects.

INTRODUCTION TO BASIC STAMP PROJECTS.

For BASIC Stamp projects (consisting of multiple programs), the $STAMP directive has an option to specify additional filenames. The syntax below demonstrates this form of the $STAMP directive:

USING THE $STAMP DIRECTIVE TO DEFINE MULTI-FILE PROJECTS.

```
'  { $STAMP  BS2e, file2, file3, …, file8 }
```

Use this form of the $STAMP directive if a project, consisting of multiple files, is desired. This form of the directive must be entered only into the first program (to be downloaded into program slot 0). The *file2*, *file3*, etc. items should be the actual name (and optionally the path) of the other files in the project. *File2* refers to the program that should be downloaded into program slot 1, *file3* is the program that should be downloaded into program slot 2, etc. If no path is given, the filename is given the path of program 0 when loading them into the editor.

Up to seven filenames can be included, bringing the total to eight files in the project all together. Upon loading, tokenizing, running or viewing program 0 in the Memory Map, the editor will read the $STAMP directive, determine if the indicated files exist, will load them if necessary and change their captions to indicate the project they belong to and their associated program number. After the directive is tokenized properly, and all associated files are labeled properly, tokenizing, running or viewing any program in the Memory Map will result in that program's entire project being tokenized, downloaded or viewed.

When program #0 of a multi-file project is opened from diskette, the entire project will be loaded (all referenced files) as well. When a file that is part of a multi-file project is closed, the entire project (all the associated files) will be closed as well.

To create a project consisting of multiple files, follow these steps:

1. Create the first file in the editor and save it (we'll call it Sample.bsx). This will be the program that is downloaded into program slot 0.
2. Create at least one other file in the editor and save it also (we'll call it NextProgram.bsx).

Note: At this point the editor tabs will be:

> 0:Sample.bsx   and   0:NextProgram.bsx.

indicating that there are two unrelated files open "Sample.bsx" and "NextProgram.bsx" and each will be downloaded into program slot 0.

3. Go back to the first program and enter or modify the $STAMP directive using the project format. Use "NextProgram" as the *File2* argument. For example:

```
' {$STAMP BS2sx, NextProgram.bsx}
```

4. Then tokenize the code by pressing F7 or selecting Run → Check Syntax from the menu.

At this point, the BASIC Stamp Editor will see the $STAMP directive and realize that this file (Sample.bsx) is the first file in a project and that the second file should be NextProgram.bsx. It will then search for the file on the hard drive (to verify its path is correct), will see that it is already loaded, and then will change the editor tabs to indicate the project relationship. At this point the editor tabs will be:

> 0:Sample.bsx   and   [Sample] 1:NextProgram.bsx.

indicating that there are two related files open; "Sample.bsx" and "NextProgram.bsx". NextProgram.bsx belongs to the "Sample" project and it will be downloaded into program slot 1 and Sample.bsx will be downloaded into program slot 0.

Using the BASIC Stamp Editor

The editor has the ability to treat projects as one logical unit and can download each of the associated source code files at once. In order to minimize download time for large projects a Project Download Mode is available in the Preferences window. The available modes are: "Modified" (the default), "All" or "Current" and are explained below. This item only affects download operations for the BS2e, BS2sx, BS2p and BS2pe. See Table 3.7.

PROJECT DOWNLOAD MODES.

Download Mode	Function
Modified (default)	This mode will cause only the source code files that were modified since the last download to be downloaded next time. If no files have been modified since the last download, or the entire project has just been loaded into the editor, all the files will be downloaded next time. This mode decreases the delay during downloading projects and should help speed development and testing.
All	This mode will cause all the source code files to be downloaded each time. This will be noticeably slow with large projects.
Current	This mode will cause only the current source code file to be downloaded, ignoring all the others. This mode can be helpful, but can lead to development errors if you forget to download a required program.

Table 3.7: Project Download Modes.

Regardless of the download mode selected, the programs will be downloaded into the program slot indicated in their tab.

Some source code may be suitable for multiple uses but requires changing a set of constants as needed for each case. For example, you may want to run the same program on a BS2 and a BS2sx, but the resolution of time-sensitive commands is different, requiring slight code modifications. Several conditional compile directives exist in PBASIC 2.5 to assist with this situation. Table 3.8 lists the available directives.

CONDITIONAL COMPILE DIRECTIVES.

Directive	Function
#DEFINE	Allows the programmer to create custom symbols for use within conditional compilation control structures.
#IF...#THEN...#ELSE	Evaluate Condition and, if it is True, compile the statement(s) following #THEN, otherwise compile the statements following #ELSE.
#SELECT...#CASE	Evaluate Expression and then conditionally compile a block of code based on comparison to Condition(s). If no conditions are found True and a #CASE ELSE block is included, the #CASE #ELSE code statements will compiled.
#ERROR	Allows the programmer to create a custom error dialog.

Table 3.8: Conditional Compile Directives.

NOTE: These directives require PBASIC 2.5.

Lets look at the syntax and examples for each conditional compile directive. For an explanation of syntax conventions, see page 128.

#DEFINE SYNTAX.

#DEFINE Symbol { = Value }

#DEFINE allows the programmer to create custom, compile-time, symbols for use within conditional compile control structures.

- **Symbol** is a unique symbol name that will optionally represent a *Value*.
- **Value** is an optional constant/expression specifying the value of *Symbol*. If the value parameter is omitted, *Symbol* is defined as true (-1).

Example:

```
' {$PBASIC 2.5}

#DEFINE DebugMode

#IF DebugMode #THEN DEBUG "Debugging."
STOP
```

In the example above, the #DEFINE statement defines *DebugMode* to be "true" (-1), since there is no *Value* argument provided. The second line is another conditional compile statement, #IF...#THEN (see below for more information) which evaluates the state of *DebugMode,* determines it is true and then allows the following DEBUG statement to be compiled into the program. The last line, STOP, is compiled into the program afterwards. The result of compiling this example is a program with only two executable statements, DEBUG "Debugging", CR and STOP. The real power of this example, however, is more obvious when you comment out, or remove, the #DEFINE line. Look at the next example, below:

```
' {$PBASIC 2.5}

' #DEFINE DebugMode

#IF DebugMode #THEN DEBUG "Dubugging."
STOP
```

Here we commented out the #DEFINE line, effectively removing that line from the program. This means that the symbol *DebugMode* will be undefined, and undefined conditional compile symbols are treated as

False (0). Upon compiling this example, the #IF…#THEN statement will evaluate *DebugMode*, which is False (because it is undefined) and then will not allow the DEBUG statement to be compiled. Only the STOP command will be compiled into the program in this example. This is a very powerful feature for quickly removing many DEBUG statements (or other statements) from a program when you're done developing it, but leaving the possibility of re-enabling all those statements should further maintenance be required at a later time.

The optional *Value* argument can be used, for example, to select modes of operation:

```
' {$PBASIC 2.5}

#DEFINE SystemMode = 2

#IF SystemMode = 1 #THEN
  HIGH 1
#ELSE
  LOW 1
#ENDIF
```

In the example above, the first line defines *SystemMode* to be equal to 2. The #IF…#THEN statement evaluates the state of *SystemMode*, determines it is 2, so the condition is false, and then it skips the statement after #THEN and allows the statement following #ELSE to be compiled into the program.

Note, conditional compile directives are evaluated just before the program is compiled, so variables and named constants cannot be referenced within a conditional compile definition. Compile-time symbols created with #DEFINE can, however, be referenced by conditional compile commands.

#IF *Condition(s)* #THEN
    Statement(s)
{ #ELSE
    ***Statement(s)* }**
#ENDIF

#IF…#THEN SYNTAX.

#IF...#THEN is a conditional compile structure similar to the run-time IF...THEN command except that, at compile time, #IF...#THEN evaluates *Condition(s)* and, if it is True, compiles the *Statement(s)* following #THEN, otherwise it compiles the *Statement(s)* following #ELSE.

- **Condition** is a statement that can be evaluated as True or False during compile-time.
- **Statement** is any valid PBASIC instruction.

Example:

```
' {$PBASIC 2.5}

' set Baud for 9600-N81

#IF ($STAMP = BS2sx) OR ($STAMP = BS2p) #THEN
  Baud   CON   16624
#ELSE

  #IF ($STAMP = BS2px)
    Baud   CON   16780
  #ELSE
    Baud   CON   16468
  #ENDIF

#ENDIF
```

In this example, the constant *Baud* is set to an appropriate value for the BASIC Stamp that is specified in the $STAMP directive (not shown). This code will work with the BS2, BS2e, BS2sx, BS2p, BS2pe, and BS2px.

One important thing to note is that the $STAMP directive is used here as a compile-time symbol, as if it were defined by #DEFINE. The compiler treats all the editor directives, $STAMP, $PBASIC and $PORT as "defined" compile-time symbols set equal to the respective value used in their declaration. At the time of this writing, using $PBASIC in this fashion is pointless since the conditional-compile directives are only supported in PBASIC 2.5, and would cause an error if compiled in any other version of the language.

#SELECT *Expression*
   #CASE *Condition(s)*
    Statement(s)
  { **#CASE** *Condition(s)*
    Statement(s)
  #CASE #ELSE
    Statement(s) }
#ENDSELECT

#SELECT...#CASE is a conditional compile structure similar to the run-time SELECT...CASE command except that, at compile time, #SELECT...#CASE evaluates *Expression* and then conditionally compiles a block of code based on comparison to *Condition(s)*. If no *Conditions* are found to be True and a #CASE #ELSE block is included, the *Statement(s)* in the #CASE #ELSE block will be compiled.

- **Expression** is a statement that can be evaluated as True or False during compile-time.
- **Condition** is a statement, that when compared to *Expression*, can be evaluated as True or False. Multiple conditions within the same CASE can be separated by commas (,).
- **Statement** is any valid PBASIC instruction.

Example:

```
' {$PBASIC 2.5}

#SELECT $STAMP
  #CASE BS2, BS2e, BS2sx
    GOSUB LCD_Write
  #CASE #ELSE
    LCDOUT LCDpin, cmd, [char]
#ENDSELECT
```

This example checks the $STAMP directive at compile-time and either compiles

```
GOSUB LCD_Write
```

- or –

```
LCDOUT LCDpin, cmd, [char]
```
into the program.

#ERROR SYNTAX.

#ERROR *Message*

#ERROR displays a compile-time error. This allows the programmer to flag fatal errors during compilation.

- *Message* is the error message string, enclosed in quotes.

Example:

```
' {$PBASIC 2.5}

#DEFINE I2CReady = (($STAMP = BS2p) OR ($STAMP = BS2pe) OR ($STAMP = BS2px))

#IF NOT I2CReady #THEN
  #ERROR "BS2p, BS2pe, or BS2px is required for this program."
#ENDIF
```

When compiled, this example will cause the editor to halt compilation and display the dialog below if you attempt to compile for a BASIC Stamp model other than the BS2p, BS2pe, or BS2px:

Figure 3.27: Custom Error Message using the #ERROR directive.

Features for Developers

The BASIC Stamp Editor has several features that are designed to support the needs of developers. Note: when installing the BASIC Stamp editor, you can instruct the installer to include additional developer resources by selecting the "Custom" option from the "Setup Type" prompt.

GENERATE OBJECT CODE FEATURE.

The Generate Object Code feature allows you to tokenize a PBASIC program and save it to a file in the tokenized form. This allows you to send your BASIC Stamp object code (the actual binary data that is downloaded to the BASIC Stamp module) to other people without having to reveal your PBASIC source code. If you are a developer who has customers using BASIC Stamp-based products, you can release firmware updates to them in this manner.

Object code can be saved as a separate .obj file (downloadable with the StampLoader.exe program) or as a single executable (integrated with the StampLoader.exe inside of it). The single executable method provides a simpler way to pass your firmware update on to your customers.

Any syntactically correct PBASIC source code can be used with the Generate Object Code feature; this includes BS1 and BS2 code as well as BS2e, BS2sx, BS2p, BS2pe, and BS2px code that is either a single file or a multi-file project. Note: The original DOS-based software for the BS1 included a directive called BSAVE; when used it would cause the software to generate an object file. In the BASIC Stamp Windows Editor, the Generate Object Code feature replaces and enhances the BSAVE feature; the reserved word BSAVE is still accepted in BS1 source code, but is simply ignored. Old BS1 object code saved via the BSAVE option is not compatible with the StampLoader.exe program so you must regenerate the object file using the BASIC Stamp Windows Editor.

If you don't have the StampLoader.exe program, it can be automatically generated for you by selecting the second output file option, "Object Code and Stamp Loader", in the Generate Object Code window. Additionally, firmware, product, company and related info can be embedded in the object code or single executable file for your customers to view before downloading.

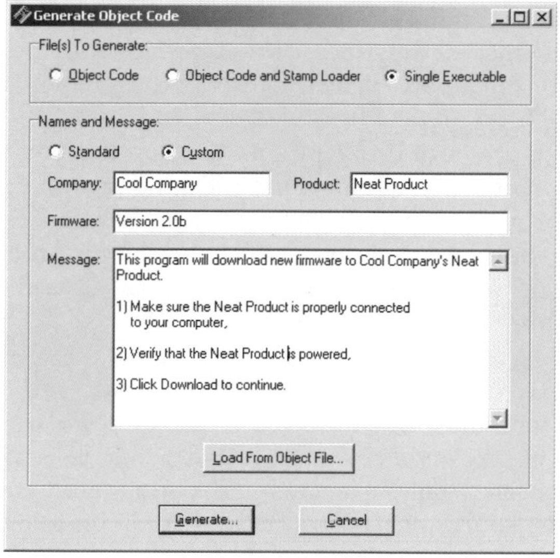

Figure 3.28: The Generate Object Code Window.

In the example above, we chose to generate a single executable with custom names and messages as shown. Then we clicked the Generate… button (which prompted us for a file name) and the file was created. When a user runs the file we just generated, they see a screen similar to the figure below:

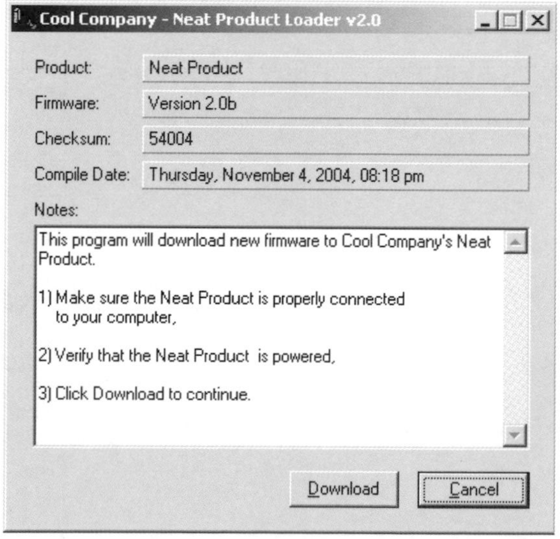

Figure 3.29: Example customized StampLoader.exe file.

Using the BASIC Stamp Editor

Another feature of interest to some developers is the BASIC Stamp Editor's Command Line interface. This interface provides for command line, batch file or third-party driven control of the editor.

The Stampw.exe program is a Win32 application that can be run through any standard method. When run with the command-line options, however, it provides special features that developers and product manufacturing managers may find useful. While this program can be run from a command prompt on a Windows system, it will not work on a DOS-only system.

The Stampw.exe supports redirection of its input and output via the standard pipe mechanisms. If its output is redirected via the command-line (ex: Stampw.exe myfile.bs2 > Test1.txt) the designated output file, *Test1.txt* in this case, will be created and various information about the processing of the source file will be stored there. This information directly reflects the information available on the GUI prompts, interactions with the user and downloading status. This feature can be combined with the /NoDebug and /NoPrompts switches for various levels of GUI interaction with the user; including completely hidden operation.

The following is the syntax of the BASIC Stamp Editor's command-line switches.

```
Stampw.exe {/Com#} {{/ReadOnly}  source_file}

Stampw.exe {/Com#} /Download {/Updates}{/NoDebug}{/NoPrompts} source_file > output_file

Stampw.exe {/Com#} /Identify {/NoPrompts} > output_file

Stampw.exe /Tokenize source_file > output_file

Stampw.exe /Pipe master_file

Stampw.exe /Help
```

Table 3.9 gives a function description for each command-line switch.

Table 3.9: Command Line Switches

Command	Function
/Com#	Specify com port (serial port) to download to. # is a valid com port number. NOTE: must be one word, i.e.: Com2 indicates com port 2.
/ReadOnly	Open *source_file* in read-only mode. The Ctrl key acts as a download key when in read-only mode. Requires *source_file* argument. This command option is not available if double-piped communication is established.
/Identify	Identify BASIC Stamp modules on COM ports. Requires redirection to *output_file*.
/Tokenize	Tokenize source code. No prompts will be displayed. Requires *source_file* argument and redirection to *output_file*.
/Download	Tokenize source code, and download it (if tokenization successful). Requires *source_file* argument and redirection to *output_file*.
/Updates	Provides program slot number (if applicable) and download-percentage-complete status updates during download.
/NoDebug	No Debug Terminal opens after downloading (even if code contains DEBUGs) and COM port is immediately closed after downloading. This option requires /Download switch. Note: This switch will have no effect if Debug Terminal is already open from a previous operation.
/NoPrompts	No screen prompts at all (except for Debug Terminal). This option requires /Download switch.
/Pipe master_file	Start up *master_file* (must be .exe) and establish bi-directional communication pipes (double-piped communication) for master-program-controlled execution. Stampw.exe remains open until *master_file* breaks pipe. This command option is not available once double-piped communication is established.
/Help	Display command-line help. This command option is not available if double-piped communication is established.

When the output of the BASIC Stamp Editor is piped to a file or a master program, it displays all of its messages in a specific, predefined format. Each message has a unique 3-digit number. Detailed information about the use of command-line options, including a table of all messages with their ID numbers, can be found in the "What's New in Stamp.exe" document included with the typical installation of the Stamp Editor.

Using the BASIC Stamp Editor

BASIC Stamp Architecture Introduction This chapter provides detail on the architecture (RAM usage) and math functions of the BS1, BS2, BS2e, BS2sx, BS2p, BS2pe, and BS2px.

The following icons will appear to indicate where there are differences among the various BASIC Stamp models:

 One or more of these icons indicates the item applies only to the BS1, BS2, BS2e, BS2sx, BS2p, BS2pe, or BS2px respectively.

If an item applies to the all of the models in the BS2 family, this icon is used.

MEMORY ORGANIZATION

The BASIC Stamp has two kinds of memory; RAM (for variables used by your program) and EEPROM (for storing the program itself). EEPROM may also be used to store long-term data in much the same way that desktop computers use a hard drive to hold both programs and files.

An important distinction between RAM and EEPROM is this:

- RAM loses its contents when the BASIC Stamp loses power; when power returns, all RAM locations are cleared to 0s.
- EEPROM retains the contents of memory, with or without power, until it is overwritten (such as during the program-downloading process or with a WRITE instruction.)

RAM ORGANIZATION (BS1)

The BS1 has 16 bytes (8 words) of RAM space arranged as shown in Table 4.1 The first word, called PORT, is used for I/O pin control. It consists of two bytes, PINS and DIRS. The bits within PINS correspond to each of the eight I/O pins on the BS1. Reading PINS effectively reads the I/O pins directly, returning an 8-bit set of 1's and 0's corresponding to the high and low state of the respective I/O pin at that moment. Writing to PINS will store a high or low value on the respective I/O pins (though only on pins that are set to outputs).

THE INPUT/OUTPUT VARIABLES.

The second byte of PORT, DIRS, controls the direction of the I/O pins. Each bit within DIRS corresponds to an I/O pin's direction. A high bit (1) sets the corresponding I/O pin to an output direction and a low bit (0) sets the corresponding I/O pin to an input direction.

The remaining words (W0 – W6) are available for general-purpose use. Each word consists of separately addressable bytes and the first two bytes (B0 and B1) are bit addressable as well.

You may assign other names (symbols) to these RAM registers as shown in section "Defining and Using Variables", below.

When the BS1 is powered up, or reset, all memory locations are cleared to 0, so all pins are inputs (DIRS = %00000000). Also, if the PBASIC program sets all the I/O pins to outputs (DIRS = %11111111), then they will initially output low, since the output latch (PINS) is cleared to all zeros upon power-up or reset, as well.

Word Name	Byte Names	Bit Names	Special Notes
PORT	PINS	PIN0 – PIN7	I/O pins; bit addressable.
	DIRS	DIR0 – DIR7	I/O pins directions; bit addressable.
W0	B0	BIT0 – BIT7	Bit addressable.
	B1	BIT8 – BIT15	Bit addressable.
W1	B2		
	B3		
W2	B4		
	B5		
W3	B6		
	B7		
W4	B8		
	B9		
W5	B10		
	B11		
W6	B12		Used by GOSUB instruction.
	B13		Used by GOSUB instruction.

Table 4.1: BS1 RAM Organization. Note: There are eight words, consisting of two bytes each for a total of 16 bytes. The bits within the upper two words are individually addressable.

The BS2, BS2e, and BS2sx models have 32 bytes of Variable RAM space arranged as shown in Table 4.2. Of these, the first six bytes are reserved for input, output, and direction control of the I/O pins. The remaining 26 bytes are available for general-purpose use as variables.

The BS2p, BS2pe, and BS2px models have an extra set of INS, OUTS, and DIRS registers for a total of 38 bytes of variable RAM. These are "shadow" registers that are switched in and out of the memory map with the AUXIO, MAINIO, and IOTERM commands. While this feature exists in the variable RAM for these models, only the BS2p40 module has the extra 16 I/O pins for which this feature is intended.

THE INPUT/OUTPUT VARIABLES.

The word variable INS is unique in that it is read-only. The 16 bits of INS reflect the state of I/O pins P0 through P15. It may only be read, not written. OUTS contains the states of the 16 output latches. DIRS controls the direction (input or output) of each of the 16 I/O pins.

A 0 in a particular DIRS bit makes the corresponding pin an input and a 1 makes the corresponding pin an output. So if bit 5 of DIRS is 0 and bit 6 of DIRS is 1, then I/O pin 5 (P5) is an input and I/O pin 6 (P6) is an output. A pin that is an input is at the mercy of circuitry outside the BASIC Stamp; the BASIC Stamp cannot change its state. A pin that is an output is set to the state indicated by the corresponding bit of the OUTS register.

When the BASIC Stamp is powered up, or reset, all memory locations are cleared to 0, so all pins are inputs (DIRS = %0000000000000000). Also, if the PBASIC program sets all the I/O pins to outputs (DIRS = %1111111111111111), then they will initially output low, since the output latch (OUTS) is cleared to all zeros upon power-up or reset, as well.

Table 4.2: RAM Organization for all BS2 models.

NOTE: There are 16 words, of two bytes each for a total of 32 bytes*. All bits are individually addressable through variable modifiers; the bits within the upper three words are also individually addressable though the pre-defined names shown. All registers are word, byte, nibble and bit addressable.

*The BS2p, BS2pe, and BS2px have an additional set of INS, OUTS, and DIRS registers that are switched in and out of the memory map in place of the main INS, OUTS, and DIRS registers by using AUXIO, MAINIO, and IOTERM. Only the BS2p40 has the required extra I/O pins this feature is intended for.

Word Name	Byte Names	Nibble Names	Bit Names	Special Notes
INS*	INL, INH	INA, INB INC, IND	IN0 – IN7 IN8 – IN15	Input pins
OUTS*	OUTL, OUTH	OUTA, OUTB OUTC, OUTD	OUT0 – OUT7 OUT8 – OUT15	Output pins
DIRS*	DIRL, DIRH	DIRA, DIRB DIRC, DIRD	DIR0 – DIR7 DIR8 – DIR15	I/O pin direction control
W0	B0, B1			
W1	B2, B3			
W2	B4, B5			
W3	B6, B7			
W4	B8, B9			
W5	B10, B11			
W6	B12, B13			
W7	B14, B15			
W8	B16, B17			
W9	B18, B19			
W10	B20, B21			
W11	B22, B23			
W12	B24, B25			

The INS variable always shows the state of the I/O pins themselves, regardless of the direction of each I/O pin. We call this, "reading the pins". If a pin was set to an input mode (within DIRS) and an external circuit connected the I/O pin to ground, the corresponding bit of INS would be low. If a pin was set to an output mode and the pin's state was set to a high level (within OUTS), the corresponding bit of INS would be high. If, however, that same pin was externally connected directly to ground, the corresponding bit of INS would be low; since we're reading the state of the pin itself and the BASIC Stamp cannot override a pin that is driven to ground or 5 volts externally. Note: The last example is an error, is a direct short and can cause damage to the BASIC Stamp! Do not intentionally connect output pins directly to an external power source or you risk destroying your BASIC Stamp.

To summarize: DIRS determines whether a pin's state is set by external circuitry (input, 0) or by the state of OUTS (output, 1). INS always matches the actual states of the I/O pins, whether they are inputs or outputs. OUTS holds bits that will only appear on pins whose DIRS bits are set to output.

SUMMARY OF THE FUNCTION OF DIRS, INS AND OUTS.

In programming the BASIC Stamp, it's often more convenient to deal with individual bytes, nibbles or bits of INS, OUTS and DIRS rather than the entire 16-bit words. PBASIC has built-in names for these elements, shown in Table 4.2.

Here's an example of what is described in Table 4.2. The INS register is 16-bits (corresponding to I/O pins 0 though 15). The INS register consists of two bytes, called INL (the Low byte) and INH (the High byte). INL corresponds to I/O pins 0 through 7 and INH corresponds to I/O pins 8 though 15. INS can also be thought of as containing four nibbles, INA, INB, INC and IND. INA is I/O pins 0 though 3, INB is I/O pins 4 though 7, etc. In addition, each of the bits of INS can be accessed directly using the names IN0, IN1, IN2… IN5.

The same naming scheme holds true for the OUTS and DIRS variables as well.

As Table 4.2 shows, the BASIC Stamp module's memory is organized into 16 words of 16 bits each. The first three words are used for I/O. The remaining 13 words are available for use as general-purpose variables.

PREDEFINED "FIXED" VARIABLES.

The 40-pin BS2p uses the first three words for I/O even though it has twice as many I/O pins. This is done with the AUXIO, MAINIO, and IOTERM commands, which effectively switch the auxiliary I/O registers in and out of the INS, OUTS, and DIRS locations.

Just like the I/O variables, the general-purpose variables have predefined names: W0 through W12 and B0 through B25. B0 is the low byte of W0; B1 is the high byte of W0; and so on through W12 (B24=low byte, B25=high byte). Unlike I/O variables, there's no reason that your program variables have to be stuck in a specific position in the BASIC Stamp's physical memory. A byte is a byte regardless of its location. And if a program uses a mixture of variables of different sizes, it can be difficult to logically dole them out or allocate storage.

More importantly, mixing fixed variables with automatically allocated variables (discussed in the next section) is an invitation to bugs. A fixed variable can overlap an allocated variable, causing data meant for one variable to show up in another! The fixed variable names (of the general-purpose variables) are only provided for power users who require absolute access to a specific location in RAM.

We recommend that you avoid using the fixed variables in most situations. Instead, let PBASIC allocate variables as described in the next section. The editor software will organize your storage requirements to make optimal use of the available memory.

DEFINING AND USING VARIABLES (VAR).

Before you can use a variable in a PBASIC program you must declare it. "Declare" means letting the BASIC Stamp know that you plan to use a variable, what you want to call it, and how big it is. Although PBASIC does have predefined variables that you can use without declaring them first (see previous sections), the preferred way to set up variables is to use the directive SYMBOL (for the BS1) or VAR (for all BS2 models). Here is the syntax for a variable declaration:

```
SYMBOL     name  =  RegisterName
```

-- or --

```
name VAR  Size
```

where *name* is the name by which you will refer to the variable, *RegisterName* is the "fixed" name for the register and *size* indicates the number of bits of storage for the variable. NOTE: The top example is for the BS1 and the bottom example is for all BS2 models.

There are certain rules regarding symbol names. Symbols must start with a letter or underscore, can contain a mixture of letters, numbers, and underscore (_) characters, and must not be the same as PBASIC reserved words, or labels used in your program. Additionally, symbols can be up to 32 characters long. See Appendix B for a list of PBASIC reserved words. PBASIC does not distinguish between upper and lower case, so the names MYVARIABLE, myVariable, and MyVaRiAbLe are all equivalent.

THE RULES OF SYMBOL NAMES.

For the BS1, the register name is one of the predefined "fixed" variable names, such as W0, W1, B0, B1, etc. Here are a few examples of variable declarations on the BS1:

```
SYMBOL    temporary = W0         ' value can be 0 to 65535
SYMBOL    counter   = B1         ' value can be 0 to 255
SYMBOL    result    = B2         ' value can be 0 to 255
```

The above example will create a variable called *temporary* whose contents will be stored in the RAM location called W0. Also, the variable *counter* will be located at RAM location B1 and *result* at location B2. Note that *temporary* is a word-sized variable (because that's what size W0 is) while the other two are both byte-sized variables. Throughout the rest of the program, we can use the names *temporary*, *counter*, and *result* instead of W0, B1 and B2, respectively. This makes the code much more readable; it's easier to determine what *counter* is used for than it would be to figure out what the name B1 means. Please note that *counter* resides at location B1, and B1 happens to be the high byte of W0. This means than changing *counter* will also change *temporary* since they overlap. A situation like this usually is a mistake and results in strange behavior, but is also a powerful feature if used carefully.

For all BS2 models, the *Size* argument has four choices: 1) Bit (1 bit), 2) Nib (nibble; 4 bits), 3) Byte (8 bits), and 4) Word (16 bits). Here are some examples of variable declarations on the BS2 models:

```
mouse    VAR    BIT     ' Value can be 0 or 1.
cat      VAR    NIB     ' Value can be 0 to 15.
dog      VAR    BYTE    ' Value can be 0 to 255.
rhino    VAR    WORD    ' Value can be 0 to 65535.
```

The above example will create a bit-sized variable called *mouse*, and nibble-sized variable called *cat*, a byte-sized variable called *dog* and a word-sized variable called *rhino*. Unlike in the BS1, these variable declarations don't point to a specific location in RAM. Instead, we only specified the desired size for each variable; the BASIC Stamp will arrange them in RAM as it sees fit. Throughout the rest of the program, we can use the names *mouse, cat, dog* and *rhino* to set or retrieve the contents of these variables.

A variable should be given the smallest size that will hold the largest value that will ever be stored in it. If you need a variable to hold the on/off status (1 or 0) of switch, use a bit. If you need a counter for a FOR...NEXT loop that will count from 1 to 100, use a byte. And so on.

If you assign a value to a variable that exceeds its size, the excess bits will be lost. For example, suppose you use the byte variable *dog*, from the example above, and write dog = 260 (%100000100 binary). What will *dog* contain? It will hold only the lowest 8 bits of 260: %00000100 (4 decimal).

DEFINING ARRAYS.

| All 2 |

On all BS2 models, you can also define multipart variables called arrays. An array is a group of variables of the same size, and sharing a single name, but broken up into numbered cells, called elements. You can define an array using the following syntax:

```
name      VAR    Size(n)
```

where *name* and *Size* are the same as described earlier. The new argument, (n), tells PBASIC how many elements you want the array to have. For example:

```
myList    VAR    Byte(10)            ' Create a 10-byte array.
```

Once an array is defined, you can access its elements by number. Numbering starts at 0 and ends at n-1. For example:

```
myList(3)  =   57
DEBUG  ?  myList(3)
```

This code will display "myList(3) = 57" on the PC screen. The real power of arrays is that the index value can be a variable itself. For example:

```
myBytes           VAR     Byte(10)        ' Define 10-byte array
idx               VAR     Nib             ' Define 4-bit var

FOR idx = 0 TO 9                          ' Repeat with idx = 0, 1, 2...9
  myBytes(idx) = idx * 13                 ' Write idx * 13 to each cell
NEXT

FOR idx = 0 TO 9                          ' Repeat with idx = 0, 1, 2...9
  DEBUG ? myBytes(idx)                    ' Show contents of each cell
NEXT
STOP
```

If you run this program, DEBUG will display each of the 10 values stored in the elements of the array: myBytes(0) = 0*13 = 0, myBytes(1) = 1*13 = 13, myBytes(2) = 2*13 = 26 ... myBytes(9) = 9*13 = 117.

A word of caution about arrays: If you're familiar with other BASICs and have used their arrays, you have probably run into the "subscript out of range" error. Subscript is another term for the index value. It is out-of-range when it exceeds the maximum value for the size of the array. For instance, in the example above, myBytes is a 10-cell array. Allowable index numbers are 0 through 9. If your program exceeds this range, PBASIC will not respond with an error message. Instead, it will access the next RAM location past the end of the array. If you are not careful about this, it can cause all sorts of bugs.

If accessing an out-of-range location is bad, why does PBASIC allow it? Unlike a desktop computer, the BASIC Stamp doesn't always have a display device connected to it for displaying error messages. So it just continues the best way it knows how. It's up to the programmer (you!) to prevent bugs. Clever programmers, can take advantage of this feature, however, to perform tricky effects.

Another unique property of PBASIC arrays is this: You can refer to the 0th cell of the array by using just the array's name without an index value. For example:

```
myBytes           VAR     Byte(10)        ' Define 10-byte array

myBytes(0) = 17                           ' Store 17 to 0th cell
DEBUG ? myBytes(0)                        ' Display contents of 0th cell
DEBUG ? myBytes                           ' Also displays 0th cell
```

All 2

This feature is how the "string" capabilities of the DEBUG and SEROUT command expect to work. A string is simply a byte array used to store text.   See "Displaying Strings (Byte Arrays)" in the DEBUG command description on page 166 for more information.

ALIASES AND VARIABLE MODIFIERS.

An *alias* is an alternative name for an existing variable. For example:

```
SYMBOL   cat          = B0           ' Create a byte-sized variable
SYMBOL   tabby        = cat          ' Create alias for cat
```

-- or --

```
cat           VAR     Byte           ' Create a byte-sized variable
tabby         VAR     cat            ' Create alias for cat
```

In this example, *tabby* is an alias to the variable *cat*. Anything stored in *cat* shows up in *tabby* and vice versa. Both names refer to the same physical piece of RAM. This kind of alias can be useful when you want to reuse a temporary variable in different places in your program, but also want the variable's name to reflect its function in each place. Use caution, because it is easy to forget about the aliases; during debugging, you might end up asking 'How did that value get here?!' The answer is that it was stored in the variable's alias.

On all the BS2 models, an alias can also serve as a window into a portion of another variable. This is done using "modifiers."   Here the alias is assigned with a modifier that specifies what part to reference:

```
rhino         VAR     Word         ' A 16-bit variable
head          VAR     rhino.HIGHBYTE ' Highest 8 bits of rhino
tail          VAR     rhino.LOWBYTE  ' Lowest 8 bits of rhino
```

Given that example, if you write the value %1011000011111101 to *rhino*, then *head* would contain %10110000 and *tail* would contain %11111101.

Table 4.3 lists all the variable modifiers. PBASIC 2.0 and 2.5 lets you apply these modifiers to any variable name and to combine them in any fashion that makes sense. For example, it will allow:

```
rhino         VAR     Word                    ' A 16-bit variable
eye           VAR     rhino.HIGHBYTE.LOWNIB.BIT1 ' A bit
```

Symbol	Definition
LOWBYTE	low byte of a word
HIGHBYTE	high byte of a word
BYTE0	byte 0 (low byte) of a word
BYTE1	byte 1 (high byte) of a word
LOWNIB	low nibble of a word or byte
HIGHNIB	high nibble of a word or byte
NIB0	nib 0 of a word or byte
NIB1	nib 1 of a word or byte
NIB2	nib 2 of a word
NIB3	nib 3 of a word
LOWBIT	low bit of a word, byte, or nibble
HIGHBIT	high bit of a word, byte, or nibble
BIT0	bit 0 of a word, byte, or nibble
BIT1	bit 1 of a word, byte, or nibble
BIT2	bit 2 of a word, byte, or nibble
BIT3	bit 3 of a word, byte, or nibble
BIT4 … BIT7	bits 4 though 7 of a word or byte
BIT8 … Bit15	bits 8 through 15 of a word

Table 4.3: Variable Modifiers for all BS2 models.

The common sense rule for combining modifiers is that they must get progressively smaller from left to right. It would make no sense to specify, for instance, the low byte of a nibble, because a nibble is smaller than a byte! And just because you can stack up modifiers doesn't mean that you should unless it is the clearest way to express the location of the part you want get at. The example above might be improved:

```
rhino          VAR     Word            ' A 16-bit variable
eye            VAR     rhino.BIT9      ' A bit
```

Although we've only discussed variable modifiers in terms of creating alias variables, you can also use them within program instructions:

```
rhino          VAR     Word            ' A 16-bit variable
head           VAR     rhino.HIGHBYTE  ' Highest 8 bits of rhino

rhino = 13567
DEBUG ? head                           ' Display alias variable head
DEBUG ? rhino.HIGHBYTE                 ' rhino.HIGHBYTE works too
STOP
```

Modifiers also work with arrays. For example:

```
myBytes     VAR    Byte(10)            ' Define 10-byte array

myBytes(0) = $AB                       ' Hex $AB into 0th byte
DEBUG  HEX  ?  myBytes.LOWNIB(0)       ' Show low nib ($B)
DEBUG  HEX  ?  myBytes.LOWNIB(1)       ' Show high nib ($A)
```

If you looked closely at that example, you probably thought it was a misprint. Shouldn't myBytes.LOWNIB(1) give you the low nibble of byte 1 of the array rather than the high nibble of byte 0? Well, it doesn't. The modifier changes the meaning of the index value to match its own size. In the example above, when myBytes() is addressed as a byte array, it has 10 byte-sized cells numbered 0 through 9. When it is addressed as a nibble array, using myBytes.LOWNIB(), it has 20 nibble-sized cells numbered 0 through 19. You could also address it as individual bits using myBytes.LOWBIT(), in which case it would have 80 bit-sized cells numbered 0 through 79.

What if you use something other than a "low" modifier, say myBytes.HIGHNIB()? That will work, but its effect will be to start the nibble array with the high nibble of myBytes(0). The nibbles you address with this nib array will all be contiguous, one right after the other, as in the previous example.

```
myBytes    VAR    Byte(10)              ' Define 10-byte array.

myBytes(0) = $AB                        ' Hex $AB into 0th byte
myBytes(1) = $CD                        ' Hex $CD into next byte
DEBUG   HEX   ?   myBytes.HIGHNIB(0)    ' Show high nib of cell 0 ($A)
DEBUG   HEX   ?   myBytes.HIGHNIB(1)    ' Show next nib ($D)
```

This property of modified arrays makes the names a little confusing. If you prefer, you can use the less-descriptive versions of the modifier names; BIT0 instead of LOWBIT, NIB0 instead of LOWNIB, and BYTE0 instead of LOWBYTE. These have exactly the same effect, but may be less likely to be misconstrued.

You may also use modifiers with the 0th cell of an array by referring to just the array name without the index value in parentheses. It's fair game for aliases and modifiers, both in VAR directives and in instructions.

THE MEMORY MAP

On all BS2 models, if you're working on a program and wondering how much variable space you have left, you can use the Memory Map feature of the editor (CTRL-M). See the "Memory Map" section of Chapter 3 on page 50.

The BS2e, BS2sx, BS2p, BS2pe, and BS2px have some additional RAM called Scratch Pad RAM. The BS2e and BS2sx have 64 bytes of Scratch Pad RAM (0 to 63) and the BS2p, BS2pe, and BS2px have 136 bytes of Scratch Pad RAM (0-135). Scratch Pad RAM can only be accessed with the GET and PUT commands and cannot have variable names assigned to it. Table 4.4 shows the layout of all SPRAM registers.

SCRATCH PAD RAM

Notice that the highest locations in Scratch Pad RAM (location 63 in the BS2e and BS2sx, locations 127-135 in the BS2p, BS2pe, and BS2px) are special-purpose, read-only locations that always contain special run-time information. For example, the lowest nibble of location 63 (BS2e and BS2sx) or 127 (BS2p, BS2pe, and BS2px) contains the number of the currently running program slot. This is handy for programs that need to know which program slot they exist in. In the BS2p, BS2pe, and BS2px, the high nibble of location 127 holds the slot designated for READ and WRITE; see the STORE command on page 449 for more information.

Table 4.4: Layout of SPRAM Registers.

NOTE: Scratch Pad RAM can only be accessed with the GET and PUT commands. Scratch Pad RAM cannot have variable names assigned to it.

Location	BS2e and BS2sx	BS2p, BS2pe and BS2px
0...62	General Purpose RAM	General Purpose RAM
63	Bits 0-3: Active program slot number.	General Purpose RAM
64..126	n/a	General Purpose RAM
127	n/a	Bits 0-3, Active program slot #. Bits 4-7, program slot for READ and WRITE operations.
128	n/a	Polled input trigger status of Main I/O pins 0-7 (0 = not triggered, 1 = triggered).
129	n/a	Polled input trigger status of Main I/O pins 8-15 (0 = not triggered, 1 = triggered).
130	n/a	Polled input trigger status of Auxiliary I/O pins 0-7 (0 = not triggered, 1 = triggered).
131	n/a	Polled input trigger status of Auxiliary I/O pins 8-15 (0 = not triggered, 1 = triggered).
132	n/a	Bits 0-3: Polled-interrupt mode, set by POLLMODE
133	n/a	Bits 0-2: Polled-interrupt "run" slot, set by POLLRUN.
134	n/a	Bit 0: Active I/O group; 0 =Main I/O, 1 = Auxiliary I/O.
135	n/a	Bit 0: Polled-output status (set by POLLMODE); 0 = disabled, 1= enabled. Bit 1: Polled-input status; 0 = none defined, 1 = at least one defined. Bit 2: Polled-run status (set by POLLMODE); 0 = disabled, 1 = enabled. Bit 3: Polled-output latch status; 0 = real-time mode, 1 = latch mode. Bit 4: Polled-input state; 0 = no trigger, 1 = triggered. Bit 5: Polled-output latch state; 0 = nothing latched, 1 = signal latched. Bit 6: Poll-wait state; 0 = No Event, 1 = Event Occurred. (Cleared by POLLMODE only). Bit 7: Polling status; 0 = not active, 1 = active.

Suppose you're working on a program called "Three Cheers" that flashes LEDs, makes hooting sounds, and activates a motor that crashes cymbals together, all in sets of three. A portion of your PBASIC program might contain something like:

CONSTANTS AND COMPILE-TIME EXPRESSIONS.

```
FOR   counter = 1  TO  3
    GOSUB Make_Cheers
NEXT
. . .
FOR   counter = 1  TO  3
    GOSUB Blink_LEDs
NEXT
. . .
FOR   counter = 1  TO  3
    GOSUB Crash_Cymbals
NEXT
```

The numbers 1 and 3 in the code above are called *constants*. They are constants because, while the program is running, nothing can happen to change those numbers. This distinguishes constants from variables, which can change while the program is running.

Constants are not limited to the decimal number system; PBASIC allows you to use several numbering systems. See "Number Representations" on page 96.

You can assign names to constants in a fashion similar to how variables are declared. On a BS1, it is identical to variable declarations. For all BS2 models, use the CON directive. Here is the syntax:

DEFINING AND USING CONSTANTS (CON).

```
SYMBOL    Name   =  ConstantValue
```

-- or --

```
Name      CON    ConstantValue
```

Once created, named constants may be used in place of the numbers they represent. For example:

```
SYMBOL    Cheers   =   3                    ' Number of cheers.

FOR  counter = 1  TO  Cheers
   GOSUB  Make_Cheers
NEXT
```

-- or --

```
Cheers    CON   3                           ' Number of cheers.

FOR  counter = 1  TO  Cheers
   GOSUB  Make_Cheers
NEXT
```

That code works exactly the same as the corresponding FOR...NEXT loop in the previous example. The editor software substitutes the number 3 for the symbol named *Cheers* throughout your program. Like variables, labels and instructions, constant names are not case sensitive; *CHEERS*, and *ChEErs* are identical to *Cheers*.

Using named constants does not increase the amount of code downloaded to the BASIC Stamp, and it often improves the clarity of the program. Weeks after a program is written, you may not remember what a particular number was supposed to represent—using a name may jog your memory (or simplify the detective work needed to figure it out).

Named constants also have another benefit. Suppose the "Three Cheers" program had to be upgraded to "Five Cheers." In the original example you would have to change all of the 3s to 5s. Search and replace would help, but you might accidentally change some 3s that weren't numbers of cheers, too. However, if you had made smart use of a named constant, all you would have to do is change 3 to 5 in one place, the constant's declaration:

```
SYMBOL    Cheers   = 5                       ' Number of cheers.
```

-- or --

```
Cheers    CON   5                            ' Number of cheers.
```

Now, assuming that you used the constant *Cheers* wherever your program needed 'the number of cheers,' your upgrade would be done.

On all BS2 models, you can take this idea a step further by defining constants with expressions; groups of math and/or logic operations that the editor software solves (evaluates) at compile-time (the time right after you start the download and before the BASIC Stamp starts running your program). For example, suppose the "Cheers" program also controls a pump to fill glasses with champagne. Perhaps the number of glasses to fill is always twice the number of cheers, minus 1 (another constant): `[All 2]`

```
Cheers    CON    5              ' # of cheers
Glasses   CON    Cheers*2-1     ' # of glasses
```
`[All 2]`

As you can see, one constant can be defined in terms of another. That is, the number glasses depends on the number cheers.

The expressions used to define constants must be kept fairly simple. The editor software solves them from left to right, and doesn't allow you to use parentheses to change the order of evaluation. The operators that are allowed in constant expressions are shown in Table 4.5.

Operator Symbol	Description
+	Add
-	Subtract
*	Multiply
/	Divide
<<	Shift Left
>>	Shift Right
&	Logical AND
|	Logical OR
^	Logical XOR

Table 4.5: Operators allowed in constant expressions for all BS2 models.

The BASIC Stamp, like any computer, excels at math and logic. However, being designed for control applications, the BASIC Stamp does math a little differently than a calculator or spreadsheet program. This section will help you understand BASIC Stamp numbers, math, and logic.

RUN-TIME MATH AND LOGIC. `[1] [All 2]`

In your programs, you may express a number in various ways, depending on how the number will be used and what makes sense to you. By default, the BASIC Stamp recognizes numbers like 0, 99 or 62145 as being in our

NUMBER REPRESENTATIONS.

everyday decimal (base-10) system. However, you may also use hexadecimal (base-16; also called hex) or binary (base-2).

Since the symbols used in decimal, hex and binary numbers overlap (e.g., 1 and 0 are used by all; 0 through 9 apply to both decimal and hex) the editor software needs prefixes to tell the numbering systems apart, as shown below:

```
99          ' Decimal (no prefix)
$1A6        ' Hex (prefix '$' required)
%1101       ' Binary (prefix '%' required)
```

The BASIC Stamp also automatically converts quoted text into ASCII codes, and allows you to apply names (symbols) to constants from any of the numbering systems. For example:

```
SYMBOL    LetterA   =   "A"         ' ASCII code for A (65)
SYMBOL    Cheers    =   3
SYMBOL    Hex128    =   $80
SYMBOL    FewBits   =   %1101
```

-- or --

```
LetterA   CON   "A"                 ' ASCII code for A (65)
Cheers    CON   3
Hex128    CON   $80
FewBits   CON   %1101
```

HEX TO BCD CONVERSION

Binary Coded Decimal (BCD) is a way to encode decimal digits that is easier to display or manipulate in some devices. Each digit of the decimal number (0 – 9) requires 4 bits (a nibble) to encode. For this reason, a BCD byte is always two decimal digits and a BCD word is always four decimal digits. The BASIC Stamp does not support BCD natively, however, because of the way that BCD is encoded the BS2 models' hexadecimal prefix, and Conversion Formatters can be used as a shortcut for most BCD input/output operations as long as the digits used do not exceed valid decimal digits (0 – 9). For example:

```
BCDValue        CON     $4096

DEBUG  HEX  BCDValue
```

The first line creates a symbol, *BCDValue*, that contains the binary form of the hexadecimal value $4096, which means the upper nibble contains the binary value for the decimal digit 4, the next nibble is 0, the next nibble is 9 and the last nibble is 6; this corresponds exactly to the BCD form of the decimal number 4096. The second line in the above example uses the HEX Conversion Formatter within the DEBUG command (see DEBUG, page 159) to output the BCD value 4096 to the Debug Terminal. The HEX Conversion Formatter can also be used for input operations to convert a decimal value to BCD, as long as that decimal value is no greater than 2 digits for a Byte-sized variable or 4 digits for a Word-sized variable.

For more information on constants, see the section "Constants and Compile-Time Expressions", above.

With all BS2 models, some of the math or logic operations in a program are solved by the BASIC Stamp. The editor software solves operations that define constants before the program is downloaded to the BASIC Stamp. The preprocessing that takes place before the program is downloaded is referred to as "compile-time."

WHEN IS RUN-TIME?

All 2

After the download is complete, the BASIC Stamp starts executing your program; this is referred to as "run-time." At run-time the BASIC Stamp processes math and logic operations involving variables, or any combination of variables and constants.

Because compile-time and run-time expressions appear similar, it can be hard to tell them apart.
A few examples will help:

All 2

```
result        VAR    Byte          ' Compile-time assignment

Cheers        CON    3             ' Compile-time
Glasses       CON    Cheers * 2 - 1 ' Compile-time
OneNinety     CON    100 + 90      ' Compile-time
NotWorking    CON    3 * result    ' ERROR: Variables not allowed here

result = Glasses                   ' Run-time
result = 99 + Glasses              ' Run-time
result = OneNinety + 1             ' "100 + 90" solved at compile-time
                                   ' OneNinety + 1 solved at run-time
result = 100 + 90                  ' 100 + 90 solved at run-time
```

Notice that the last example is solved at run-time, even though the math performed could have been solved at compile-time since it involves two constants. If you find something like this in your own programs, you can save some program space in the EEPROM by converting the run-time expression 100+90 into a compile-time expression like OneNinety CON 100+90.

To sum up: compile-time expressions are those that involve only constants; once a variable is involved, the expression must be solved at run-time. That's why the line "NotWorking CON 3 * result" would generate an error message. The CON directive works only at compile-time and *result* is a variable; variables are not allowed in compile-time expressions.

DEFINING AND USING PINS WITH THE PIN DIRECTIVE.

Now we know now to create variables and constants (with VAR and CON) but there is a third option if you're using PBASIC 2.5; pin-type symbols (with PIN). PIN is like VAR and CON put together and represents an I/O pin.

There are some situations where it is handy to refer to a pin using a variable (like IN2 or OUT2) and also as a constant (2, in this case). The PIN directive lets you define a context-sensitive symbol representing an I/O pin. Depending on where and how this pin-type symbol is used determines whether it is treated as an I/O pin input variable, and I/O pin output variable or as a constant representing the pin number.

Let's explore a simple example to see where this is useful. It is common practice to define constants for any number used in many places so that changing that number doesn't create a maintenance hassle later on. If we were to use a constant symbol to represent an I/O pin, we might do something like this:

```
' {$PBASIC 2.5}

signal    CON   1              ' constant-type symbol representing I/O 1

INPUT   signal                 ' set signal pin to input

Wait:
  IF signal = 0 THEN Wait      ' wait until signal pin = 1
```

Here we define *signal* to represent our desired I/O pin, then we use the INPUT command to set it to the input direction and later we check the state of the signal pin and loop (wait) while it is equal to logic 0. This code has a common bug, however; the INPUT command works as expected, because its *Pin* argument requires a number representing the I/O pin, but the *Condition* argument in the IF…THEN statement will always evaluate to false because *signal* is a constant equal to 1, and "1 = 0" is false. What the user really meant to happen is something like: IF IN1 = 0 THEN Wait because *IN1* is the input variable representing the current state of I/O pin 1. This situation is perfect for the PIN directive:

```
' {$PBASIC 2.5}

signal PIN 1              ' pin-type symbol representing I/O 1

INPUT  signal            ' set signal pin to input

Wait:
  IF signal = 0 THEN Wait    ' wait until signal = 1
```

All 2

We only changed one thing in this code: the CON directive was changed to PIN. Now *signal* is a context-sensitive symbol that will be treated as a constant or as a variable depending on where it is used. In the INPUT command *signal* is used as the *Pin* argument, and since that argument requires a number representing the pin number, *signal* is treated as a constant equal to 1. In the IF…THEN statement, *signal* is compared to another value (which implies that what *signal* represents is expected to change at run-time; i.e.: *signal's* value is "variable") so *signal* is treated as a variable equal to the input variable for the defined pin (IN1 in this case).

As another example, consider the following code:

```
' {$PBASIC 2.5}

signal    CON   2        ' constant-type symbol representing I/O 2

OUTPUT  signal           ' set signal pin to output
signal = 1               ' set signal high
```

Here, again, this is a common bug; the OUTPUT command will work as expected, but the signal = 1 statement generates a syntax error at compile-time. Why the error? This is an assignment statement, meant to assign the value 1 to the item on the left, but the item on the left is a constant, not a variable, so it can not be changed at run-time. What the user was thinking when writing this was: OUT2 = 1 which sets the value of the output variable representing I/O pin 2 to logical 1 (high). Here's the solution:

```
' {$PBASIC 2.5}

signal    PIN   2        ' pin-type symbol representing I/O 2

OUTPUT  signal           ' set signal pin to output
signal = 1               ' set signal high
```

The OUTPUT command treats *signal* as a constant equal to 2 and the signal = 1 statement treats *signal* as a variable equal to the output variable for the defined pin (OUT2 in this case).

You might be wondering why "signal = 0" in the IF…THEN statement of our first example treats *signal* as the input variable *IN1* and yet "signal = 1" in our last example treats *signal* as the output variable *OUT2*. The distinction is that the first example is a comparison and the second example is an assignment. Comparisons need to "read" expressions and then evaluate the comparison while assignments need to read expressions and then "write" the results. Since *signal* is to the left of the equal sign (=) in our assignment statement, it must be a variable we can write to, thus it must be treated as OUT2, in this case.

What happens if our pin-type symbol is to the right of the equal sign in an assignment statement? Example:

```
' {$PBASIC 2.5}

signal1   PIN   1        ' pin-type symbol representing I/O 1
signal2   PIN   2        ' pin-type symbol representing I/O 2

INPUT  signal1           ' set signal1 pin to input
OUTPUT signal2           ' set signal2 pin to output
signal2 = signal1        ' set signal2 pin to signal1 pin's state
```

In this case *signal2* is treated as OUT2 and *signal1* is treated as IN1; left side must be written to and right side must be read from.

If a pin-type symbol is used in a command, but not in the *Pin* argument of that command, it will be treated as an input variable (i.e.: INx). NOTE: It is very rare that you'll need to use a pin-type symbol in this way.

The following is a summary of behaviors and uses of pin-type symbols.

PIN_Symbol behaves like a constant:
1. when used in a command's *Pin* argument. Example:

    ```
    OUTPUT   PIN_Symbol
    ```

2. when used in the index of an array. Example:

    ```
    myArray(PIN_Symbol) = 25
    ```

PIN_Symbol behaves like an input variable (INx):
1. when used in a command's non-*Pin* argument that expects to read a variable/constant/expression. Example:

    ```
    DEBUG BIN PIN_Symbol
    ```

2. when used in a command's *Condition* argument. Example:

    ```
    IF PIN_Symbol = 1 THEN...
    ```

3. when used to the right of the equal sign (=) in an assignment statement. Example:

    ```
    ex: myVariable = PIN_Symbol + 1
    ```

PIN_Symbol behaves like an output variable (OUTx):
1. when used in a command's non-*Pin* argument that expects to write a result to a variable. Example:

    ```
    LOOKUP index, [0, 1, 1, 0, 1], PIN_Symbol
    ```

2. when used to the left of the equal sign (=) in an assignment statement. Example:

    ```
    PIN_Symbol = 1
    ```

Let's talk about the four basic operations of arithmetic: addition (+), subtraction (-), multiplication (*), and division (/).

BASIC ARITHMETIC OPERATIONS

1 All 2

You may recall that the order in which you do a series of additions and subtractions doesn't affect the result. The expression 12+7-3+22 works out the same as 22-3+12+7. However, when multiplication or division are involved, it's a different story; 12+3*2/4 is not the same as 2*12/4+3. In fact, you may have the urge to put parentheses around portions of those equations to clear things up.

ORDER OF OPERATIONS.

The BASIC Stamp solves math problems in the order they are written: from left to right. The result of each operation is fed into the next operation. So to compute 12+3*2/4, the BASIC Stamp goes through a sequence like this:

$$12 + 3 = 15$$
$$15 * 2 = 30$$
$$30 / 4 = 7$$

Since the BASIC Stamp performs integer math (whole numbers only) 30 / 4 results in 7, not 7.5. We'll talk more about integers in the next section.

Some other dialects of BASIC would compute that same expression based on their precedence of operators, which requires that multiplication and division be done before addition. So the result would be:

$$3 * 2 = 6$$
$$6 / 4 = 1$$
$$12 + 1 = 13$$

Once again, because of integer math, the fractional portion of 6 / 4 is dropped, so we get 1 instead of 1.5.

1 The BS1 does not allow parenthesis in expressions. Unfortunately, all expressions have to be written so that they evaluate as intended strictly from left to right.

All 2 All BS2 models, however, allow parentheses to be used to change the order of evaluation. Enclosing a math operation in parentheses gives it priority over other operations. To make the BASIC Stamp compute the previous expression in the conventional way, you would write it as 12 + (3*2/4). Within the parentheses, the BASIC Stamp works from left to right. If you wanted to be even more specific, you could write 12 + ((3*2)/4). When there are parentheses within parentheses, the BASIC Stamp works from the innermost parentheses outward. Parentheses placed within parentheses are called "nested parentheses."

INTEGER MATH.

The BASIC Stamp performs all math operations by the rules of positive integer math. That is, it handles only whole numbers, and drops any fractional portions from the results of computations. The BASIC Stamp handles negative numbers using two's complement rules.

BASIC Stamp Architecture – Math and Operators

All BS2 models can interpret twos complement negative numbers correctly [All 2] in DEBUG and SEROUT instructions using formatters like SDEC (for signed decimal). In calculations, however, it assumes that all values are positive. This yields correct results with two's complement negative numbers for addition, subtraction, and multiplication, but not for division.

The standard operators we just discussed: +, - ,* and / all work on two values; as in 1 + 3 or 26 * 144. The values that operators process are referred to as arguments. So we say that the add, subtract, multiply and divide operators take two arguments.

UNARY AND BINARY OPERATORS.

Operators that take two arguments are called "binary" operators, and those that take only one argument are called "unary" operators. Please note that the term "binary operator" has nothing to do with binary numbers; it's just an inconvenient coincidence that the same word, meaning 'involving two things' is used in both cases.

The minus sign (-) is a bit of a hybrid. It can be used as a binary operator, as in 8-2 = 6, or it can be used as a unary operator to represent negative numbers, such as -4.

Unary operators take precedence over binary operators; the unary operation is always performed first. For example, on all BS2 models, SQR is the unary operator for square root. In the expression 10 - SQR 16, the BASIC Stamp first takes the square root of 16, then subtracts it from 10.

Most of the descriptions that follow say something like "computes (some function) of a 16-bit value." This does not mean that the operator does not work on smaller byte or nibble values, but rather that the computation is done in a 16-bit workspace. If the value is smaller than 16 bits, the BASIC Stamp pads it with leading 0s to make a 16-bit value. If the 16-bit result of a calculation is to be packed into a smaller variable, the higher-order bits are discarded (truncated).

NOTES ABOUT THE 16-BIT WORKSPACE.

Keep this in mind, especially when you are working with two's complement negative numbers, or moving values from a larger variable to a smaller one. For example, look at what happens when you move a two's complement negative number into a byte (rather than a word):

```
[All 2]   value     VAR     Byte

          value = - 99
          DEBUG  SDEC  ?  value              ' Show signed decimal result (157)
```

[1] [All 2] We expected -99 to be displayed but what we got was 157. How did -99 become 157? Let's look at the bits: 99 is %01100011 binary. When the BASIC Stamp negates 99, it converts the number to 16 bits %0000000001100011, and then takes the two's complement, %1111111110011101. Since we've asked for the result to be placed in an 8-bit (byte) variable, the upper eight bits are truncated and the lower eight bits stored in the byte: %10011101.

Now for the second half of the story. DEBUG's SDEC modifier (for all BS2 models) expects a 16-bit, two's complement value, but we've only given it a byte to work with. As usual, it creates a 16-bit value by padding the leading eight bits with 0s: %0000000010011101. And what's that in signed decimal? 157.

To fix this problem, always store values that are intended to be signed into a word-sized variable.

UNARY OPERATORS.

Table 4.1 lists the available Unary Operators. Note: the BS1 only supports negative (-).

Table 4.1: Unary Operators. Note: the BS1 only supports the negative (-) unary operator.

Operator	Description	Supported By:
ABS	Returns absolute value	All except BS1
COS	Returns cosine in twos complement binary radians	All except BS1
DCD	2^n-power decoder	All except BS1
~	Inverse	All except BS1
-	Negative	All
NCD	Priority encoder of a 16-bit value	All except BS1
SIN	Returns sine in twos complement binary radians	All except BS1
SQR	Returns square root of value	All except BS1

ABSOLUTE VALUE: ABS

[All 2] The Absolute Value operator (ABS) converts a signed (two's complement) 16-bit number to its absolute value. The absolute value of a number is a positive number representing the difference between that number and 0. For example, the absolute value of -99 is 99. The absolute value of 99 is also 99. ABS works on two's complement negative numbers. Examples of ABS at work:

```
result            VAR     Word

result = -99                           ' Put -99 into result
                                       ' ...(2's complement format)
DEBUG SDEC ? result                    ' Display as a signed #
DEBUG SDEC ? ABS result                ' Display as a signed #
```

The Cosine operator (COS) returns the two's complement, 16-bit cosine of an angle specified as an 8-bit "binary radian" (0 to 255) angle. COS is the same as SIN in all respects, except that the cosine function returns the x distance instead of the y distance. See "Sine: SIN", below, for a code example and more information.

COSINE: COS

[All 2]

The Decoder operator (DCD) is a 2^n-power decoder of a four-bit value. DCD accepts a value from 0 to 15, and returns a 16-bit number with the bit, described by value, set to 1. For example:

DECODER: DCD

[All 2]

```
result    VAR     Word

result  =  DCD   12                    ' Set bit 12
DEBUG BIN16 ?   result                 ' Display result (%0001000000000000)
```

The Inverse operator (~) complements (inverts) the bits of a number. Each bit that contains a 1 is changed to 0 and each bit containing 0 is changed to 1. This process is also known as a "bitwise NOT" and "ones complement". For example:

INVERSE: ~

```
result    VAR     Byte

result = %11110001                     ' Store bits in byte result.
DEBUG  BIN8  ?  result                 ' Display in binary (%11110001)
result = ~ result                      ' Complement result
DEBUG  BIN8  ?  Result                 ' Display in binary (%00001110)
```

The Negative operator (-) negates a 16-bit number (converts to its twos complement).

NEGATIVE: -

[1]

```
SYMBOL  result         = W1

result = -99                           ' Put -99 into result
                                       ' ...(2's complement format)
result = result + 100                  ' Add 100 to it
DEBUG result                           ' Display result (1)
```

-- or --

```
[All 2]  result          VAR     Word

         result = 99                        ' Put -99 into result
                                            ' ...(2's complement format)
         DEBUG SDEC ? result                ' Display as a signed #
         result = -result                   ' Negate the value
         DEBUG SDEC ? result                ' Display as a signed #
```

ENCODER: NCD

[All 2] The Encoder operator (NCD) is a "priority" encoder of a 16-bit value. NCD takes a 16-bit value, finds the highest bit containing a 1 and returns the bit position plus one (1 through 16). If the input value is 0, NCD returns 0. NCD is a fast way to get an answer to the question "what is the largest power of two that this value is greater than or equal to?" The answer NCD returns will be that power, plus one. Example:

```
         result          VAR     Word

         result = %1101                     ' Highest bit set is bit 3
```

SINE: SIN

[All 2] `DEBUG ? NCD result                     ' Show the NCD of result (4)`The Sine operator (SIN) returns the two's complement, 16-bit sine of an angle specified as an 8-bit binary radian (0 to 255) angle.

To understand the SIN operator more completely, let's look at a typical sine function. By definition: given a circle with a radius of 1 unit (known as a unit circle), the sine is the y-coordinate distance from the center of the circle to its edge at a given angle. Angles are measured relative to the 3-o'clock position on the circle, increasing as you go around the circle counterclockwise.

At the origin point (0 degrees) the sine is 0, because that point has the same y (vertical) coordinate as the circle center. At 45 degrees the sine is 0.707. At 90 degrees, sine is 1. At 180 degrees, sine is 0 again. At 270 degrees, sine is -1.

The BASIC Stamp SIN operator breaks the circle into 0 to 255 units instead of 0 to 359 degrees. Some textbooks call this unit a "binary radian" or "brad." Each brad is equivalent to 1.406 degrees. And instead of a unit circle, which results in fractional sine values between 0 and 1, BASIC Stamp SIN is based on a 127-unit circle. Results are given in two's complement form in order to accommodate negative values. So, at the origin, SIN is 0. At 45 degrees (32 brads), sine is 90. At 90 degrees (64 brads), sine is 127. At 180 degrees (128 brads), sine is 0. At 270 degrees (192 brads), sine is -127.

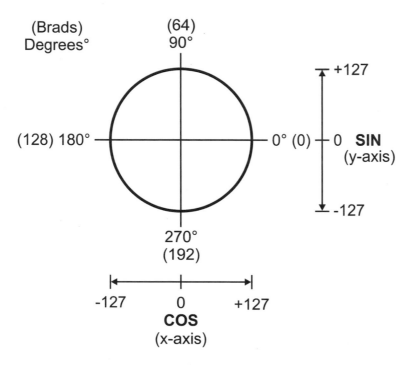

Figure 4.1: 127-Unit Circle

To convert brads to degrees, multiply by 180 then divide by 128, or simply multiply with "*/ 360". To convert degrees to brads, multiply by 128, then divide by 180. Here's a small program that demonstrates the SIN and COS operators:

```
degr    VAR Word
brads   VAR Byte

DEBUG 2, 4, 0,"ANGLE", TAB, "COS", TAB, "SIN", CR
DEBUG "DEGREES", TAB,"BRADS", TAB, "(X)", TAB,"(Y)", CR

FOR degr = 0 TO 359 STEP 45                  ' Increment degrees
  brads = degr * 128 / 180                   ' Convert to brads
   DEBUG CR, DEC3 degr, TAB, DEC3 brads, TAB ' Display angle
   DEBUG SDEC COS brads, TAB, SDEC SIN brads ' Display COS & SIN
NEXT
```

SQUARE ROOT: SQR

The Square Root operator (SQR) computes the integer square root of an unsigned 16-bit number. (The number must be unsigned since the square root of a negative number is an 'imaginary' number.) Remember that most square roots have a fractional part that the BASIC Stamp discards when doing its integer-only math. So it computes the square root of 100 as 10 (correct), but the square root of 99 as 9 (the actual is close to 9.95). Example:

```
DEBUG ? SQR 100          ' Display square root of 100 (10)
DEBUG ? SQR 99           ' Display of square root of 99
                         ' ...(9 due to truncation)
```

BINARY OPERATORS.

Table 4.6 lists the available Binary (two-argument) Operators.

Table 4.6: Binary Operators. Note: some binary operators are not supported by all BASIC Stamp models.

Operator	Description	Supported By:
+	Addition	All
-	Subtraction	All
*	Multiplication	All
**	Multiplication (returns upper 16-bits)	All
*/	Multiply by 8-bit integer, 8-bit fraction	All BS2 models
/	Division	All
//	Modulus (Remainder of division)	All
ATN	Returns arctangent of X/Y vector	All BS2 models
HYP	Returns hypotenuse of X/Y vector	All BS2 models
MIN	Limits a value to a specified low	All
MAX	Limits a value to a specified high	All
DIG	Returns specified digit of number	All BS2 models
<<	Shift bits left by specified amount	All BS2 models
>>	Shift bits right by specified amount	All BS2 models
REV	Reverse specified number of bits	All BS2 models
&	Bitwise AND	All
		Bitwise OR	All
^	Bitwise XOR	All
&/	Logical AND NOT	BS1 Only
|/	Logical OR NOT	BS1 Only
^/	Logical XOR NOT	BS1 Only

ADD: +

The Addition operator (+) adds variables and/or constants, returning a 16-bit result. It works exactly as you would expect with unsigned integers from 0 to 65535. If the result of addition is larger than 65535, the carry bit will be lost. If the values added are signed 16-bit numbers and the destination is a 16-bit variable, the result of the addition will be correct in both sign and value.

For example:

```
SYMBOL    value1  =  W0
SYMBOL    value2  =  W1

value1 = - 99
value2 = 100
value1 = value1 + value2        ' Add the numbers
DEBUG  value1                   ' Show the result (1)
```

-- or --

```
value1    VAR    Word
value2    VAR    Word

value1 = - 1575
value2 = 976
value1 = value1 + value2        ' Add the numbers
DEBUG  SDEC  ?  value1          ' Show the result (-599)
```

The Subtraction operator (-) subtracts variables and/or constants, SUBTRACT: -
returning a 16-bit result. It works exactly as you would expect with
unsigned integers from 0 to 65535. If the result is negative, it will be
correctly expressed as a signed 16-bit number. For example:

```
SYMBOL    value1  =  W0
SYMBOL    value2  =  W1

value1 = 199
value2 = 100
value1 = value1 - value2        ' Subtract the numbers
DEBUG  value1                   ' Show the result (99)
```

-- or --

```
value1    VAR    Word
value2    VAR    Word

value1 = 1000
value2 = 1999
value1 = value1 - value2        ' Subtract the numbers
DEBUG  SDEC  ?  value1          ' Show the result (-999)
```

The Multiply operator (*) multiplies variables and/or constants, returning MULTIPLY: *
the low 16 bits of the result. It works exactly as you would expect with
unsigned integers from 0 to 65535. If the result of multiplication is larger
than 65535, the excess bits will be lost. Multiplication of signed variables
will be correct in both number and sign, provided that the result is in the
range -32767 to +32767.

```
⌐1   SYMBOL    value1    =    W0
     SYMBOL    value2    =    W1

     value1 = 1000
     value2 = 19
     value1 = value1 * value2            ' Multiply value1 by value2
     DEBUG  value1                       ' Show the result (19000)
```

-- or --

```
All 2  value1    VAR    Word
       value2    VAR    Word
       value1 = 1000
       value2 = - 19
       value1 = value1 * value2          ' Multiply value1 by value2
       DEBUG  SDEC  ?  value1            ' Show the result (-19000)
```

MULTIPLY HIGH: **

⌐1 All 2   The Multiply High operator (**) multiplies variables and/or constants, returning the high 16 bits of the result. When you multiply two 16-bit values, the result can be as large as 32 bits. Since the largest variable supported by PBASIC is a word (16 bits), the highest 16 bits of a 32-bit multiplication result are normally lost. The ** (double-star) instruction gives you these upper 16 bits. For example, suppose you multiply 65000 ($FDE8) by itself. The result is 4,225,000,000 or $FBD46240. The * (star, or normal multiplication) instruction would return the lower 16 bits, $6240. The ** instruction returns $FBD4.

```
⌐1   SYMBOL    value1    =    W0
     SYMBOL    value2    =    W1

     value1 = $FDE8
     value2 = value1 ** value1           ' Multiply $FDE8 by itself
     DEBUG  $value2                      ' Return high 16 bits ($FBD4)
```

-- or --

```
All 2  value1    VAR    Word
       value2    VAR    Word

       value1 = $FDE8
       value2 = value1 ** value1         ' Multiply $FDE8 by itself
       DEBUG HEX ? value2                ' Return high 16 bits  ($FBD4)
```

An interesting application of the ** operator allows you no multiply a number by a fractional value less than one. The fraction must be expressed in units of 1/65536. To find the fractional ** argument, multiply the fraction part by 65536. For example, 0.72562 is represented by 47554, which is 0.72562 * 65536.

```
SYMBOL   Frac          = 47554          ' = 0.72562 x 65536
SYMBOL   value         = W0

value = 10000
value = value ** Frac                   ' Multiply 10000 by 0.72562
DEBUG value                             ' Show result (7256)
```

-- or --

```
Frac             CON     47554          ' = 0.72562 x 65536
value            VAR     Word

value = 10000
value = value ** Frac                   ' Multiply 10000 by 0.72562
DEBUG ? value                           ' Show result (7256)
```

The Multiply Middle operator (*/) multiplies variables and/or constants, returning the middle 16 bits of the 32-bit result. This has the effect of multiplying a value by a whole number and a fraction. The whole number is the upper byte of the multiplier (0 to 255 whole units) and the fraction is the lower byte of the multiplier (0 to 255 units of 1/256 each). The */ (star-slash) instruction gives you an excellent workaround for the BASIC Stamp's integer-only math. Suppose you want to multiply a value by 1.5. The whole number, and therefore the upper byte of the multiplier, would be 1, and the lower byte (fractional part) would be 128, since 128/256 = 0.5. It may be clearer to express the */ multiplier in hex—as $0180—since hex keeps the contents of the upper and lower bytes separate.   Here's an example:

MULTIPLY MIDDLE: */

```
value1    VAR    Word

value1 = 100
value1 = value1*/ $0180                 ' Multiply by 1.5 [1 + (128/256)]
DEBUG ? value1                          ' Show result (150)
```

To calculate the constant for use with the */ operator, multiply the target (mixed) value by 256 and convert to an integer. For instance, take Pi (π, 3.14159). The */ constant would be INT(3.14159 * 256) = 804 ($0324). So the constant Pi for use with */ would be $0324. This isn't a perfect match for Pi, but the error is only about 0.1%. Note that the */ operator can be used to multiply by mixed values up to about 255.996.

DIVIDE: /

The Divide operator (/) divides variables and/or constants, returning a 16-bit result. Works exactly as you would expect with unsigned integers from 0 to 65535. Use / only with positive values; signed values do not provide correct results. Here's an example of unsigned division:

```
SYMBOL    value1    =   W0
SYMBOL    value2    =   W1
value1 = 1000
value2 = 5

value1 = value1 / value2          ' Divide the numbers
DEBUG  value1                     ' Show the result (200)
```

-- or --

```
value1    VAR    Word
value2    VAR    Word

value1 = 1000
value2 = 5
value1 = value1 / value2          ' Divide the numbers
DEBUG  DEC  ?  value1             ' Show the result (200)
```

A workaround to the inability to divide signed numbers is to have your program divide absolute values, then negate the result if one (and only one) of the operands was negative. All values must lie within the range of -32767 to +32767. Here is an example:

```
sign           VAR      Bit            ' Bit to hold the result sign
value1         VAR      Word
value2         VAR      Word

value1 = 100
value2 = -3200

sign = value1.BIT15 ^ value2.BIT15    ' Determine sign of result
value2 = ABS value2 / ABS value1      ' Divide absolute values
IF (sign = 1) THEN value2 = -value2   ' Negate result if sign = 1
DEBUG SDEC ? value2                   ' Show the result (-32)
```

MODULUS: //

The Modulus operator (//) returns the remainder left after dividing one value by another. Some division problems don't have a whole-number result; they return a whole number and a fraction. For example, 1000/6 = 166.667. Integer math doesn't allow the fractional portion of the result, so 1000/6 = 166. However, 166 is an approximate answer, because 166*6 = 996. The division operation left a remainder of 4. The // (double-slash) returns the remainder, 4 in this example. Naturally, numbers that divide evenly, such as 1000/5, produce a remainder of 0.

Example:

```
SYMBOL   value1        = W0
SYMBOL   value2        = W1

value1 = 1000
value2 = 6
value1 = value1 // value2          ' Get remainder of value1 / value2
DEBUG value1                       ' Show the result (4)
```

-- or --

```
value1         VAR     Word
value2         VAR     Word

value1 = 1000
value2 = 6
value1 = value1 // value2          ' Get remainder of value1 / value2
DEBUG ? value1                     ' Show the result (4)
```

The Arctangent operator (ATN) returns the angle to the vector specified by X and Y coordinate values. The syntax of ATN is:

ARCTANGENT: ATN

All 2

```
xCoord ATN yCoord
```

where xCoord and yCoord are the coordinates of the target vector point.

In the BASIC Stamp, the angle is returned in binary radians (0 to 255) instead of degrees (0 to 359). See the explanation of the SIN operator for more information about binary radians. Coordinate input values are limited to -127 to 127 (signed bytes) as shown in the diagram of the PBASIC Unit Circle (Figure 4.2).

```
brads          VAR     Word         ' angle in brads
degr           VAR     Word         ' angle in degrees

brads = 4 ATN 4                     ' get angle
degr = brads */ 360                 ' convert to degrees
DEBUG SDEC ? brads                  ' display brads (32)
DEBUG SDEC ? degr                   ' display degrees (45)
```

Figure 4.2: ATN and HYP operators in the PBASIC unit circle

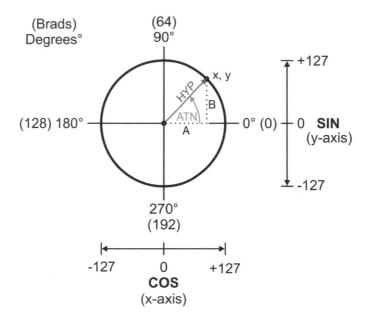

HYPOTENUSE: HYP

[All 2] The Hypotenuse operator (HYP) returns the length of the hypotenuse of a right triangle with sides of length A and B. The syntax of HYP is:

```
SideA HYP SideB
```

where SideA and SideB are the side lengths of a right-triangle (the order isn't important). Another application of HYP is to calculate the distance between the origin (0, 0) and a point (X, Y) in a Cartesian coordinate system. Side length (vector) input values are limited to -127 to 127 (signed bytes). See diagram with ATN operator, Figure 4.2.

```
DEBUG ? 3 HYP 4                  ' hypotenuse of 3x4 triangle (5)
```

MINIMUM: MIN

[1] [All 2] The Minimum operator (MIN) limits a value to a specified 16-bit positive minimum. The syntax of MIN is:

```
value  MIN  limit
```

where *value* is a constant or variable value to perform the MIN function upon and *limit* is the minimum value that *value* is allowed to be. Its logic is, 'if *value* is less than *limit*, then make result = *limit*; if *value* is greater than or equal to *limit*, make result = *value*.'

MIN works in positive math only; its comparisons are not valid when used on two's complement negative numbers, since the positive-integer representation of a number like -1 ($FFFF or 65535 in unsigned decimal) is larger than that of a number like 10 ($000A or 10 decimal). Use MIN only with unsigned integers. Because of the way fixed-size integers work, you should be careful when using an expression involving MIN 0. For example, 0-1 MIN 0 will result in 65535 because of the way fixed-size integers wrap around.

```
SYMBOL  value1        = W0
SYMBOL  value2        = W1

FOR value1 = 100 TO 0 STEP -10        ' Walk value1 from 100 to 0
  value2 = value1 MIN 50              ' Use MIN to clamp at 50
  DEBUG value2                        ' Show "clamped" value
NEXT
-- or --

value           VAR     Word

FOR value = 100 TO 0 STEP 10          ' Walk value from 100 to 0
  DEBUG ? value MIN 50                ' Show value1, use MIN to clamp at 50
NEXT
```

1

All 2

The Maximum operator (MAX) limits a value to a specified 16-bit positive maximum. The syntax of MAX is:

MAXIMUM: MAX

1 All 2

```
value   MAX  Limit
```

Where *value* is a constant or variable value to perform the MAX function upon and *limit* is the maximum value that *value* is allowed to be. Its logic is, 'if *value* is greater than *limit*, then make result = *limit*; if *value* is less than or equal to *limit*, make result = *value*.' MAX works in positive math only; its comparisons are not valid when used on two's complement negative numbers, since the positive-integer representation of a number like -1 ($FFFF or 65535 in unsigned decimal) is larger than that of a number like 10 ($000A or 10 decimal). Use MAX only with unsigned integers. Because of the way fixed-size integers work, you should be careful when using an expression involving MAX 65535. For example, 65535+1 MAX 65535 will result in 0 because of the way fixed-size integers wrap around.

```
▓1   SYMBOL   value1          = W0
     SYMBOL   value2          = W1

     FOR value1 = 0 TO 100 STEP 10          ' Walk value1 from 0 to 100
       value2 = value1 MAX 50               ' Use MAX to clamp at 50
       DEBUG value2                         ' Show "clamped" value
     NEXT
```

-- or --

```
All 2   value            VAR     Word

        FOR value = 0 TO 100 STEP 10         ' Walk value from 0 to 100
          DEBUG ? value MAX 50               ' Show value, use MAX clamp at 50
        NEXT
```

DIGIT: DIG

All 2 The Digit operator (DIG) returns the specified decimal digit of a 16-bit positive value. Digits are numbered from 0 (the rightmost digit) to 4 (the leftmost digit of a 16-bit number; 0 to 65535).

Example:

```
value            VAR     Word
idx              VAR     Byte

value = 9742
DEBUG ? value DIG 2                    ' Show digit 2 (7)
FOR idx = 4 TO 0
  DEBUG ? value DIG idx                ' Show digits 0 through 4 (09742)
NEXT
```

SHIFT LEFT: <<

All 2 The Shift Left operator (<<) shifts the bits of a value to the left a specified number of places. Bits shifted off the left end of a number are lost; bits shifted into the right end of the number are 0s. Shifting the bits of a value left n number of times has the same effect as multiplying that number by 2 to the nth power. For instance $100 << 3$ (shift the bits of the decimal number 100 left three places) is equivalent to $100 * 2^3$. Here's an example:

```
value            VAR     Word
idx              VAR     Byte

value = %1111111111111111
FOR idx = 1 TO 16                      ' Repeat with idx = 1 to 16
  DEBUG BIN16 ? value << idx           ' Shift value left idx places
NEXT
```

SHIFT RIGHT: >>

All 2 The Shift Right operator (>>) shifts the bits of a value to the right a specified number of places. Bits shifted off the right end of a number are lost; bits shifted into the left end of the number are 0s. Shifting the bits of a value right n number of times has the same effect as dividing that number by 2 to the nth power. For instance $100 >> 3$ (shift the bits of the decimal number 100 right three places) is equivalent to $100 / 2^3$. Here's an example:

```
value          VAR     Word
idx            VAR     Byte

value = %1111111111111111
FOR idx = 1 TO 16                    ' Repeat with idx = 1 to 16
  DEBUG BIN16 ? value >> idx         ' Shift value right idx places
NEXT
```

The Reverse operator (REV) returns a reversed (mirrored) copy of a specified number of bits of a value, starting with the right-most bit (least significant bit or "lsb"). For instance, %10101101 REV 4 would return %1011, a mirror image of the right-most four bits of the value. Example:

REVERSE: REV

```
DEBUG BIN4 ? %10101101 REV 4      ' Mirror 1st 4 bits (%1011)
```

The And operator (&) returns the bitwise AND of two values. Each bit of the values is subject to the following logic:

AND: &

    0 AND 0 = 0
    0 AND 1 = 0
    1 AND 0 = 0
    1 AND 1 = 1

The result returned by & will contain 1s in only those bit positions in which both input values contain 1s. Example:

```
SYMBOL  value1      = B2
SYMBOL  value2      = B3
SYMBOL  result      = B4

value1 = %00001111
value2 = %10101101
result = value1 & value2
DEBUG %result                       ' Show result of AND (%00001101)
-- or --

DEBUG BIN8 ? %00001111 & %10101101  ' Show result of AND (%00001101)
```

The OR operator (|) returns the bitwise OR of two values. Each bit of the values is subject to the following logic:

OR: |

$$0 \text{ OR } 0 = 0$$
$$0 \text{ OR } 1 = 1$$
$$1 \text{ OR } 0 = 1$$
$$1 \text{ OR } 1 = 1$$

The result returned by | will contain 1s in any bit positions in which one or the other (or both) input values contain 1s. Example:

```
SYMBOL   value1        = B2
SYMBOL   value2        = B3
SYMBOL   result        = B4

value1 = %00001111
value2 = %10101001
result = value1 | value2
DEBUG %result                          ' Show result of OR (%10101111)
```

-- or --

```
DEBUG  BIN  ?  %00001111  |  %10101001   ' Show result of OR (%10101111)
```

XOR: ^

The Xor operator (^) returns the bitwise XOR of two values. Each bit of the values is subject to the following logic:

$$0 \text{ XOR } 0 = 0$$
$$0 \text{ XOR } 1 = 1$$
$$1 \text{ XOR } 0 = 1$$
$$1 \text{ XOR } 1 = 0$$

The result returned by ^ will contain 1s in any bit positions in which one or the other (but not both) input values contain 1s. Example:

```
SYMBOL   value1        = B2
SYMBOL   value2        = B3
SYMBOL   result        = B4

value1 = %00001111
value2 = %10101001
result = value1 ^ value2
DEBUG %result                          ' Show result or XOR (%10100110)
```

-- or --

```
DEBUG BIN8 ? %00001111 ^ %10101001      ' Show result of XOR (%10100110)
```
All 2

The And Not operator (&/) returns the bitwise AND NOT of two values. AND NOT: &/
Each bit of the values is subject to the following logic:

> 0 AND NOT 0 = 0
> 0 AND NOT 1 = 0
> 1 AND NOT 0 = 1
> 1 AND NOT 1 = 0

The result returned by &/ will contain 1s in any bit positions in which the
first value is 1 and the second value is 0. Example:

```
SYMBOL  value1          = B2
SYMBOL  value2          = B3
SYMBOL  result          = B4

value1 = %00001111
value2 = %10101001
result = value1 &/ value2
DEBUG %result                   ' Show result of AND NOT (%00000110)
```

The Or Not operator (| /) returns the bitwise OR NOT of two values. Each OR NOT: |/
bit of the values is subject to the following logic:

> 0 OR NOT 0 = 1
> 0 OR NOT 1 = 0
> 1 OR NOT 0 = 1
> 1 OR NOT 1 = 1

The result returned by | / will contain 1s in any bit positions in which the
first value is 1 or the second value is 0. Example:

```
SYMBOL  value1          = B2
SYMBOL  value2          = B3
SYMBOL  result          = B4

value1 = %00001111
value2 = %10101001
result = value1 |/ value2
DEBUG %result                           ' Show result of OR NOT (%01011111)
```

XOR NOT: ^/

The Xor Not operator (^/) returns the bitwise XOR NOT of two values. Each bit of the values is subject to the following logic:

0 XOR NOT 0 = 1
0 XOR NOT 1 = 0
1 XOR NOT 0 = 0
1 XOR NOT 1 = 1

The result returned by ^/ will contain 1s in any bit positions in which the first value and second values are equal.

Example:

```
SYMBOL   value1       = B2
SYMBOL   value2       = B3
SYMBOL   result       = B4

value1 = %00001111
value2 = %10101001
result = value1 ^/ value2
DEBUG %result                              ' Show result of OR NOT (%01011001)
```

Introduction

This chapter provides details on all three versions of the PBASIC Programming Language. A categorical listing of all available PBASIC commands is followed by an alphabetized command reference with syntax, functional descriptions, and example code for each command.

PBASIC LANGUAGE VERSIONS

There are three forms of the PBASIC language: PBASIC 1.0 (for the BS1), PBASIC 2.0 (for all BS2 models) and PBASIC 2.5 (for all BS2 models). You may use any version of the language that is appropriate for your BASIC Stamp module; however, when using any BS2 model, we suggest you use PBASIC 2.5 for any new programs you write because of the advanced control and flexibility it allows. PBASIC 2.5 is backward compatible with almost every existing PBASIC 2.0-based program, and code that is not 100% compatible can easily be modified to work in PBASIC 2.5.

This chapter gives details on every command for every BASIC Stamp model. Be sure to pay attention to any notes in the margins and body text regarding supported models and PBASIC language versions wherever they apply.

The BASIC Stamp Editor for Windows defaults to using PBASIC 1.0 (for the BS1) or PBASIC 2.0 (for all BS2 models). If you wish to use the default language for your BASIC Stamp model you need not do anything special. If you wish to use PBASIC 2.5, you must specify that fact, using the $PBASIC directive in your source code, for example:

```
' {$PBASIC 2.5}
```

Review the Compiler Directives section of Chapter 3 for more details on this directive. Note: you may also specify either 1.0 or 2.0 using the $PBASIC directive if you wish to explicitly state those desired languages.

Please note that the reserved word set will vary with each version of PBASIC, with additional reserved words for some BASIC Stamp models. Please see the reserved words tables in Appendix B for the complete lists. PBASIC 2.5 features many enhancements. Table 5.1 gives a brief summary of these items, with references to more information given elsewhere.

BASIC Stamp Command Reference

Feature Categories	New Items	Description
Additional Commands	DEBUGIN, DO...LOOP, EXIT, ON. SELECT...CASE	Allows easier user input and program control. See individual command descriptions.
Enhanced Commands	IF...THEN, GET, PUT, READ, WRITE	Improves program control, and SPRAM and EEPROM access. See individual command descriptions.
Additional Directive	PIN	Provides flexible, context-sensitive I/O pin references; see page 99.
Conditional Compile Directives	#DEFINE, #ERROR, #IF...#THEN...#ELSE, #SELECT...CASE	Encourages development of source code that is compatible with multiple BASIC Stamp models and helpful user hints; see page 70.
Additional Predefined Constants	CLRDN, CLREOL, CRSRDN, CRSRLF, CRSRRT, CRSRUP, CRSRX, CRSRXY, CRSRY, LF	Symbols for control characters supported by the Debug Terminal. See Table 5.13 in the DEBUG command description, page 168.
Syntax Enhancements	, and :	Any line can be continued to the next line after the comma (,) character wherever commas are normally used. Colons are required on label declarations.

Table 5.1: PBASIC 2.5 Enhancements.

CATEGORICAL LISTING OF COMMANDS

This section lists all available PBASIC commands for all BASIC Stamp models, grouped by category. Commands with PBASIC 2.5 enhanced syntax options are marked with (*); commands that exist only in PBASIC 2.5 are indicated with ($^{2.5}$).

 One or more of these icons indicates the item applies to the BS1, BS2, BS2e, BS2sx, BS2p, BS2pe, or BS2px respectively.

 If an item applies to all of the models in the BS2 family, this icon is used.

BRANCHING / PROGRAM CONTROL

|⅁| |All 2| BRANCH   Jump to address specified by offset.

|⅁| |All 2| IF...THEN*   Conditionally execute one or more blocks of code.

|⅁| |All 2| GOTO   Jump to address.

|⅁| |All 2| GOSUB   Jump to subroutine at address.

[All 2] ON[2.5]	Jump to address or subroutine specified by an offset.	
[1] [All 2] RETURN	Return from subroutine.	
[e/sx] [2p] [2pe] [2px] RUN	Switch execution to another program slot.	
[2p] [2pe] [2px] POLLRUN	Switch execution to another program page upon the occurrence of a polled interrupt.	
[All 2] SELECT ...CASE[2.5]	Evaluate expression and conditionally execute a block of code based on comparison to multiple conditions.	
[All 2] STOP	Halt program execution until BASIC Stamp is reset.	

LOOPING STRUCTURES

[All 2] DO...LOOP[2.5]	Execute code block repetitively, with optional, conditional exit.
[All 2] EXIT[2.5]	Terminate execution of a looping code block (DO...LOOP or FOR...NEXT).
[1] [All 2] FOR...NEXT	Execute code block repetitively, a finite number of times using a counter.

EEPROM ACCESS

[1] EEPROM	Store data in EEPROM during program download.
[All 2] DATA	Store data in EEPROM during program download.
[1] [All 2] READ*	Read EEPROM value into variable.
[1] [All 2] WRITE*	Write value into EEPROM.
[2b] [2pe] [2px] STORE	Switch READ/WRITE access to different program slot.

RAM ACCESS

[2e/sx] [2b] [2pe] [2px] GET*	Read Scratch Pad RAM value into variable.
[2e/sx] [2b] [2pe] [2px] PUT*	Write value into Scratch Pad RAM.

BASIC Stamp Command Reference

NUMERICS

[1] LET	Optional instruction to perform variable assignments.
[1] [All 2] LOOKUP	Look up data specified by offset and store in variable. This instruction provides a means to make a lookup table.
[1] [All 2] LOOKDOWN	Find target's matching value in table and store match number (0-N) in variable.
[1] [All 2] RANDOM	Generate a pseudo-random number.

DIGITAL I/O

[2] CONFIGPIN	Configure pin properties.
[1] [All 2] INPUT	Make pin an input.
[1] [All 2] OUTPUT	Make pin an output.
[1] [All 2] REVERSE	Reverse direction of a pin.
[1] [All 2] LOW	Make pin output low.
[1] [All 2] HIGH	Make pin output high.
[1] [All 2] TOGGLE	Make pin an output and toggle state.
[1] [All 2] PULSIN	Measure width of an input pulse.
[1] [All 2] PULSOUT	Output a pulse by inverting a pin for a given amount of time.
[1] [All 2] BUTTON	Debounce button, perform auto-repeat, and branch to address if button is in target state.
[All 2] COUNT	Count cycles on a pin for a given amount of time.
[All 2] XOUT	Generate X-10 power line control codes.
[2][2][2] AUXIO	Switch control to auxiliary I/O pin group.
[2][2][2] MAINIO	Switch control to main I/O pin group.
[2][2][2] IOTERM	Switch control to specified I/O pin group.
[2][2][2] POLLIN	Specify pin and state for a polled-interrupt.
[2][2][2] POLLOUT	Specify pin and state for output upon a polled-interrupt.
[2][2][2] POLLMODE	Specify the polled-interrupt mode.

ASYNCHRONOUS SERIAL I/O

[1] [All 2] SERIN	Input data in an asynchronous serial stream.
[1] [All 2] SEROUT	Output data in an asynchronous serial stream.
OWIN	Input data from a 1-wire device.
OWOUT	Output data to a 1-wire device.

SYNCHRONOUS SERIAL I/O

[1] [All 2] SHIFTIN	Shift data in from synchronous serial device.
[1] [All 2] SHIFTOUT	Shift data out to synchronous serial device.
I2CIN	Input data from I²C serial device.
I2COUT	Output data to I²C serial device.

PARALLEL I/O

LCDCMD	Write a command to an LCD.
LCDIN	Read data from an LCD.
LCDOUT	Write data to an LCD.

ANALOG I/O

[1] [All 2] PWM	Output using pulse width modulation, then return pin to input.
[1] POT	Read a 5 kΩ - 50 kΩ potentiometer and scale result.
[All 2] RCTIME	Measure a variable resistance or capacitance.
COMPARE	Compare two 0-5 V analog voltages.

TIME

[1] [All 2] PAUSE	Pause execution for 0–65535 milliseconds.
POLLWAIT	Pause until a polled-interrupt occurs.

SOUND

[1] SOUND	Generate tones or white noise.
[All 2] FREQOUT	Generate one or two sine waves of specified frequencies.
[All 2] DTMFOUT	Generate DTMF telephone tones.

BASIC Stamp Command Reference

POWER CONTROL

:1: [All 2] NAP	Nap for a short period. Power consumption is reduced.
:1: [All 2] SLEEP	Sleep for 1-65535 seconds. Power consumption is reduced.
:1: [All 2] END	Sleep until the power cycles or the PC connects. Power consumption is reduced.

PROGRAM DEBUGGING

:1: [All 2] DEBUG	Send information to the PC for viewing in the Debug Terminal's Receive windowpane.
[All 2] DEBUGIN[2.5]	Retrieve information from the user via the PC, entered into the Debug Terminal's Transmit windowpane.

SYNTAX CONVENTIONS

BOLD UPPER CASE – any word that appears bold with all capital letters must be typed exactly as shown. These are all reserved words.

Italics – italicized words must be replaced with your content.

[ ] – square brackets must be typed, in the position shown around the given syntax element. Only used with PBASIC 2.0 and 2.5.

( ) – parentheses must be typed in the position shown around the given syntax element; only used this way with PBASIC 1.0.**

{ } – curly braces indicate optional syntax items. They are not typed as part of any syntax other than compiler directives.

| – vertical line separates mutually exclusive syntax elements.

, \ # = – where they appear, commas, backslashes, pound signs, and equal signs must be typed in the positions shown.

**NOTE: You may use parentheses to enclose expressions in PBASIC 2.0 and 2.5, but they are not necessary. Used within an expression, parentheses will change the order of evaluation. See page 103 for details and examples.

AUXIO

BS1	BS2	BS2e	BS2sx	BS2p	BS2pe	BS2px

AUXIO

Function

Switch from control of main I/O pins to auxiliary I/O pins (on the BS2p40 only).

Quick Facts

Table 5.2: AUXIO Quick Facts.

	BS2p, BS2pe, and BS2px
I/O pin IDs	0 – 15 (just like main I/O, but after AUXIO command, all references affect physical pins 21 – 36).
Special Notes	The BS2p, BS2pe, and BS2px 24-pin modules accept this command, however, only the BS2p40 gives access to the auxiliary I/O pins.
Related Commands	MAINIO and IOTERM

Explanation

The BS2p, BS2pe, and BS2px are available as 24-pin modules that are pin compatible with the BS2, BS2e and BS2sx. Also available is a 40-pin module called the BS2p40, with an additional 16 I/O pins (for a total of 32). The BS2p40's extra, or auxiliary, I/O pins can be accessed in the same manner as the main I/O pins (by using the IDs 0 to 15) but only after issuing an AUXIO or IOTERM command. The AUXIO command causes the BASIC Stamp to affect the auxiliary I/O pins instead of the main I/O pins in all further code until the MAINIO or IOTERM command is reached, or the BASIC Stamp is reset or power-cycled. AUXIO is also used when setting the DIRS register for auxiliary I/O pins on the BS2p40.

When the BASIC Stamp module is reset, all RAM variables including DIRS and OUTS are cleared to zero. This affects both main and auxiliary I/O pins. On the BS2p24, BS2pe, and BS2px, the auxiliary I/O pins from the interpreter chip are not connected to physical I/O pins on the BASIC Stamp module. While not connected to anything, these pins do have internal pull-up resistors activated, effectively connecting them to Vdd. After reset, reading the auxiliary I/O from a BS2p24, BS2pe24, or BS2px24 will return all 1s.

Here is a simple AUXIO example:

```
HIGH 0                         ' make P0 high
AUXIO                          ' select auxiliary pins
LOW 0                          ' make X0 low
```

The first line of the above example will set I/O pin 0 of the main I/O pins (P0, physical pin 5) high. Afterward, the AUXIO command tells the BASIC Stamp that all commands following it should affect the auxiliary I/O pins. The following LOW command will set I/O pin 0 of the auxiliary I/O pins (X0, physical pin 21) low.

Note that the main I/O and auxiliary I/O pins are independent of each other; the states of the main I/O pins remain unchanged while the program affects the auxiliary I/O pins, and vice versa.

Other commands that affect I/O group access are MAINIO and IOTERM.

Demo Program (AUX_MAIN_TERM.bsp)

```
' AUX_MAIN_TERM.bsp
' This program demonstrates the use of the AUXIO, MAINIO and IOTERM
' commands to affect I/O pins in the auxiliary and main I/O groups.

' {$STAMP BS2p}
' {$PBASIC 2.5}

#SELECT $STAMP
  #CASE BS2, BS2E, BS2SX
    #ERROR "Program requires BS2p40"
  #CASE BS2P, BS2PE, BS2PX
    DEBUG "Note: This program designed for the BS2p40.", CR
#ENDSELECT

port             VAR     Bit


Main:
  DO
    MAINIO                        ' Switch to main I/O pins
    TOGGLE 0                      ' Toggle state of I/O pin P0
    PWM 1, 100, 40                ' Generate PWM on I/O pin P1

    AUXIO                         ' Switch to auxiliary I/O pins
    TOGGLE 0                      ' Toggle state of I/O pin X0
    PULSOUT 1, 1000               ' Generate a pulse on I/O pin X1
    PWM 2, 100, 40                ' Generate PWM on I/O pin X2
```

NOTE: This example program will tokenize with the 24-pin BS2p , BS2pe, and BS2px, but its effects can only be seen on the BS2p40. This program uses conditional compilation techniques; see Chapter 3 for more information.

```
    IOTERM port                      ' Switch to main or aux I/Os
                                     ' -- depending on port
    TOGGLE 3                         ' Toggle state of I/O pin 3
                                     ' -- on main and aux, alternately
    port = ~port                     ' Invert port
    PAUSE 1000                       ' 1 second delay
LOOP
END
```

BRANCH

BRANCH *Offset,* (*Address0, Address1, ...AddressN*)

BRANCH *Offset,* [*Address0, Address1, ...AddressN*]

NOTE: Expressions are not allowed as arguments on the BS1.

Function

Go to the address specified by offset (if in range).

- **Offset** is a variable/constant/expression (0 – 255) that specifies the index of the address, in the list, to branch to (0 – N).

- **Addresses** are labels that specify where to go. BRANCH will ignore any list entries beyond offset 255.

Quick Facts

Table 5.3: BRANCH Quick Facts.

	BS1	All BS2 Models
Limit of **Address** Entries	Limited only by memory	256
Related Commands	None	ON...GOTO

Explanation

The BRANCH instruction is useful when you want to write something like this:

```
IF value = 0 THEN Case_0        ' when value is 0, jump to Case_0
IF value = 1 THEN Case_1        ' when value is 1, jump to Case_1
IF value = 2 THEN Case_2        ' when value is 2, jump to Case_2
```

BS1 syntax not shown here.

You can use BRANCH to organize this into a single statement:

```
BRANCH value, [Case_0, Case_1, Case_2]
```

This works exactly the same as the previous IF...THEN example. If the value isn't in range (in this case if *value* is greater than 2), BRANCH does nothing and the program continues with the next instruction after BRANCH.

BRANCH can be teamed with the LOOKDOWN instruction to create a simplified SELECT...CASE statement. See LOOKDOWN for an example.

Demo Program (BRANCH.bs1)

```
' BRANCH.bs1
' This program shows how the value of idx controls the destination of the
' BRANCH instruction.

' {$STAMP BS1}
' {$PBASIC 1.0}

SYMBOL  idx            = B2


Main:
  DEBUG "idx: ", #idx, " "
  BRANCH idx, (Task_0, Task_1, Task_2)        ' branch to task
  DEBUG "BRANCH target error...", CR, CR       ' ... unless out of range

Next_Task:
  idx = idx + 1 // 4                           ' force idx to be 0..3
  GOTO Main

Task_0:
  DEBUG "BRANCHed to Task_0", CR
  GOTO Next_Task

Task_1:
  DEBUG "BRANCHed to Task_1", CR
  GOTO Next_Task

Task_2:
  DEBUG "BRANCHed to Task_2", CR
  GOTO Next_Task
```

Demo Program (BRANCH.bs2)

All 2

NOTE: This example program can be used with all BS2 models by changing the $STAMP directive accordingly.

```
' BRANCH.bs2
' This program shows how the value of idx controls the destination of the
' BRANCH instruction.

' {$STAMP BS2}
' {$PBASIC 2.5}

idx             VAR     Nib


Main:
  DEBUG "idx: ", DEC1 idx, " "
  BRANCH idx, [Task_0, Task_1, Task_2]         ' branch to task
  DEBUG "BRANCH target error...", CR, CR        ' ... unless out of range

Next_Task:
  idx = idx + 1 // 4                            ' force idx to be 0..3
```

```
    PAUSE 250
    GOTO Main

Task_0:
  DEBUG "BRANCHed to Task_0", CR
  GOTO Next_Task

Task_1:
  DEBUG "BRANCHed to Task_1", CR
  GOTO Next_Task

Task_2:
  DEBUG "BRANCHed to Task_2", CR
  GOTO Next_Task
```

BUTTON | BS1 | BS2 | BS2e | BS2sx | BS2p | BS2pe | BS2px |

1 All 2

BUTTON *Pin, DownState, Delay, Rate, Workspace, TargetState, Address*

Function

Monitor and process a pushbutton input, perform auto-repeat, and branch to address if button is in target state. Button circuits may be active-low or active-high.

1
NOTE: Expressions are not allowed as arguments on the BS1. The range of the *Pin* argument on the BS1 is 0 – 7.

- **Pin** is a variable/constant/expression (0–15) that specifies the I/O pin to use. This pin will be set to input mode.

- **DownState** is a variable/constant/expression (0 or 1) that specifies which logical state occurs when the button is pressed.

- **Delay** is a variable/constant/expression (0 – 255) that specifies how long the button must be pressed before auto-repeat starts. The delay is measured in cycles of the BUTTON routine. Delay has two special settings: 0 and 255. If Delay is 0, BUTTON performs no debounce or auto-repeat. If Delay is 255, BUTTON performs debounce, but no auto-repeat.

- **Rate** is a variable/constant/expression (0 – 255) that specifies the number of cycles between auto-repeats. The rate is expressed in cycles of the BUTTON routine.

- **Workspace** is a byte variable used by BUTTON for workspace. It must be cleared to 0 before being used by BUTTON for the first time and should not be adjusted outside of the BUTTON command. **NOTE: All RAM is cleared to 0 by default upon power-up or reset of the BASIC Stamp module.**

- **TargetState** is a variable/constant/expression (0 or 1) that specifies which state the button should be in for a branch to occur. (0=not pressed, 1=pressed)

- **Address** is a label that specifies where to branch if the button is in the target state.

Explanation

When you press a button or flip a switch, the contacts make or break a connection. A brief (1 to 20-ms) burst of noise occurs as the contacts scrape and bounce against each other. By scanning an input within a loop to ensure that the contact remains in a specified state for a minimum duration, spurious multiple inputs caused by contact noise can be eliminated. The BUTTON instruction helps prevent this noise from being interpreted as more than one switch action; this is the function of the *Delay* parameter. For a demonstration of switch bounce, see the demo program for the COUNT instruction. *Delay*, combined with the *Rate* argument, allows the programmer to control the rate at which multiple inputs are accepted by the BASIC Stamp.

BUTTON also lets PBASIC react to a button press the way your computer keyboard does to a key press. When you press a key, a character immediately appears on the screen. If you hold the key down, there's a delay, then a rapid-fire stream of characters appears on the screen. BUTTON's auto-repeat function can be set up to work much the same way.

BUTTON is designed for use inside a program loop. Each time through the loop, BUTTON checks the state of the specified pin. When it first matches *DownState*, BUTTON begins the *Delay* countdown for auto-repeat. Then, in accordance with *TargetState*, it either branches to *Address* (TargetState = 1) or doesn't (TargetState = 0).

If the switch stays in *DownState*, BUTTON counts the number of program loops that execute. When this count equals *Delay*, BUTTON once again triggers the action specified by *TargetState* and *Address*. Hereafter, if the switch remains in *DownState*, BUTTON waits *Rate* number of cycles between actions. The *Workspace* variable is used by BUTTON to keep track of how many cycles have occurred since the *Pin* switched to *TargetState* or since the last auto-repeat.

BUTTON does not stop program execution. In order for its delay and auto-repeat functions to work properly, BUTTON must be executed from within a program loop.

Figure 5.1: Sample BUTTON circuits. Active-high (left) and active-low (right).

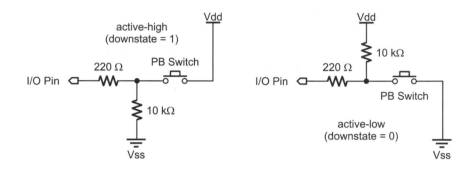

Demo Program (BUTTON.bs1)

```
' BUTTON.bs1
' Connect an active-low circuit to pin P0 of the BS1. When you press the
' button, the DEBUG screen will display an asterisk (*). The program, as
' shown below, will print an asterisk at the first button press, then
' delay approximately one second (200 x 5 ms PAUSE) before auto-repeating
' at a rate of approximately 100 ms (5 x 20 ms).  Feel free to modify the
' program to see the effects of your changes on the way BUTTON responds.

' {$STAMP BS1}
' {$PBASIC 1.0}

SYMBOL   Btn              = 0

SYMBOL   btnWrk           = B2


Main:
    ' Try changing the Delay value (200) in BUTTON to see the effect of
    ' its modes: 0 = no delay; 1-254 = varying delays before auto-repeat;
    ' 255 = no auto-repeat (only one action per button press)
    '
    ' The BUTTON instruction will cause the program to branch to
    ' No_Press unless P0 = 0

    PAUSE 5
    BUTTON Btn, 0, 200, 20, btnWrk, 0, No_Press
    DEBUG "*"

No_Press:
    GOTO Main
```

BUTTON – BASIC Stamp Command Reference

Demo Program (BUTTON.bs2)

NOTE: This example program can be used with all BS2 models by changing the $STAMP directive accordingly.

```
' BUTTON.bs2
' Connect an active-low circuit to pin P0 of the BS2. When you press the
' button, the DEBUG screen will display an asterisk (*). The program, as
' shown below, will print an asterisk at the first button press, then
' delay approximately one second (200 x 5 ms PAUSE) before auto-repeating
' at a rate of approximately 100 ms (5 x 20 ms).  Feel free to modify the
' program to see the effects of your changes on the way BUTTON responds.

' {$STAMP BS2}
' {$PBASIC 2.5}

Btn             PIN     0

btnWrk          VAR     Byte


Main:
  ' Try changing the Delay value (200) in BUTTON to see the effect of
  ' its modes: 0 = no delay; 1-254 = varying delays before auto-repeat;
  ' 255 = no auto-repeat (only one action per button press)
  '
  ' The BUTTON instruction will cause the program to branch to
  ' No_Press unless P0 = 0

  PAUSE 5
  BUTTON Btn, 0, 200, 20, btnWrk, 0, No_Press
  DEBUG "*"

No_Press:
  GOTO Main
```

COMPARE

COMPARE *Mode, Variable*

Function

Enable or disable comparator, compare voltages on P1 and P2 and retrieve comparison result to store in *Variable*.

- *Mode* is a variable/constant/expression (0 – 2) that enables or disables the comparator (input pins P1 and P2) and determines if the optional comparator output pin (pin P0) is enabled or not. See Table 5.4 for an explanation of the *Mode* values.

- *Variable* is a variable (usually a bit) in which the comparison result is stored.

Quick Facts

Table 5.4: COMPARE Quick Facts.

	BS2px
***Mode* Values**	0: Disables comparator
	1: Enables comparator with P0 as result output
	2: Enables comparator without P0 as result output
***Variable* Values**	0: Voltage P1 > P2; P0 optionally outputs 0
	1: Voltage P1 < P2; P0 optionally outputs 1

Explanation

The COMPARE command enables or disables the built-in comparator hardware on the BS2px's I/O pins P0, P1, and P2. I/O pins P1 and P2 are the comparator inputs and P0 is optionally the comparator result output pin.

By default, the comparator feature is disabled. Using the COMPARE command with a *Mode* argument of 1 or 2 enables the comparator feature (using input pins P1 and P2) and returns the result of the comparison in *Variable*. If *Mode* is 1, the result of the comparison is also output on I/O pin P0. The following is an example of the COMPARE command:

```
Result   VAR   Bit
COMPARE  1,    Result
```

This example enables the comparator (setting P0 to output the result, with P1 and P2 as the comparator inputs) and writes the result of the comparison into *Result*. Both *Result* and the output pin P0 will be 0 if the

input voltage on P1 was greater than that of P2. *Result* and the output pin
P0 will be 1 if the input voltage on P1 was less than that of P2.

Note that the comparator hardware operates independently of the
execution speed of the BS2px and will continue to run and update P0 if
Mode = 1, even during sleep mode (execution of END, NAP, POLLWAIT 8,
or SLEEP commands). To avoid spurious current draw during sleep
mode, disable the comparator first.

Demo Program (COMPARE.bpx)

NOTE: This example program can be
used only with the BS2px.

```
' COMPARE.bpx
' This example demonstrates the use of the COMPARE command.
' Connect two variable voltage sources (0 to 5 volts) on I/O pins
' P1 and P2 (or a button on each pin connected to ground).  Run the program
' and watch the Debug Terminal display as you adjust the variable voltage
' or press the buttons.

' {$STAMP BS2px}
' {$PBASIC 2.5}

Result VAR Bit

#IF $STAMP <> BS2PX #THEN
  #ERROR "This program requires a BS2px."
#ENDIF

Setup:
  CONFIGPIN DIRECTION, %0000000000000001    'P0 = output, all others = input
  CONFIGPIN PULLUP,    %0000000000000110    'Enable pull-ups on P1 and P2
  DEBUG "BS2px COMPARATOR DEMONSTRATION", CR,
        "==============================", CR,
        "Input Voltage: P1 > P2", CR,
        "Output State:  P0 = 0"

Main:
DO                                    'Display P1/P2 comparison
  COMPARE 1, Result
  IF Result = 0 THEN
    DEBUG CRSRXY,18,2,">"
  ELSE
    DEBUG CRSRXY,18,2,"<"
  ENDIF
  DEBUG CRSRXY,20,3,BIN1 Result
LOOP
```

CONFIGPIN

CONFIGPIN *Mode, PinMask*

Function

Configure special properties of I/O pins.

- **Mode** is a variable/constant/expression (0 – 3), or one of four predefined symbols, that specifies the I/O pin property to configure: Schmitt Trigger, Logic Threshold, Pull-up Resistor or Output Direction. See Table 5.5 for an explanation of *Mode* values.

- **PinMask** is a variable/constant/expression (1 – 65535) that indicates how *Mode* is applied to I/O pins. Each bit of *PinMask* corresponds to an individual I/O pin. A high bit (1) enables the *Mode* and a low bit (0) disables the *Mode* on the corresponding I/O pin.

Quick Facts

Table 5.5: CONFIGPIN Quick Facts.

	BS2px
Mode Values	0 (or SCHMITT): Schmitt Trigger
	1 (or THRESHOLD): Logic Threshold
	2 (or PULLUP): Pull-up Resistor
	3 (or DIRECTION): Output Direction
Related Commands (For DIRECTION Mode)	INPUT and OUTPUT, and the DIRx = # assignment statement

Explanation

The CONFIGPIN command enables or disables special I/O pin properties on all 16 I/O pins at once. There are four properties, or modes, available: Schmitt Trigger, Logic Threshold, Pull-up Resistor, and Output Direction. Each I/O pin on the BS2px contains special hardware dedicated to each of these properties.

OUTPUT DIRECTION.

By default, all BASIC Stamp I/O pins are set to inputs. Enabling the Output Direction mode sets an I/O pin's direction to output. Disabling the Output Direction mode sets an I/O pin's direction to input. This has the same effect as using the OUTPUT or INPUT commands, or the DIRx = # assignment statement to configure I/O pin directions. The following is an example of the CONFIGPIN command using the Output Direction mode:

```
CONFIGPIN DIRECTION, %0000000100010011
```

Every high bit (1) in the *PinMask* argument enables the output direction for the corresponding I/O pin while every low bit (0) disables the output direction. In the above example, I/O pins 8, 4, 1, and 0 are set to the output direction and all other I/O pins are set to the input direction. This is similar to the following statement:

```
DIRS = %0000000100010011
```

Pull-up resistors are commonly used in circuitry where a component, such PULL-UP RESISTORS. as a button, provides an open/drain signal; the signal is either floating (open) or is driven to ground (drain). Since the BASIC Stamp input pins must always be connected to either 5 volts or ground (0 volts) in order to read a reliable logic state with them, a pull-up resistor is required on circuitry, such as the button circuit mentioned above, so that the signal is never left floating (electrically disconnected).

The following example enables internal pull-up resistors on I/O pins 15, 12, 6, and 3, and disables internal pull-up resistors on all other I/O pins:

```
CONFIGPIN  PULLUP, %1001000001001000
```

Note that the internal pull-up resistors are intentionally weak, about 20 kΩ. Additionally, the internal pull-up resistors can be activated for all pins, regardless of pin direction, but really matter only when the associated pin is set to input mode.

An input pin's logic threshold determines the voltage levels that are LOGIC THRESHOLD. interpreted as logic high (1) and logic low (0). Most microcontrollers, and other integrated circuits use one of two types of logic threshold: TTL Level or CMOS Level. The BASIC Stamp I/O pins are, by default, configured for TTL level logic thresholds. Figure 5.2 is an illustration of the difference between TTL and CMOS logic levels.

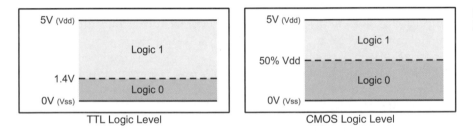

Figure 5.2: TTL and CMOS Logic Level Threshold Voltages

The logic threshold for TTL is 1.4 volts; a voltage below 1.4 is considered to be a logic 0 while a voltage above 1.4 is considered to be a logic 1. The logic threshold for CMOS is 50% of Vdd; a voltage below ½ Vdd is considered a logic 0 while a voltage above ½ Vdd is considered a logic 1.

For the CONFIGPIN command's THRESHOLD mode, a high bit (1) in the *PinMask* argument sets the corresponding I/O pin to CMOS threshold level, and a low bit sets it to a TTL threshold level. The following example sets CMOS threshold level on I/O pins 3, 2, 1, and 0, and TTL threshold level on all other I/O pins.

```
CONFIGPIN  THRESHOLD, %0000000000001111
```

The threshold level can be set for all pins, regardless of pin direction, but really matters only when the associated pin is set to input mode.

SCHMITT TRIGGER

Normally, if a signal on an input pin is somewhat noisy (the voltage level randomly rises and falls beyond the logic threshold boundary) then reading that pin's input value will result in spurious highs and lows (1s and 0s). Schmitt Triggers are circuits that make inputs more steady and reliable by adding a region of hysteresis around the logic threshold that the signal must completely traverse before the logic level is interpreted as being changed. By default BASIC Stamp I/O pins are set to normal input mode, but the BS2px can be configured for Schmitt Trigger mode as well. Figure 5.3 illustrates Schmitt Trigger characteristics.

Figure 5.3: Schmitt Trigger Characteristics

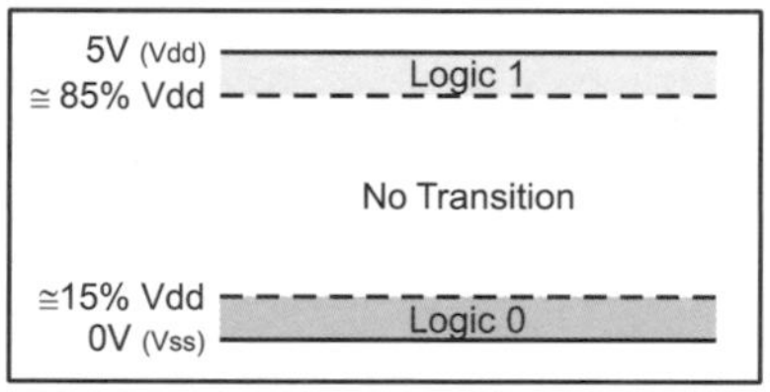

In Schmitt Trigger mode, the threshold for a logic 0 is approximately 15% of Vdd and the threshold for a logic 1 is approximately 85% of Vdd. The input pin defaults to an unknown state until the initial voltage crosses a logic 0 or logic 1 boundary. Thereafter, the voltage must cross above 85% of Vdd to be interpreted as a logic 1 and must cross below 15% of Vdd to be interpreted as a logic 0. If the voltage transitions somewhere between the two thresholds, the interpreted logic state remains the same as the previous state.

For the CONFIGPIN command's SCHMITT mode, a high bit (1) in the *PinMask* argument enables the Schmitt Trigger on the corresponding I/O pin and a low bit (0) disables the Schmitt Trigger. The following example sets Schmitt Triggers on I/O pins 7, 6, 5, and 4, and sets all other I/O pins to normal mode.

```
CONFIGPIN  SCHMITT, %0000000011110000
```

Schmitt Trigger mode can be activated for all pins, regardless of pin direction, but really matters only when the associated pin is set to input mode.

Demo Program (CONFIGPIN.bpx)

NOTE: This example program can be used only with the BS2px.

```
' CONFIGPIN.BPX
' This example demonstrates the use of the CONFIGPIN command.
' All I/O pins are set to inputs with various combinations of
' Pull-Up Resistor, Logic Threshold and Schmitt-Trigger properties.
' While running, this program will constantly display the state of all
' input pins along with an indication of the configuration for each group
' of pins.  Try connecting different input signals to the I/O pins (such as
' buttons, a function generator with a slowing sweeping signal (0 to 5
' VDC)) or simply running your fingers across the I/O pins and note how
' they react based upon their configured property.

' {$STAMP BS2px}
' {$PBASIC 2.5}

#IF $STAMP <> BS2PX #THEN
  #ERROR "This program requires a BS2px."
#ENDIF

Setup:
  CONFIGPIN DIRECTION, %0000000000000000     'Set all I/O pins to inputs
  CONFIGPIN PULLUP,    %1111111111110000     'Enable pull-ups on pins 4 - 15
  CONFIGPIN THRESHOLD, %0000111100000000     'Set P8-P11 to CMOS, others TTL
  CONFIGPIN SCHMITT,   %1111000000000000     'Enable Schmitt-Triggers P12-P15

  DEBUG CLS
  DEBUG "        BS2px INPUT PIN CONFIGURATION TEST", CR,
        "========================================================", CR,
        "        P15-P12: Pull-Up Resistors, TTL & Schmitt-Triggers", CR,
        "       /", CR,
        "      /    P11-P8: Pull-Up Resistors & CMOS", CR,
        "     /    /", CR,
        "    |    /     P7-P4: Pull-Up Resistors & TTL", CR,
        "    |    |    /", CR,
        "    |    |    |    P3-P0: Normal", CR,
        "    |    |    |    /", CR,
```

```
            "  |     |     |     |", CR,
            "---- ---- ---- ----"

Main:
DO
  'Display input pin states
  DEBUG CRSRXY,0,12, BIN4 IND, " ", BIN4 INC, " ", BIN4 INB, " ", BIN4 INA
LOOP
```

COUNT

 COUNT *Pin, Duration, Variable*

Function

Count the number of cycles (0-1-0 or 1-0-1) on the specified pin during the *Duration* time frame and store that number in *Variable*.

- **Pin** is a variable/constant/expression (0 – 15) that specifies the I/O pin to use. This pin will be set to input mode.

- **Duration** is a variable/constant/expression (1 – 65535) specifying the time during which to count. The unit of time for *Duration* is described in Table 5.6.

- **Variable** is a variable (usually a word) in which the count will be stored.

Quick Facts

Table 5.6: COUNT Quick Facts.

NOTE: All timing values are approximate.

	BS2, BS2e	BS2sx	BS2p	BS2pe	BS2px
Units in *Duration*	1 ms	400 µs	287 µs	720 µs	287 µs
Duration range	1 ms to 65.535 s	400 µs to 26.214 s	287 µs to 18.809 s	720 µs to 47.18 s	287 µs to 18.809 s
Minimum pulse width	4.16 µs	1.66 µs	1.20 µs	3.0 µs	1.20 µs
Maximum frequency (square wave)	120,000 Hz	300,000 Hz	416,700 Hz	166,667 Hz	416,700 Hz
Related Command	PULSIN				

Explanation

The COUNT instruction makes the *Pin* an input, then for the specified *Duration* of time, counts cycles on that pin and stores the total in *Variable*. A cycle is a change in state from 1 to 0 to 1, or from 0 to 1 to 0.

According to Table 5.6, COUNT on the BS2 can respond to transitions (pulse widths) as small as 4.16 microseconds (µs). A cycle consists of two transitions (e.g., 0 to 1, then 1 to 0), so COUNT (on the BS2) can respond to square waves with periods as short as 8.32 µs; up to 120 kilohertz (kHz) in frequency. For non-square waves (those whose high time and low time are unequal), the shorter of the high and low times must be at least 4.16 µs in width (on the BS2). Refer to Table 5.6 for data on other BASIC Stamp models.

If you use COUNT on slowly changing analog waveforms like sine waves, you may find that the value returned is higher than expected. This is because the waveform may pass through the BASIC Stamp module's logic threshold slowly enough that noise causes false counts. You can fix this by passing the signal through a Schmitt Trigger, like one of the inverters of a 74HCT14. Or, you may use the BS2px's built-in Schmitt-Trigger pin property; see the CONFIGPIN section beginning on page 143 for details.

Demo Program (COUNT.bs2)

All 2

NOTE: This example program can be used with all BS2 models. This program uses conditional compilation techniques; see Chapter 3 for more information.

```
' COUNT.bs2
' Connect an active-low button circuit shown in the BUTTON command
' description to pin P0 of the BS2. The DEBUG screen will prompt you to
' press the button as quickly as possible for a 1-second count.  When the
' count is done, the screen will display your "score," the total number of
' cycles registered by COUNT.  Note that this score will almost always
' be greater than the actual number of presses because of switch contact
' bounce.

' {$STAMP BS2}
' {$PBASIC 2.5}

PushBtn         PIN    0                   ' pushbutton on P0

#SELECT $STAMP
  #CASE BS2, BS2E
    DurAdj      CON    $100                ' / 1
  #CASE BS2SX
    DurAdj      CON    $280                ' / 0.400
  #CASE BS2P, BS2PX
    DurAdj      CON    $37B                ' / 0.287
  #CASE BS2PE
    DurAdj      CON    $163                ' / 0.720
#ENDSELECT

Capture         CON    1000                ' 1 second

cycles          VAR    Word                ' counted cycles


Main:
  DO
    DEBUG CLS,
          "How many times can you press the button in 1 second?", CR
    PAUSE 1000
    DEBUG "Ready, set... "
```

```
    PAUSE 500
    DEBUG "GO!", CR
    COUNT PushBtn, (Capture */ DurAdj), cycles
    DEBUG CR, "Your score: ", DEC cycles, CR
    PAUSE 3000
    DEBUG "Press button to go again."
    DO : LOOP UNTIL (PushBtn = 0)          ' wait for button press
LOOP
END
```

DATA

BS1	BS2	BS2e	BS2sx	BS2p	BS2pe	BS2px

1 **(See EEPROM)**

All 2 { *Symbol* } **DATA** *DataItem* { , *DataItem...* }

Function

Write data to the EEPROM during program download.

- *Symbol* is an optional, unique symbol name that will be automatically defined as a constant equal to the location number of the first data item.

- *DataItem* is a constant/expression (0 – 65535) indicating a value, and optionally how to store the value.

Quick Facts

Table 5.7: DATA Quick Facts.

	All BS2 Models
Special Notes	Writes values to EEPROM during download in blocks of 16 bytes. Writes byte or word-sized values. Can be used to decrease program size.
Related Commands	READ and WRITE

Explanation

When you download a program into the BASIC Stamp, it is stored in the EEPROM starting at the highest address (2047) and working towards the lowest address. Most programs don't use the entire EEPROM, so the lower portion is available for other uses. The DATA directive allows you to define a set of data to store in the available EEPROM locations. It is called a "directive" rather than a "command" because it performs an activity at compile-time rather than at run-time (i.e.: the DATA directive is not downloaded to the BASIC Stamp, but the data it contains is downloaded).

WRITING SIMPLE, SEQUENTIAL DATA.

The simplest form of the DATA directive is something like the following:

```
DATA        100, 200, 52, 45
```

This example, when downloaded, will cause the values 100, 200, 52 and 45 to be written to EEPROM locations 0, 1, 2 and 3, respectively. You can then use the READ and WRITE commands in your code to access these locations and the data you've stored there.

DATA – BASIC Stamp Command Reference

DATA uses a counter, called a pointer, to keep track of available EEPROM addresses. The value of the pointer is initially 0. When a program is downloaded, the DATA directive stores the first byte value at the current pointer address, then increments (adds 1 to) the pointer. If the program contains more than one DATA directive, subsequent DATAs start with the pointer value left by the previous DATA. For example, if the program contains:

```
DATA        72, 69, 76, 76, 79
DATA        104, 101, 108, 108, 111
```

The first DATA directive will start at location 0 and increment the pointer for each data value it stores (1, 2, 3, 4 and 5). The second DATA directive will start with the pointer value of 5 and work upward from there. As a result, the first 10 bytes of EEPROM will look like the following:

	EEPROM Location (address)									
	0	**1**	**2**	**3**	**4**	**5**	**6**	**7**	**8**	**9**
Contents	72	69	76	76	79	104	101	108	108	111

Table 5.8: Example EEPROM Storage.

What if you don't want to store values starting at location 0? Fortunately, the DATA directive has an option to specify the next location to use. You can specify the next location number (to set the pointer to) by inserting a *DataItem* in the form @x ;where x is the location number. The following code writes the same data in Table 5.8 to locations 100 through 109:

```
DATA        @100, 72, 69, 76, 76, 79, 104, 101, 108, 108, 111
```

In this example, the first *DataItem* is @100. This tells the DATA directive to store the following *DataItem(s)* starting at location 100. All the *DataItems* to the right of the @100 are stored in their respective locations (100, 101, 102... 109).

In addition, the DATA directive allows you to specify new starting locations at any time within the *DataItem* list. If, for example, you wanted to store 56 at location 100 and 47 at location 150 (while leaving every other location intact), you could type the following:

```
DATA        @100, 56, @150, 47
```

If you have multiple DATA directives in your program, it may be difficult to remember exactly what locations contain the desired data. For this reason, the DATA directive can optionally be prefixed with a unique symbol name. This symbol becomes a constant that is set equal to the location number of the first byte of data within the directive. For example,

```
MyNumbers    DATA    @100, 72, 73
```

This would store the values 72 and 73 starting with location 100 and will create a constant, called *MyNumbers*, which is set equal to 100. Your program can then use the *MyNumbers* constant as a reference to the start of the data within a READ or WRITE command. Each DATA directive can have a unique symbol preceding it, allowing you to reference the data defined at different locations.

RESERVING EEPROM LOCATIONS. There may be a time when you wish to reserve a section of EEPROM for use by your BASIC code, but not necessarily store data there to begin with. To do this, simply specify a *DataItem* within parentheses, as in:

```
DATA         @100, (20)
```

The above DATA directive will reserve 20 bytes of EEPROM, starting with location 100. It doesn't store any values there, rather it simply leaves the data as it is and increments DATA's location pointer by 20. A good reason to do this is when you have a program already downloaded into the BASIC Stamp that has created or manipulated some data in EEPROM. To protect that section of EEPROM from being overwritten by your next program (perhaps a new version of the same program) you can reserve the space as shown above. The EEPROM's contents from locations 100 to 119 will remain intact. NOTE: This only "reserves" the space for the program you are currently downloading; the BASIC Stamp does not know to "reserve" the space for future programs. In other words, make sure use this feature of the DATA directive in every program you download if you don't want to risk overwriting valuable EEPROM data.

IMPORTANT CONCEPT: HOW DATA AND PROGRAMS ARE DOWNLOADED INTO EEPROM. It is important to realize that EEPROM is not overwritten during programming unless it is needed for program storage, or is filled by a DATA directive specifying data to be written. **During downloading, EEPROM is always written in 16-byte sections if, and only if, any location within that section needs writing.**

WRITING A BLOCK OF THE SAME VALUE. DATA can also store the same number in a block of consecutive locations. This is similar to reserving a block of EEPROM, above, but with a value added before the first parenthesis.

For example,

```
DATA        @100, 0 (20)
```

This statement writes the value 0 in all the EEPROM locations from 100 to 119.

A common use for DATA is to store strings; sequences of bytes representing text. PBASIC converts quoted text like "A" into the corresponding ASCII character code (65 in this case). To make data entry easier, you can place quotes around a whole chunk of text used in a DATA directive, and PBASIC will understand it to mean a series of bytes (see the last line of code below). The following three DATA directives are equivalent:

WRITING TEXT STRINGS.

```
DATA        72, 69, 76, 76, 79
DATA        "H", "E", "L", "L", "O"
DATA        "HELLO"
```

All three lines of code, above, will result in the numbers 72, 69, 76, 76, and 79 being stored into EEPROM upon downloading. These numbers are simply the ASCII character codes for "H", "E", "L", "L", and "O", respectively. See the Demo program, below, for an example of storing and reading multiple text strings.

The EEPROM is organized as a sequential set of byte-sized memory locations. By default, the DATA directive stores bytes into EEPROM. If you try to store a word-sized value (ex: DATA 1125) only the lower byte of the value will be stored. This does not mean that you can't store word-sized values, however. A word consists of two bytes, called a low-byte and a high-byte. If you wanted to store the value 1125 using the DATA directive, simply insert the prefix "word" before the number, as in:

WRITING WORD VALUES VS. BYTE VALUES.

```
DATA        Word 1125
```

The directive above will automatically break the word-sized value into two bytes and store them into two sequential EEPROM locations (the low-byte first, followed by the high-byte). In this case, the low-byte is 101 and the high byte is 4 and they will be stored in locations 0 and 1, respectively. If you have multiple word-sized values, you must prefix each value with "word", as in:

```
DATA        Word 1125, Word 2000
```

To retrieve a word-sized value, you'll need to use the WORD modifier in the READ command and a word-sized variable.

Finally, a *DataItem* may be defined using a simple expression with the binary operators shown in Table 4.5. For example,

```
MinLvl          CON     10

myLvl           VAR     Byte

Level1          DATA    MinLvl + 10
Level2          DATA    MinLvl * 5 + 21

READ Level2, myLvl                          ' read EE location Level2
DEBUG DEC myLvl                             ' show value of myLvl (71)
```

[All 2] Demo Program (DATA.bs2)

NOTE: This example program can be used with all BS2 models by changing the $STAMP directive accordingly.

```
' DATA.bs2
' This program stores a number of large text strings into EEPROM with the
' DATA directive and then sends them, one character at a time via the DEBUG
' command.  This is a good demonstration of how to save program space by
' storing large amounts of data in EEPROM directly, rather than embedding
' the data into DEBUG commands.

' {$STAMP BS2}
' {$PBASIC 2.5}

idx         VAR     Word            ' current location number
phrase      VAR     Nib             ' current phrase number
char        VAR     Byte            ' character to print

' ----- Define all text phrases (out of order, just for fun!) -----
'
Text1       DATA    "Here is the first part of a large chunk of textual "
            DATA    "data ", CR, "that needs to be transmitted.  There's "
            DATA    "a 5 second delay", CR, "between text paragraphs. ", CR
            DATA    CR, 0

Text3       DATA    "The alternative (having multiple DEBUGs or SEROUTs, "
            DATA    "each ", CR, "with their own line of text) consumes "
            DATA    "MUCH more EEPROM ", CR, "(program) space. ", CR
            DATA    CR, 0

Text6       DATA    "The 0 is used by this program to indicate we've "
            DATA    "reached the ", CR, "End of Text.  The Main routine "
            DATA    "pauses in between each block of", CR, "text,and then "
            DATA    "uses a LOOKUP command to retrieve the location ", CR
            DATA    "of the next desired block of text to print. ", 0
```

```
Text4     DATA    CLS, "This program also demonstrates retrieving data "
          DATA    "out of order ", CR, "in relation to the way it is "
          DATA    "stored in EEPROM. Additionally,", CR, "control codes "
          DATA    "(like carriage-returns, clear-screens, etc) can ", CR
          DATA    "be embedded right in the data, as it is here. ", CR
          DATA    CR, 0

Text2     DATA    "This is an example of a good way to save space in "
          DATA    "your ", CR, "BASIC Stamp's program by storing data "
          DATA    "into EEPROM and ", CR, "retrieving it, one byte at a "
          DATA    "time, and transmitting it ", CR, "with just a single "
          DATA    "DEBUG (or SEROUT) command.", CR, CR, 0

Text5     DATA    "The Print_It routine simply takes the idx variable, "
          DATA    "retrieves", CR, "the character at the EEPROM location "
          DATA    "pointed to by it, and ", CR, "prints it to the screen "
          DATA    "until it finds a byte with a value of 0.", CR, CR, 0


Main:
  DEBUG CLS                             ' Clear DEBUG window
  FOR phrase = 1 TO 6                   ' Print blocks one by one
    LOOKUP (phrase - 1),
           [Text1, Text2, Text3, Text4, Text5, Text6], idx
    GOSUB Print_It
    PAUSE 5000                          ' Pause for 5 seconds
  NEXT
  END

Print_It:
  DO
    READ idx, char                      ' Get next character
    idx = idx + 1                       ' Point to next location
    IF (char = 0) THEN EXIT             ' If 0, we're done with block
    DEBUG char                          ' Otherwise, transmit it
  LOOP
  RETURN                                ' Return to the main routine
```

DEBUG

BS1	BS2	BS2e	BS2sx	BS2p	BS2pe	BS2px

`1` `All 2` **DEBUG** *OutputData* { *, OutputData* }

Function

Display information on the PC screen within the BASIC Stamp Editor's Debug Terminal. This command can be used to display text or numbers in various formats on the PC screen in order to follow program flow (called debugging) or as part of the functionality of the BASIC Stamp application.

`1`
NOTE: Expressions are not allowed as arguments on the BS1. The only constant allowed for the BS1 DEBUG command is a text string.

• **OutputData** is a variable/constant/expression (0 – 65535) that specifies the information to output. Valid data can be ASCII characters (text strings and control characters), decimal numbers (0 - 65535), hexadecimal numbers ($0000 - $FFFF) or binary numbers (up to %1111111111111111). Data can be modified with special formatters as explained below.

Quick Facts

Table 5.9: DEBUG Quick Facts.

	BS1	BS2, BS2e, BS2sx BS2p, BS2pe	BS2px
Serial Protocol	Asynchronous 4800, N, 8, 1 True polarity Custom packetized format	Asynchronous 9600, N, 8, 1 Inverted polarity Raw data	Asynchronous 19200, N, 8, 1 Inverted polarity Raw data
Related Commands	None	SEROUT and DEBUGIN	

Explanation

DEBUG provides a convenient way for your BASIC Stamp to send messages to the PC screen while running. The name "debug" suggests its most popular use; debugging programs by showing you the value of a variable or expression, or by indicating what portion of a program is currently executing. DEBUG is also a great way to rehearse programming techniques. Throughout this manual, we use DEBUG to give you immediate feedback on the effects of instructions. The following example demonstrates using the DEBUG command to send the text string message "Hello World!".

```
DEBUG   "Hello, World!"
```

After you download this one-line program, the BASIC Stamp Editor will open a Debug Terminal on your PC screen and wait for a response from

DEBUG – BASIC Stamp Command Reference

the BASIC Stamp. A moment later, the phrase "Hello World!" will appear. Note that if you close the Debug Terminal, your program keeps executing, but you can't see the DEBUG data anymore.

Multiple pieces of data can be sent with one DEBUG command by separating the data with commas (,). The following example produces exactly the same results as the example above.

```
DEBUG "Hello ", "World!"
```

DEBUG can also print and format numbers (values) from both constants and variables. The formatting methods for DEBUG are very different for the BS1, than for any other BASIC Stamp. Please read the appropriate sections, below, carefully.

BASIC Stamp 1 Formatting

DISPLAYING DECIMAL NUMBERS (BS1).

On the BS1, the DEBUG command, by default, displays numbers in the format "symbol = value" (followed by a carriage return), using the decimal number system. For example,

```
SYMBOL  x = B2

x = 75
DEBUG x
```

displays "x = 75" on the screen. To display the value, in decimal, without the "x =" text, use the value formatter (#) before the variable name. For example, the following code displays "75" on the screen.

```
SYMBOL  x = B2

x = 75
DEBUG #x
```

To display numbers in hexadecimal or binary form, use the $ or % formatter, respectively. The code below displays the same number in its hexadecimal and binary forms.

DISPLAYING HEXADECIMAL OR BINARY NUMBERS (BS1).

```
SYMBOL  x = B2

x = 75
DEBUG $x, %x
```

After running the above code, "x = $4B" and "x = %01001011" should appear on the screen. To display hexadecimal or binary values without the "symbol = " preface, use the value formatter (#) before the $ and %, as shown below:

```
SYMBOL   x = B2

x = 75
DEBUG #x, "as HEX is ", #$x        ' displays "75 as HEX is $4B"
DEBUG #x, "as BINARY is ", #%x     ' displays "75 as BINARY is %01001011"
```

DISPLAYING ASCII CHARACTERS (BS1). To display a number as its ASCII character equivalent, use the ASCII formatter (@).

```
SYMBOL   x = B2

x = 75
DEBUG @x
```

Table 5.10: DEBUG Formatters for the BASIC Stamp 1.

Formatter	Description
#	Suppresses the "symbol = x" format and displays only the 'x' value. The default format is decimal but may be combined with any of the formatters below (ex: #x to display: x value)
@	Displays "symbol = 'x'" + carriage return; where x is an ASCII character.
$	Hexadecimal text.
%	Binary text.

USING CR AND CLS (BS1). Two pre-defined symbols, CR and CLS, can be used to send a carriage-return or clear-screen command to the Debug Terminal. The CR symbol will cause the Debug Terminal to start a new line and the CLS symbol will cause the Debug Terminal to clear itself and place the cursor at the top-left corner of the screen. The following code demonstrates this.

```
DEBUG  "You can not see this.", CLS, "Here is line 1", CR, "Here is line 2"
```

When the above is run, the final result is "Here is line 1" on the first line of the screen and "Here is line 2" on the second line. You may or may not have seen "You can not see this." appear first. This is because it was immediately followed by a clear-screen symbol, CLS, which caused the display to clear the screen before displaying the rest of the information.

NOTE: The rest of this discussion does not apply to the BASIC Stamp 1.

BASIC Stamp 2, 2e, 2sx, 2p, 2pe, and 2px Formatting

On the all BASIC Stamp models except the BS1, the DEBUG command, by default, displays everything as ASCII characters. What if you want to display a number? You might think the following example would do this:

All 2

DISPLAYING ASCII CHARACTERS.

```
x       VAR     Byte

x = 65
DEBUG   x                       ' Try to show decimal value of x
```

Since we set *x* equal to 65 (in line 2), you might expect the DEBUG line to display "65" on the screen. Instead of "65", however, you'll see the letter "A" if you run this example. The problem is that we never told the BASIC Stamp how to output *x*, and it defaults to ASCII (the ASCII character at position 65 is "A"). Instead, we need to tell it to display the "decimal form" of the number in *x*. We can do this by using the decimal formatter (DEC) before the variable. The example below will display "65" on the screen.

DISPLAYING DECIMAL NUMBERS.

```
x       VAR     Byte

x = 65
DEBUG   DEC x                   ' Show decimal value of x
```

In addition to decimal (DEC), DEBUG can display numbers in hexadecimal (HEX) and binary (BIN). See Table 5.11 and Table 5.12 for a complete list of formatters.

DISPLAYING HEXADECIMAL AND BINARY NUMBERS.

Expressions are allowed within the DEBUG command arguments as well. In the above code, DEBUG DEC x+25 would yield "90" and DEBUG DEC x*10/2-3 would yield "322".

EXPRESSIONS IN DEBUG COMMANDS.

Table 5.11: DEBUG Special Formatters for all BS2 models.

Special Formatter	Action
?	Displays "symbol = x' + carriage return; where x is a number. Default format is decimal, but may be combined with conversion formatters (ex: BIN ? x to display "x = binary_number").
ASC ?	Displays "symbol = 'x'" + carriage return; where x is an ASCII character.
STR ByteArray {\L}	Send character string from an array. The optional \L argument can be used to limit the output to L characters, otherwise, characters will be sent up to the first byte equal to 0 or the end of RAM space is reached.
REP Byte \L	Send a string consisting of Byte repeated L times (ex: REP "X"\10 sends "XXXXXXXXXX").

Table 5.12: DEBUG Conversion Formatters for all BS2 models.

Conversion Formatter	Type of Number	Notes
DEC{1..5}	Decimal, optionally fixed to 1 – 5 digits	1
SDEC{1..5}	Signed decimal, optionally fixed to 1 – 5 digits	1,2
HEX{1..4}	Hexadecimal, optionally fixed to 1 – 4 digits	1,3
SHEX{1..4}	Signed hexadecimal, optionally fixed to 1 – 4 digits	1,2
IHEX{1..4}	Indicated hexadecimal, optionally fixed to 1 – 4 digits ($ prefix)	1
ISHEX{1..4}	Signed, indicated hexadecimal, optionally fixed to 1 – 4 digits ($ prefix)	1,2
BIN{1..16}	Binary, optionally fixed to 1 – 16 digits	1
SBIN{1..16}	Signed binary, optionally fixed to 1 – 16 digits	1,2
IBIN{1..16}	Indicated binary, optionally fixed to 1 – 16 digits (% prefix)	1
ISBIN{1..16}	Signed, indicated binary, optionally fixed to 1 – 16 digits (% prefix)	1,2

1 Fixed-digit formatters like DEC4 will pad the number with leading 0s if necessary; ex: DEC4 65 sends 0065. If a number is larger than the specified number of digits, the leading digits will be dropped; ex: DEC4 56422 sends 6422.
2 Signed modifiers work under two's complement rules.
3 The HEX modifier can be used for BCD to Decimal Conversion. See "Hex to BCD Conversion" on page 97.

DISPLAYING "INDICATED" NUMBERS.

As seen in Table 5.12, special versions of the DEC, HEX and BIN formatters allow for the display of indicated, signed and fixed-width numbers. The term "indicated" simply means that a special symbol is displayed, before the number, indicating what number system it belongs to. For example,

```
x        VAR      Byte

x = 65
DEBUG   HEX x                         ' Show hexadecimal value of x
```

displays "41" (65, in decimal, is 41, in hexadecimal). You might see a problem here... unless you knew the number was supposed to be hexadecimal, you might think it was 41, in decimal... a totally different number. To help avoid this, use the IHEX formatter (the "I" stands for indicated). Changing the DEBUG line to read: DEBUG IHEX x would print "$41" on the screen. A similar formatter for binary also exists, IBIN, which prints a "%" before the number.

Signed numbers are preceded with a space ( ) or a minus sign (-) to indicate a positive or negative number, respectively. Normally, any number displayed by the BASIC Stamp is shown in its unsigned (positive) form without any indicator. The signed formatters allow you to display the number as a signed (rather than unsigned) value. **NOTE: Only Word-sized variables can be used for signed number display.** The code below demonstrates the difference in all three numbering schemes.

DISPLAYING SIGNED VS. UNSIGNED NUMBERS.

```
x        VAR    Word

x = -65
DEBUG  "Signed: ", SDEC  x, "  ", ISHEX  x, "  ", ISBIN  x, CR
DEBUG  "Unsigned: ", DEC  x, "  ", IHEX  x, "  ", IBIN  x
```

This code will generate the display shown below:

```
Signed:  -65     -$41     -%1000001
Unsigned:  65471    $FFBF    %1111111110111111
```

The signed form of the number –65 is shown in decimal, hexadecimal and then in binary on the top line. The unsigned form, in all three number systems, is shown on the bottom line. If the unsigned form looks strange to you, it's because negative numbers are stored in twos complement format within the BASIC Stamp.

Suppose that your program contained several DEBUG instructions showing the contents of different variables. You would want some way to tell them apart. One possible way is to do the following:

AUTOMATIC NAMES IN THE DISPLAY.

```
x        VAR    Byte
y        VAR    Byte

x = 100
y = 250
DEBUG "X = ", DEC x, CR           ' Show decimal value of x
DEBUG "Y = ", DEC y, CR           ' Show decimal value of y
```

but typing the name of the variables in quotes (for the display) can get a little tedious. A special formatter, the question mark (?), can save you a lot of time. The code below does exactly the same thing (with less typing):

```
x        VAR      Byte
y        VAR      Byte

x = 100
y = 250
DEBUG DEC ? x                    ' Show decimal value of x
DEBUG DEC ? y                    ' Show decimal value of y
```

The display would look something like this:

```
x = 100
y = 250
```

The ? formatter always displays data in the form "symbol = value" (followed by a carriage return). In addition, it defaults to displaying in decimal, so we really only needed to type: DEBUG ? x for the above code. You can, of course, use any of the three number systems. For example: DEBUG HEX ? x or DEBUG BIN ? y.

It's important to note that the "symbol" it displays is taken directly from what appears to the right of the ?. If you were to use an expression, for example: DEBUG ? x*10/2+3 in the above code, the display would show: "x*10/2+3 = 503".

A special formatter, ASC, is also available for use only with the ? formatter to display ASCII characters, as in: DEBUG ASC ? x.

What if you need to display a table of data; multiple rows and columns? The Signed/Unsigned code (above) approaches this but, if you notice, the columns don't line up. The number formatters (DEC, HEX and BIN) have some useful variations to make the display fixed-width (see Table 5.12). Up to 5 digits can be displayed for decimal numbers. To fix the value to a specific number of decimal digits, you can use DEC1, DEC2, DEC3, DEC4 or DEC5. For example:

```
x        VAR      Byte

x = 165
DEBUG DEC5 x                     ' Show decimal value of x in 5 digits
```

displays "00165". Notice that leading zeros? The display is "fixed" to 5 digits, no more and no less. Any unused digits will be filled with zeros.

Using DEC4 in the same code would display "0165". DEC3 would display "165". What would happen if we used DEC2? Regardless of the number, the BASIC Stamp will ensure that it is always the exact number of digits you specified. In this case, it would truncate the "1" and only display "65".

Using the fixed-width version of the formatters in the Signed/Unsigned code above, may result in the following code:

```
x       VAR     Word

x = -65
DEBUG "Signed:    ", SDEC5 x, "   ", ISHEX4 x, "   ", ISBIN16 x, CR
DEBUG "Unsigned: ", DEC5 x, "   ", IHEX4 x, "   ", IBIN16 x
```

and displays:

```
Signed:    -00065    -$0041    -%0000000001000001
Unsigned:  65471     $FFBF     %1111111110111111
```

Note: The columns don't line up exactly (due to the extra "sign" characters in the first row), but it certainly looks better than the alternative.

If you have a string of characters to display (a byte array), you can use the STR formatter to do so. The STR formatter has two forms (as shown in Table 5.11) for variable-width and fixed-width data. The example below is the variable-width form.

DISPLAYING STRINGS (BYTE ARRAYS).

VARIABLE-WIDTH STRINGS.

```
x       VAR     Byte(5)

x(0) = "A"
x(1) = "B"
x(2) = "C"
x(3) = "D"
x(4) = 0
DEBUG STR x
```

This code displays "ABCD" on the screen. In this form, the STR formatter displays each character contained in the byte array until it finds a character that is equal to 0 (value 0, not "0"). This is convenient for use with the SERIN command's STR formatter, which appends 0's to the end of variable-width character string inputs. NOTE: If your byte array doesn't end with 0, the BASIC Stamp will read and output all RAM register contents until it finds a 0 or until it cycles through all RAM locations.

FIXED-WIDTH STRINGS.

To specify a fixed-width format for the STR formatter, use the form STR x\n; where x is the byte array and n is the number of characters to print. Changing the DEBUG line in the example above to: DEBUG STR x\2 would display "AB" on the screen.

REPEATING CHARACTERS.

If you need to display the same ASCII character multiple times, the REP (repeat) formatter can help. REP takes the form: REP x\n ;where x is the character and n is the number of times to repeat it. For example:

```
DEBUG  REP "-"\10
```

would display 10 hyphens on the screen, "----------".

SPECIAL CONTROL CHARACTERS.

Since individual DEBUG instructions can grow to be fairly complicated, and since a program can contain many DEBUGS, you'll probably want to control the character positioning of the Debug Terminal screen. DEBUG supports a number of different control characters, some with pre-defined symbols (see Table 5.13).

All of the control characters have pre-defined symbols associated with them. In your DEBUG commands, you can use those symbols, for example: DEBUG "Hello", CR displays "Hello" followed by a carriage return. You can always use the ASCII value for any of the control characters, however. For example: DEBUG "Hello", 13 is exactly the same as the code above.

The Move To (x,y) control character allows positioning to a specific column and row of the display. If the Debug Terminal receives this character, it expects to see an x and y position value to follow (in the next two characters received). The following line moves the cursor to column number 4 in row number 5 and displays "Hello":

```
' {$PBASIC 2.5}

DEBUG CRSRXY, 4, 5, "Hello"
```

DEBUG – BASIC Stamp Command Reference

The upper-left cursor position is 0,0 (that is column 0, row 0). The right-most cursor positions depend on the size of the Debug Terminal window (which is user adjustable). If a character position that is out of range is received, the Debug Terminal wraps back around to the opposite side of the screen.

The Move To Column (x) and Move To Row (y) control characters work similarly to Move To (x,y) except they only expect a singe position value to follow.

The Clear Right (CLREOL) control character clears the characters that appear to the right of, and on, the cursor's current position. The cursor is not moved by this action.

The Clear Down (CRLDN) control character clears the characters that appear below, and on, the cursor's current line. The cursor is not moved by this action.

Name	Symbol	ASCII Value	Description
Clear Screen	CLS	0	Clear the screen and place cursor at home position.
Home	HOME	1	Place cursor at home in upper-left corner of the screen.
Move To (x,y)	CRSRXY [2.5]	2	Move cursor to specified location. Must be followed by two values (x and then y)
Cursor Left	CRSRLF [2.5]	3	Move cursor one character to left.
Cursor Right	CRSRRT [2.5]	4	Move cursor one character to right.
Cursor Up	CRSRUP [2.5]	5	Move cursor one character up.
Cursor Down	CRSRDN [2.5]	6	Move cursor one character down.
Bell	BELL	7	Beep the PC speaker.
Backspace	BKSP	8	Back up cursor to left one space.
Tab	TAB	9	Tab to the next column.
Line Feed	LF [2.5]	10	Move cursor down one line.
Clear Right	CLREOL [2.5]	11	Clear line contents to the right of cursor.
Clear Down	CLRDN [2.5]	12	Clear screen contents below cursor.
Carriage Return	CR	13	Move cursor to the first column of the next line (shift any data on the right down to that line as well).
Move To Column X	CRSRX [2.5]	14	Move cursor to specified column. Must be followed by byte value (x) for the column (0 is the left-most column).
Move To Row Y	CRSRY [2.5]	15	Move cursor to specified row. Must be followed by byte value (y) for the row (0 is the top-most row).

Table 5.13: Special DEBUG Control Characters for all BS2 models.

NOTE: ([2.5]) indicates this control character requires the PBASIC 2.5 compiler directive.

TECHNICAL BACKGROUND

⟦All 2⟧ On all the BS2 models, DEBUG is actually a special case of the SEROUT instruction. It is set for inverted (RS-232-compatible) serial output through the programming connector (the SOUT pin) at 9600 baud, no parity, 8 data bits, and 1 stop bit. For example,

```
DEBUG "Hello"
```

is exactly like:

⟦2⟧
```
' {$STAMP BS2}

SEROUT 16, $4054, ["Hello"]
```

in terms of function on a BS2. The DEBUG line actually takes less program space, and is obviously easier to type.

Another method to decrease program space is to reduce the number of DEBUG instructions by spreading DEBUG data across multiple lines. To do this, each line that wraps around must end with a comma as in the example below:

```
' {$PBASIC 2.5}

DEBUG "This is line 1", CR,
      "This is line 2"
```

The example above works identically to, but uses less program space than this version:

```
DEBUG "This is line 1", CR
DEBUG "This is line 2"
```

Note that spreading a DEBUG statement across multiple lines requires the declaration of PBASIC 2.5 syntax.

You may view DEBUG's output using a terminal program set to the above parameters, but you may have to modify either your development board or the serial cable to temporarily disconnect pin 3 of the BASIC Stamp (pin 4 of the DB-9 connector). See the SEROUT command for more detail.

A demo program for all BS2 models that uses DEBUG and DEBUGIN commands can be found at the end of the DEBUGIN section, next.

DEBUGIN

DEBUGIN *InputData* { , *InputData* }

Function
Accept information from the user via the Debug Terminal within the BASIC Stamp Editor program.

- **InputData** is list of variables and formatters that tells DEBUGIN what to do with incoming data. DEBUGIN can store data in a variable or array, interpret numeric text (decimal, binary, or hex) and store the corresponding value in a variable, wait for a fixed or variable sequence of bytes, or ignore a specified number of bytes. These actions can be combined in any order in the *InputData* list.

Quick Facts

Table 5.14: DEBUGIN Quick Facts.

	BS2, BS2e, BS2sx, BS2p, BS2pe	BS2px
Serial Protocol	Asynchronous 9600 baud N, 8, 1 Inverted Polarity, Raw Data	Asynchronous 19200 baud N, 8, 1 Inverted Polarity, Raw Data
Related Commands	SERIN and DEBUG	

Explanation
DEBUGIN provides a convenient way for your BASIC Stamp to accept input from the user via the Debug Terminal. DEBUGIN can wait for, filter and convert incoming data in powerful ways, using the same techniques and modifiers as SERIN.

DEBUGIN is actually a special case of the SERIN instruction. It is set for inverted (RS-232-compatible) serial input through the programming connector (the SIN pin) at 9600 baud (19200 baud on BS2px), no parity, 8 data bits, and 1 stop bit.

For example:

```
DEBUGIN DEC1 myNum
```

is exactly like:

```
' {$STAMP BS2}

SERIN 16, $4054, [DEC1 myNum]
```

⌗2

in terms of function on a BS2. The DEBUGIN line actually takes less program space, and is obviously easier to type. Example:

```
' {$PBASIC 2.5}

myNum    VAR      Nib

DEBUG CLS, "Enter a number (1 - 5)? --> "
DEBUGIN DEC1 myNum
IF ((myNum >= 1) AND (myNum <= 5)) THEN
  DEBUG CLS, "You entered: ", DEC1 myNum
ELSE
  DEBUG CLS, "Sorry, number out of range"
ENDIF
END
```

The tables below list all the special formatters and conversion formatters available to the DEBUGIN command. See the SERIN instruction for additional information and examples of their use.

Special Formatter	Action
STR ByteArray \L {\E}	Input a character string of length L into an array. If specified, an end character E causes the string input to end before reaching length L. Remaining bytes are filled with 0s (zeros).
WAIT (Value)	Wait for a sequence of bytes specified by value. Value can be numbers separated by commas or quoted text (ex: 65, 66, 67 or "ABC"). The WAIT formatter is limited to a maximum of six characters.
WAITSTR ByteArray {\L}	Wait for a sequence of bytes matching a string stored in an array variable, optionally limited to L characters. If the optional L argument is left off, the end of the array-string must be marked by a byte containing a zero (0).
SKIP Length	Ignore Length bytes of characters.

Table 5.15: DEBUGIN Special Formatters.

There is an additional special formatter for the BS2p, BS2pe, and BS2px: ⌗2p ⌗2pe ⌗2px

Special Formatter	Action
SPSTR L	Input a character string of length L bytes (up to 126) into Scratch Pad RAM, starting at location 0. Use GET to retrieve the characters.

Table 5.16: DEBUGIN Additional Special Formatter for the BS2p, BS2pe, and BS2px.

Table 5.17: DEBUGIN Conversion Formatters.

Conversion Formatter	Type of Number	Numeric Characters Accepted	Notes
DEC{1..5}	Decimal, optionally limited to 1 – 5 digits	0 through 9	1
SDEC{1..5}	Signed decimal, optionally limited to 1 – 5 digits	-, 0 through 9	1,2
HEX{1..4}	Hexadecimal, optionally limited to 1 – 4 digits	0 through 9, A through F	1,3,5
SHEX{1..4}	Signed hexadecimal, optionally limited to 1 – 4 digits	-, 0 through 9, A through F	1,2,3
IHEX{1..4}	Indicated hexadecimal, optionally limited to 1 – 4 digits	$, 0 through 9, A through F	1,3,4
ISHEX{1..4}	Signed, indicated hexadecimal, optionally limited to 1 – 4 digits	-, $, 0 through 9, A through F	1,2,3,4
BIN{1..16}	Binary, optionally limited to 1 – 16 digits	0, 1	1
SBIN{1..16}	Signed binary, optionally limited to 1 – 16 digits	-, 0, 1	1,2
IBIN{1..16}	Indicated binary, optionally limited to 1 – 16 digits	%, 0, 1	1,4
ISBIN{1..16}	Signed, indicated binary, optionally limited to 1 – 16 digits	-, %, 0, 1	1,2,4
NUM	Generic numeric input (decimal, hexadecimal or binary); hexadecimal or binary number must be indicated	$, %, 0 through 9, A through F	1, 3, 4
SNUM	Similar to NUM with value treated as signed with range -32768 to +32767	-, $, %, 0 through 9, A through F	1,2,3,4

1 All numeric conversions will continue to accept new data until receiving either the specified number of digits (ex: three digits for DEC3) or a non-numeric character.

2 To be recognized as part of a number, the minus sign (-) must immediately precede a numeric character. The minus sign character occurring in non-numeric text is ignored and any character (including a space) between a minus and a number causes the minus to be ignored.

3 The hexadecimal formatters are not case-sensitive; "a" through "f" means the same as "A" through "F".

4 Indicated hexadecimal and binary formatters ignore all characters, even valid numerics, until they receive the appropriate prefix ($ for hexadecimal, % for binary). The indicated formatters can differentiate between text and hexadecimal (ex: ABC would be interpreted by HEX as a number but IHEX would ignore it unless expressed as $ABC). Likewise, the binary version can distinguish the decimal number 10 from the binary number %10. A prefix occurring in non-numeric text is ignored, and any character (including a space) between a prefix and a number causes the prefix to be ignored. Indicated, signed formatters require that the minus sign come before the prefix, as in -$1B45.

5 The HEX modifier can be used for Decimal to BCD Conversion. See "Hex to BCD Conversion" on page 97.

For examples of all conversion formatters and how they process incoming data, see Appendix C.

Demo Program (DEBUGIN.bs2)

```
' DEBUGIN.bs2
' This program demonstrates the ability to accept user input from the
' Debug Terminal, and to accept numeric entry in any valid format.

' {$STAMP BS2}
' {$PBASIC 2.5}

myNum    VAR     Word


Main:
  DO
    DEBUG CLS, "Enter any number: "    ' prompt user
    DEBUGIN SNUM myNum                 ' retrieve number in any format

    DEBUG CLS,                         ' display number in all formats
         SDEC ? myNum,
         SHEX ? myNum,
         SBIN ? myNum
    PAUSE 3000
  LOOP                                 ' do it again
  END
```

All 2

NOTE: This example program can be used with all BS2 models by changing the $STAMP directive accordingly.

DO...LOOP

BS1	BS2	BS2e	BS2sx	BS2p	BS2pe	BS2px

All 2

DO { WHILE | UNTIL *Condition(s)* }
    Statement(s)
LOOP { WHILE | UNTIL *Condition(s)* }

NOTE: DO...LOOP requires the PBASIC 2.5 compiler directive.

Function

Create a repeating loop that executes the *Statement(s)*, one or more program lines that form a code block, between DO and LOOP, optionally testing *Condition(s)* before or after the *Statement(s)*.

- **Condition** is an optional variable/constant/expression (0 - 65535) which determines whether the loop will run or terminate. *Condition* must follow WHILE or UNTIL.

- **Statement** is any valid PBASIC instruction.

Quick Facts

Table 5.18: DO...LOOP Quick Facts.

	All BS2 Models
Maximum Nested Loops	16
WHILE *Condition* Evaluation	Run loop if *Condition* evaluates as true
UNTIL *Condition* Evaluation	Terminate loop if *Condition* evaluates as true
Related Commands	FOR...NEXT and EXIT

Explanation

DO...LOOP loops let a program execute a series of instructions indefinitely or until a specified condition terminates the loop. The simplest form is shown here:

```
' {$PBASIC 2.5}

DO
  DEBUG "Error...", CR
  PAUSE 2000
LOOP
```

In this example the error message will be printed on the Debug screen every two seconds until the BASIC Stamp is reset. Simple DO...LOOP loops can be terminated with EXIT.

For example:

```
' {$PBASIC 2.5}

AckPin    PIN    0
Pressed   CON    1

DO
  DEBUG "Error...", CR
  IF (AckPin = Pressed) THEN EXIT       ' wait for user button press
  PAUSE 2000
LOOP
GOTO Initialize                         ' re-initialize system
```

In this case the DO...LOOP will continue until the pin called *AckPin* is equal to *Pressed* (1), and then the loop will terminate and continue at the line GOTO Initialize.

More often than not, you will want to test some condition to determine whether the code block should run or continue to run. A loop that tests the condition before running code block is constructed like this:

```
' {$PBASIC 2.5}

reps    VAR    Nib

DO WHILE (reps < 3)                     ' test before loop statements
  DEBUG "*"
  reps = reps + 1
LOOP
```

In this program the instructions DEBUG "*" and reps = reps + 1 will not run unless the WHILE condition evaluates as True. Another way to write the loop is like this:

```
' {$PBASIC 2.5}

reps    VAR    Nib

DO
  DEBUG "*"
  reps = reps + 1
LOOP UNTIL (reps >= 3)                  ' test after loop statements
```

The difference is that with this loop, the code block will always be run at least once before the condition is tested and will continue to run as long as the UNTIL condition evaluates as False.

Note that the WHILE test (loop runs WHILE *Condition* is True) and UNTIL test (loop runs UNTIL *Condition* is True) can be interchanged, but they are generally used as illustrated above.

NOTE: This example program can be used with all BS2 models by changing the $STAMP directive accordingly.

All 2 **Demo Program (DO-LOOP.bs2)**

```
' DO-LOOP.bs2
' This program creates a little guessing game.  It starts by creating
' a (pseudo) random number between 1 and 10.  The inner loop will run
' until the answer is guessed or 10 tries have been attempted.  The
' outer loop has no condition and will cause the inner loop code to
' run until the BASIC Stamp is reprogrammed.

' {$STAMP BS2}
' {$PBASIC 2.5}

rVal            VAR     Word            ' random value
answer          VAR     Byte            ' game answer
guess           VAR     Byte            ' player guess
tries           VAR     Nib             ' number of tries


Main:
  DO
    RANDOM rVal
    answer = rVal.LOWBYTE */ 10 + 1      ' create 1 - 10 answer
    tries = 0

    DO                                   ' get answer until out of tries
      DEBUG CLS,
            "Guess a number (1 - 10): "
      DEBUGIN DEC guess                  ' get new guess
      tries = tries + 1                  ' update tries count
    LOOP UNTIL ((tries = 10) OR (guess = answer))

    IF (guess = answer) THEN             ' test reason for loop end
      DEBUG CR, "You got it!"
    ELSE
      DEBUG CR, "Sorry ... the answer was ", DEC answer, "."
    ENDIF
    PAUSE 1000
  LOOP                                   ' run again
  END
```

DTMFOUT

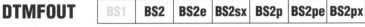

All 2 **DTMFOUT** *Pin,* { *OnTime, OffTime,* } [*Tone* {, *Tone...*}]

Function

Generate dual-tone, multifrequency tones (DTMF, i.e., telephone "touch" tones).

- **Pin** is a variable/constant/expression (0 – 15) that specifies the I/O pin to use. This pin will be set to output mode during generation of tones and set to input mode afterwards.

- **OnTime** is an optional variable/constant/expression (0 – 65535) specifying a duration of the tone. The unit of time and the default time for *OnTime* is described in Table 5.19.

- **OffTime** is an optional variable/constant/expression (0 – 65535) specifying the length of silent pause after a tone (or between tones, if multiple tones are specified). The unit of time and the default time for *OffTime* is described in Table 5.19.

- **Tone** is a variable/constant/expression (0 – 15) specifying the DTMF tone to generate. Tones 0 through 11 correspond to the standard layout of the telephone keypad, while 12 through 15 are the fourth-column tones used by phone test equipment and in ham-radio applications.

Quick Facts

Table 5.19: DMTFOUT Quick Facts.

	BS2, BS2e	BS2sx	BS2p	BS2pe	BS2px
Default *OnTime*	200 ms	80 ms	55 ms	196 ms	34 ms
Default *OffTime*	50 ms	50 ms	50 ms	50 ms	50 ms
Units in *OnTime*	1 ms	0.4 ms	0.265 ms	1 ms	0.166 ms
Units in *OffTime*	1 ms	1 ms	1 ms	1 ms	1 ms
Related Command	FREQOUT				

Explanation

DTMF tones are used to dial the phone or remotely control certain radio equipment. The BASIC Stamp can generate these tones digitally using the DTMFOUT instruction. Figure 5.4 shows how to connect a speaker or audio amplifier to hear these tones and Figure 5.5 shows how to connect the BASIC Stamp to the phone line.

DTMFOUT – BASIC Stamp Command Reference

The following DTMFOUT instruction will generate DTMF tones on I/O pin 10:

```
DTMFOUT 10, [6, 2, 4, 8, 3, 3, 3]          ' Call Parallax
```

If the BASIC Stamp is connected to the phone line properly, the above command would be equivalent to dialing 624-8333 from a phone keypad. If you wanted to slow the pace of the dialing to accommodate a noisy phone line or radio link, you could use the optional *OnTime* and *OffTime* values:

```
DTMFOUT 10, 500, 100, [ 6, 2, 4, 8, 3, 3, 3]   ' Call Parallax, slowly
```

In this example, on a BS2 the *OnTime* is set to 500 ms (1/2 second) and *OffTime* to 100 ms (1/10th second).

Tone Value	Corresponding Telephone Key
0 – 9	Digits 0 through 9
10	Star (*)
11	Pound (#)
12 – 15	Fourth column tones A through D

Table 5.20: DTMF Tones and Corresponding Telephone Keys.

Driving an Audio Amplifier

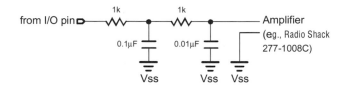

Figure 5.4: Example RC Filter Circuits for Driving an Audio Amplifier (top) or a Speaker (bottom).

Driving a Speaker

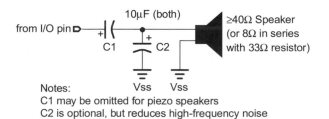

Notes:
C1 may be omitted for piezo speakers
C2 is optional, but reduces high-frequency noise

TECHNICAL BACKGROUND.

The BASIC Stamp microcontroller is a purely digital device. DTMF tones are analog waveforms, consisting of a mixture of two sine waves at different audio frequencies. So how does a digital device generate analog output? The BASIC Stamp creates and mixes the sine waves mathematically, then uses the resulting stream of numbers to control the duty cycle of a very fast pulse-width modulation (PWM) routine. So what's actually coming out of the I/O pin is a rapid stream of pulses. The purpose of the filtering arrangements shown in Figure 5.4 and Figure 5.5 is to smooth out the high-frequency PWM, leaving only the lower frequency audio behind.

Keep this in mind if you want to interface BASIC Stamp's DTMF output to radios and other equipment that could be adversely affected by the presence of high-frequency noise on the input. Make sure to filter the DTMF output thoroughly. The circuits in Figure 5.4 are only a starting point; you may want to use an active low-pass filter with a roll-off point around 2 kHz.

Figure 5.5: Example DAA Circuit to Interface to a Standard Telephone Line.

Interfacing to the Telephone Line

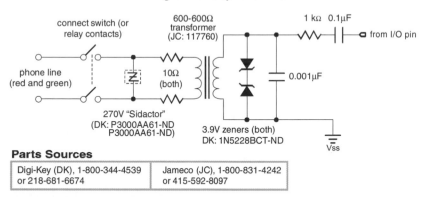

Parts Sources

Digi-Key (DK), 1-800-344-4539 or 218-681-6674	Jameco (JC), 1-800-831-4242 or 415-592-8097

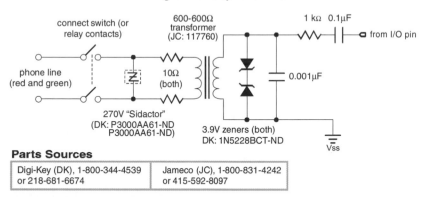

Demo Program (DTMFOUT.bs2)

NOTE: This example program can be used with all BS2 models. This program uses conditional compilation techniques; see Chapter 3 for more information.

```
' DTMFOUT.bs2
' This demo program is a rudimentary memory dialer. Since DTMF digits fit
' within a nibble (four bits), the program below packs two DTMF digits into
' each byte of three EEPROM data tables. The end of phone number is marked
' by the nibble $F, since this is not a valid phone-dialing digit.
' Conditional compilation sets the timing adjustment factor so that the
' output will sound the same on any BS2 model.
```

```
' {$STAMP BS2}
' {$PBASIC 2.5}

Spkr            PIN     10                  ' DTMF output on pin 10

#SELECT $STAMP
  #CASE BS2, BS2E, BS2PE
    TmAdj       CON     $100                ' x 1.0 (time adjust)
  #CASE BS2SX
    TmAdj       CON     $280                ' x 2.5
  #CASE BS2P
    TmAdj       CON     $3C5                ' x 3.77
  #CASE BS2PX
    TmAdj       CON     $607                ' x 6.03
#ENDSELECT

eeLoc           VAR     Byte                ' EEPROM address of stored number
eeByte          VAR     Byte                ' Byte containing two DTMF digits
dtDig           VAR     eeByte.NIB1         ' Digit to dial
phone           VAR     Nib                 ' Pick a phone #
hiLo            VAR     Bit                 ' Bit to select upper and lower nib

Parallax        DATA    $19,$16,$62,$48,$33,$3F   ' Phone: 1-916-624-8333
ParallaxFax     DATA    $19,$16,$62,$48,$00,$3F   ' Phone: 1-916-624-8003
Information     DATA    $15,$20,$55,$51,$21,$2F   ' Phone: 1-520-555-1212


Main:
  FOR phone = 0 TO 2
    ' retrieve address
    LOOKUP phone, [Parallax, ParallaxFax, Information], eeLoc
    GOSUB Dial_Number
    PAUSE 2000
  NEXT
  END

Dial_Number:
  DO
    READ eeLoc, eeByte                      ' Retrieve byte from EEPROM
    eeLoc = eeLoc + 1                       ' point to next pair of digits
    FOR hiLo = 0 TO 1                       ' Dial upper and lower digits
      IF (dtDig = $F) THEN EXIT             ' Hex $F is end-of-number flag
      DTMFOUT Spkr,                         ' dial digit
              150 */ TmAdj, 25, [dtDig]     ' 150 ms on, 25 ms off
      eeByte = eeByte << 4                  ' Shift in next digit
    NEXT
  LOOP UNTIL (dtDig = $F)
  RETURN
```

EEPROM

EEPROM { *Location,* } (*DataItem* {, *DataItem...*})

(See DATA)

Function

Write data to the EEPROM during program download.

- **Location** is an optional variable/constant (0 – 255) that specifies the starting location in the EEPROM at which data should be stored. If no location is given, data is written starting at the next available location.

- **DataItem** is a constant (0 – 255) to be stored in EEPROM.

Quick Facts

Table 5.21: EEPROM Quick Facts.

	BS1
Special Notes	Writes values to EEPROM during download. Can be used to decrease program size.
Related Commands	READ and WRITE

Explanation

When you download a program into the BASIC Stamp 1, it is stored in the EEPROM starting at the highest address (255) and working towards the lowest address. Most programs don't use the entire EEPROM, so the lower portion is available for other uses. The EEPROM directive allows you to define a set of data to store in the available EEPROM locations. It is called a "directive" rather than a "command" because it performs an activity at compile-time rather than at run-time (i.e.: the EEPROM directive is not downloaded to the BASIC Stamp 1, but the data it contains is downloaded).

WRITING SIMPLE, SEQUENTIAL DATA.

The simplest form of the EEPROM directive is something like the following:

```
EEPROM    (100, 200, 52, 45)
```

This example, when downloaded, will cause the values 100, 200, 52 and 45 to be written to EEPROM locations 0, 1, 2 and 3, respectively. You can then use the READ and WRITE commands in your code to access these locations and the data you've stored there.

The EEPROM directive uses a counter, called a pointer, to keep track of available EEPROM addresses. The value of the pointer is initially 0. When a program is downloaded, the EEPROM directive stores the first byte value at the current pointer address, then increments (adds 1 to) the pointer. If the program contains more than one EEPROM directive, subsequent EEPROM directives start with the pointer value left by the previous EEPROM directive. For example, if the program contains:

THE EEPROM POINTER (COUNTER).

```
EEPROM    (72, 69, 76, 76, 79)
EEPROM    (104, 101, 108, 108, 111)
```

The first EEPROM directive will start at location 0 and increment the pointer for each data value it stores (1, 2, 3, 4 and 5). The second EEPROM directive will start with the pointer value of 5 and work upward from there. As a result, the first 10 bytes of EEPROM will look like the following:

	EEPROM Location (address)									
	0	1	2	3	4	5	6	7	8	9
Contents	72	69	76	76	79	104	101	108	108	111

Table 5.22: Example EEPROM Storage.

What if you don't want to store values starting at location 0? Fortunately, the EEPROM directive has an option to specify the next location to use. You can specify the next location number (to set the pointer to) by using the optional *Location* argument before the list of *DataItems*. The following code writes the same data in Table 5.22 to locations 50 through 59:

WRITING DATA TO OTHER LOCATIONS.

```
EEPROM    50, (72, 69, 76, 76, 79, 104, 101, 108, 108, 111)
```

In this example, the *Location* argument is given and tells the EEPROM directive to store the following *DataItem(s)* starting at location 50. The *DataItems* in the list are stored in their respective locations (50, 51, 52... 59).

It is important to realize that the entire BASIC Stamp 1 EEPROM is overwritten during programming. Any EEPROM location not containing a PBASIC program or *DataItems* from an EEPROM directive is written with a 0.

IMPORTANT CONCEPT: HOW DATA AND PROGRAMS ARE DOWNLOADED INTO EEPROM.

A common use for EEPROM is to store strings; sequences of bytes representing text. PBASIC converts quoted text like "A" into the corresponding ASCII character code (65 in this case). To make data entry easier, you can place quotes around a whole chunk of text used in an

WRITING TEXT STRINGS.

EEPROM directive, and PBASIC will understand it to mean a series of bytes (see the last line of code below). The following three EEPROM directives are equivalent:

```
EEPROM    (72, 69, 76, 76, 79)
EEPROM    ("H", "E", "L", "L", "O")
EEPROM    ("HELLO")
```

All three lines of code, above, will result in the numbers 72, 69, 76, 76, and 79 being stored into EEPROM upon downloading. These numbers are simply the ASCII character codes for "H", "E", "L", "L", and "O", respectively. See the demo program, below, for an example of storing and reading multiple text strings.

WRITING WORD VALUES VS. BYTE VALUES.

The EEPROM is organized as a sequential set of byte-sized memory locations. The EEPROM directive only stores bytes into EEPROM. If you try to store a word-sized value, for example: EEPROM (1125), only the lower byte of the value will be stored (in this case, 101). This does not mean that you can't store word-sized values, however. A word consists of two bytes, called a low-byte and a high-byte. If you wanted to store the value 1125 using the EEPROM directive you'll have to calculate the low-byte and the high-byte and insert them in the list in the proper order, as in:

```
EEPROM    (101, 4)
```

The directive above will store the two bytes into two sequential EEPROM locations (the low-byte first, followed by the high-byte). We calculated this in the following manner: 1) high-byte is INT(value / 256) and 2) low-byte is value – (high-byte * 256).

To retrieve a word-sized value, you'll need to use two READ commands and a word-sized variable. For example,

```
SYMBOL   result        = W0           ' word-sized variable
SYMBOL   resultLo      = B0           ' B0 is the low-byte of W0
SYMBOL   resultHi      = B1           ' B1 is the high-byte of W0

EEPROM  (101, 4)

READ  0, resultLo
READ  1, resultHi
DEBUG #result
```

This code would write the low-byte and high-byte of the number 1125 into locations 0 and 1 during download. When the program runs, the two

READ commands will read the low-byte and high-byte out of EEPROM (reconstructing it in a word-sized variable) and then display the value on the screen. See the READ and WRITE commands for more information.

Demo Program (EEPROM.bs1)

```
' EEPROM.bs1
' This program stores a couple of text strings into EEPROM with the EEPROM
' directive and then sends them, one character at a time via the SEROUT
' command.  This is a good demonstration of how to save program space by
' storing large amounts of data in EEPROM directly, rather than embedding
' the data into SEROUT commands.

' {$STAMP BS1}
' {$PBASIC 1.0}

SYMBOL  SOut          = 0             ' serial output

SYMBOL  idx           = B2            ' Holds current location number
SYMBOL  phrase        = B3
SYMBOL  char          = B4            ' Holds current character to print

Phrases:
  EEPROM ("Here is a long message that needs to be transmitted.", 13, 0)
  EEPROM ("Here is some more text to be transmitted.", 13, 0)


Main:
  idx = 0
  FOR phrase = 1 TO 2                 ' select phrase
    GOSUB Print_It                    ' print the phrase
    PAUSE 3000                        ' Pause for 3 seconds
  NEXT
  END

Print_It:
  READ idx, char                      ' get next character
  idx = idx + 1                       ' point to next EEPROM location
  IF char = 0 THEN Print_Done         ' if 0, we're done with this block
  SEROUT SOut, N2400, (char)          ' otherwise, transmit it
  'DEBUG #@char                       ' -- for demo with DEBUG (slower)
  GOTO Print_It

Print_Done:
  RETURN                              ' return to caller
```

END

BS1	BS2	BS2e	BS2sx	BS2p	BS2pe	BS2px

END

Function

End the program, placing the BASIC Stamp into low-power mode indefinitely. This is equivalent to having a program that does not loop continuously; once the BASIC Stamp reaches the end of the PBASIC program, it enters low-power mode indefinitely. The END command is optional.

Quick Facts

Table 5.23: END Quick Facts.

Note: Current measurements are based on 5-volt power, no extra loads, and 75°F ambient temperature.

	BS1	BS2	BS2e	BS2sx	BS2p	BS2pe	BS2px
Current Draw During Run	1 mA	3 mA	25 mA	60 mA	40 mA	15 mA	55 mA
Current Draw During Sleep	25 µA	50 µA	200 µA	500 µA	350 µA	36 µA	450 µA
Related Commands	NAP and SLEEP	NAP, SLEEP and STOP			NAP, SLEEP, STOP and POLLWAIT		

Explanation

END puts the BASIC Stamp into its inactive, low-power mode. In this mode the Stamp's current draw (excluding loads driven by the I/O pins) is reduced to the amount shown in Table 5.23. END keeps the BASIC Stamp inactive until the reset line is activated, the power is cycled off and back on or the PC downloads another program.

Just as with the SLEEP command, pins will retain their input or output settings after the BASIC Stamp is deactivated by END. For example, if the BASIC Stamp is powering an LED when END executes, the LED will stay lit after END, but every 2.3 seconds, there will be a visible wink of the LED as the output pin switches to the input direction for 18 ms (60 µs on the BS2pe). (See the SLEEP command for more information).

EXIT

BS1	BS2	BS2e	BS2sx	BS2p	BS2pe	BS2px

<u>All 2</u> **EXIT**

NOTE: EXIT requires the PBASIC 2.5 compiler directive.

Function

Causes the immediate termination of a loop construct (DO...LOOP, FOR...NEXT).

Quick Facts

Table 5.24: EXIT Quick Facts.

	All BS2 Models
Maximum EXITs per Loop	16
Related Commands	DO...LOOP and FOR...NEXT

Explanation

The EXIT instruction allows a program to terminate a loop structure before the loop limit test is executed. While not required, EXIT is usually used as part of an IF...THEN construct to test a secondary condition for terminating a loop, or for testing a termination condition of an unconditional DO...LOOP structure.

For example, the following subroutine will send characters from a DATA statement to a serial port until a 0 byte is encountered in the data:

```
' {$PBASIC 2.5}

DO
  READ eeAddr, char             ' get character from DATA statement
  eeAddr = eeAddr + 1           ' update address pointer
  IF (char = 0) THEN EXIT       ' if 0, end of string
  DEBUG char                    ' otherwise, transmit the character
LOOP                            ' get next character
RETURN
```

<u>All 2</u> **Demo Program (EXIT.bs2)**

NOTE: This example program can be used with all BS2 models by changing the $STAMP directive accordingly.

```
' EXIT.bs2
' This program demonstrates the early termination of DO...LOOP and
' FOR..NEXT loop structures.  IF...THEN is used to test a condition
' and when true, EXIT will terminate the loop.

' {$STAMP BS2}
' {$PBASIC 2.5}

col             VAR     Nib
```

```
row                VAR    Nib

Setup:
  col = 0

Main:
  DO WHILE (col < 10)                ' attempt 10 iterations
    FOR row = 0 TO 15                ' attempt 16 iterations
      IF (row > 9) THEN EXIT         ' terminate when row > 9
      DEBUG CRSRXY, (col * 8), row,  ' print col/row at location
            DEC col, "/", DEC row, CR
    NEXT
    col = col + 1                    ' update column
    IF (col = 3) THEN EXIT           ' terminate when col = 3
  LOOP
  END
```

FOR...NEXT

 **FOR** *Counter* = *StartValue* **TO** *EndValue* { **STEP** {-} *StepValue* }

    Statement(s)

NEXT { *Counter* }

All 2 **FOR** *Counter* = *StartValue* **TO** *EndValue* { **STEP** *StepValue* }

    Statement(s)

NEXT { *Counter* }

Function

Create a repeating loop that executes the *Statement(s)*, one or more program lines that form a code block, between FOR and NEXT, incrementing or decrementing *Counter* according to *StepValue* until the value of the *Counter* variable passes the *EndValue*.

NOTE: Expressions are not allowed as arguments on the BS1.

- **Counter** is a variable (usually a byte or a word) used as a counter.

- **StartValue** is a variable/constant/expression (0 – 65535) that specifies the initial value of the variable (*Counter*).

- **EndValue** is a variable/constant/expression (0 – 65535) that specifies the end value of the variable (*Counter*). When the value of *Counter* is outside of the range *StartValue* to *EndValue*, the FOR...NEXT loop stops executing and the program goes on to the instruction after NEXT.

NOTE: Use a minus sign to indicate negative *StepValues* on the BS1.

- **StepValue** is an optional variable/constant/expression (0 – 65535) by which the *Counter* increases or decreases with each iteration through the FOR...NEXT loop. On the BS1, use a minus sign (-) in front of the *StepValue* to indicate a negative step. On all BS2 models, if *StartValue* is larger than *EndValue*, PBASIC understands *StepValue* to be negative, even though no minus sign is used.

- **Statement** is any valid PBASIC instruction.

Quick Facts

	BS1	All BS2 Models
Max. Nested Loops	8	16
To Decrement *Counter* Variable	Set *StartValue* > *EndValue* and enter negative *StepValue**	Set *StartValue* > *EndValue*
Counter Comparison	Exit loop if *Counter* exceeds *EndValue*	Exit loop if *Counter* outside range set by *StartValue* to *EndValue*
Related Commands	None	DO...LOOP and EXIT

Table 5.25: FOR...NEXT Quick Facts.

*NOTE: For the BS1, direction (increment or decrement) cannot be changed at run-time.

Explanation

FOR...NEXT loops let your program execute a series of instructions for a specified number of repetitions (called iterations). By default, each time through the loop, the *Counter* variable is incremented by 1. It will continue to loop until the value of *Counter* is outside of the range set by *StartValue* and *EndValue*. Also, FOR...NEXT loops always execute at least once. The simplest form is shown here:

SIMPLEST FORM OF FOR...NEXT.

NOTE: On the BS1, the loop will continue until *Counter* has gone past *EndValue*.

```
reps     VAR     Nib                ' counter for the FOR/NEXT loop

FOR reps = 1 TO 3                    ' repeat with reps = 1, 2, 3
   DEBUG  "*"                        ' put * on screen for each repetition
NEXT
```

NOTE: Replace the first line with **SYMBOL reps = B0** on the BS1.

PROCESSING A FOR...NEXT LOOP.

In the above code, the FOR command sets *reps* = 1. Then the DEBUG line (within the FOR...NEXT loop) is executed; printing an asterisk (*) on the screen. When the BASIC Stamp sees the NEXT command, it goes back to the previous FOR command, adds 1 to *reps* and compares the result to the range set by *StartValue* and *EndValue*. If *reps* is still within range, it executes the code in the loop again. Each time the FOR...NEXT loop executes, the value of *reps* is updated (incremented by 1) and the code within the loop (the DEBUG line) is executed; printing another asterisk on the screen. This code will run through the loop three times; setting *reps* to 1, 2 and 3, and printing three asterisks on the screen. After the third loop, again the BASIC Stamp goes back up to the FOR command, adds 1 to *reps* and compares the result (4 in this case) to the range. Since the range is 1 to 3 and the value is 4 (outside the range) the FOR...NEXT loop is done and the BASIC Stamp will jump down to the first line of code following the NEXT command.

You can view the changing values of *reps* by including the *reps* variable in a DEBUG command within the loop:

NOTE: Change the first line as noted above and replace line 3 with **DEBUG #Reps, CR**

```
reps      VAR      Nib                    ' counter for the FOR/NEXT loop

FOR reps = 1 TO 3                         ' repeat with reps = 1, 2, 3
  DEBUG DEC reps, CR                      ' print rep number
NEXT
```

Running this example should display "1" , "2", and "3" on the screen.

DECREMENTING THE COUNTER INSTEAD OF INCREMENTING IT.

FOR...NEXT can also be made to decrement (rather than increment) the *Counter* variable. The BS1 does this when you specify a negative *StepValue* (as well as a *StartValue* that is greater than the *EndValue*). All other BASIC Stamp models do this automatically when the *StartValue* is greater than the *EndValue*. Examples of both are shown below:

```
SYMBOL  reps    = B0                      ' counter for the FOR/NEXT loop

FOR reps = 3 TO 1 STEP -1                 ' repeat with reps = 3, 2, 1
  DEBUG #reps, CR                         ' print reps number
NEXT
```

-- or --

```
reps      VAR      Nib                    ' counter for the FOR/NEXT loop

FOR reps = 3 TO 1                         ' repeat with reps = 3, 2, 1
  DEBUG DEC reps, CR                      ' print reps number
NEXT
```

Note that the code for all the BS2 models did not use the optional STEP argument. This is because we wanted to decrement by positive 1 anyway (the default unit) and the BASIC Stamp realizes it needs to decrement because the *StartValue* is greater than the *EndValue*. A negative *StepValue* on any BS2 model would be treated as its positive, twos complement counterpart. For example, –1 in twos complement is 65535. So the following code executes only once:

```
reps      VAR      Nib                    ' counter for the FOR/NEXT loop

FOR reps = 3 TO 1 STEP -1                 ' try to decrement 3 by 65535
  DEBUG DEC reps, CR                      ' print reps number
NEXT
```

The above code would run through the loop once with *reps* set to 3. The second time around, it would decrement *reps* by 65535 (-1 is 65535 in twos complement) effectively making the number –65532 (4 in twos complement) which is outside the range of the loop.

All the arguments in the FOR...NEXT command can be constants, variables or expressions on all BS2 models. This leads to some interesting uses. For example, if you make the *StartValue* and *EndValue* a variable, and change their values within the loop, you'll change the behavior of the loop itself. Try the following:

USING VARIABLES AS ARGUMENTS.

```
{' $PBASIC 2.5}

reps            VAR     Byte        ' counter for the FOR/NEXT loop
startVal        VAR     Byte
endVal          VAR     Byte

startVal = 1                        ' initialize startVal to 1
endVal = 3                          ' initialize endVal to 3

FOR reps = startVal TO endVal       ' repeat for 1 to 3
  DEBUG DEC reps, CR
  IF (reps = 3) THEN                ' if reps =3, swap startVal/endVal
    startVal = 3                    '  otherwise continue loop
    endVal = 1
  ENDIF
NEXT
```

All 2

NOTE: The increment/decrement direction of the FOR...NEXT loop cannot be changed on the BS1.

Here the loop starts with a range of 1 to 3. First, the DEBUG line prints the value of *reps*. Then the IF...THEN line makes a decision; if *reps* is equal to 3, then swap the order of *startVal* and *endVal*, otherwise continue the loop execution. The next time through the loop (after *startVal* and *endVal* have been swapped), *reps* will be decremented instead of incremented because *startVal* is greater than *endVal*. The result is a display on the screen of the numbers 1, 2, 3, 2, 1.

The following example uses the value of *reps* as the *StepValue*. This creates a display of power's of 2 (1, 2, 4, 8, 16, 32, 64, etc):

```
reps    VAR     Word                ' counter for the loop

FOR reps = 1 TO 256 STEP reps       ' each loop add current value of reps
  DEBUG DEC ? reps                  ' show reps in Debug window
NEXT
```

NOTE: For BS1's, change line 1 to
SYMBOL reps = W0
and line 3 to
DEBUG reps

There is a potential bug that you should be careful to avoid. The BASIC Stamp uses unsigned 16-bit integer math for any math operation it performs, regardless of the size of values or variables. The maximum value the BASIC Stamp can internally calculate is 65535 (the largest 16-bit

WATCH OUT FOR 16-BIT ROLLOVER, OR VARIABLE RANGE, ERRORS.

number). If you add 1 to 65535, you get 0 as the 16-bit register rolls over (like a car's odometer does when you exceed the maximum mileage it can display). Similarly, if you subtract 1 from 0, you'll get 65535 as the 16-bit register rolls under (a rollover in the opposite direction).

If you write a FOR...NEXT loop who's *StepValue* would cause *Counter* to go past 65535, this rollover may cause the loop to execute more times than you expect. Try the following example:

NOTE: For BS1's, change line 1 to
SYMBOL reps = W0
and line 3 to
DEBUG reps

```
reps    VAR     Word                    ' counter for the loop

FOR reps = 0 TO 65535 STEP 3000         ' each loop add 3000
  DEBUG DEC ? reps                      ' show reps in Debug window
NEXT
```

The value of *reps* increases by 3000 each trip through the loop. As it approaches the *EndValue*, an interesting thing happens; *reps* is: 57000, 60000, 63000, 464, 3464... It passes the *EndValue*, rolls over and keeps going. That's because the result of the calculation 63000 + 3000 exceeds the maximum capacity of a 16-bit number and then rolls over to 464. When the result of 464 is tested against the range ("Is Reps > 0 and is Reps < 65535?") it passes the test and the loop continues.

A similar symptom can be seen in a program who's *EndValue* is mistakenly set higher than what the counter variable can hold. The example below uses a byte-sized variable, but the *EndValue* is set to a number greater than what will fit in a byte:

```
SYMBOL  reps    = B2                    ' counter for the loop

FOR reps = 0 TO 300                     ' each loop add 1
  DEBUG reps                            ' show reps in Debug window
NEXT
```

-- or --

```
reps    VAR     Byte                    ' counter for the loop

FOR reps = 0 TO 300                     ' each loop add 1
  DEBUG DEC ? reps                      ' show reps in Debug window
NEXT
```

Here, *reps* is a byte variable; which can only hold the number range 0 to 255. The *EndValue* is set to 300, however; greater than 255. This code will loop endlessly because when *reps* is 255 and the FOR...NEXT loop adds 1, *reps* becomes 0 (bytes will rollover after 255 just like words will rollover after 65535). The result, 0, is compared against the range (0 – 255) and it is found to be within the range, so the FOR...NEXT loop continues.

It's important to realize that on all the BS2 models, the test is against the entire range, not just the *EndValue*. The code below is a slight modification of the previous example (the *StartValue* is 10 instead of 0) and will not loop endlessly.

NOTE: On the BS1, the loop will continue until *Counter* has gone past *EndValue*. The rollover error will still occur if the BS1 cannot determine if *Counter* went past *EndValue*.

```
reps     VAR     Byte                ' counter for the loop

FOR reps = 10 TO 300                 ' each loop add 1
  DEBUG DEC ? reps                   ' show reps in Debug window
NEXT
```

reps still rolls over to 0, as before, however, this time it is outside the range of 10 to 255. The loop stops, leaving *reps* at 0. Note that this code is still in error since *reps* will never reach 300 until it is declared as a Word.

Demo Program (FOR-NEXT.bs1)

```
' FOR-NEXT.bs1
' This example uses a FOR...NEXT loop to churn out a series of sequential
' squares (numbers 1, 2, 3, 4... raised to the second power) by using a
' variable to set the FOR...NEXT StepValue, and incrementing StepValue
' within the loop.  Sir Isaac Newton is generally credited with the
' discovery of this technique.

' {$STAMP BS1}
' {$PBASIC 1.0}

SYMBOL   square      = B2            ' FOR/NEXT counter
SYMBOL   stepSize    = B3            ' step size increases by 2 each loop


Setup:
  stepSize = 1
  square = 1

Main:
  FOR square = 1 TO 250 STEP stepSize ' show squares up to 250
    DEBUG square                      ' display on screen
    stepSize = stepSize + 2           ' add 2 to stepSize
  NEXT                                ' loop until square > 250
  END
```

All 2 **Demo Program (FOR-NEXT.bs2)**

NOTE: This example program can be used with all BS2 models by changing the $STAMP directive accordingly.

```
' FOR-NEXT.bs2
' This example uses a FOR...NEXT loop to churn out a series of sequential
' squares (numbers 1, 2, 3, 4... raised to the second power) by using a
' variable to set the FOR...NEXT StepValue, and incrementing StepValue
' within the loop.  Sir Isaac Newton is generally credited with the
' discovery of this technique.

' {$STAMP BS2}
' {$PBASIC 2.5}

square          VAR       Byte              ' FOR/NEXT counter
stepSize        VAR       Byte              ' step size increases by 2 each loop


Setup:
  stepSize = 1
  square = 1

Main:
  FOR square = 1 TO 250 STEP stepSize       ' show squares up to 250
    DEBUG DEC ? square                      ' display on screen
    stepSize = stepSize + 2                 ' add 2 to stepSize
  NEXT                                      ' loop until square > 250
  END
```

FREQOUT	BS1	BS2	BS2e	BS2sx	BS2p	BS2pe	BS2px

1 (See SOUND)

All 2 FREQOUT *Pin, Duration, Freq1* { , *Freq2* }

Function

Generate one or two sine-wave tones for a specified *Duration*.

- *Pin* is a variable/constant/expression (0 – 15) that specifies the I/O pin to use. This pin will be set to output mode.

- *Duration* is a variable/constant/expression (0 - 65535) specifying the amount of time to generate the tone(s). The unit of time for *Duration* is described in Table 5.26.

- *Freq1* is a variable/constant/expression (0 – 32767) specifying frequency of the first tone. The unit of *Freq1* is described in Table 5.26.

- *Freq2* is an optional argument exactly like *Freq1*. When specified, two frequencies will be mixed together on the specified I/O pin.

Quick Facts

Table 5.26: FREQOUT Quick Facts.

	BS2, BS2e	BS2sx	BS2p	BS2pe	BS2px
Units in Duration	1 ms	0.4 ms	0.265 ms	1 ms	0.166 ms
Units in Freq1 and Freq2	1 Hz	2.5 Hz	3.77 Hz	1.51 Hz	6.03 Hz
Range of Frequency	0 to 32767 Hz	0 to 81917 Hz	0 to 123531 Hz	0 to 49478 Hz	0 to 197585 Hz
Related Commands	DTMFOUT and PWM				

Explanation

FREQOUT generates one or two sine waves using a pulse-width modulation algorithm. The circuits shown in Figure 5.6 will filter the signal in order to play the tones through a speaker or audio amplifier. Here's a simple FREQOUT command:

SIMPLEST FORM OF FREQOUT.

```
FREQOUT 2, 1000, 2500
```

On the BS2, this command generates a 2500 Hz tone for 1 second (1000 ms) on I/O pin 2. See Table 5.26 for timing data on other BASIC Stamp models.

To play two tones on the same I/O pin at once:

```
FREQOUT 2, 1000, 2500, 3000
```

GENERATING TWO TONES AT ONCE.

This will generate a 2500 Hz and 3000 Hz tone for 1 second. The frequencies will mix together for a chord- or bell-like sound. To generate a silent pause, specify frequency value(s) of 0.

Driving an Audio Amplifier

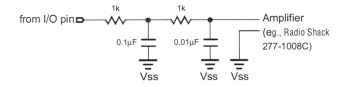

Figure 5.6: Example RC filter circuits for driving an audio amplifier(top) or a speaker (bottom).

Driving a Speaker

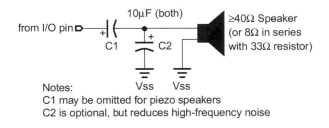

Notes:
C1 may be omitted for piezo speakers
C2 is optional, but reduces high-frequency noise

The circuits in Figure 5.6 work by filtering out the high-frequency PWM used to generate the sine waves. FREQOUT works over a very wide range of frequencies (as shown in Table 5.26) so at the upper end of its range, those PWM filters will also filter out most of the desired frequency. You may find it necessary to reduce values of the parallel capacitors shown in the circuit, or to devise a custom active filter for your application.

FREQUENCY CONSIDERATIONS.

NOTE: This example program can be used with all BS2 models. This program uses conditional compilation techniques; see Chapter 3 for more information.

All 2

Demo Program (FREQOUT.bs2)

```
' FREQOUT.bs2
' This program demonstrates sound-effects generation by the BASIC Stamp.
' Conditional compilation sets timing and frequency adjustment factors so
' that the output will sound the same on any BS2 model.

' {$STAMP BS2}
' {$PBASIC 2.5}

Spkr            PIN    10              ' output pin for FREQOUT

#SELECT $STAMP
  #CASE BS2, BS2E
    TmAdj       CON    $100            ' x 1.0 (time adjust)
    FrAdj       CON    $100            ' x 1.0 (freq adjust)
  #CASE BS2SX
    TmAdj       CON    $280            ' x 2.5
    FrAdj       CON    $066            ' x 0.4
  #CASE BS2P
    TmAdj       CON    $3C5            ' x 3.77
    FrAdj       CON    $044            ' x 0.265
  #CASE BS2PE
    TmAdj       CON    $100            ' x 1.0
    FrAdj       CON    $0A9            ' x 0.662
  #CASE BS2PX
    TmAdj       CON    $607            ' x 6.03
    FrAdj       CON    $2A             ' x 0.166
#ENDSELECT

Main:
  DEBUG "Let's make a call...", CR
  ' combine 350 Hz & 440 Hz
  FREQOUT Spkr, 2000 */ TmAdj, 350 */ FrAdj, 440 */ FrAdj
  ' dial number (digits 150 ms on, 25 ms off)
  DTMFOUT Spkr, 150 */ TmAdj, 25, [5, 5, 5, 1, 2, 1, 2]
  PAUSE 500

  ' bad connection (SIT sequence)
  FREQOUT Spkr, 375 */ TmAdj, 985 */ FrAdj
  FREQOUT Spkr, 375 */ TmAdj, 1371 */ FrAdj
  FREQOUT Spkr, 375 */ TmAdj, 1777 */ FrAdj

  DEBUG "Oops! -- try again...", CR
  PAUSE 1000
  DTMFOUT Spkr, 150 */ TmAdj, 25, [5, 5, 5, 2, 2, 2, 2]
  DEBUG "Ringing"
  FREQOUT Spkr, 2000 */ TmAdj, 440 */ FrAdj, 480 */ FrAdj
  PAUSE 4000
  FREQOUT Spkr, 2000 */ TmAdj, 440 */ FrAdj, 480 */ FrAdj
  INPUT Spkr
  END
```

GET

		BS2e	BS2sx	BS2p	BS2pe	BS2px
~~BS1~~	~~BS2~~	BS2e	BS2sx	BS2p	BS2pe	BS2px

 GET *Location,* { **WORD** } *Variable* { , { **WORD** } *Variable...* }

NOTE: The optional arguments require PBASIC 2.5.

Function

Read the value from Scratch Pad RAM (SPRAM) *Location* and store in *Variable*.

- **Location** is a variable/constant/expression (0 – 63 for BS2e and BS2sx and 0 – 131 for BS2p, BS2pe, and BS2px) that specifies the SPRAM location to read from.

- **Variable** is a variable (usually a byte, or word if using the optional WORD modifier) in which to store the value.

Quick Facts

Table 5.27: GET Quick Facts.

	BS2e and BS2sx	BS2p, BS2pe, and BS2px
Scratch Pad RAM Size and Organization	64 bytes (0 – 63). Organized as bytes only.	136 bytes (0 – 135). Organized as bytes only.
General Purpose Locations	0 - 62	0 – 126
Special Use Location	Location 63: Active program slot number (read only).	Location 127: READ/WRITE slot and Active Program slot (read only). Locations 128-135: Polled Interrupt status (read only).
Related Commands	PUT	PUT and STORE, and SPSTR formatter.
PBASIC 2.5 Syntax Options	Multiple sequential variables may be read from the Scratch Pad RAM. The optional WORD modifier may be specified to retrieve 16-bit values.	

Explanation

The GET command reads a value from the specified Scratch Pad RAM location and stores it into *Variable*. All values in all locations can be retrieved from within any of the 8 program slots.

USES FOR SCRATCH PAD RAM.

SPRAM is useful for passing data to programs in other program slots and for additional workspace. It is different than regular RAM in that symbol names cannot be assigned directly to locations and each location is always configured as a byte only. The following code will read the value at location 25, store it in a variable called *temp* and display it:

```
temp      VAR      Byte

GET 25, temp                            ' retrieve byte from location 25
DEBUG DEC temp
```

When using the PBASIC 2.5 directive, multiple sequential variables may be read from the Scratch Pad RAM, starting at *Location*, and the WORD modifier may be specified to retrieve 16-bit values.

```
' {$PBASIC 2.5}

temp      VAR      Byte
temp2     VAR      Word

GET 25, temp, Word temp2                ' retrieve byte from location 25
                                        '  and word from locations 26 and 27

DEBUG DEC temp, CR
DEBUG DEC temp2
```

The low nibble of location 63 (BS2e and BS2sx) and location 127 (BS2p, BS2pe, and BS2px) is a special, read-only location that always contains the number of the currently running program slot. On the BS2p, BS2pe, and BS2px, the high nibble of location 127 also contains the current program slot that will be used for the READ and WRITE commands. See the demo program below for an example of use.

Table 5.28 shows the layout of all SPRAM registers.

Table 5.28: Layout of SPRAM Registers.

NOTE: Scratch Pad RAM can only be accessed with the GET and PUT commands. Scratch Pad RAM cannot have variable names assigned to it.

Location	BS2e and BS2sx	BS2p, BS2pe, and BS2px
0...62	General Purpose RAM	General Purpose RAM
63	Bits 0-3: Active program slot number.	General Purpose RAM
64..126	n/a	General Purpose RAM
127	n/a	Bits 0-3, Active program slot #. Bits 4-7, program slot for READ and WRITE operations.
128	n/a	Polled input trigger status of Main I/O pins 0-7 (0 = not triggered, 1 = triggered).
129	n/a	Polled input trigger status of Main I/O pins 8-15 (0 = not triggered, 1 = triggered).
130	n/a	Polled input trigger status of Auxiliary I/O pins 0-7 (0 = not triggered, 1 = triggered).
131	n/a	Polled input trigger status of Auxiliary I/O pins 8-15 (0 = not triggered, 1 = triggered).
132	n/a	Bits 0-3: Polled-interrupt mode, set by POLLMODE
133	n/a	Bits 0-2: Polled-interrupt "run" slot, set by POLLRUN.
134	n/a	Bit 0: Active I/O group; 0 = Main I/O, 1 = Auxiliary I/O.
135	n/a	Bit 0: Polled-output status (set by POLLMODE); 0 = disabled, 1= enabled. Bit 1: Polled-input status; 0 = none defined, 1 = at least one defined. Bit 2: Polled-run status (set by POLLMODE); 0 = disabled, 1 = enabled. Bit 3: Polled-output latch status; 0 = real-time mode, 1 = latch mode. Bit 4: Polled-input state; 0 = no trigger, 1 = triggered. Bit 5: Polled-output latch state; 0 = nothing latched, 1 = signal latched. Bit 6: Poll-wait state; 0 = No Event, 1 = Event Occurred. (Cleared by POLLMODE only). Bit 7: Polling status; 0 = not active, 1 = active.

Demo Program (GET_PUT1.bsx)

NOTE: This is written for the BS2sx but can be used with the BS2e, BS2p, BS2pe and BS2px also. This program uses conditional compilation techniques; see Chapter 3 for more information.

```
' GET_PUT1.bsx
' This example demonstrates the use of the GET and PUT commands.  First,
' slot location is read using GET to display the currently running program
' number.  Then a set of values are written (PUT) into locations 0 TO 9.
' Afterwards, program number 1 is RUN.  This program is a BS2SX project
' consisting of GET_PUT1.BSX and GET_PUT2.BSX, but will run on the BS2e,
' BS2p, BS2pe and BS2px without modification.

' {$STAMP BS2sx, GET_PUT2.BSX}
' {$PBASIC 2.5}
```

```
#SELECT $STAMP
  #CASE BS2
    #ERROR "BS2e or greater required."
  #CASE BS2E, BS2SX
    Slot         CON      63
  #CASE BS2P, BS2PE, BS2PX
    Slot         CON      127
#ENDSELECT


value          VAR      Byte
idx            VAR      Byte


Setup:
  GET Slot, value
  DEBUG "Program Slot #", DEC value.NIB0, CR

Main:
  FOR idx = 0 TO 9
    value = (idx + 3) * 8
    PUT idx, value
    DEBUG " Writing: ", DEC2 value, " to location: ", DEC2 idx, CR
  NEXT
  DEBUG CR
  RUN 1
  END
```

Demo Program (GET_PUT2.bsx)

```
' GET_PUT2.bsx
' This example demonstrates the use of the GET and PUT commands.  First,
' the Slot location is read using GET to display the currently running
' program number.  Then a set of values are read (GET) from locations
' 0 to 9 and displayed on the screen for verification.  This program is a
' BS2SX project consisting of GET_PUT1.BSX and GET_PUT2.BSX, but will run
' on the BS2e, BS2p, BS2pe, and BS2px without modification.

' {$STAMP BS2sx}
' {$PBASIC 2.5}

#SELECT $STAMP
  #CASE BS2
    #ERROR "BS2e or greater required."
  #CASE BS2E, BS2SX
    Slot         CON      63
  #CASE BS2P, BS2PE, BS2PX
    Slot         CON      127
#ENDSELECT

value          VAR      Byte
idx            VAR      Byte
```

NOTE: This is written for the BS2sx but can be used with the BS2e, BS2p, BS2pe and BS2px also. This program uses conditional compilation techniques; see Chapter 3 for more information.

```
Setup:
  GET Slot, value
  DEBUG "Program Slot #", DEC value.NIB0, CR

Main:
  FOR idx = 0 TO 9
    GET idx, value
    DEBUG "  Reading: ", DEC2 value, " from location: ", DEC2 idx, CR
  NEXT
  END
```

GOSUB

| BS1 | BS2 | BS2e | BS2sx | BS2p | BS2pe | BS2px |

GOSUB *Address*

Function

Store the address of the next instruction after GOSUB, then go to the point in the program specified by *Address*; with the intention of returning to the stored address.

- **Address** is a label that specifies where to go.

Quick Facts

Table 5.29: GOSUB Quick Facts.

	BS1	**All BS2 Models**
Max. GOSUBs per program	16	255
Max. nested GOSUBs	4	4
Related Commands	GOTO	ON...GOSUB and GOTO

Explanation

GOSUB is a close relative of GOTO, in fact, its name means, "GO to a SUBroutine". When a PBASIC program reaches a GOSUB, the program executes the code beginning at the specified address label. Unlike GOTO, GOSUB also stores the address of the instruction immediately following itself. When the program encounters a RETURN command, it interprets it to mean, "go to the instruction that follows the most recent GOSUB." In other words, a GOSUB makes the BASIC Stamp do a similar operation as you do when you see a table or figure reference in this manual; 1) you remember where you are, 2) you go to the table or figure and read the information there, and 3) when you've reached the end of it, you "return" to the place you were reading originally.

GOSUB CAN SAVE EEPROM (PROGRAM) SPACE.

GOSUB is mainly used to execute the same piece of code from multiple locations. If you have, for example, a block of three lines of code that need to be run from 10 different locations in your entire program you could simply copy and paste those three lines to each of those 10 locations. This would amount to a total of 30 lines of repetitive code (and extra space wasted in the program memory). A better solution is to place those three lines in a separate routine, complete with it's own label and followed by a

RETURN command, then just use a GOSUB command at each of the 10 locations to access it. This technique can save a lot of program space.

Try the example below:

```
Main:
  GOSUB Hello
  DEBUG "How are you?"
  END

Hello:
  DEBUG "Hello, my friend!", CR
  RETURN
```

The above code will start out by GOSUB'ing to the section of code beginning with the label *Hello*. It will print "Hello, my friend!" on the screen then RETURN to the line after the GOSUB… which prints "How are you?" and ENDs. Note: colons (:) are placed after labels, as in " "Main: " and "Hello:" but the colon is not used on references to these labels such as in the "GOSUB Hello" line.

There's another interesting lesson here; what would happen if we removed the END command from this example? Since the BASIC Stamp reads the code from left to right / top to bottom (like the English language) once it had returned to and run the "How are you?" line, it would naturally "fall into" the *Hello* routine again. Additionally, at the end of the *Hello* routine, it would see the RETURN again (although it didn't GOSUB to that routine this time) and because there wasn't a previous place to return to, the BASIC Stamp will start the entire program over again. This would cause an endless loop. The important thing to remember here is to always make sure your program doesn't allow itself to "fall into" a subroutine.

WATCH OUT FOR SUBROUTINES THAT YOUR PROGRAM CAN "FALL INTO."

NOTE: On the BS1, a RETURN without a GOSUB will return the program to the last GOSUB (or will end the program if no GOSUB was executed).

A limited number of GOSUBs are allowed per program (as shown in Table 5.29), and they may be nested only four levels deep. In other words, the subroutine that's the destination of a GOSUB can contain a GOSUB to another subroutine, and so on, to a maximum depth (total number of GOSUBS before the first RETURN) of four. Any deeper, and the program will "forget" its way back to the starting point (the instruction following the very first GOSUB).

GOSUB LIMITATIONS.

When GOSUBS are nested, each RETURN takes the program back to the instruction after the most-recent GOSUB. As is mentioned above, if the

BASIC Stamp encounters a RETURN without a previous GOSUB, the entire program starts over from the beginning. Take care to avoid these phenomena.

Demo Program (GOSUB.bs1)

```
' GOSUB.bs1
' This program is a guessing game that generates a random number in a
' subroutine called Pick_A_Number. It is written to stop after ten
' guesses. To see a common bug associated with GOSUB, delete or comment
' out the line beginning with END after the FOR-NEXT loop. This means
' that after the loop is finished, the program will wander into the
' Pick_A_Number subroutine. When the RETURN at the end executes, the
' program will go back to the beginning of the program. This will cause
' the program to execute endlessly. Make sure that your programs can't
' accidentally execute subroutines!

' {$STAMP BS1}
' {$PBASIC 1.0}

SYMBOL   rounds       = B2          ' number of reps
SYMBOL   numGen       = W0          ' random number holder
SYMBOL   myNum        = B3          ' random number, 1-10


Setup:
  numGen = 11500                    ' initialize random "seed"

Main:
  FOR rounds = 1 TO 10
    DEBUG CLS, "Pick a number from 1 to 10", CR
    GOSUB Pick_A_Number
    PAUSE 2000                      ' dramatic pause
    DEBUG "My number was: ", #myNum ' show the number
    PAUSE 1000                      ' another pause.
  NEXT
  DEBUG CLS, "Done"
  END                               ' end program

' Random-number subroutine. A subroutine is just a piece of code with
' the RETURN instruction at the end. Always make sure your program enters
' subroutines with a GOSUB. If you don't, the RETURN won't have the
' correct address, and your program will have a bug!

Pick_A_Number:
  RANDOM numGen                     ' stir up the bits of NumGen.
  DEBUG numGen, CR
  myNum = numGen / 6550 MIN 1       ' scale to fit 1-10 range.
  RETURN                            ' go back to 1st instruction
                                    ' after GOSUB that got us here
```

Demo Program (GOSUB.bs2)

All 2

NOTE: This example program can be used with all BS2 models by changing the $STAMP directive accordingly.

```
' GOSUB.bs2
' This program is a guessing game that generates a random number in a
' subroutine called Pick_A_Number. It is written to stop after ten
' guesses. To see a common bug associated with GOSUB, delete or comment
' out the line beginning with END after the FOR-NEXT loop. This means
' that after the loop is finished, the program will wander into the
' Pick_A_Number subroutine. When the RETURN at the end executes, the
' program will go back to the beginning of the program. This will cause
' the program to execute endlessly. Make sure that your programs can't
' accidentally execute subroutines!

' {$STAMP BS2}
' {$PBASIC 2.5}

rounds          VAR     Byte            ' number of reps
numGen          VAR     Word            ' random number holder
myNum           VAR     Byte            ' random number, 1-10


Setup:
  numGen = 11500                        ' initialize random "seed"

Main:
  FOR rounds = 1 TO 10
    DEBUG CLS, "Pick a number from 1 to 10", CR
    GOSUB Pick_A_Number
    PAUSE 2000                          ' dramatic pause
    DEBUG "My number was: ", DEC myNum  ' show the number
    PAUSE 1000                          ' another pause.
  NEXT
  DEBUG CLS, "Done"
  END                                   ' end program

' Random-number subroutine. A subroutine is just a piece of code with
' the RETURN instruction at the end. Always make sure your program enters
' subroutines with a GOSUB. If you don't, the RETURN won't have the
' correct address, and your program will have a bug!

Pick_A_Number:
  RANDOM numGen                         ' stir up the bits of NumGen.
  DEBUG DEC ? numGen
  myNum = numGen / 6550 MIN 1           ' scale to fit 1-10 range.
  RETURN                                ' go back to 1st instruction
                                        ' after GOSUB that got us here
```

GOTO

BS1	BS2	BS2e	BS2sx	BS2p	BS2pe	BS2px

GOTO *Address*

Function

Go to the point in the program specified by *Address*.
- **Address** is a label that specifies where to go.

Quick Facts

Table 5.30: GOTO Quick Facts.

	BS1	**All BS2 Models**
Related Commands	BRANCH and GOSUB	ON...GOTO, BRANCH and GOSUB
Max. GOTOs per Program	Unlimited, but good programming practices suggest using the least amount possible.	

Explanation

The GOTO command makes the BASIC Stamp execute the code that starts at the specified *Address* location. The BASIC Stamp reads PBASIC code from left to right / top to bottom, just like in the English language. The GOTO command forces the BASIC Stamp to jump to another section of code.

A common use for GOTO is to create endless loops; programs that repeat a group of instructions over and over. For example:

```
Start:
  DEBUG  "Hi", CR
GOTO  Start
```

The above code will print "Hi" on the screen, over and over again. The GOTO Start line simply tells it to go back to the code that begins with the label *Start*. Note: colons (:) are placed after labels, as in "Start:" to further indicate that they are labels, but the colon is not used on references to labels such as in the "GOTO Start" line.

Demo Program (GOTO.bs2)

NOTE: This is written for the BS2 but can be used for the BS1 and all other BS2 models as well, by modifying the $STAMP directive accordingly.

```
' GOTO.bs2
' This program is not very practical, but demonstrates the use of GOTO to
' jump around the code.  This code jumps between three different routines,
' each of which print something different on the screen.  The routines are
' out of order for this example.
```

```
'{$STAMP  BS2}

GOTO Routine1

Routine2:
  DEBUG "We're in routine #2",CR
  PAUSE 1000
GOTO Routine3

Routine1:
  DEBUG "We're in routine #1",CR
  PAUSE 1000
GOTO Routine2

Routine3:
  DEBUG "We're in routine #3",CR
  PAUSE 1000
GOTO Routine1
```

HIGH

BS1	BS2	BS2e	BS2sx	BS2p	BS2pe	BS2px	BS2px

HIGH *Pin*

Function

Make the specified pin output high.

- **Pin** is a variable/constant/expression (0 – 15) that specifies which I/O pin to set high. This pin will be placed into output mode.

NOTE: Expressions are not allowed as arguments on the BS1. The range of the *Pin* argument on the BS1 is 0 – 7.

Quick Facts

Table 5.31: HIGH Quick Facts.

	BS1 and all BS2 Models
Related Commands	LOW and TOGGLE

Explanation

The HIGH command sets the specified pin to 1 (a +5 volt level) and then sets its mode to output. For example,

```
HIGH 6
```

does exactly the same thing as:

```
OUT6 = 1
DIR6 = 1
```

Using the HIGH command is faster and more concise, in this case.

Connect an LED and a resistor as shown in Figure 5.7 for demo program HIGH.bs2, below.

Figure 5.7: Example LED Circuit.

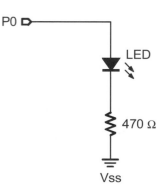

Demo Program (HIGH.bs2)

```
' HIGH.bs2
' This simple program sets I/O pin 0 high for 1/2 second and low for
' 1/2 second in an endless loop.  Connect an LED to P0 for a simple
' blinker.

' {$STAMP BS2}


Main:
  HIGH 0
  PAUSE 500
  LOW 0
  PAUSE 500
  GOTO Main
  END
```

1 All 2

NOTE: This is written for the BS2 but can be used for the BS1 and all other BS2 models as well, by modifying the $STAMP directive accordingly.

I2CIN

I2CIN *Pin, SlaveID,* **{** *Address* **{** *\LowAddress* **},** **}** **[** *InputData* **]**

Function

Receive data from a device using the I²C protocol.

- **Pin** is a variable/constant/expression (0 or 8) that specifies which I/O pins to use. I²C devices require two I/O pins to communicate. The *Pin* argument serves a double purpose; specifying the first pin (for connection to the chip's SDA pin) and, indirectly, the other required pin (for connection to the chip's SCL pin). See explanation below. Both I/O pins will be toggled between output and input mode during the I2CIN command and both will be set to input mode by the end of the I2CIN command.

- **SlaveID** is a variable/constant/expression (0 – 255) indicating the unique ID of the I²C chip.

- **Address** is an optional variable/constant/expression (0 – 255) indicating the desired address within the I²C chip to receive data from. The *Address* argument may be used with the optional *LowAddress* argument to indicate a word-sized address value.

- **LowAddress** is an optional variable/constant/expression (0 – 255) indicating the low-byte of the word-sized address within the I²C chip to receive data from. This argument must be used along with the *Address* argument.

- **InputData** is a list of variables and modifiers that tells I2CIN what to do with incoming data. I2CIN can store data in a variable or array, interpret numeric text (decimal, binary, or hex) and store the corresponding value in a variable, wait for a fixed or variable sequence of bytes, or ignore a specified number of bytes. These actions can be combined in any order in the *InputData* list.

Quick Facts

	BS2p, BS2pe, and BS2px	
Values for *Pin*	*Pin* = 0	*Pin* = 8
I/O Pin Arrangement	0: Serial Data (SDA) pin 1: Serial Clock (SCL) pin	8: Serial Data (SDA) pin 9: Serial Clock (SCL) pin
Transmission Rate	Approximately 81 kbits/sec on a BS2p, 45 kbits/sec on a BS2pe, and 83 kbits/sec on a BS2px (not including overhead).	
Special Notes	Both the SDA and SCL pins must have 1 kΩ - 4.7 kΩ pull-up resistors. The I2CIN command does not allow for multiple masters. The BASIC Stamp cannot operate as an I²C slave device.	
Related Command	I2COUT	

Table 5.32: I2CIN Quick Facts.

Explanation

The I²C protocol is a form of synchronous serial communication developed by Phillips Semiconductors. It only requires two I/O pins and both pins can be shared between multiple I²C devices. The I2CIN command allows the BASIC Stamp to receive data from an I²C device.

The following is an example of the I2CIN command:

A SIMPLE I2CIN EXAMPLE.

```
result  VAR    Byte
I2CIN 0, $A1, 0, [result]
```

This code will transmit a "read" command to an I²C device (connected to I/O pins 0 and 1) and then will receive one byte and store it in the variable *result*. Though it may seem strange, the I2CIN command first transmits some data and then receives data. It must first transmit information (ID, read/write and address) in order to tell the I²C device what information it would like to receive. The exact information transmitted ($A1, 0) depends on the I²C device that is being used.

NOTE: The I2C command will make up to 8 attempts to connect to the addressed device. If the device does not properly respond, the I2C command will timeout and the *InputData* will remain unchanged..

The above example will read a byte of data from location 0 of a 24LC16B EEPROM from Microchip. Figure 5.8 shows the proper wiring for this example to work. The *SlaveID* argument ($A1) is both the ID of the chip and the command to read from the chip; the 1 means read. The *Address* argument (0) is the EEPROM location to read from.

Figure 5.8: Example Circuit for the I2CIN command and a 24LC16B EEPROM.

Note: The 4.7 kΩ resistors are required for the I2CIN command to function properly.

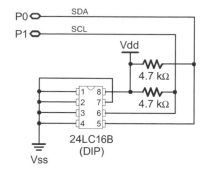

RECEIVING FORMATTED DATA.

The I2CIN command's *InputData* argument is similar to the SERIN command's *InputData* argument. This means data can be received as ASCII character values, decimal, hexadecimal and binary translations and string data as in the examples below. (Assume the 24LC16B EEPROM is used and it has the string, "Value: 3A:101" stored, starting at location 0).

```
value    VAR    Byte(13)

I2CIN 0, $A1, 0, [value]          ' receive the ASCII value for "V"
I2CIN 0, $A1, 0, [DEC value]      ' receive the number 3
I2CIN 0, $A1, 0, [HEX value]      ' receive the number $3A
I2CIN 0, $A1, 0, [BIN value]      ' receive the number %101
I2CIN 0, $A1, 0, [STR value\13]   ' receive the string "Value: 3A:101"
```

Table 5.33 and Table 5.34 below list all the available special formatters and conversion formatters available to the I2CIN command. See the SERIN command for additional information and examples of their use.

Table 5.33: I2CIN Special Formatters.

Special Formatter	Action
SKIP *Length*	Ignore *Length* bytes of characters.
SPSTR L	Input a character stream of length L bytes (up to 126) into Scratch Pad RAM, starting at location 0. Use GET to retrieve the characters.
STR *ByteArray* \L {\E}	Input a character string of length L into an array. If specified, an end character E causes the string input to end before reaching length L. Remaining bytes are filled with 0s (zeros).
WAITSTR *ByteArray* {\L}	Wait for a sequence of bytes matching a string stored in an array variable, optionally limited to L characters. If the optional L argument is left off, the end of the array-string must be marked by a byte containing a zero (0).

Conversion Formatter	Type of Number	Numeric Characters Accepted	Notes
DEC{1..5}	Decimal, optionally limited to 1 – 5 digits	0 through 9	1
SDEC{1..5}	Signed decimal, optionally limited to 1 – 5 digits	-, 0 through 9	1,2
HEX{1..4}	Hexadecimal, optionally limited to 1 – 4 digits	0 through 9, A through F	1,3,5
SHEX{1..4}	Signed hexadecimal, optionally limited to 1 – 4 digits	-, 0 through 9, A through F	1,2,3
IHEX{1..4}	Indicated hexadecimal, optionally limited to 1 – 4 digits	$, 0 through 9, A through F	1,3,4
ISHEX{1..4}	Signed, indicated hexadecimal, optionally limited to 1 – 4 digits	-, $, 0 through 9, A through F	1,2,3,4
BIN{1..16}	Binary, optionally limited to 1 – 16 digits	0, 1	1
SBIN{1..16}	Signed binary, optionally limited to 1 – 16 digits	-, 0, 1	1,2
IBIN{1..16}	Indicated binary, optionally limited to 1 – 16 digits	%, 0, 1	1,4
ISBIN{1..16}	Signed, indicated binary, optionally limited to 1 – 16 digits	-, %, 0, 1	1,2,4
NUM	Generic numeric input (decimal, hexadecimal or binary); hexadecimal or binary number must be indicated	$, %, 0 through 9, A through F	1, 3, 4
SNUM	Similar to NUM with value treated as signed with range -32768 to +32767	-, $, %, 0 through 9, A through F	1,2,3,4

Table 5.34: I2CIN Conversion Formatters.

1 All numeric conversions will continue to accept new data until receiving either the specified number of digits (ex: three digits for DEC3) or a non-numeric character.
2 To be recognized as part of a number, the minus sign (-) must immediately precede a numeric character. The minus sign character occurring in non-numeric text is ignored and any character (including a space) between a minus and a number causes the minus to be ignored.
3 The hexadecimal formatters are not case-sensitive; "a" through "f" means the same as "A" through "F".
4 Indicated hexadecimal and binary formatters ignore all characters, even valid numerics, until they receive the appropriate prefix ($ for hexadecimal, % for binary). The indicated formatters can differentiate between text and hexadecimal (ex: ABC would be interpreted by HEX as a number but IHEX would ignore it unless expressed as $ABC). Likewise, the binary version can distinguish the decimal number 10 from the binary number %10. A prefix occurring in non-numeric text is ignored, and any character (including a space) between a prefix and a number causes the prefix to be ignored. Indicated, signed formatters require that the minus sign come before the prefix, as in -$1B45.
5 The HEX modifier can be used for Decimal to BCD Conversion. See "Hex to BCD Conversion" on page 97.

For examples of all conversion formatters and how they process incoming data, see Appendix C.

The I²C protocol has a well-defined standard for the information passed at the start of each transmission. First of all, any information sent must be transmitted in units of 1 byte (8-bits). The first byte, we call the *SlaveID*, is an 8-bit pattern whose upper 7-bits contain the unique ID of the device you wish to communicate with. The lowest bit indicates whether this is a write operation (0) or a read operation (1). Figure 5.9 shows this format.

Figure 5.9: Slave ID Format.

7	6	5	4	3	2	1	0
A_6	A_5	A_4	A_3	A_2	A_1	A_0	R/W

The second byte, immediately following the SlaveID, is the optional *Address*. It indicates the 8-bit address (within the device) containing the data you would like to receive. Note that the *Address* argument is optional and may be left unspecified for devices that don't require an *Address* argument.

USING LONG ADDRESSES.

Some devices require more than 8 bits of address. For this case, the optional *LowAddress* argument can be used for the low-byte of the required address. When using the *LowAddress* argument, the *Address* argument is effectively the high-byte of the address value. For example, if the entire address value is 2050, use 8 for the *Address* argument and 2 for the *LowAddress* argument (8 * 256 + 2 = 2050).

Following the last address byte is the first byte of data. This data byte may be transmitted or received by the BASIC Stamp. In the case of the I2CIN command, this data byte is transmitted by the device and received by the BASIC Stamp. Additionally, multiple data bytes can follow the address, depending on the I²C device. Note that every device has different limitations regarding how may contiguous bytes they can receive or transmit in one session. Be aware of these device limitations and program accordingly.

START AND STOP CONDITIONS AND ACKNOWLEDGMENTS.

Every I²C transmission session begins with a Start Condition and ends with a Stop Condition. Additionally, immediately after every byte is transmitted, an extra clock cycle is used to send or receive an acknowledgment signal (ACK). All of these operations are automatically taken care of by the I2CIN command so that you need not be concerned with them. The general I²C transmission format is shown in Figure 5.10.

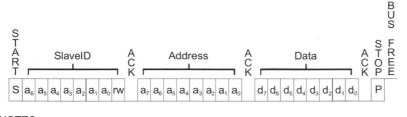

Figure 5.10: I²C Transmission Format.

NOTES:
S = Start Condition
P = Stop Condition
a = id or address bit
d = data bit (transmitted by the BASIC Stamp or the I²C device)
ACK = Acknowledge signal. (Most acknowledge signals are generated by the I²C device)

Since the I2CIN command is intended for input only, it actually overrides the "R/W" bit (bit 0) in the *SlaveID* argument. This is done so that it can use the I²C protocol's "Combined Format" for receiving data. Put simply, this means a command such as: I2CIN 0, $A1, 10, [Result] actually transmits $A0, then 10, then $A1 and then it reads the data back from the device. The $A0 means "write", the 10 is the address to write to, and finally, the $A1 indicates a change of direction; to "read" the location, instead. Even though the I2CIN command really doesn't care what the value of the *SlaveID*'s LSB is, it is suggested that you still set it appropriately for clarity.

SPECIAL NOTE ABOUT I2CIN INPLIMENTATION.

Also note that the I2CIN command does not support multiple I²C masters and the BASIC Stamp cannot operate as an I²C slave device.

Demo Program (I2C.bsp)

NOTE: This example program can be used with the BS2p, BS2pe, and BS2px. This program uses conditional compilation techniques; see Chapter 3 for more information.

```
' I2C.bsp
' This program demonstrates writing and reading every location in a 24LC16B
' EEPROM using the BS2p/BS2pe's I2C commands.  Connect the BS2p, BS2pe,  or
' BS2px to the 24LC16B DIP EEPROM as shown in the diagram in the I2CIN or
' I2COUT command description.

' {$STAMP BS2p}
' {$PBASIC 2.5}

#IF ($STAMP < BS2P) #THEN
  #ERROR "Program requires BS2p, BS2pe, or BS2px."
#ENDIF

SDA             PIN    0                ' I2C SDA pin
SCL             PIN    SDA + 1
```

```
addr              VAR      Word              ' internal address
block             VAR      Nib               ' block address in 24LC16
value             VAR      Byte              ' value to write
check             VAR      Nib               ' for checking retuned values
result            VAR      Byte(16)          ' array for returned value


Write_To_EEPROM:
  DEBUG "Writing...", CR
  PAUSE 2000
  FOR addr = 0 TO 2047 STEP 16            ' loop through all addresses
    block = addr.NIB2 << 1               ' calculate block address
    value = addr >> 4                    ' create value from upper 8 bits
    ' write 16 bytes
    I2COUT SDA, $A0 | block, addr, [REP value\16]
    PAUSE 5
    DEBUG "Addr: ", DEC4 addr, "-", DEC4 addr + 15, "  ",
          "Value: ", DEC3 value, CR
  NEXT
  PAUSE 2000

Read_From_EEPROM:
  DEBUG CR, "Reading...", CR
  PAUSE  2000
  FOR addr = 0 TO 2047 STEP 16
    block = addr.NIB2 << 1
    value = addr >> 4
    I2CIN SDA, $A1 | block, addr, [STR result\16]
    FOR check = 0 TO 15
      IF (result(check) <> value) THEN Error
    NEXT
    DEBUG "Addr: ", DEC4 addr, "-", DEC4 addr + 15, "  ",
          "Value: ", DEC3 result, CR
  NEXT
  PAUSE 100
  DEBUG CR, "All locations passed"
  END


Error:
  DEBUG "Error at location: ", DEC4 addr + check, CR,
        "Found: ", DEC3 result(check), ", Expected: ", DEC3 value
  END
```

I2COUT

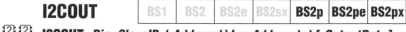

I2COUT *Pin, SlaveID, { Address { \LowAddress },} [OutputData]*

Function

Send data to a device using the I²C protocol.

- **Pin** is a variable/constant/expression (0 or 8) that specifies which I/O pins to use. I²C devices require two I/O pins to communicate. The *Pin* argument serves a double purpose; specifying the first pin (for connection to the chip's SDA pin) and, indirectly, the other required pin (for connection to the chip's SCL pin). See explanation below. Both I/O pins will be toggled between output and input mode during the I2COUT command and both will be set to input mode by the end of the I2COUT command.

- **SlaveID** is a variable/constant/expression (0 – 255) indicating the unique ID of the I²C chip.

- **Address** is an optional variable/constant/expression (0 – 255) indicating the desired address within the I²C chip to send data to. The *Address* argument may be used with the optional *LowAddress* argument to indicate a word-sized address value.

- **LowAddress** is an optional variable/constant/expression (0 – 255) indicating the low-byte of the word-sized address within the I²C chip to receive data from. This argument must be used along with the *Address* argument.

- **OutputData** is a list of variables, constants, expressions and formatters that tells I2COUT how to format outgoing data. I2COUT can transmit individual or repeating bytes, convert values into decimal, hexadecimal or binary text representations, or transmit strings of bytes from variable arrays. These actions can be combined in any order in the *OutputData* list.

Quick Facts

	BS2p, BS2pe, and BS2px	
Values for *Pin*	*Pin* = 0	*Pin* = 8
I/O Pin Arrangement	0: Serial Data (SDA) pin 1: Serial Clock (SCL) pin	8: Serial Data (SDA) pin 9: Serial Clock (SCL) pin
Transmission Rate	Approximately 81 kbits/sec on a BS2p, 45 kbits/sec on a BS2pe, and 83 kbits/sec on a BS2px (not including overhead).	
Special Notes	The SDA and SCL pins must have 1 kΩ - 4.7 kΩ pull-up resistors. The I2CIN command does not allow for multiple masters. The BASIC Stamp cannot operate as an I²C slave device.	
Related Command	I2CIN	

Table 5.35: I2COUT Quick Facts.

Explanation

The I²C protocol is a form of synchronous serial communication developed by Phillips Semiconductors. It only requires two I/O pins and both pins can be shared between multiple I²C devices. The I2COUT command allows the BASIC Stamp to send data to an I²C device.

The following is an example of the I2COUT command:

A SIMPLE I2COUT EXAMPLE.

```
I2COUT 0, $A0, 5, [100]
```

This code will transmit a "write" command to an I²C device (connected to I/O pins 0 and 1), followed by an address of 5 and finally will transmit the number 100.

The above example will write a byte of data to location 5 of a 24LC16B EEPROM from Microchip. Figure 5.11 shows the proper wiring for this example to work. The *SlaveID* argument ($A0) is both the ID of the chip and the command to write to the chip; the 0 means write. The *Address* argument (5) is the EEPROM location to write to.

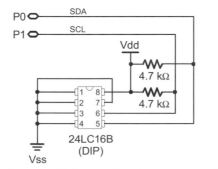

Figure 5.11: Example Circuit for the I2COUT command and a 24LC16B EEPROM.

Note: The 4.7 kΩ resistors are required for the I2COUT command to function properly.

SENDING AND FORMATTING DATA.

The I2COUT command's *OutputData* argument is similar to the DEBUG and SEROUT command's *OutputData* argument. This means data can be sent as literal text, ASCII character values, repetitive values, decimal, hexadecimal and binary translations and string data as in the examples below. (Assume the 24LC16B EEPROM is being used).

```
value    VAR    Byte
value = 65

I2COUT 0, $A0, 0, [value]            ' send "A"
I2COUT 0, $A0, 0, [REP value\5]      ' send "AAAAA"
I2COUT 0, $A0, 0, [DEC value]        ' send "6" and "5"
I2COUT 0, $A0, 0, [HEX value]        ' send "4" and "1"
I2COUT 0, $A0, 0, [BIN value]        ' send "1000001"
```

Table 5.36 and Table 5.37 list all the available formatters for the I2COUT command. See the DEBUG and SEROUT commands for additional information and examples of their use.

Table 5.36: I2COUT Conversion Formatters.

Conversion Formatter	Type of Number	Notes
DEC{1..5}	Decimal, optionally fixed to 1 – 5 digits	1
SDEC{1..5}	Signed decimal, optionally fixed to 1 – 5 digits	1,2
HEX{1..4}	Hexadecimal, optionally fixed to 1 – 4 digits	1,3
SHEX{1..4}	Signed hexadecimal, optionally fixed to 1 – 4 digits	1,2
IHEX{1..4}	Indicated hexadecimal, optionally fixed to 1 – 4 digits ($ prefix)	1
ISHEX{1..4}	Signed, indicated hexadecimal, optionally fixed to 1 – 4 digits ($ prefix)	1,2
BIN{1..16}	Binary, optionally fixed to 1 – 16 digits	1
SBIN{1..16}	Signed binary, optionally fixed to 1 – 16 digits	1,2
IBIN{1..16}	Indicated binary, optionally fixed to 1 – 16 digits (% prefix)	1
ISBIN{1..16}	Signed, indicated binary, optionally fixed to 1 – 16 digits (% prefix)	1,2

1 Fixed-digit formatters like DEC4 will pad the number with leading 0s if necessary; ex: DEC4 65 sends 0065. If a number is larger than the specified number of digits, the leading digits will be dropped; ex: DEC4 56422 sends 6422.
2 Signed modifiers work under two's complement rules.
3 The HEX modifier can be used for BCD to Decimal Conversion. See "Hex to BCD Conversion" on page 97.

Special Formatter	Action
?	Displays "symbol = x' + carriage return; where x is a number. Default format is decimal, but may be combined with conversion formatters (ex: BIN ? x to display "x = binary_number").
ASC ?	Displays "symbol = 'x'" + carriage return; where x is an ASCII character.
STR ByteArray {\L}	Send character string from an array. The optional \L argument can be used to limit the output to L characters, otherwise, characters will be sent up to the first byte equal to 0 or the end of RAM space is reached.
REP Byte \L	Send a string consisting of Byte repeated L times (ex: REP "X"\10 sends "XXXXXXXXXX").

Table 5.37: I2COUT Special Formatters

The I²C protocol has a well-defined standard for the information passed at the start of each transmission. First of all, any information sent must be transmitted in units of 1 byte (8-bits). The first byte, we call the *SlaveID*, is an 8-bit pattern whose upper 7-bits contain the unique ID of the device you wish to communicate with. The lowest bit indicates whether this is a write operation (0) or a read operation (1). Figure 5.12 shows this format.

THE I²C PROTOCOL FORMAT.

7	6	5	4	3	2	1	0
A_6	A_5	A_4	A_3	A_2	A_1	A_0	R/W

Figure 5.12: Slave ID Format

The second byte, immediately following the *SlaveID*, is the optional *Address*. It indicates the 8-bit address (within the device) containing the data you would like to receive. Note that the *Address* argument is optional and may be left unspecified for devices that don't require an *Address* argument.

Some devices require more than 8 bits of address. For this case, the optional *LowAddress* argument can be used for the low-byte of the required address. When using the *LowAddress* argument, the *Address* argument is effectively the high-byte of the address value. For example, if the entire address value is 2050, use 8 for the *Address* argument and 2 for the *LowAddress* argument (8 * 256 + 2 = 2050).

USING LONG ADDRESSES.

Following the last address byte is the first byte of data. This data byte may be transmitted or received by the BASIC Stamp. In the case of the I2COUT command, this data byte is transmitted by the BASIC Stamp and received by the device. Additionally, multiple data bytes can follow the address, depending on the I²C device. Note that every device has different limitations regarding how may contiguous bytes they can receive or transmit in one session. Be aware of this, and program accordingly.

START AND STOP CONDITIONS AND ACKNOWLEDGMENTS.

Every I²C transmission session begins with a Start Condition and ends with a Stop Condition. Additionally, immediately after every byte is transmitted, an extra clock cycle is used to send or receive an acknowledgment signal (ACK). All of these operations are automatically taken care of by the I2COUT command so that you need not be concerned with them. The general I²C transmission format is shown in Figure 5.13.

Figure 5.13: I²C Transmission Format

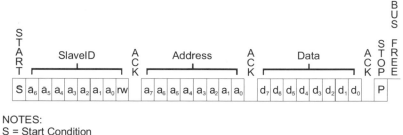

NOTES:
S = Start Condition
P = Stop Condition
a = id or address bit
d = data bit (transmitted by the BASIC Stamp or the I²C device)
ACK = Acknowledge signal. (Most acknowledge signals are generated by the I²C device)

SPECIAL NOTE ABOUT I2COUT INPLIMENTATION.

Since the I2COUT command is intended for output only, it actually overrides the "R/W" bit (bit 0) in the *SlaveID* argument. This is done to avoid device conflicts should the value be mistyped. Put simply, this means commands such as: I2COUT 0, $A0, 10, [0] and I2COUT 0, $A1, 10, [0] both transmit the same thing ($A0, then 10, then the data). Even though the I2COUT command really doesn't care what the value of the *SlaveID*'s LSB is, it is suggested that you still set it appropriately for clarity.

Also note that the I2COUT command does not support multiple I²C masters and the BASIC Stamp cannot operate as an I²C slave device.

Demo Program (I2C.bsp)

NOTE: This example program can be used with the BS2p, BS2pe and BS2px. This program uses conditional compilation techniques; see Chapter 3.

```
' I2C.bsp
' This program demonstrates writing and reading every location in a 24LC16B
' EEPROM using the BS2p/BS2pe's I2C commands.  Connect the BS2p, BS2pe, or
' BS2px to the 24LC16B DIP EEPROM as shown in the diagram in the I2CIN or
```

```
' I2COUT command description.

' {$STAMP BS2p}
' {$PBASIC 2.5}

#IF ($STAMP < BS2P) #THEN
  #ERROR "Program requires BS2p, BS2pe or BS2px."
#ENDIF

SDA            PIN      0                ' I2C SDA pin
SCL            PIN      SDA + 1

addr           VAR      Word             ' internal address
block          VAR      Nib              ' block address in 24LC16
value          VAR      Byte             ' value to write
check          VAR      Nib              ' for checking retuned values
result         VAR      Byte(16)         ' array for returned value

Write_To_EEPROM:
  DEBUG "Writing...", CR
  PAUSE 2000
  FOR addr = 0 TO 2047 STEP 16           ' loop through all addresses
    block = addr.NIB2 << 1               ' calculate block address
    value = addr >> 4                     ' create value from upper 8 bits
    ' write 16 bytes
    I2COUT SDA, $A0 | block, addr, [REP value\16]
    PAUSE 5
    DEBUG "Addr: ", DEC4 addr, "-", DEC4 addr + 15, "  ",
          "Value: ", DEC3 value, CR
  NEXT
  PAUSE 2000

Read_From_EEPROM:
  DEBUG CR, "Reading...", CR
  PAUSE  2000
  FOR addr = 0 TO 2047 STEP 16
    block = addr.NIB2 << 1
    value = addr >> 4
    I2CIN SDA, $A1 | block, addr, [STR result\16]
    FOR check = 0 TO 15
      IF (result(check) <> value) THEN Error
    NEXT
    DEBUG "Addr: ", DEC4 addr, "-", DEC4 addr + 15, "  ",
          "Value: ", DEC3 result, CR
  NEXT
  PAUSE 100
  DEBUG CR, "All locations passed"
  END

Error:
  DEBUG "Error at location: ", DEC4 addr + check, CR,
        "Found: ", DEC3 result(check), ", Expected: ", DEC3 value
  END
```

IF...THEN

BS1	BS2	BS2e	BS2sx	BS2p	BS2pe	BS2px

⌶1 All 2   **IF** *Condition(s)* **THEN** *Address*

All 2   **IF** *Condition(s)* **THEN** *Statement(s)* { **ELSE** *Statement(s)* }

All 2   **IF** *Condition(s)* **THEN**
  Statement(s)
{ **ELSEIF** *Condition(s)* **THEN**
    Statement(s)... }
{ **ELSE**
    Statement(s) }
ENDIF

Function

Evaluate *Condition(s)* and, if true, go to the *Address* or execute the *Statement(s)* following THEN, otherwise process the ELSEIF/ELSE block(s), if provided. ELSEIF is optional and works just like IF, but is only evaluated if the *Condition(s)* in the preceding IF is false. The ELSE block is optional and is executed if all *Condition(s)* in all preceding IF/ELSEIFs are false. The program will continue at the next line of code (single-line syntax) or the line that follows ENDIF (multi-line syntax) unless *Address* or *Statement(s)* are executed that cause the program to jump.

- **Condition** is a statement, such as "x = 7" that can be evaluated as true or false. *Condition* can be a very simple or very complex relationship, as described below.

- **Address** is a label that specifies where to go in the event that *Condition(s)* is true.

- **Statement** is any valid PBASIC instruction. Multiple statements may be placed on the same line (though not recommended) by separating each statement with a colon (:).

Quick Facts

Table 5.38: IF...THEN Quick Facts.

	BS1	All BS2 Models
Comparison Operators	=, <>, >, <, >=, <=	=, <>, >, <, >=, <=
Conditional Logic Operators	AND, OR	NOT, AND, OR, XOR
Format of Condition	*Variable Comparison Value*; where *Value* is a variable or constant	*Value1 Comparison Value2*; where *Value1* and *Value2* can by any of variable, constant or expression
Parentheses	Not Allowed	Allowed
Max nested IF...THENs	n/a	16
Max ELSEIFs per IF	n/a	16
Max ELSEs per IF	n/a	1
Related Command	None	SELECT...CASE

Explanation

IF...THEN is PBASIC's decision maker that allows one block of code or another to run based on the value (True or False) of a condition. The condition that IF...THEN tests is written as a mixture of comparison and logic operators. The available comparison operators are:

Table 5.39: IF...THEN Comparison Operators.

Comparison Operator Symbol	Definition
=	Equal
<>	Not Equal
>	Greater Than
<	Less Than
>=	Greater Than or Equal To
<=	Less Than or Equal To

Comparisons are always written in the form: Value1 Comparison Value2. The values to be compared can be any combination of variables (any size), constants, or expressions.

NOTE: On the BS1, expressions are not allowed as arguments. Also, the Value1 (to the left of comparison) must be a variable.

The following example is an IF...THEN command with a simple condition:

A SIMPLE FORM OF IF...THEN

```
IF value < 4000 THEN Main
```

This code will compare the value of *value* to the number 4000. If *value* is less than 4000, the condition is true and the program will jump (implied

GOTO) to the label called *Main*. This is the simplest form of IF...THEN and is the only form supported by PBASIC 1.0 and PBASIC 2.0.

ALL ABOUT *CONDITION(S)*.

The *Condition(s)* argument is very powerful and flexible. In the next few pages we'll demonstrate this flexibility in great detail and afterwards we'll discuss the additional, optional arguments allowed by PBASIC 2.5.

Here's a complete example of IF...THEN in action:

NOTE: For BS1's, change line 1 to
SYMBOL value = W0
and line 4 to
DEBUG #value, CR

```
value     VAR      Word

Main:
  PULSIN 0, 1, value
  DEBUG DEC value, cr
  IF value < 4000 THEN Main
  DEBUG "Pulse value was greater than 3999!"
```

Here, the BASIC Stamp will look for and measure a pulse on I/O pin 0, then compare the result, *value*, against 4000. If *value* is less than (<) 4000, it will jump back to Main. Each time through the loop, it displays the measured value and once it is greater than or equal to 4000, it displays, "Value was greater than 3999!"

[All 2] On all BS2 models, the values can be expressions as well. This leads to very flexible and sophisticated comparisons. The IF...THEN statement below is functionally the same as the one in the program above:

```
IF value < (45 * 100 - (25 * 20)) THEN Val_Low
```

[All 2] Here the BASIC Stamp evaluates the expression: 45 * 100 = 4500, 25 * 20 = 500, and 4500 – 500 = 4000. Then the BASIC Stamp performs the comparison: is *value* < 4000? Another example that is functionally the same:

```
IF (value / 100) < 40 THEN Val_Low
```

WATCH OUT FOR UNSIGNED MATH
COMPARISON ERRORS

[All 2] It's important to realize that all comparisons are performed using unsigned, 16-bit math. This can lead to strange results if you mix signed and unsigned numbers in IF...THEN conditions. Watch what happens here when we include a signed number (–99):

```
Test:
 IF -99 < 100 THEN Is_Less
 DEBUG "Greater than or equal to 100"
 END

Is_Less:
 DEBUG "Less than 100"
 END
```

Although –99 is obviously less than 100, the program will say it is greater. The problem is that –99 is internally represented as the two's complement value 65437, which (using unsigned math) is greater than 100. This phenomena will occur whether or not the negative value is a constant, variable or expression.

IF...THEN supports the conditional logic operators NOT, AND, OR, and XOR to allow for more sophisticated conditions, such as multi-part conditions. See Table 5.38 for a list of the operators and Table 5.40 for their effects.

LOGICAL OPERATORS (NOT, AND, OR AND XOR).

The NOT operator inverts the outcome of a condition, changing false to true, and true to false. The following IF...THENs are equivalent:

NOTE: The NOT and XOR operators are not available on the BS1.

```
IF x <> 100 THEN Not_Equal
IF NOT x = 100 THEN Not_Equal
```

The operators AND, OR, and XOR can be used to join the results of two conditions to produce a single true/false result. AND and OR work the same as they do in everyday speech. Run the example below once with AND (as shown) and again, substituting OR for AND:

NOTE: For BS1's, change lines 1 and 2 to:
SYMBOL value1 = B2
SYMBOL value2 = B3

```
value1          VAR     Byte
value2          VAR     Byte

Setup:
  value1 = 5
  value2 = 9

Main:
  IF value1 = 5 AND value2 = 10 THEN Is_True
  DEBUG "Statement is False"
  END

Is_True:
  DEBUG "Statement is True"
  END
```

The condition "value1 = 5 AND value2 = 10" is not true. Although value1 is 5, value2 is not 10. The AND operator works just as it does in English; both conditions must be true for the statement to be true. The OR operator also works in a familiar way; if one or the other or both conditions are true, then the statement is true. The XOR operator (short for exclusive-OR) may not be familiar, but it does have an English counterpart: If one condition or the other (but not both) is true, then the statement is true.

NOTE: On the BS1, parentheses are not allowed within arguments.

Table 5.40 below summarizes the effects of the conditional logic operators. On all BS2 models you can alter the order in which comparisons and logical operations are performed by using parentheses. Operations are normally evaluated left-to-right. Putting parentheses around an operation forces PBASIC 2.0 and PBASIC 2.5 to evaluate it before operations that are not in parentheses.

Table 5.40: Conditional Logic Operators Truth Tables.

NOTE: The NOT and XOR operators are not available on the BS1.

Truth Table for Logical Operator: NOT	
Condition A	NOT A
False	True
True	False

Truth Table for Logical Operator: AND		
Condition A	Condition B	A AND B
False	False	False
False	True	False
True	False	False
True	True	True

Truth Table for Logical Operator: OR		
Condition A	Condition B	A OR B
False	False	False
False	True	True
True	False	True
True	True	True

Truth Table for Logical Operator: XOR		
Condition A	Condition B	A XOR B
False	False	False
False	True	True
True	False	True
True	True	False

Internally, the BASIC Stamp defines "false" as 0 and "true" as any value other than 0. Consider the following instructions:

INTERNAL REPRESENTATION OF BOOLEAN VALUES (TRUE VS. FALSE).

```
flag    VAR    Bit

Setup:
  flag = 1

Test:
  IF flag THEN Is_True
  DEBUG  "False"
  END

Is_True:
  DEBUG "True"
  END
```

Since *flag* is 1, IF...THEN would evaluate it as true and print the message "True" on the screen. Suppose you changed the IF...THEN command to read "IF NOT flag THEN Is_True." That would also evaluate as true. Whoa! Isn't NOT 1 the same thing as 0? No, at least not in the 16-bit world of the BASIC Stamp.

Internally, the BASIC Stamp sees a bit variable containing 1 as the 16-bit number %0000000000000001. So it sees the NOT of that as %1111111111111110. Since any non-zero number is regarded as true, NOT 1 is true. Strange but true.

The easiest way to avoid the kinds of problems this might cause is to always use a conditional operator with IF...THEN. Change the example above to read IF flag = 1 THEN is_True. The result of the comparison will follow IF...THEN rules. Also, the logical operators will work as they should; IF NOT Flag = 1 THEN is_True will correctly evaluate to false when *flag* contains 1.

AVOIDING ERRORS WITH BOOLEAN RESULTS.

This also means that you should only use the "named" conditional logic operators NOT, AND, OR, and XOR with IF...THEN. The conditional logic operators format their results correctly for IF...THEN instructions. The other logical operators, represented by symbols ~, &, |, and ^ do not; they are binary logic operators.

The remainder of this discussion only applies to the extended IF...THEN syntax supported by PBASIC 2.5.

IF...THEN WITH A SINGLE *STATEMENT*   In addition to supporting everything discussed above, PBASIC 2.5 provides enhancements to the IF...THEN command that allow for more powerful, structured programming. In prior examples we've only used the first syntax form of this command: IF *Condition(s)* THEN *Address*. That form, while handy in some situations, can be quite limiting in others. For example, it is common to need to perform a single instruction based on a condition. Take a look at the following code:

```
' {$PBASIC 2.5}

x   VAR   Byte

FOR x = 1 TO 20                              ' count to 20
  DEBUG CR, DEC x                            ' display num
  IF (x // 2) = 0 THEN DEBUG " EVEN"         ' even num?
NEXT
```

This example prints the numbers 1 through 20 on the screen but every even number is also marked with the text " EVEN." The IF...THEN command checks to see if *x* is even or odd and, if it is even (i.e.: x // 2 = 0), then it executes the statement to the right of THEN: DEBUG " EVEN." If it was odd, it simply continued at the following line, NEXT.

Suppose you also wanted to mark the odd numbers. You could take advantage of the optional ELSE clause, as in:

```
' {$PBASIC 2.5}

x   VAR   Byte

FOR x = 1 TO 20                              ' count to 20
  DEBUG CR, DEC x
  IF (x // 2) = 0 THEN DEBUG " EVEN" ELSE DEBUG " ODD"
NEXT
```

This example prints the numbers 1 through 20 with " EVEN" or " ODD" to the right of each number. For each number (each time through the loop) IF...THEN asks the question, "Is the number even?" and if it is it executes DEBUG " EVEN" (the instruction after THEN) or, if it is not even it executes DEBUG " ODD" (the instruction after ELSE). It's important to note that this form of IF...THEN always executes code as a result of *Condition(s)*; it either does "this" (THEN) or "that" (ELSE).

The IF...THEN in the previous example is called a "single-line" syntax. It is most useful where you only have one instruction to run as the result of a *Condition*. Sometimes this form may be a little hard to read, like in our above example. For these cases, it would be better to use the "multi-line" syntax of IF...THEN. The multi-line format allows the same flexibility as the single-line format, but is easier to read in most cases and requires an ENDIF statement at the end. For example, our IF...THEN line above could be re-written as:

```
IF (x // 2) = 0 THEN
  DEBUG " EVEN"                      ' even number
ELSE
  DEBUG " ODD"                       ' odd number
ENDIF
```

This example runs exactly the same way, is much easier to read and also leaves extra room to add some helpful comments on the right. We also indented the *Statement(s)* for clarity and suggest you do the same.

Did you notice that multi-line syntax requires ENDIF to mark the end of the IF...THEN...ELSE construct? That is because the *Statement(s)* argument can be multiple instructions on multiple lines, so without ENDIF there is no way to know just where the IF...THEN...ELSE ends.

Occasionally, it may be necessary to have compound IF statements. One way to achieve this is through nested IF...THEN...END constructs:

```
' {$PBASIC 2.5}

value           VAR     Word

DO
  PULSIN 0, 1, value                ' measure pulse input
  DEBUG DEC value, CR
  IF (value > 4000) THEN            ' evaluate duration
    DEBUG "Value was greater than 4000"
  ELSE
    IF (value = 4000) THEN
      DEBUG "Value was equal to 4000"
    ELSE
      DEBUG "Value was less than 4000"
    ENDIF
  ENDIF
  DEBUG CR, CR
  PAUSE 1000
LOOP
```

Here, the BASIC Stamp will look for and measure a pulse on I/O pin 0, then compare the result, *value*, against 4000. Based on this comparison, a message regarding the pulse width value will be printed.

If *value* is greater than 4000, "Value was greater than 4000" is printed to the screen. Look what happens if *value* is <u>not</u> greater than 4000... the code in the ELSE block is run, which is another IF...THEN...ELSE statement. This "nested" IF...THEN statement checks if *value* is equal to 4000 and if it is, it prints "Value was equal to 4000" or, if it was not equal, the last ELSE code block executes, printing "Value was less than 4000." Up to sixteen (16) IF...THENs can be nested like this.

USING THE ELSEIF CLAUSE

The nesting option is great for many situations, but, like single-line syntax, may be a little hard to read, especially if there are multiple nested statements or there is more than one instruction in each of the *Statement(s)* arguments. Additionally, every multi-line IF...THEN construct must end with ENDIF, resulting in two ENDIFs right near each other in our example; one for the innermost IF...THEN and one for the outermost IF...THEN. For this reason, IF...THEN supports an optional ELSEIF clause. The ELSEIF clause takes the place of a nested IF...THEN and removes the need for multiple ENDIFs. Our IF...THEN construction from the example above could be rewritten to:

```
' {$PBASIC 2.5}

IF (value > 4000) THEN                    ' evaluate duration
  DEBUG "Value was greater than 4000"
ELSEIF (value = 4000) THEN
  DEBUG "Value was equal to 4000"
ELSE
  DEBUG "Value was less than 4000"
ENDIF
```

This IF...THEN construct does the same thing as in the previous example:
1) if value is greater than 4000:
    it displays "Value was greater than 4000"
2) else, if value is equal to 4000 (the ELSEIF part):
    it displays "Value was equal to 4000"
3) and finally (ELSE) if none of the above were true:
    it displays "Value was less than 4000"

Note that an IF...THEN construct can have as many as sixteen (16) ELSEIF clauses, but a maximum of only one (1) ELSE clause.

There are three demo programs below. The first two demonstrate the PBASIC 1.0 (BS1) and PBASIC 2.0 (all BS2 models) form of the IF...THEN command. The last example demonstrates the PBASIC 2.5 (all BS2 models) form of IF...THEN.

Demo Program (IF-THEN.bs1)

```
' IF-THEN.bs1
' The program below generates a series of 16-bit random numbers and tests
' each to determine whether they're evenly divisible by 3. If a number is
' evenly divisible by 3, then it is printed, otherwise, the program
' generates another random number.  The program counts how many numbers it
' prints, and quits when this number reaches 10.

' {$STAMP BS1}
' {$PBASIC 1.0}

SYMBOL   sample        = W0        ' Random number to be tested
SYMBOL   samps         = B2        ' Number of samples taken
SYMBOL   temp          = B3        ' Temporary workspace


Setup:
  sample = 11500

Mult3:
  RANDOM sample                    ' Put a random number into sample
  temp = sample // 3
  IF temp <> 0 THEN Mult3          ' Not multiple of 3? -- try again
    DEBUG #sample, "divides by 3", CR  ' show sample divisible by 3
    samps = samps + 1              ' Count multiples of 3
    IF samps = 10 THEN Done        ' Quit with 10 samples
  GOTO Mult3                       ' keep checking

Done:
  DEBUG CR, "All done."
  END
```

Demo Program (IF-THEN.bs2)

NOTE: This example program can be used with all BS2 models by changing the $STAMP directive accordingly.

```
' IF-THEN.bs2
' The program below generates a series of 16-bit random numbers and tests
' each to determine whether they're evenly divisible by 3. If a number is
' evenly divisible by 3, then it is printed, otherwise, the program
' generates another random number.  The program counts how many numbers it
' prints, and quits when this number reaches 10.
```

```
' {$STAMP BS2}
' {$PBASIC 2.0}


sample          VAR     Word        ' Random number to be tested
samps           VAR     Nib         ' Number of samples taken
temp            VAR     Nib         ' Temporary workspace


Setup:
  sample = 11500

Mult3:
  RANDOM sample                     ' Put a random number into sample
  temp = sample // 3
  IF temp <> 0 THEN Mult3           ' Not multiple of 3? -- try again
    DEBUG DEC5 sample, " divides by 3", CR
    samps = samps + 1               ' Count multiples of 3
    IF samps = 10 THEN Done         ' Quit with 10 samples
  GOTO Mult3                        ' keep checking

Done:
  DEBUG CR, "All done."
  END
```

All 2 ## Demo Program (IF-THEN-ELSE.bs2)

NOTE: This example program can be used with all BS2 models by changing the $STAMP directive accordingly.

```
' IF-THEN-ELSE.bs2
' The program below generates a series of 16-bit random numbers and tests
' each to determine whether they're evenly divisible by 3. If a number is
' evenly divisible by 3, then it is printed, otherwise, the program
' generates another random number. The program counts how many numbers it
' prints, and quits when this number reaches 10.

' {$STAMP BS2}
' {$PBASIC 2.5}                     ' version 2.5 required

sample          VAR     Word        ' Random number to be tested
hits            VAR     Nib         ' Number of hits
misses          VAR     Word        ' Number of misses


Setup:
  sample = 11500

Main:
  DO
    RANDOM sample                   ' Put a random number into sample
    IF ((sample // 3) = 0) THEN     ' divisible by 3?
      DEBUG DEC5 sample,            ' - yes, print value and message
            " is divisible by 3", CR
```

```
      hits = hits + 1                    ' count hits (divisible by 3)
   ELSE
      misses = misses + 1                ' count misses
   ENDIF
LOOP UNTIL (hits = 10)                    ' quit after 10 hits

DEBUG CR,
      "All done.", CR, CR,                ' display results
      "Hits:    ", DEC hits, CR,
      "Misses:  ", DEC misses, CR,
      "Samples: ", DEC (hits + misses)
END
```

INPUT

BS1	BS2	BS2e	BS2sx	BS2p	BS2pe	BS2px

⌷1 ⌷All 2 **INPUT** *Pin*

⌷1
NOTE: Expressions are not allowed as arguments on the BS1. The range of the PIN argument on the BS1 is 0 – 7.

Function

Make the specified pin an input.

- *Pin* is a variable/constant/expression (0 – 15) that specifies which I/O pin to set to input mode.

Quick Facts

Table 5.41: INPUT Quick Facts.

	BS1	All BS2 Models
Input Pin Variables	PINS; PIN0 through PIN7	INS; IN0 through IN15
Related Commands	OUTPUT and REVERSE	

Explanation

There are several ways to make a pin an input. When a program begins, all of the BASIC Stamp's pins are inputs. Commands that rely on input pins, like PULSIN and SERIN, automatically change the specified pin to input. Writing 0s to particular bits of the variable DIRS makes the corresponding pins inputs. And then there's the INPUT command.

When a pin is an input, your program can check its state by reading the corresponding INS variable (PINS on the BS1). For example:

⌷All 2
```
INPUT 4

Hold:
  IF IN4 = 0 THEN Hold                    ' stay here until P4 = 1
```

The code above will read the state of P4 as set by external circuitry. If nothing is connected to P4, it will alternate between states (1 or 0) apparently at random.

What happens if your program writes to the OUTS bit (PINS bit on the BS1) of a pin that is set up as an input? The value is stored in OUTS (PINS on the BS1), but has no effect on the outside world. If the pin is changed to output, the last value written to the corresponding OUTS bit (or PINS bit

on the BS1) will appear on the pin. The demo program shows how this
works.

Demo Program (INPUT.bs1)

```
' INPUT.bs1
' This program demonstrates how the input/output direction of a pin is
' determined by the corresponding bit of DIRS. It also shows that the
' state of the pin itself (as reflected by the corresponding bit of PINS)
' is determined by the outside world when the pin is an input, and by the
' corresponding bit of OUTS when it's an output. To set up the demo,
' connect a 10k resistor from +5V to P7 on the BASIC Stamp. The resistor
' to +5V puts a high (1) on the pin when it's an input. The BASIC Stamp
' can override this state by writing a low (0) to bit 7 of OUTS and
' changing the pin to output.

' {$STAMP BS1}
' {$PBASIC 1.0}

Main:
  INPUT 7                           ' Make P7 an input
  DEBUG "State of P7: ", #PIN7, CR

  PIN7 = 0                          ' Write 0 to output latch
  DEBUG "After 0 written to OUT7: "
  DEBUG #PIN7, CR

  OUTPUT 7                          ' Make P7 an output
  DEBUG "After P7 changed to output: "
  DEBUG #PIN7
```

Demo Program (INPUT.bs2)

NOTE: This example program can be used with all BS2 models by changing the $STAMP directive accordingly.

```
' INPUT.bs2
' This program demonstrates how the input/output direction of a pin is
' determined by the corresponding bit of DIRS. It also shows that the
' state of the pin itself (as reflected by the corresponding bit of INS)
' is determined by the outside world when the pin is an input, and by the
' corresponding bit of OUTS when it's an output. To set up the demo,
' connect a 10k resistor from +5V to P7 on the BASIC Stamp. The resistor
' to +5V puts a high (1) on the pin when it's an input. The BASIC Stamp
' can override this state by writing a low (0) to bit 7 of OUTS and
' changing the pin to output.

' {$STAMP BS2}
' {$PBASIC 2.5}

Main:
  INPUT 7                           ' Make P7 an input
  DEBUG "State of P7: ",
```

```
      BIN1 IN7, CR

OUT7 = 0                              ' Write 0 to output latch
DEBUG "After 0 written to OUT7: ",
      BIN1 IN7, CR

OUTPUT 7                              ' Make P7 an output
DEBUG "After P7 changed to output: ",
      BIN1 IN7
```

IOTERM

IOTERM *Port*

BS1	BS2	BS2e	BS2sx	BS2p	BS2pe	BS2px

Function
Switch control to main I/O pins or auxiliary I/O pins (on the BS2p40 only) depending on state of *Port*.

• *Port* is a variable/constant/expression (0 – 1) that specifies which I/O port to use.

Quick Facts

Table 5.42: IOTERM Quick Facts.

	BS2p, BS2pe, and BS2px
Values for *Port*	0 = switch to main I/O group, 1 = switch to auxiliary I/O group.
I/O pin IDs	0 – 15 (after IOTERM command, all references affect physical pins 5 – 20 or 21 – 36 depending on state of *Port*).
Special Notes	Both the BS2p and BS2pe 24-pin modules accept this command, however, only the BS2p40 gives access to the auxiliary I/O pins.
Related Commands	AUXIO and MAINIO

Explanation
The BS2p, BS2pe and BS2px are available as 24-pin modules that are pin compatible with the BS2, BS2e and BS2sx. Also available is a 40-pin module called the BS2p40, with an additional 16 I/O pins (for a total of 32). The BS2p40's I/O pins are organized into two groups, called main and auxiliary. The I/O pins in each group can be accessed in the same manner (by referencing I/O pins 0 – 15) but access is only possible within one group at a time. The IOTERM command causes the BASIC Stamp to affect either the main or auxiliary I/O pins in all further code until the MAINIO, AUXIO or another IOTERM command is reached, or the BASIC Stamp is reset or power-cycled. The value of *Port* determines which group of I/O pins will be referenced. Using 0 for *Port* will switch to the main I/O group and using 1 for *Port* will switch to the auxiliary group.

A SIMPLE IOTERM EXAMPLE.

The following example illustrates this:

```
HIGH 0              ' make P0 high
IOTERM 1            ' Port = 1, so switch to auxiliary pins
LOW 0               ' make X0 low
```

The first line of the above example will set I/O pin 0 of the main I/O pins (physical pin 5) high. Afterward, the IOTERM command tells the BASIC

IOTERM – BASIC Stamp Command Reference

Stamp that all commands following it should affect the auxiliary I/O pins (*Port = 1*). The following LOW command will set I/O pin 0 of the auxiliary I/O pins (physical pin 21) low.

Note that the main I/O and auxiliary I/O pins are independent of each other; the states of the main I/O pins remain unchanged while the program affects the auxiliary I/O pins, and vice versa.

MAIN I/O AND AUXILIARY I/O PINS ARE INDEPENDENT AND UNAFFECTED BY CHANGES IN THE OPPOSITE GROUP.

Other commands that affect I/O group access are AUXIO and MAINIO.

Demo Program (AUX_MAIN_TERM.bsp)

NOTE: This example program will tokenize with the 24-pin BS2p, BS2pe, and BS2px but its effects can only be seen on the BS2p40. This program uses conditional compilation techniques; see Chapter 3 for more information.

```
' AUX_MAIN_TERM.bsp
' This program demonstrates the use of the AUXIO, MAINIO and IOTERM
' commands to affect I/O pins in the auxiliary and main I/O groups.

' {$STAMP BS2p}
' {$PBASIC 2.5}

#SELECT $STAMP
  #CASE BS2, BS2E, BS2SX
    #ERROR "Program requires BS2p40"
  #CASE BS2P, BS2PE, BS2PX
    DEBUG "Note: This program designed for the BS2p40.", CR
#ENDSELECT

port            VAR     Bit

Main:
  DO
    MAINIO                          ' Switch to main I/O pins
    TOGGLE 0                        ' Toggle state of I/O pin P0
    PWM 1, 100, 40                  ' Generate PWM on I/O pin P1

    AUXIO                           ' Switch to auxiliary I/O pins
    TOGGLE 0                        ' Toggle state of I/O pin X0
    PULSOUT 1, 1000                 ' Generate a pulse on I/O pin X1
    PWM 2, 100, 40                  ' Generate PWM on I/O pin X2

    IOTERM port                     ' Switch to main or aux I/Os
                                    ' -- depending on port
    TOGGLE 3                        ' Toggle state of I/O pin 3
                                    ' -- on main and aux, alternately
    port = ~port                    ' Invert port
    PAUSE 1000                      ' 1 second delay
  LOOP
  END
```

LCDCMD

| BS1 | BS2 | BS2e | BS2sx | **BS2p** | **BS2pe** | **BS2px** |

LCDCMD *Pin, Command*

Function

Send a command to an LCD display.

- **Pin** is a variable/constant/expression (0 – 1 or 8 – 9) that specifies which I/O pins to use. The LCD requires, at most, seven I/O pins to operate. Note that LCDCMD, LCDIN and LCDOUT use a 4-bit interface to the LCD which requires a specific initialization sequence before LCDIN and LCDOUT can be used. Specifics on the initialization sequence will follow. The *Pin* argument serves a double purpose; specifying the first pin and, indirectly, the group of other required pins. See explanation below. All I/O pins will be set to output mode.

- **Command** is a variable/constant/expression (0 – 255) indicating the LCD command to send.

Quick Facts

Table 5.43: LCDCMD Quick Facts.

	BS2p, BS2pe, and BS2px
Values for *Pin*	0, 1, 8 or 9
I/O Pin Arrangement when *Pin* is 0 or 1	0 or 1 (depending on pin): LCD Enable (E) pin 2: LCD Read/Write (R/W) pin 3: LCD Register Select (RS) pin 4 – 7: LCD Data Buss (DB4 – DB7, respectively) pins
I/O Pin Arrangement when *Pin* is 8 or 9	8 or 9 (depending on pin): LCD Enable (E) pin 10: LCD Read/Write (R/W) pin 11: LCD Register Select (RS) pin 12 – 15: LCD Data Buss (DB4 – DB7, respectively) pins
Special Notes	LCDCMD is designed to use the LCD's 4-bit mode only.
Related Commands	LCDIN and LCDOUT

Explanation

NOTE: LCDCMD, LCDIN and LCDOUT use a 4-bit interface to the LCD which requires a specific initialization sequence before LCDIN and LCDOUT can be used; read more below.

The three LCD commands (LCDCMD, LCDIN and LCDOUT) allow the BS2p, BS2pe, and BS2px to interface directly to standard LCD displays that feature a Hitachi 44780 controller (part #HD44780A). This includes many 1 x 16, 2 x 16 and 4 x 20 character LCD displays.

The Hitachi 44780 LCD controller supports a number of special instructions for initializing the display, moving the cursor, changing the default layout, etc. The LCDCMD command is used to send one of these instructions to the LCD. It is most commonly used to initialize the display upon a power-up or reset condition.

The following is an example of the LCDCMD command:

A SIMPLE LCDCMD EXAMPLE.

```
LCDOUT 0, 24
```

The above code will send the Scroll Left command (represented by the number 24) to the LCD whose enable pin is connected to I/O pin 0. This will cause the LCD display to scroll, or shift, the entire display one character to the left.

You may have noticed that the *Pin* argument in the example above was 0. The LCDCMD command actually uses more than just this I/O pin, however. The LCDCMD command requires seven I/O pins. This is because the standard LCD displays have a parallel interface, rather than a serial one. The *Pin* argument can be the numbers 0, 1, 8 or 9 and will result in the use of the I/O pins shown in Table 5.43. Figure 5.14 shows the required wiring for the above command to work.

WIRING THE BASIC STAMP TO AN LCD.

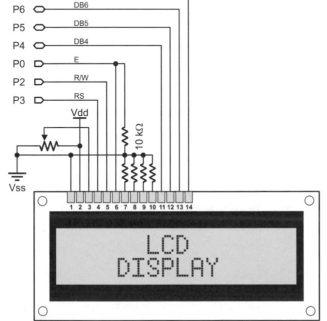

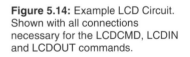

Figure 5.14: Example LCD Circuit. Shown with all connections necessary for the LCDCMD, LCDIN and LCDOUT commands.

Note that we could have used 1 for the *Pin* argument and moved the LCD's Enable pin (pin 6) to I/O pin 1. Similarly, using 9 for the *Pin* argument would have required us to wire the LCD's pins to I/O pins 9 through 15, rather than I/O pins 0 and 2 through 7.

INITIALIZING THE LCD; THE MOST IMPORTANT STEP!

When the LCD is first powered-up, it defaults to an 8-bit interface and must be configured for a 4-bit buss before sending commands like the one shown above. This process is known as initializing the LCD and is the first thing your program should do upon starting up. The following code is a good example of LCD initialization.

```
Init_LCD:
  PAUSE 1000                    ' allow LCD to self-initialize first
  LCDCMD 0, %00110000           ' send wakeup sequence to LCD
  PAUSE 5                       ' pause required by LCD specs
  LCDCMD 0, %00110000
  PAUSE 0                       ' pause required by LCD specs
  LCDCMD 0, %00110000
  PAUSE 0                       ' pause required by LCD specs
  LCDCMD 0, %00100000           ' set data bus to 4-bit mode
  LCDCMD 0, %00101000           ' set to 2-line mode with 5x8 font
  LCDCMD 0, %00001100           ' display on without cursor
  LCDCMD 0, %00000110           ' auto-increment cursor
```

This initialization code is the most commonly used sequence for a 2 x 16 and 4 x 20 LCD display (the 2-line mode instruction sets the 4 x 20 to 4-line mode). The PAUSE 1000 command is optional, but only if your program takes more than approximately 700 ms before it executes the InitLCD code above. Without it, upon powering your circuit, the BASIC Stamp may talk to the LCD too early, the LCD will then miss some of the commands and the display will operate strangely, or not at all.

Do not change the "wake-up" and "4-bit mode" sequence commands. However, the commands below the line that says, "Set data bus to 4-bit mode" may be modified to set other desired modes.

COMMON LCD COMMANDS.

Table 5.44 shows the most commonly used LCD commands. Here's an example:

```
LCDCMD 0, 16
```

This will make the LCD's cursor move left by one character (16 is the Cursor Left command), even if the cursor is not visible. The next character printed on the display (with the LCDOUT command) will appear at the current cursor's location. Here's another example:

```
LCDCMD 0, 128 + 64
```

The above command will move the cursor to the first character position on the second line (on a 2 x 16 display). 128 is the Move To Display Address command and 64 is the location number. See the "Character Positioning" section, below, for more information.

	Command (in decimal)	Description
Do Nothing	0	Don't perform any special operation.
Clear Display	1	Clear the display and move cursor to home position.
Home Display	2	Move cursor and display to home position.
Inc Cursor	6	Set cursor direction to right, without a display shift.
Display Off	8	Turn off display (display data is retained).
Display On	12	Turn on display without cursor (display is restored).
Blinking Cursor	13	Turn on display with blinking cursor.
Underline Cursor	14	Turn on display with underline cursor.
Cursor Left	16	Move cursor left one character.
Cursor Right	20	Move cursor right one character.
Scroll Left	24	Scroll display left one character.
Scroll Right	28	Scroll display right one character.
Move To CGRAM Address	64 + address	Move pointer to character RAM location.
Move To DDRAM Address	128 + address	Move cursor to Display Data RAM location.

Table 5.44: Common LCD Commands. These are supported by LCDs with the Hitachi 44780 controller.

While most users will only need the commands shown in Table 5.44 above, Table 5.45 below details all of the instructions supported by the LCD (for advanced users). Many instructions are multipurpose, depending on the state of special bits. Clever manipulation of the instruction bits will allow for powerful control of the LCD.

A NOTE ABOUT ADVANCED LCD COMMANDS.

The last command shown above (Move To DDRAM Address) is used to move the cursor to a specific position on the LCD. The LCD's DDRAM (Display Data RAM) is a fixed size with a unique position number for each character cell. The viewable portion of the DDRAM depends on the LCD's logical view position (which can be altered with the Scroll Display command). The default view position is called the Home position; it means that the display's upper left character corresponds to DDRAM

CHARACTER POSITIONING: MOVING THE CURSOR.

location 0. Figure 5.15 indicates the position numbers for characters on the LCD screen.

Table 5.45: All LCD Commands (for advanced users). These are supported by LCDs with the Hitachi 44780 controller.

	Command Code (in binary)								Description
	7	6	5	4	3	2	1	0	
Clear Display	0	0	0	0	0	0	0	1	Clear entire display and move cursor home (address 0).
Home Display	0	0	0	0	0	0	1	0	Move cursor home and return display to home position.
Entry Mode	0	0	0	0	0	1	M	S	Sets cursor direction (M: 0=left, 1=right) and display scrolling (S: 0=no scroll, 1=scroll)
Display/Cursor	0	0	0	0	1	D	U	B	Sets display on/off (D), underline cursor (U) and blinking block cursor (B). (0=off, 1=on)
Scroll Display / Shift Cursor	0	0	0	1	C	M	0	0	Shifts display or cursor (C: 0=cursor, 1=display) left or right (M: 0=left, 1=right).
Function Set	0	0	1	B	L	F	0	0	Sets buss size (B: 0=4-bits, 1=8-bits), number of lines (L: 0=1-line, 1=2-lines) and font size (F: 0=5x8, 1=5x10)
Move To CGRAM Address	0	1	A	A	A	A	A	A	Move pointer to character RAM location specified by address (A)
Move To DDRAM Address	1	A	A	A	A	A	A	A	Move cursor to display RAM location specified by address (A)

Note that Figure 5.15 shows the most common DDRAM mapping, though some LCD's may have organized the DDRAM differently. A little experimentation with your LCD may reveal this.

Figure 5.15: LCD Character Positions.

NOTE: Many 1 x 16 displays conform to the position numbers shown on Line 1 of the 2 x 16 display.

2 x 16 Display

On-screen positions*   Off-screen positions*

Line 1: 0 1 2 3 4 5 6 7 8 9 10 11 12 13 14 15 16 ··· 39
Line 2: 64 65 66 67 68 69 70 71 72 73 74 75 76 77 78 79 80 ··· 103

4 x 20 Display

Line 1: 0 1 2 3 4 5 6 7 8 9 10 11 12 13 14 15 16 17 18 19
Line 2: 64 65 66 67 68 69 70 71 72 73 74 75 76 77 78 79 80 81 82 83
Line 3: 20 21 22 23 24 25 26 27 28 29 30 31 32 33 34 35 36 37 38 39
Line 4: 84 85 86 87 88 89 90 91 92 93 94 95 96 97 98 99 100 101 102 103

*Assuming the display is in the home position.

On a standard 2 x 16 character display, the following command would move the cursor to the third column of the second line:

```
LCDCMD 0, 128 + 66
```

The number 128 tells the LCD we wish to move the cursor and 66 is the location number of the desired position. Similarly, sending just 128 (128 + 0) would move the cursor to the first character of the first line (the upper left character if the display is at the home position).

You may have noticed that the 2 x 16 display has many locations that are not visible; they are beyond the right edge of the screen. These locations (16 – 39 and 80 to 103) become important for scrolling operations. For example, it is possible to move the cursor to location 16, print some text there and then issue a number of Scroll Left instructions (LCDCMD 0, 24) to slowly scroll the text onto the display from right to left. If you did so, the DDRAM positions that were on the left of the screen would now be past the left edge of the screen. For example,

SCROLLING THE DISPLAY.

```
LCDCMD 0, 24
LCDCMD 0, 24
```

would cause the screen to scroll to the left by two characters. At this point, the upper-left character in the display would actually be DDRAM location 2 and the lower-left character would be DDRAM location 66. Locations 0, 1, 64 and 65 would be off the left edge of the LCD and would no longer be visible. Some interesting effects can be achieved by taking advantage of this feature.

The 4 x 20 LCD has a strange DDRAM map. The upper-right character is location 19 and the next location, 20, appears as the first character of the third line. This strange mapping is due to constraints in the LCD controller and the manufacturers design, and unfortunately makes the scrolling features virtually useless on the 4 x 20 displays.

NOTES ON DDRAM MAPPING FOR 4 x 20 LCDS.

Even though the LCD requires many pins to talk to it, only the Enable pin needs to remain dedicated to the LCD and all the other pins can be multiplexed (shared) with certain other devices (if wired carefully). In addition, the I/O pin connected to the LCD's R/W pin is only necessary if the LCDIN command will be used in the application. If the LCDIN command will not be used, LCD pin 5 (R/W pin) can be connected to

DETAILS ON LCD WIRING.

ground, the 4 resistors on LCD pins 7-10 may be removed (connecting pins 7-10 directly to ground). Note that even though this change will leave BASIC Stamp I/O pin 2 disconnected, it will still be set to output mode for each LCDCMD and LCDOUT command executed.

Demo Program (LCDINIT.bsp)

NOTE: This example program can be used with the BS2p, BS2pe, and BS2px by changing the $STAMP directive accordingly.

```
' LCDINIT.bsp
' This program demonstrates initialization and printing on a 2 x 16
' character LCD display. The set of "LCD constants", below, are provided
' as pre-defined and useful LCD commands, though not all are actually
' used in this program.

' {$STAMP BS2p}
' {$PBASIC 2.5}

#IF ($STAMP < BS2P) #THEN
  #ERROR "Program requires BS2p, BS2pe or BS2px."
#ENDIF

Lcd             PIN     0

LcdCls          CON     $01     ' clear the LCD
LcdHome         CON     $02     ' move cursor home
LcdCrsrL        CON     $10     ' move cursor left
LcdCrsrR        CON     $14     ' move cursor right
LcdDispL        CON     $18     ' shift chars left
LcdDispR        CON     $1C     ' shift chars right
LcdDDRam        CON     $80     ' Display Data RAM
LcdCGRam        CON     $40     ' Character Generator RAM
LcdLine1        CON     $80     ' DDRAM address of line 1
LcdLine2        CON     $C0     ' DDRAM address of line 2


Init_LCD:
  PAUSE 1000                    ' allow LCD to self-initialize first
  LCDCMD Lcd, %00110000         ' send wakeup sequence to LCD
  PAUSE 5                       ' pause required by LCD specs
  LCDCMD Lcd, %00110000
  PAUSE 0                       ' pause required by LCD specs
  LCDCMD Lcd, %00110000
  PAUSE 0                       ' pause required by LCD specs
  LCDCMD Lcd, %00100000         ' set data bus to 4-bit mode
  LCDCMD Lcd, %00101000         ' set to 2-line mode with 5x8 font
  LCDCMD Lcd, %00001100         ' display on without cursor
  LCDCMD Lcd, %00000110         ' auto-increment cursor

Main:
  DO
    LCDOUT Lcd, LcdCls, ["Hello, World!"]
    LCDOUT Lcd, LcdLine2, ["How are you?"]
```

```
   PAUSE 3000
   LCDCMD Lcd, LcdCls
   PAUSE 500
LOOP
END
```

LCDIN

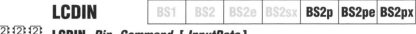

LCDIN *Pin, Command,* [*InputData*]

Function

Receive data from an LCD display.

- **Pin** is a variable/constant/expression (0 – 1 or 8 – 9) that specifies which I/O pins to use. The LCD requires, at most, seven I/O pins to operate. The *Pin* argument serves a double purpose; specifying the first pin and, indirectly, the group of other required pins. See explanation below. All I/O pins will be set to output mode initially and the upper I/O pins (4 – 7 or 12 – 15) will be set to input mode by the end of the LCDIN command.

- **Command** is a variable/constant/expression (0 – 255) indicating the LCD command to send.

- **InputData** is a list of variables and formatters that tells LCDIN what to do with incoming data. LCDIN can store data in a variable or array, interpret numeric text (decimal, binary, or hex) and store the corresponding value in a variable, wait for a fixed or variable sequence of bytes, or ignore a specified number of bytes. These actions can be combined in any order in the *InputData* list.

Quick Facts

Table 5.46: LCDIN Quick Facts.

	BS2p, BS2pe, and BS2px		
Values for *Pin*	0, 1, 8 or 9		
I/O Pin Arrangement when *Pin* is 0 or 1	0 or 1 (depending on pin): LCD Enable (E) pin 2: LCD Read/Write (R/W) pin 3: LCD Register Select (RS) pin 4 – 7: LCD Data Buss (DB4 – DB7, respectively) pins		
I/O Pin Arrangement when *Pin* is 8 or 9	8 or 9 (depending on pin): LCD Enable (E) pin 10: LCD Read/Write (R/W) pin 11: LCD Register Select (RS) pin 12 – 15: LCD Data Buss (DB4 – DB7, respectively) pins		
Special Notes	LCDIN is designed to use the LCD's 4-bit mode only.		
Related Commands	LCDCMD and LCDOUT		

LCDIN – BASIC Stamp Command Reference

Explanation

The three LCD commands (LCDCMD, LCDIN and LCDOUT) allow the BS2p, BS2pe, and BS2px to interface directly to standard LCD displays that feature a Hitachi 44780 controller (part #HD44780A). This includes many 1 x 16, 2 x 16 and 4 x 20 character LCD displays.

NOTE: LCDCMD, LCDIN and LCDOUT use a 4-bit interface to the LCD which requires a specific initialization sequence before LCDIN and LCDOUT can be used; read more below.

The LCDIN command is used to send one instruction and then receive at least one data byte from the LCD's Character Generator RAM or Display Data RAM. The following is an example of the LCDIN command:

A SIMPLE LCDIN EXAMPLE.

```
char     VAR   Byte
LCDIN  0, 128, [char]
```

The above code will read the character value at location 0 of the DDRAM. See the "Character Positioning" section, of the LCDCMD command description on page 252 for more information.

The LCDIN command actually uses more than just the I/O pin specified by the *Pin* argument. The LCDIN command requires seven I/O pins. This is because the standard LCD displays have a parallel interface, rather than a serial one. The *Pin* argument can be the numbers 0, 1, 8 or 9 and will result in the use of the I/O pins shown in Table 5.46. Please refer to the LCDCMD command description for information on page properly wiring the LCD display.

TWO VERY IMPORTANT STEPS:
1) WIRING THE BASIC STAMP TO AN LCD.
2) INITIALIZING THE LCD.

When the LCD is first powered-up, it defaults to an 8-bit interface and must be properly configured for a 4-bit buss before sending commands like the one shown above. This process is known as initializing the LCD and is the first thing your program should do upon starting up. Please refer to the LCDCMD command description for information on properly initializing the LCD display.

The LCDIN command's *InputData* argument is similar to the SERIN command's *InputData* argument. This means data can be received as ASCII character values, decimal, hexadecimal and binary translations and string data as in the examples below (assume the LCD display has "Value: 3A:101" starting at the first character of the first line on the screen).

RECEIVING FORMATTED DATA.

Page 258 • *BASIC Stamp Syntax and Reference Manual 2.2* • *www.parallax.com*

```
value      VAR  Byte(13)
LCDIN  0, 128, [value]                    'receive the ASCII value for "V"
LCDIN  0, 128, [DEC  value]               'receive the number 3.
LCDIN  0, 128, [HEX  value]               'receive the number $3A.
LCDIN  0, 128, [BIN  value]               'receive the number %101.
LCDIN  0, 128, [STR value\13]             'receive the string "Value: 3A:101"
```

Table 5.47 and Table 5.48 list all the special formatters and conversion formatters available to the LCDIN command. See the SERIN command for additional information and examples of their use.

Some possible uses of the LCDIN command are 1) in combination with the LCDOUT command to store and read data from the unused DDRAM or CGRAM locations (as extra variable space), 2) to verify that the data from a previous LCDOUT command was received and processed properly by the LCD, and 3) to read character data from CGRAM for the purposes of modifying it and storing it as a custom character.

Table 5.47: LCDIN Special Formatters.

Special Formatter	Action
SPSTR L	Input a character string of length L bytes (up to 126) into Scratch Pad RAM, starting at location 0. Use GET to retrieve the characters.
STR *ByteArray* \L {\E}	Input a character string of length L into an array. If specified, an end character E causes the string input to end before reaching length L. Remaining bytes are filled with 0s (zeros).
WAIT (*Value*)	Wait for a sequence of bytes specified by value. Value can be numbers separated by commas or quoted text (ex: 65, 66, 67 or "ABC"). The WAIT formatter is limited to a maximum of six characters.
WAITSTR *ByteArray* {\L}	Wait for a sequence of bytes matching a string stored in an array variable, optionally limited to L characters. If the optional L argument is left off, the end of the array-string must be marked by a byte containing a zero (0).
SKIP *Length*	Ignore *Length* bytes of characters.

Conversion Formatter	Type of Number	Numeric Characters Accepted	Notes
DEC{1..5}	Decimal, optionally limited to 1 – 5 digits	0 through 9	1
SDEC{1..5}	Signed decimal, optionally limited to 1 – 5 digits	-, 0 through 9	1,2
HEX{1..4}	Hexadecimal, optionally limited to 1 – 4 digits	0 through 9, A through F	1,3,5
SHEX{1..4}	Signed hexadecimal, optionally limited to 1 – 4 digits	-, 0 through 9, A through F	1,2,3
IHEX{1..4}	Indicated hexadecimal, optionally limited to 1 – 4 digits	$, 0 through 9, A through F	1,3,4
ISHEX{1..4}	Signed, indicated hexadecimal, optionally limited to 1 – 4 digits	-, $, 0 through 9, A through F	1,2,3,4
BIN{1..16}	Binary, optionally limited to 1 – 16 digits	0, 1	1
SBIN{1..16}	Signed binary, optionally limited to 1 – 16 digits	-, 0, 1	1,2
IBIN{1..16}	Indicated binary, optionally limited to 1 – 16 digits	%, 0, 1	1,4
ISBIN{1..16}	Signed, indicated binary, optionally limited to 1 – 16 digits	-, %, 0, 1	1,2,4
NUM	Generic numeric input (decimal, hexadecimal or binary); hexadecimal or binary number must be indicated	$, %, 0 through 9, A through F	1, 3, 4
SNUM	Similar to NUM with value treated as signed with range -32768 to +32767	-, $, %, 0 through 9, A through F	1,2,3,4

Table 5.48: LCDIN Conversion Formatters

1 All numeric conversions will continue to accept new data until receiving either the specified number of digits (ex: three digits for DEC3) or a non-numeric character.
2 To be recognized as part of a number, the minus sign (-) must immediately precede a numeric character. The minus sign character occurring in non-numeric text is ignored and any character (including a space) between a minus and a number causes the minus to be ignored.
3 The hexadecimal formatters are not case-sensitive; "a" through "f" means the same as "A" through "F".
4 Indicated hexadecimal and binary formatters ignore all characters, even valid numerics, until they receive the appropriate prefix ($ for hexadecimal, % for binary). The indicated formatters can differentiate between text and hexadecimal (ex: ABC would be interpreted by HEX as a number but IHEX would ignore it unless expressed as $ABC). Likewise, the binary version can distinguish the decimal number 10 from the binary number %10. A prefix occurring in non-numeric text is ignored, and any character (including a space) between a prefix and a number causes the prefix to be ignored. Indicated, signed formatters require that the minus sign come before the prefix, as in -$1B45.
5 The HEX modifier can be used for Decimal to BCD Conversion. See "Hex to BCD Conversion" on page 97.

For examples of all conversion formatters and how they process incoming data see Appendix C.

NOTE: This example program can be used with the BS2p, BS2pe, and BS2px. This program uses conditional compilation techniques; see Chapter 3 for more information.

Demo Program (LCDIN.bsp)

```
' LCDIN.bsp
' This program demonstrates initialization, printing and reading
' from a 2 x 16 character LCD display.

' {$STAMP BS2p}
' {$PBASIC 2.5}

#IF ($STAMP < BS2P) #THEN
  #ERROR "Program requires BS2p, BS2pe or BS2px."
#ENDIF

Lcd            PIN     0

LcdCls         CON     $01      ' clear the LCD
LcdHome        CON     $02      ' move cursor home
LcdCrsrL       CON     $10      ' move cursor left
LcdCrsrR       CON     $14      ' move cursor right
LcdDispL       CON     $18      ' shift chars left
LcdDispR       CON     $1C      ' shift chars right
LcdDDRam       CON     $80      ' Display Data RAM
LcdCGRam       CON     $40      ' Character Generator RAM
LcdLine1       CON     $80      ' DDRAM address of line 1
LcdLine2       CON     $C0      ' DDRAM address of line 2

char           VAR     Byte(16)

Init_LCD:
  PAUSE 1000                    ' allow LCD to self-initialize first
  LCDCMD Lcd, %00110000         ' send wakeup sequence to LCD
  PAUSE 5                       ' pause required by LCD specs
  LCDCMD Lcd, %00110000
  PAUSE 0                       ' pause required by LCD specs
  LCDCMD Lcd, %00110000
  PAUSE 0                       ' pause required by LCD specs
  LCDCMD Lcd, %00100000         ' set data bus to 4-bit mode
  LCDCMD Lcd, %00101000         ' set to 2-line mode with 5x8 font
  LCDCMD Lcd, %00001100         ' display on without cursor
  LCDCMD Lcd, %00000110         ' auto-increment cursor

Main:
  DO
    LCDOUT Lcd, LcdCls, ["Hello!"]
    GOSUB Read_LCD_Screen
    PAUSE 3000
    LCDOUT Lcd, LcdCls, ["I'm a 2x16 LCD!"]
    GOSUB Read_LCD_Screen
    PAUSE 3000
  LOOP
```

```
Read_LCD_Screen:
  DEBUG "LCD now says: "
  LCDIN Lcd, LcdLine1, [STR char\16]
  DEBUG STR char\16, CR
  RETURN
```

LCDOUT

| BS1 | BS2 | BS2e | BS2sx | BS2p | BS2pe | BS2px |

LCDOUT *Pin, Command,* **[** *OutputData* **]**

Function

Send data to an LCD display.

- **Pin** is a variable/constant/expression (0 – 1 or 8 – 9) that specifies which I/O pins to use. The LCD requires, at most, seven I/O pins to operate. The *Pin* argument serves a double purpose; specifying the first pin and, indirectly, the group of other required pins. See explanation below. All I/O pins will be set to output mode.

- **Command** is a variable/constant/expression (0 – 255) indicating an LCD command to send.

- **OutputData** is a list of variables, constants, expressions and formatters that tells LCDOUT how to format outgoing data. LCDOUT can transmit individual or repeating bytes, convert values into decimal, hex or binary text representations, or transmit strings of bytes from variable arrays. These actions can be combined in any order in the *OutputData* list.

Quick Facts

Table 5.49: LCDOUT Quick Facts.

	BS2p, BS2pe, and BS2px
Values for *Pin*	0, 1, 8 or 9
I/O Pin Arrangement when *Pin* is 0 or 1	0 or 1 (depending on pin): LCD Enable (E) pin 2: LCD Read/Write (R/W) pin 3: LCD Register Select (RS) pin 4 – 7: LCD Data Buss (DB4 – DB7, respectively) pins
I/O Pin Arrangement when *Pin* is 8 or 9	8 or 9 (depending on pin): LCD Enable (E) pin 10: LCD Read/Write (R/W) pin 11: LCD Register Select (RS) pin 12 – 15: LCD Data Buss (DB4 – DB7, respectively) pins
Special Notes	LCDOUT is designed to use the LCD's 4-bit mode only.
Related Commands	LCDCMD and LCDIN

Explanation

NOTE: LCDCMD, LCDIN and LCDOUT use a 4-bit interface to the LCD which requires a specific initialization sequence before LCDIN and LCDOUT can be used; read more below.

The three LCD commands (LCDCMD, LCDIN and LCDOUT) allow the BS2p, BS2pe, and BS2px to interface directly to standard LCD displays that feature a Hitachi 44780 controller (part #HD44780A). This includes many 1 x 16, 2 x 16 and 4 x 20 character LCD displays.

LCDOUT – BASIC Stamp Command Reference

The LCDOUT command is used to send one instruction followed by at least one data byte to the LCD. The data that is output is written to the LCD's Character Generator RAM or Display Data RAM. The following is an example of the LCDOUT command: A SIMPLE LCDOUT EXAMPLE.

```
LCDOUT  0, 1, ["Hello World!"]
```

The above code will clear the LCD screen and then send "Hello World!" to the screen. The first argument (0) is the starting I/O pin number and the second argument (1) is the LCD's instruction for Clear Screen.

The LCDOUT command actually uses more than just the I/O pin specified by the *Pin* argument. The LCDOUT command requires seven I/O pins. This is because the standard LCD displays have a parallel interface, rather than a serial one. The *Pin* argument can be the numbers 0, 1, 8 or 9 and will result in the use of the I/O pins shown in Table 5.49. Please refer to the LCDCMD command description for information on properly wiring the LCD display. TWO VERY IMPORTANT STEPS: 1) WIRING THE BASIC STAMP TO AN LCD. 2) INITIALIZING THE LCD.

When the LCD is first powered-up, it defaults to an 8-bit interface and must be properly configured for a 4-bit buss before sending commands like the one shown above. This process is known as initializing the LCD and is the first thing your program should do upon starting up. Please refer to the LCDCMD command description for information on properly initializing the LCD display.

The LCDOUT command's *OutputData* argument is exactly like that of the DEBUG and SEROUT command's *OutputData* argument. This means data can be sent as literal text, ASCII character values, repetitive values, decimal, hexadecimal and binary translations and string data as in the examples below. SENDING AND FORMATTING DATA.

```
value   VAR    Byte

value = 65

LCDOUT 0, 0, [value]            ' send "A"
LCDOUT 0, 0, [REP value\5]      ' send "AAAAA"
LCDOUT 0, 0, [DEC value]        ' send "6" and "5"
LCDOUT 0, 0, [HEX value]        ' send "4" and "1"
LCDOUT 0, 0, [BIN value]        ' send "1000001"
```

Table 5.50 and Table 5.51 list all the available conversion formatters and special formatters available to the LCDOUT command. See the DEBUG and SEROUT commands for additional information and examples of their use.

Table 5.50: LCDOUT Conversion Formatters.

Conversion Formatter	Type of Number	Notes
DEC{1..5}	Decimal, optionally fixed to 1 – 5 digits	1
SDEC{1..5}	Signed decimal, optionally fixed to 1 – 5 digits	1,2
HEX{1..4}	Hexadecimal, optionally fixed to 1 – 4 digits	1,3
SHEX{1..4}	Signed hexadecimal, optionally fixed to 1 – 4 digits	1,2
IHEX{1..4}	Indicated hexadecimal, optionally fixed to 1 – 4 digits ($ prefix)	1
ISHEX{1..4}	Signed, indicated hexadecimal, optionally fixed to 1 – 4 digits ($ prefix)	1,2
BIN{1..16}	Binary, optionally fixed to 1 – 16 digits	1
SBIN{1..16}	Signed binary, optionally fixed to 1 – 16 digits	1,2
IBIN{1..16}	Indicated binary, optionally fixed to 1 – 16 digits (% prefix)	1
ISBIN{1..16}	Signed, indicated binary, optionally fixed to 1 – 16 digits (% prefix)	1,2

1 Fixed-digit formatters like DEC4 will pad the number with leading 0s if necessary; ex: DEC4 65 sends 0065. If a number is larger than the specified number of digits, the leading digits will be dropped; ex: DEC4 56422 sends 6422.
2 Signed modifiers work under two's complement rules.
3 The HEX modifier can be used for BCD to Decimal Conversion. See "Hex to BCD Conversion" on page 97.

Table 5.51: LCDOUT Special Formatters.

Special Formatter	Action
?	Displays "symbol = x' + carriage return; where x is a number. Default format is decimal, but may be combined with conversion formatters (ex: BIN ? x to display "x = binary_number").
ASC ?	Displays "symbol = 'x'" + carriage return; where x is an ASCII character.
STR ByteArray {\L}	Send character string from an array. The optional \L argument can be used to limit the output to L characters, otherwise, characters will be sent up to the first byte equal to 0 or the end of RAM space is reached.
REP Byte \L	Send a string consisting of Byte repeated L times (ex: REP "X"\10 sends "XXXXXXXXXX").

USING THE *COMMAND* ARGUMENT.

The *Command* argument is useful for proceeding a set of data with a special LCD instruction. For example, the code below will move the cursor to location 64 (the first character on the second line) and print "Hi":

```
LCDOUT  0, 128 + 64, ["Hi"]
```

The next example, below, will turn on the blinking block cursor and print "Yo!":

LCDOUT – BASIC Stamp Command Reference

```
LCDOUT 0, 13, ["Yo!"]
```

Most of the time, you will want to send data without preceding it with a command. To do this, simply use 0 for the *Command* argument, as in:

```
LCDOUT 0, 0, ["Hello there!"]
```

Another use for the LCDOUT command is to access and create custom characters. The Hitachi 44780 controller has a built-in character set that is similar to the ASCII character set (at least for the first 128 characters). Most of these characters are stored in ROM and are not changeable, however, the first eight characters (ASCII 0 though 7) are programmable.

CREATING CUSTOM CHARACTERS.

Each of the programmable characters is five pixels wide and eight pixels tall. It takes eight bytes to describe each character; one byte per row (the left-most three bits are ignored). For example, the character at ASCII location 0 is defined by the bit patterns stored in bytes 0 through 7 of Character Generator RAM (CGRAM). The character at ASCII location 1 is defined by the bit patterns stored in bytes 8 through 15 of CGRAM, and so on.

To create a custom character, use some graph paper to plot out the bit pattern (on and off pixels) in a 5 x 8 pattern, as shown in Figure 5.16. Then calculate the corresponding binary value of the bit pattern for each of the eight rows of character data.

Character Cell Structure and Data

Figure 5.16: LCD Character Structure.

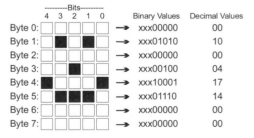

After the data is calculated for each character (8 byte values per character), use the LCDOUT command with the "Move To CGRAM Address" instruction to insert the data into the character's CGRAM locations. For example, the code below will store the character shown in Figure 5.16 into character 0's CGRAM data locations. Then it will place the cursor back on the display (DDRAM) and print the character on the screen.

```
LCDOUT  0,  64+0, [00, 10, 00, 04, 17, 14, 00, 00]
LCDOUT  0, 128+0, ["Custom Char: ", 0]
```

The number 64 in the *Command* argument is the LCD's "Move to CGRAM Address" instruction and the 0 that is added to it is the location of the first row of data for the character 0. The LCDOUT command will write the first *OutputData* value (00) to this location, the second *OutputData* value (10) to location 1, etc. If we wanted this custom character to affect character 1, instead of 0, we'd have to adjust the value of the "Move To..." command, i.e.: 64+8. To affect character 2, we'd use 64+16.

To try the example above, don't forget to execute the LCD initialization code (shown in the LCDCMD description) first and never forget to move the cursor back to the screen (as with the last command, above) when you're done writing the character data to CGRAM.

Demo Program (LCDOUT.bsp)

NOTE: This example program can be used with the BS2p, BS2pe, and BS2px. This program uses conditional compilation techniques; see Chapter 3 for more information.

```
' LCDOUT.bsp
' This program demonstrates initialization and printing on a 2x16
' character LCD display.

' {$STAMP BS2p}
' {$PBASIC 2.5}

#IF ($STAMP < BS2P) #THEN
  #ERROR "Program requires BS2p, BS2pe or BS2px."
#ENDIF

Lcd           PIN     0

LcdCls        CON     $01     ' clear the LCD
LcdHome       CON     $02     ' move cursor home
LcdCrsrL      CON     $10     ' move cursor left
LcdCrsrR      CON     $14     ' move cursor right
LcdDispL      CON     $18     ' shift chars left
LcdDispR      CON     $1C     ' shift chars right
LcdDDRam      CON     $80     ' Display Data RAM
LcdCGRam      CON     $40     ' Character Generator RAM
LcdLine1      CON     $80     ' DDRAM address of line 1
LcdLine2      CON     $C0     ' DDRAM address of line 2


Init_LCD:
  PAUSE 1000                  ' allow LCD to self-initialize first
```

```
LCDCMD Lcd, %00110000          ' send wakeup sequence to LCD
PAUSE 5                        ' pause required by LCD specs
LCDCMD Lcd, %00110000
PAUSE 0                        ' pause required by LCD specs
LCDCMD Lcd, %00110000
PAUSE 0                        ' pause required by LCD specs
LCDCMD Lcd, %00100000          ' set data bus to 4-bit mode
LCDCMD Lcd, %00101000          ' set to 2-line mode with 5x8 font
LCDCMD Lcd, %00001100          ' display on without cursor
LCDCMD Lcd, %00000110          ' auto-increment cursor

LCDOUT Lcd, LcdCGRam,          ' load custom character map
       [$00, $0A, $0A, $00, $11, $0E, $06, $00]

Main:
  DO
    LCDOUT Lcd, LcdCls, ["Hello my friend."]
    PAUSE 750
    LCDOUT Lcd, LcdLine2, ["How are you?"]
    PAUSE 1500
    LCDCMD Lcd, LcdCls
    LCDOUT Lcd, LcdLine1 + 1, ["I'm doing just"]
    LCDOUT Lcd, LcdLine2 + 4, ["fine!  ", 0]
    PAUSE 2000
  LOOP
  END
```

LET

BS1	BS2	BS2e	BS2sx	BS2p	BS2pe	BS2px

1 **{ LET }** *Variable* **=** *Value*

Function

Sets *Variable* equal to the value of *Value*.

- *Value* is a variable/constant/expression. (0-65535).

- *Variable* is a variable which will be set equal to *Value*.

Explanation

LET is an optional instruction for the BASIC Stamp 1 that can be used with variable assignment statements, such as A = 5 and B = A + 2, etc. This instruction is not required and only exists on the BASIC Stamp 1. LET was a commonly used command in early forms of BASIC, and was originally included in the BS1 command set to accommodate programmers from that generation. Parallax recommends that all new BASIC Stamp 1 programs use assignment statements without the LET command.

1 **Demo Program (LET.bs1)**

```
' LET.bs1
' This example demonstrates the use of LET in assignment statements, which
' is optional and not recommended.  Note that the Lunchtime and
' Dinnertime routines do essentially the same thing, but the Dinnertime
' method is recommended(even though the pricing scheme is not!)

' {$PBASIC 1.0}
' {$STAMP BS1}

SYMBOL salad    = B1
SYMBOL bread    = B2
SYMBOL soup     = B3
SYMBOL lunch    = B4
SYMBOL dinner   = B5

Lunchtime:
  LET salad     = 3
  LET bread     = 1
  LET soup      = 4
  LUNCH = salad + bread + soup
  DEBUG "lunch = $", #lunch, "plus local tax.", CR

Dinnertime:
  salad    = 4
  bread    = 2
  soup     = 5
```

```
dinner = salad + bread + soup
DEBUG "Dinner = $",# lunch, "plus local tax.", CR
```

LOOKDOWN

BS1	BS2	BS2e	BS2sx	BS2p	BS2pe	BS2px

 1   **LOOKDOWN** *Target,* (*Value0, Value1, ...ValueN*), *Variable*

All **2**   **LOOKDOWN** *Target,* { *ComparisonOp* } [*Value0, Value1, ...ValueN*], *Variable*

Function

Compare *Target* value to a list of values and store the index number of the first value that matches into *Variable*. If no value in the list matches, *Variable* is left unaffected. On all BS2 models, the optional *ComparisonOp* is used as criteria for the match; the default criteria is "equal to."

1

NOTE: Expressions are not allowed as arguments on the BS1.

- **Target** is a variable/constant/expression (0 – 65535) to be compared to the values in the list.

All **2**

- **ComparisonOp** is an optional comparison operator (as described in Table 5.53) to be used as the criteria when comparing values. When no *ComparisonOp* is specified, equal to (=) is assumed. This argument is not available on the BS1.

- **Values** are variables/constants/expressions (0 – 65535) to be compared to *Target*.

- **Variable** is a variable (usually a byte) that will be set to the index (0 – 255) of the matching value in the *Values* list. If no matching value is found, *Variable* is left unaffected.

Quick Facts

Table 5.52: LOOKDOWN Quick Facts.

	BS1 and all BS2 Models
Limit of *Value* Entries	256
Starting Index Number	0
If value list contains no match...	Variable is left unaffected
Related Command	LOOKUP

Explanation

LOOKDOWN works like the index in a book. In an index, you search for a topic and get the page number. LOOKDOWN searches for a target value in a list, and stores the index number of the first match in a variable. For example:

```
SYMBOL     value   =   B0
SYMBOL     result  =   B1
value   =  17
result  =  15

LOOKDOWN  value, (26, 177, 13, 1, 0, 17, 99), result
DEBUG  "Value matches item ", #result, "in list"
```

-- or --

```
value      VAR   Byte
result     VAR   Nib
value   =  17
result  =  15

LOOKDOWN  value, [26, 177, 13, 1, 0, 17, 99], result
DEBUG  "Value matches item ", DEC  result, " in list"
```

DEBUG prints, "Value matches item 5 in list" because the value (17) matches item 5 of [26, 177, 13, 1, 0, 17, 99]. Note that index numbers count up from 0, not 1; that is, in this list, 26 is item 0.

THE INDEX NUMBER OF THE FIRST ITEM IS 0, NOT 1.

What happens if the value doesn't match any of the items in the list? Try changing "Value = 17" to "Value = 2." Since 2 is not on the list, LOOKDOWN leaves *result* unaffected. Since *result* contained 15 before LOOKDOWN executed, DEBUG prints "Value matches item 15 in list." By strategically setting the initial value of *result*, as we have here, your program can be written to detect when an item was not found in the list.

Don't forget that text phrases are just lists of byte values, so they too are eligible for LOOKDOWN searches, as in this example:

USING TEXT IN THE VALUE LIST.

```
SYMBOL     value =    B0
SYMBOL     result=    B1

value   =  "f"
result  =  255

LOOKDOWN  value, ("The quick brown fox"), result
DEBUG  "Value matches item ", #result, "in list"
```

-- or --

```
All 2   value    VAR    Byte
        result   VAR    Nib

        value   =  "f"
        result  =  255

LOOKDOWN  value, ["The quick brown fox"], result
DEBUG  "Value matches item ", DEC  result, " in list"
```

DEBUG prints, "Value matches item 16 in list" because the character at index item 16 is "f" in the phrase, "The quick brown fox".

LOOKDOWN CAN USE VARIABLES AND EXPRESSIONS IN THE VALUE LIST.

The examples above show LOOKDOWN working with lists of constants, but it also works with variables and expressions also. Note, however, that expressions are not allowed as argument on the BS1.

USING LOOKDOWN'S COMPARISON OPERATORS.

All 2

On all BS2 models, the LOOKDOWN command can also use another criteria (other than "equal to") for its list. All of the examples above use LOOKDOWN's default comparison operator, =, that searches for an exact match. The entire list of *ComaprisonOps* is shown in Table 5.53. The "greater than" comparison operator (>) is used in the following example:

```
value    VAR    Byte
result   VAR    Nib

value   =  17
result  =  15

LOOKDOWN  value, >[26, 177, 13, 1, 0, 17, 99], result
DEBUG  "Value greater than item ", DEC  result, " in list"
```

DEBUG prints, "Value greater than item 2 in list" because the first item the value 17 is greater than is 13 (which is item 2 in the list). *Value* is also greater than items 3 and 4, but these are ignored, because LOOKDOWN only cares about the first item that matches the criteria. This can require a certain amount of planning in devising the order of the list. See the demo program below.

WATCH OUT FOR UNSIGNED MATH ERRORS WHEN USING THE COMPARISON OPERATORS.

LOOKDOWN comparison operators (Table 5.53) use unsigned 16-bit math. They will not work correctly with signed numbers, which are represented internally as two's complement (large 16-bit integers). For example, the two's complement representation of -99 is 65437. So although -99 is certainly less than 0, it would appear to be larger than zero to the LOOKDOWN comparison operators. The bottom line is: Don't used signed numbers with LOOKDOWN comparisons.

ComparisonOp Symbol	Description
=	Find the first value Target is equal to
<>	Find the first value Target is not equal to
>	Find the first value Target is greater than
<	Find the first value Target is less than
>=	Find the first value Target is greater than or equal to
<=	Find the first value Target is less than or equal to

Table 5.53: LOOKDOWN Comparison Operators.

A common application for LOOKDOWN is to use it in conjunction with the BRANCH, ON...GOTO, or ON...GOSUB commands to create selective jumps based on a simple variable input:

USING LOOKDOWN WITH BRANCH, ON...GOTO OR ON...GOSUB TO JUMP BASED ON VALUES.

All 2

```
' {$PBASIC 2.5}

cmd       VAR       Byte

DO
  DEBUG CLS, "Enter cmd (SLMH): "
  DEBUGIN cmd
  LOOKDOWN cmd, ["SLMH"], cmd
  ON cmd GOSUB _Stop, _Low, _Medium, _High
  IF cmd > 3 THEN DEBUG CLS, "Command not in list"
  PAUSE 2000
  END
LOOP

_Stop:
  DEBUG CLS, "Stop"
  RETURN

_Low:
  DEBUG CLS, "Low"
  RETURN

_Medium:
  DEBUG CLS, "Medium"
  RETURN

_High:
  DEBUG CLS, "High"
  RETURN
```

In this example, the program waits for a key. Here's what happens when "M" is pressed and *cmd* contains "M" (ASCII 77). LOOKDOWN finds that this is item 2 of a list of one-character commands and stores 2 into *cmd*. ON...GOSUB then goes to item 2 of its list, which is the program label

"_Medium" at which point DEBUG prints "Medium" on the PC screen then returns to the main loop. This is a powerful method for interpreting user input, and a lot neater than the alternative IF...THEN instructions.

USING LOOKDOWN WITH LOOKUP TO "MAP" NON-CONTIGUOUS SETS OF NUMBERS.

Another great use of LOOKDOWN is in combination with LOOKUP to "map" non-contiguous sets of numbers together. For example, you may have an application where certain numbers are received by the BASIC Stamp and, in response, the BASIC Stamp needs to send a specific set of numbers. This may be easy to code if the numbers are contiguous, or follow some known algebraic equations... but what if they don't? The table below shows some sample, non-contiguous inputs and the corresponding outputs the BASIC Stamp needs to respond with:

Table 5.54: Non-Contiguous Number Example.

Each of these values received (inputs):	Needs to result in each of these values sent (outputs):
5	16
14	17
1	18
43	24
26	10
22	12
30	11

So, if we receive the number 5, we need to output 16. If we received 43, we need to output 24, and so on. These numbers are not contiguous and they don't appear to be derived from any simple algorithm. We can solve this problem with two lines of code, as follows:

```
LOOKDOWN  value, [5, 14, 1, 43, 26, 22, 30], value
LOOKUP  value, [16, 17, 18, 24, 10, 12, 11], value
```

Assuming our received number is in *value*, the first line (LOOKDOWN) will find the value in the list and store the index of the location that matches back into *value*. (This step "maps" the non-contiguous numbers: 5, 14, 1, etc, to a contiguous set of numbers: 0, 1, 2, etc). The second line (LOOKUP) takes our new *value*, finds the number at that location and stores it back into *value*. If the received value was 14, LOOKDOWN stores 1 into *value* and LOOKUP looks at the value at location 1 and stores 17 in *value*. The number 43 gets mapped to 3, 3 gets mapped to 24, and so on. This is a quick and easy fix for a potentially messy problem!

Demo Program (LOOKDOWN.bs1)

```
' LOOKDOWN.bs1
' This program uses LOOKDOWN followed by LOOKUP to map the numbers:
' 0, 10, 50, 64, 71 and 98 to 35, 40, 58, 62, 79, and 83,
' respectively. All other numbers are mapped to 255.

' {$STAMP BS1}
' {$PBASIC 1.0}

SYMBOL   num     = W0                  ' holds current number
SYMBOL   result  = W1                  ' holds mapped result

Main:
  FOR num = 0 TO 100
    result = 255                       ' default value for no match
    LOOKDOWN num, (0, 10, 50, 64, 71, 98), result
    LOOKUP result, (35, 40, 58, 62, 79, 83), result
    DEBUG "Num = ", #num, "Result = ", #result, CR
    PAUSE 100
  NEXT
  END
```

Demo Program (LOOKDOWN.bs2)

```
' LOOKDOWN.bs2
' This program uses LOOKDOWN to determine the number of decimal
' digits in a number. Since LOOKDOWN uses a zero-indexed table, the
' output will be the number of digits minus one, so this gets
' corrected in the following line.  Note that zero is considered a
' valid number and has one digit.

' {$STAMP BS2}
' {$PBASIC 2.5}

aNum            VAR     Word            ' the number to study
stpSz           VAR     Word            ' FOR-NEXT step size
numDig          VAR     Nib             ' digits in aNum

Setup:
stpSz = 2

Main:
  FOR aNum = 0 TO 15000 STEP stpSz
    LOOKDOWN aNum, <[0, 10, 100, 1000, 10000, 65535], numDig
    ' right-justify output
    DEBUG "aNum = ", REP " "\(5-numDig), DEC aNum, TAB,
        "Digits = ", DEC numDig, CR
    PAUSE 250
    LOOKDOWN aNum, <[0, 10, 100, 1000, 10000, 65535], stpSz
    LOOKUP stpSz, [2, 2, 5, 25, 250, 500, 1000], stpSz
  NEXT
  END
```

All 2

NOTE: This example program can be used with all BS2 models by changing the $STAMP directive accordingly.

LOOKUP

BS1	BS2	BS2e	BS2sx	BS2p	BS2pe	BS2px

1 **LOOKUP** *Index,* **(** *Value0, Value1, ...ValueN* **),** *Variable*

All 2 **LOOKUP** *Index,* **[** *Value0, Value1, ...ValueN* **],** *Variable*

Function

1

NOTE: Expressions are not allowed as arguments on the BS1.

Find the value at location *Index* and store it in *Variable*. If *Index* exceeds the highest index value of the items in the list, *Variable* is left unaffected.

- **Index** is a variable/constant/expression (0 – 255) indicating the list item to retrieve.

- **Values** are variables/constants/expressions (0 – 65535).

- **Variable** is a variable that will be set to the value at the *Index* location. If *Index* exceeds the highest location number, *Variable* is left unaffected.

Quick Facts

Table 5.55: LOOKUP Quick Facts.

	BS1 and all BS2 Models
Limit of Value Entries	256
Starting Index Number	0
If index exceeds the highest location...	Variable is left unaffected
Related Command	LOOKDOWN

Explanation

LOOKUP retrieves an item from a list based on the item's position, *Index*, in the list. For example:

1
```
SYMBOL   index   = B2
SYMBOL   result  = B3

index = 3
result = 255

LOOKUP index, (26, 177, 13, 1, 0, 17, 99), result
DEBUG  "Item ", #index, "is: ", #result

-- or --
```

```
index    VAR    Byte
result   VAR    Byte

index = 3
result = 255

LOOKUP index, [26, 177, 13, 1, 0, 17, 99], result
DEBUG  "Item ", DEC index, " is: ", DEC result
```

All 2

In this example, DEBUG prints "Item 3 is: 1." Note that the first location number is 0. In the list above, item 0 is 26, item 1 is 177, etc.

THE INDEX NUMBER OF THE FIRST ITEM IS 0, NOT 1.

If *index* is beyond the end of the list, the result variable is unchanged. In the example above, if *index* were greater than 6, the message would have reported the result to be 255, because that's what *result* contained before LOOKUP executed.

Don't forget that text phrases are just lists of byte values, so they too are eligible for LOOKUP searches, as in this example:

USING TEXT IN THE VALUE LIST.

```
SYMBOL  index   = B2
SYMBOL  result  = B3

index  = 16
result = " "

LOOKUP index, ("The quick brown fox"), result
DEBUG @result
```

1

-- or --

```
index    VAR    Byte
result   VAR    Byte

index  = 16
result = " "

LOOKUP index, ["The quick brown fox"], result
DEBUG ASC ? result
```

All 2

DEBUG prints, "Result = 'f' " because the character at index item 16 is "f" in the phrase, "The quick brown fox".

The examples above show LOOKUP working with lists of constants, but it also works with variables and expressions also. Note, however, that expressions are not allowed as argument on the BS1.

LOOKUP CAN USE VARIABLES AND EXPRESSIONS IN THE VALUE LIST.

USING LOOKUP WITH LOOKDOWN TO "MAP" NON-CONTIGUOUS SETS OF NUMBERS.

A great use of LOOKUP is in combination with LOOKDOWN to "map" non-contiguous sets of numbers together. For example, you may have an application where certain numbers are received by the BASIC Stamp and, in response, the BASIC Stamp needs to send a specific set of numbers. This may be easy to code if the numbers are contiguous, or follow some known algebraic equations... but what if they don't? The table below shows some sample, non-contiguous inputs and the corresponding outputs the BASIC Stamp needs to respond with:

Table 5.56: Non-Contiguous Number Example.

Each of these values received (inputs):	Needs to result in each of these values sent (outputs):
5	16
14	17
1	18
43	24
26	10
22	12
30	11

So, if we receive the number 5, we need to output 16. If we received 43, we need to output 24, and so on. These numbers are not contiguous and they don't appear to be derived from any simple algorithm. We can solve this problem with two lines of code, as follows:

```
LOOKDOWN value, [5, 14, 1, 43, 26, 22, 30], value
LOOKUP value, [16, 17, 18, 24, 10, 12, 11], value
```

Assuming our received number is in *value*, the first line (LOOKDOWN) will find the value in the list and store the index of the location that matches back into *value*. (This step "maps" the non-contiguous numbers: 5, 14, 1, etc, to a contiguous set of numbers: 0, 1, 2, etc). The second line (LOOKUP) takes our new *value*, finds the number at that location and stores it back into *value*. If the received value was 14, LOOKDOWN stores 1 into *value* and LOOKUP looks at the value at location 1 and stores 17 in *value*. The number 43 gets mapped to 3, 3 gets mapped to 24, and so on. This is a quick and easy fix for a potentially messy problem!

Demo Program (LOOKUP.bs1)

```
' LOOKUP.bs1
' This program uses Lookup to create a Debug-window animation of a spinning
' propeller.  The animation consists of the four ASCII characters | / - \
' which, when printed rapidly in order at a fixed location, appear to spin.
' A little imagination helps a lot here....
```

```
' {$STAMP BS1}
' {$PBASIC 1.0}

SYMBOL   idx             = B2
SYMBOL   frame           = B3


Spinner:
  LOOKUP idx, ("|/-\"), frame        ' lookup current frame character
  DEBUG CLS, "Spinner: ", #@frame    ' display
  idx = idx + 1 // 4                 ' update frame index (0..3)
  GOTO Spinner                       ' loop forever
  END
```

Demo Program (LOOKUP.bs2)

All 2

```
' LOOKUP.bs2
' This program uses LOOKUP to create a Debug-window animation of a spinning
' propeller.  The animation consists of the four ASCII characters | / - \
' which, when printed rapidly in order at a fixed location, appear to spin.
' A little imagination helps a lot here....

' {$STAMP BS2}
' {$PBASIC 2.5}

idx             VAR    Nib
frame           VAR    Byte


Spinner:
  DO
    LOOKUP idx, ["|/-\"], frame       ' lookup current frame character
    DEBUG HOME, "Spinner: ", frame    ' display
    PAUSE 150                         ' pause between frames
    idx = idx + 1 // 4                ' update frame index (0..3)
  LOOP                                ' loop forever
  END
```

NOTE: This example program can be used with all BS2 models by changing the $STAMP directive accordingly.

LOW

BS1	BS2	BS2e	BS2sx	BS2p	BS2pe	BS2px

LOW *Pin*

Function

Make the specified pin output low.

- **Pin** is a variable/constant/expression (0 – 15) that specifies which I/O pin to set low. This pin will be placed into output mode.

NOTE: Expressions are not allowed as arguments on the BS1. The range of the *Pin* argument on the BS1 is 0 – 7.

Quick Facts

Table 5.57: LOW Quick Facts.

	BS1 and all BS2 Models
Related Commands	HIGH and TOGGLE

Explanation

The LOW command sets the specified pin to 0 (a 0 volt level) and then sets its mode to output. For example,

```
LOW  6
```

does exactly the same thing as:

```
OUT6 = 0
DIR6 = 1
```

Using the LOW command is faster, in this case.

Connect an LED and a resistor as shown in Figure 5.17 for the demo program below.

Figure 5.17: Example LED Circuit.

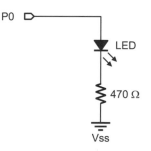

LOW – BASIC Stamp Command Reference

Demo Program (LOW.bs2)

NOTE: This example program can be used with the BS1 and all BS2 models by changing the $STAMP directive accordingly.

```
' LOW.bs2
' This simple program sets I/O pin 0 high for 1/2 second and low for
' 1/2 second in an endless loop.  Connect an LED to P0 for a simple
' blinker.

' {$STAMP BS2}


Main:
  HIGH 0
  PAUSE 500
  LOW 0
  PAUSE 500
  GOTO Main
  END
```

MAINIO

| BS1 | BS2 | BS2e | BS2sx | BS2p | BS2pe | BS2px |

MAINIO

Function

Switch from control of auxiliary I/O pins to main I/O pins (on the BS2p40 only).

Quick Facts

Table 5.58: MAINIO Quick Facts.

	BS2p, BS2pe, and BS2px
I/O pin IDs	0 – 15 (just like auxiliary I/O, but after MAINIO command, all references affect physical pins 5 – 20).
Special Notes	The 24-pin BS2p, BS2pe, and BS2px accept this command, however, only the BS2p40 gives access to the auxiliary I/O pins.
Related Commands	AUXIO and IOTERM

Explanation

The BS2p, BS2pe and BS2px are available as 24-pin modules that are pin compatible with the BS2, BS2e and BS2sx. Also available is a 40-pin module called the BS2p40, with an additional 16 I/O pins (for a total of 32). The BS2p40's extra, or auxiliary, I/O pins can be accessed in the same manner as the main I/O pins (by using the IDs 0 to 15) but only after issuing AUXIO or IOTERM commands. The MAINIO command causes the BASIC Stamp to affect the main I/O pins (the default) instead of the auxiliary I/O pins in all further code until the AUXIO or IOTERM command is reached, or the BASIC Stamp is reset or power-cycled.

A SIMPLE MAINIO EXAMPLE.

The following example illustrates this:

```
AUXIO                          ' switch to auxiliary pins
HIGH 0                         ' make X0 high
MAINIO                         ' switch to main pins
LOW 0                          ' make P0 low
```

The first line of the above example will tell the BASIC Stamp to affect the auxiliary I/O pins in the commands following it. Line 2, sets I/O pin 0 of the auxiliary I/O pins (physical pin 21) high. Afterward, the MAINIO command tells the BASIC Stamp that all commands following it should affect the main I/O pins. The last command, LOW, will set I/O pin 0 of the main I/O pins (physical pin 5) low.

Note that the main I/O and auxiliary I/O pins are independent of each other; the states of the main I/O pins remain unchanged while the program affects the auxiliary I/O pins, and vice versa.

MAIN I/O AND AUXILIARY I/O PINS ARE INDEPENDENT AND UNAFFECTED BY CHANGES IN THE OPPOSITE GROUP.

Other commands that affect I/O group access are AUXIO and IOTERM.

Demo Program (AUX_MAIN_TERM.bsp)

NOTE: This example program will tokenize with the 24-pin BS2p, BS2pe, and BS2px, but its effects can only be seen on the BS2p40. This program uses conditional compilation techniques; see Chapter 3 for more information.

```
' AUX_MAIN_TERM.bsp
' This program demonstrates the use of the AUXIO, MAINIO and IOTERM
' commands to affect I/O pins in the auxiliary and main I/O groups.

' {$STAMP BS2p}
' {$PBASIC 2.5}

#SELECT $STAMP
  #CASE BS2, BS2E, BS2SX
    #ERROR "Program requires BS2p40"
  #CASE BS2P, BS2PE, BS2PX
    DEBUG "Note: This program designed for the BS2p40.", CR
#ENDSELECT

port            VAR     Bit


Main:
  DO
    MAINIO                        ' Switch to main I/O pins
    TOGGLE 0                      ' Toggle state of I/O pin P0
    PWM 1, 100, 40                ' Generate PWM on I/O pin P1

    AUXIO                         ' Switch to auxiliary I/O pins
    TOGGLE 0                      ' Toggle state of I/O pin X0
    PULSOUT 1, 1000               ' Generate a pulse on I/O pin X1
    PWM 2, 100, 40                ' Generate PWM on I/O pin X2

    IOTERM port                   ' Switch to main or aux I/Os
                                  ' -- depending on port
    TOGGLE 3                      ' Toggle state of I/O pin 3
                                  ' -- on main and aux, alternately
    port = ~port                  ' Invert port
    PAUSE 1000                    ' 1 second delay
  LOOP
  END
```

NAP

BS1	BS2	BS2e	BS2sx	BS2p	BS2pe	BS2px

NAP *Duration*

Function

Enter sleep mode for a short time. Power consumption is reduced as indicated in Table 5.59 assuming no loads are being driven.

NOTE: Expressions are not allowed as arguments on the BS1.

- **Duration** is a variable/constant/expression (0 – 7) that specifies the duration of the reduced-power nap. The duration is (2^Duration) * 18 ms. Table 5.60 indicates the nap length for any given *Duration*.

Quick Facts

Table 5.59: NAP Quick Facts.

Note: Current measurements are based on 5-volt power, no extra loads, and 75°F ambient temperature.

	BS1	BS2	BS2e	BS2sx	BS2p	BS2pe	BS2px
Current Draw During Run	1 mA	3 mA	25 mA	60 mA	40 mA	15 mA	55 mA
Current Draw During NAP	25 µA	50 µA	200 µA	500 µA	350 µA	36 µA	450 µA
Related Commands	END and SLEEP				END, SLEEP, and POLLWAIT		
Accuracy of Nap	-50 to 100% (±10% @ 75°F with stable power supply)						

Explanation

NAP uses the same shutdown/startup mechanism as SLEEP, with one big difference. During SLEEP, the BASIC Stamp automatically compensates for variations in the speed of the watchdog timer oscillator that serves as its alarm clock. As a result, longer SLEEP intervals are accurate to approximately ±1 percent.

Table 5.60: *Duration* and Resulting Length of NAP.

Duration	Length of Nap
0	18 ms
1	36 ms
2	72 ms
3	144 ms
4	288 ms
5	576 ms
6	1152 ms (1.152 seconds)
7	2304 ms (2.304 seconds)

NAP ACCURACY NOTES.

NAP intervals are directly controlled by the watchdog timer without compensation. Variations in temperature, supply voltage, and manufacturing tolerance of the BASIC Stamp's interpreter chip can cause the actual timing to vary by as much as –50, +100 percent (i.e., a *Duration* of 0, NAP can range from 9 to 36 ms). At room temperature with a fresh battery or other stable power supply, variations in the length of a NAP will be less than ±10 percent.

One great use for NAP is in a battery-powered application where at least a small amount of time is spent doing nothing. For example, you may have a program that loops endlessly, performing some task, that pauses for approximately 100 ms each time through the loop. You could replace your PAUSE 100 with NAP 3, as long as the timing of the 100 ms pause was not critical. The NAP 3 would effectively pause your program for about 144 ms and, at the same time, would place the BASIC Stamp in low-power mode, which would extend your battery life.

A GREAT USE FOR NAP; FREE POWER SAVINGS.

If your application is driving loads (sourcing or sinking current through output-high or output-low pins) during a NAP, current will be interrupted for about 18 ms (60 µs on the BS2pe) when the BASIC Stamp wakes up. The reason is that the watchdog-timer reset that awakens the BASIC Stamp also causes all of the pins to switch to input mode for approximately 18 ms (60 µs on the BS2pe). When the interpreter firmware regains control of the processor, it restores the I/O direction dictated by your program.

TIPS FOR DRIVING LOADS DURING NAP.

If you plan to use END, NAP, POLLWAIT or SLEEP in your programs, make sure that your loads can tolerate these power outages. The simplest solution is often to connect resistors high or low (to +5V or ground) as appropriate to ensure a continuing supply of current during the reset glitch.

The demo program can be used to demonstrate the effects of the NAP glitch with an LED and resistor as shown in Figure 5.18.

Figure 5.18: Example LED Circuit.

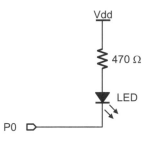

Demo Program (NAP.bs2)

```
' NAP.bs2
' The program below lights an LED by placing a low on pin 0. This completes
' the circuit from +5V, through the LED and resistor, to ground. During the
' NAP interval, the LED stays lit, but blinks off for a fraction of a sec.
' This blink is caused by the NAP wakeup mechanism during wakeup, all pins
' briefly slip into input mode, effectively disconnecting them from loads.

' {$STAMP BS2}


Setup:
  LOW 0                                    ' turn LED on

Snooze:
  NAP 4                                    ' nap for 288 ms
  GOTO Snooze
  END
```

NOTE: ON requires PBASIC 2.5. [All 2]

ON

| BS1 | BS2 | BS2e | BS2sx | BS2p | BS2pe | BS2px |

[All 2] **ON** *Offset* **GOTO** *Address1, Address2, ...AddressN*

[All 2] **ON** *Offset* **GOSUB** *Address1, Address2, ...AddressN*

Function

GOTO or GOSUB to the *Address* specified by *Offset* (if in range). ON is similar in operation to BRANCH with the exception that program execution can optionally return to the line following ON (if using ON...GOSUB).

- • **Offset** is a variable/constant/expression (0 - 255) that specifies the index (0 - N) of the address, in the list, to GOTO or GOSUB to.

- • **Address** is a label that specifies where to go for a given *Offset*. ON will ignore any list entries beyond offset 255.

Quick Facts

Table 5.61: ON Quick Facts.

	All BS2 Models
Limit of Address Entries	256
Maximum GOSUBs per Program	255 (each ON...GOSUB counts as one GOSUB, regardless of number of address list entries)
Maximum Nested GOSUBS	4
Related Commands	BRANCH, GOTO and GOSUB

Explanation

The ON instruction is like saying, "Based ON the value of *Offset*, GOTO or GOSUB to one of these *Addresses.*" ON is useful when you want to write something like this:

```
IF (value = 0) THEN GOTO Case_0        ' "GOTO" jump table
IF (value = 1) THEN GOTO Case_1
IF (value = 2) THEN GOTO Case_2

- or -

IF (value = 0) THEN GOSUB Case_0       ' "GOSUB" jump table
IF (value = 1) THEN GOSUB Case_1
IF (value = 2) THEN GOSUB Case_2
```

You can use ON to organize each of these two examples into single statements:

```
ON value GOTO Case_0, Case_1, Case_2    ' "GOTO" jump table
```

- or -

```
ON value GOSUB Case_0, Case_1, Case_2   ' "GOSUB" jump table
```

This works like the previous IF...THEN example. If the value isn't in range (in this case if value is greater than 2), ON does nothing and the program continues with the next instruction after ON.

See the GOTO and GOSUB command descriptions for more information.

Demo Program (ON-GOTO.bs2)

NOTE: This example program can be used with all BS2 models by changing the $STAMP directive accordingly.

```
' ON-GOTO.bs2
' This program shows how the value of idx controls the destination of the
' ON...GOTO instruction.

' {$STAMP BS2}
' {$PBASIC 2.5}

idx             VAR     Byte


Main:
  DEBUG "idx: ", DEC idx, " "
  ON idx GOTO Case_0, Case_1, Case_2    ' if idx = 0..2 goto label
  DEBUG "ON..GOTO target error.", CR    ' message if idx is out of range

Update:
  idx = idx + 1 // 4                    ' force idx to be 0..3
  PAUSE 1000
  GOTO Main

Case_0:
  DEBUG "Running Case_0 routine", CR
  GOTO Update

Case_1:
  DEBUG "Running Case_1 routine", CR
  GOTO Update

Case_2:
  DEBUG "Running Case_2 routine", CR
  GOTO Update
```

Demo Program (ON-GOSUB.bs2)

NOTE: This example program can be used with all BS2 models by changing the $STAMP directive accordingly.

```
' ON-GOSUB.bs2
' This program demonstrates a simple task manager that can be used
' in a variety of applications.  It is particularly useful in
' robotics and industrial applications.  The advantage of this
' design is that task code modules may be called from other places
' in the program, including other tasks, and the overall program flow
' is maintained.

' {$STAMP BS2}
' {$PBASIC 2.5}

task            VAR     Nib


Main:
  DO
    ON task GOSUB Task_0, Task_1, Task_2      ' run current task
    task = task + 1 // 3                      ' update task pointer
    PAUSE 1000
  LOOP
  END

Task_0:
  DEBUG "Running Task 0", CR
  RETURN

Task_1:
  DEBUG "Running Task 1", CR
  RETURN

Task_2:
  DEBUG "Running Task 2", CR
  RETURN
```

OUTPUT

| BS1 | BS2 | BS2e | BS2sx | BS2p | BS2pe | BS2px |

OUTPUT *Pin*

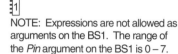

NOTE: Expressions are not allowed as arguments on the BS1. The range of the *Pin* argument on the BS1 is 0 – 7.

Function

Make the specified pin an output.

- ***Pin*** is a variable/constant/expression (0 – 15) that specifies which I/O pin to set to output mode.

Quick Facts

Table 5.62: OUTPUT Quick Facts.

	BS1 and all BS2 Models
Related Commands	INPUT and REVERSE

Explanation

There are several ways to make a pin an output. Commands that rely on output pins, like PULSOUT and SEROUT, automatically change the specified pin to output. Writing 1s to particular bits of the variable DIRS makes the corresponding pins outputs. And then there's the OUTPUT command.

When a pin is an output, your program can change its state by writing to the corresponding bit in the OUTS variable (PINS on the BS1). For example:

```
OUTPUT 4
OUT4 = 1
```

EFFECTS OF SETTING AN INPUT PIN TO AN OUTPUT.

When your program changes a pin from input to output, whatever state happens to be in the corresponding bit of OUTS (PINS on the BS1) sets the initial state of the pin. To simultaneously make a pin an output and set its state use the HIGH and LOW commands.

Demo Program (INPUT_OUTPUT.bs1)

```
' INPUT_OUTPUT.bs1
' This program demonstrates how the input/output direction of a pin is
' determined by the corresponding bit of DIRS. It also shows that the
' state of the pin itself (as reflected by the corresponding bit of PINS)
' is determined by the outside world when the pin is an input, and by the
' corresponding bit of PINS when it's an output. To set up the demo,
' connect a 10k resistor from +5V to P7 on the BASIC Stamp. The resistor
```

```
' to +5V puts a high (1) on the pin when it's an input. The BASIC Stamp
' can override this state by writing a low (0) to bit 7 of OUTS and
' changing the pin to output.

' {$STAMP BS1}
' {$PBASIC 1.0}


Main:
  INPUT 7                           ' Make P7 an input
  DEBUG "State of P7: ", #PIN7, CR

  PIN7 = 0                          ' Write 0 to output latch
  DEBUG "After 0 written to OUT7: "
  DEBUG #PIN7, CR

  OUTPUT 7                          ' Make P7 an output
  DEBUG "After P7 changed to output: "
  DEBUG #PIN7
  END
```

Demo Program (INPUT_OUTPUT.bs2)

```
' INPUT_OUTPUT.bs2
' This program demonstrates how the input/output direction of a pin is
' determined by the corresponding bit of DIRS. It also shows that the
' state of the pin itself (as reflected by the corresponding bit of INS)
' is determined by the outside world when the pin is an input, and by the
' corresponding bit of OUTS when it's an output. To set up the demo,
' connect a 10k resistor from +5V to P7 on the BASIC Stamp. The resistor
' to +5V puts a high (1) on the pin when it's an input. The BASIC Stamp
' can override this state by writing a low (0) to bit 7 of OUTS and
' changing the pin to output.

' {$STAMP BS2}
' {$PBASIC 2.5}


Main:
  INPUT 7                           ' Make P7 an input
  DEBUG "State of P7: ",
        BIN1 IN7, CR

  OUT7 = 0                          ' Write 0 to output latch
  DEBUG "After 0 written to OUT7: ",
        BIN1 IN7, CR

  OUTPUT 7                          ' Make P7 an output
  DEBUG "After P7 changed to output: ",
        BIN1 IN7
  END
```

NOTE: This example program can be used with all BS2 models by changing the $STAMP directive accordingly.

OWIN

OWIN *Pin, Mode,* **[** *InputData* **]**

Function

Receive data from a device using the 1-Wire protocol.

- *Pin* is a variable/constant/expression (0 – 15) that specifies which I/O pin to use. 1-Wire devices require only one I/O pin (called DQ) to communicate. This I/O pin will be toggled between output and input mode during the OWIN command and will be set to input mode by the end of the OWIN command.

- *Mode* is a variable/constant/expression (0 – 15) indicating the mode of data transfer. The *Mode* argument controls placement of reset pulses (and detection of presence pulses) as well as byte vs. bit input and normal vs. high speed. See explanation below.

- *InputData* is a list of variables and modifiers that tells OWIN what to do with incoming data. OWIN can store data in a variable or array, interpret numeric text (decimal, binary, or hex) and store the corresponding value in a variable, wait for a fixed or variable sequence of bytes, or ignore a specified number of bytes. These actions can be combined in any order in the *InputData* list.

Quick Facts

Table 5.63: OWIN Quick Facts.

	BS2p, BS2pe, and BS2px
Receive Rate	Approximately 20 kbits/sec (low speed, not including reset pulse)
Special Notes	The DQ pin (specified by *Pin*) must have a 4.7 KΩ pull-up resistor. The BS2pe is not capable of high-speed transfers.
Related Commands	OWOUT

Explanation

The 1-Wire protocol is a form of asynchronous serial communication developed by Dallas Semiconductor. It only requires one I/O pin and that pin can be shared between multiple 1-Wire devices. The OWIN command allows the BASIC Stamp to receive data from a 1-wire device.

A SIMPLE OWIN EXAMPLE.

The following is an example of the OWIN command:

```
result  VAR    Byte

OWIN 0, 1, [result]
```

This code will transmit a "reset" pulse to a 1-Wire device (connected to I/O pin 0) and then will detect the device's "presence" pulse and then receive one byte and store it in the variable *result*.

The *Mode* argument is used to control placement of reset pulses (and detection of presence pulses) and to designate byte vs. bit input and normal vs. high speed. Figure 5.19 shows the meaning of each of the 4 bits of Mode. Table 5.64 shows just some of the 16 possible values and their effect.

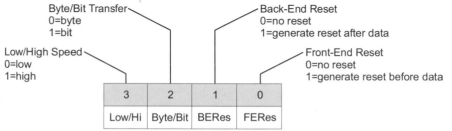

Figure 5.19: *Mode* Format.

Mode	Effect
0	No Reset, Byte mode, Low speed
1	Reset before data, Byte mode, Low speed
2	Reset after data, Byte mode, Low speed
3	Reset before and after data, Byte mode, Low speed
4	No Reset, Bit mode, Low speed
5	Reset before data, Bit mode, Low speed
8	No Reset, Byte mode, High speed
9	Reset before data, Byte mode, High speed

Table 5.64: OWIN *Mode* Values.

NOTE: The BS2pe is not capable of high-speed transfers.

The proper value for *Mode* depends on the 1-Wire device and the portion of the communication you're working on. Please consult the data sheet for the device in question to determine the correct value for *Mode*. In many cases, however, when using the OWIN command, *Mode* should be set for either No Reset (to receive data from a transaction already started by a OWOUT command) or a Back-End Reset (to terminate the session after data is received). This may vary due to device and application requirements, however.

When using the Bit (rather than Byte) mode of data transfer, all variables in the *InputData* argument will only receive one bit. For example, the following code could be used to receive two bits using this mode:

```
bitOne  VAR     Byte
bitTwo  VAR     Byte

OWIN 0, 6, [bitOne, bitTwo]
```

In the code above, we chose the value "6" for *Mode*. This sets Bit transfer and Back-End Reset modes. Also, we could have chosen to make the *bitOne* and *bitTwo* variables each a byte in size, but they still would only have received one bit each in the OWIN command (due to the *Mode* we chose).

RECEIVING FORMATTED DATA.

The OWIN command's *InputData* argument is similar to the SERIN command's *InputData* argument. This means data can be received as ASCII character values, decimal, hexadecimal and binary translations and string data as in the examples below. (Assume a 1-Wire device is used and that it transmits the string, "Value: 3A:101" every time it receives a Front-End Reset pulse).

```
value   VAR     Byte(13)

OWIN 0, 1, [value]              ' receive ASCII value for "V"
OWIN 0, 1, [DEC value]         ' receive the number 3
OWIN 0, 1, [HEX value]         ' receive the number $3A
OWIN 0, 1, [BIN value]         ' receive the number %101
OWIN 0, 1, [STR value\13]      ' receive "Value: 3A:101"
```

Table 5.65 and Table 5.66 list all the special formatters and conversion formatters available to the OWIN command. See the SERIN command for additional information and examples of their use.

Table 5.65: OWIN Special Formatters.

Special Formatter	Action
SPSTR L	Input a character string of length L bytes (up to 126) into Scratch Pad RAM, starting at location 0. Use GET to retrieve the characters.
STR *ByteArray* \L {\E}	Input a character string of length L into an array. If specified, an end character E causes the string input to end before reaching length L. Remaining bytes are filled with 0s (zeros).
WAITSTR *ByteArray* {\L}	Wait for a sequence of bytes matching a string stored in an array variable, optionally limited to L characters. If the optional L argument is left off, the end of the array-string must be marked by a byte containing a zero (0).
SKIP *Length*	Ignore *Length* bytes of characters.

\Conversion Formatter	Type of Number	Numeric Characters Accepted	Notes
DEC{1..5}	Decimal, optionally limited to 1 – 5 digits	0 through 9	1
SDEC{1..5}	Signed decimal, optionally limited to 1 – 5 digits	-, 0 through 9	1,2
HEX{1..4}	Hexadecimal, optionally limited to 1 – 4 digits	0 through 9, A through F	1,3,5
SHEX{1..4}	Signed hexadecimal, optionally limited to 1 – 4 digits	-, 0 through 9, A through F	1,2,3
IHEX{1..4}	Indicated hexadecimal, optionally limited to 1 – 4 digits	$, 0 through 9, A through F	1,3,4
ISHEX{1..4}	Signed, indicated hexadecimal, optionally limited to 1 – 4 digits	-, $, 0 through 9, A through F	1,2,3,4
BIN{1..16}	Binary, optionally limited to 1 – 16 digits	0, 1	1
SBIN{1..16}	Signed binary, optionally limited to 1 – 16 digits	-, 0, 1	1,2
IBIN{1..16}	Indicated binary, optionally limited to 1 – 16 digits	%, 0, 1	1,4
ISBIN{1..16}	Signed, indicated binary, optionally limited to 1 – 16 digits	-, %, 0, 1	1,2,4
NUM	Generic numeric input (decimal, hexadecimal or binary); hexadecimal or binary number must be indicated	$, %, 0 through 9, A through F	1, 3, 4
SNUM	Similar to NUM with value treated as signed with range -32768 to +32767	-, $, %, 0 through 9, A through F	1,2,3,4

Table 5.66: OWIN Conversion Formatters

1 All numeric conversions will continue to accept new data until receiving either the specified number of digits (ex: three digits for DEC3) or a non-numeric character.

2 To be recognized as part of a number, the minus sign (-) must immediately precede a numeric character. The minus sign character occurring in non-numeric text is ignored and any character (including a space) between a minus and a number causes the minus to be ignored.

3 The hexadecimal formatters are not case-sensitive; "a" through "f" means the same as "A" through "F".

4 Indicated hexadecimal and binary formatters ignore all characters, even valid numerics, until they receive the appropriate prefix ($ for hexadecimal, % for binary). The indicated formatters can differentiate between text and hexadecimal (ex: ABC would be interpreted by HEX as a number but IHEX would ignore it unless expressed as $ABC). Likewise, the binary version can distinguish the decimal number 10 from the binary number %10. A prefix occurring in non-numeric text is ignored, and any character (including a space) between a prefix and a number causes the prefix to be ignored. Indicated, signed formatters require that the minus sign come before the prefix, as in -$1B45.

5 The HEX modifier can be used for Decimal to BCD Conversion. See "Hex to BCD Conversion" on page 97.

For examples of all conversion formatters and how they process incoming data, see Appendix C.

THE 1-WIRE PROTOCOL FORMAT.

The 1-Wire protocol has a well-defined standard for transaction sequences. Every transaction sequence consists of four parts: 1) Initialization, 2) ROM Function Command, 3) Memory Function Command, and 4) Transaction/Data. Additionally, the ROM Function Command and Memory Function Command are always 8 bits wide (1 byte in size) and is sent least-significant-bit (LSB) first.

The Initialization part consists of a reset pulse (generated by the master) and will be followed by a presence pulse (generated by all slave devices). Figure 5.20 details the reset pulse generated by the BASIC Stamp and a typical presence pulse generated by a 1-wire slave, in response.

Figure 5.20: OWIN Reset and Presence Pulse.

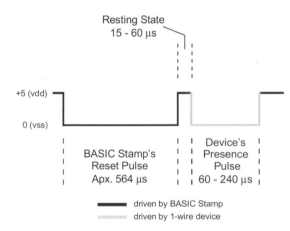

This reset pulse is controlled by the lowest two bits of the *Mode* argument in the OWIN command. It can be made to appear before the ROM Function Command (ex: *Mode* = 1), after the Transaction/Data portion (ex: *Mode* = 2), before and after the entire transaction (ex: *Mode* = 3) or not at all (ex: *Mode* = 0). See the section on *Mode*, above, for more information.

Following the Initialization part is the ROM Function Command. The ROM Function Command is used to address the desired 1-Wire device. Table 5.67 shows common ROM Function Commands. If only a single 1-Wire device is connected, the Skip ROM command may be used to address it. If more than one 1-Wire device is attached, the BASIC Stamp will ultimately have to address them individually using the Match ROM command.

Command	Value (in Hex)	Action
Read ROM	$33	Reads the 64-bit ID of the 1-Wire device. This command can only be used if there is a single 1-wire device on the line.
Match ROM	$55	This command, followed by a 64-bit ID, allows the BASIC Stamp to address a specific 1-Wire device.
Skip ROM	$CC	Address a 1-Wire device without its 64-bit ID. This command can only be used if there is a single 1-wire device on the line.
Search ROM	$F0	Reads the 64-bit IDs of all the 1-Wire devices on the line. A process of elimination is used to distinguish each unique device.

Table 5.67: 1-Wire ROM Function Commands.

The third part, the Memory Function Command, allows the BASIC Stamp to address specific memory locations, or features, of the 1-Wire device. Refer to the 1-Wire device's data sheet for a list of the available Memory Function Commands.

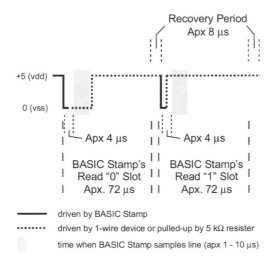

Figure 5.21: Example Read Slot.

Finally, the Transaction/Data section is used to read or write data to the 1-Wire device. The OWIN command will read data at this point in the transaction. A read is accomplished by generating a brief low-pulse and sampling the line within 15 μs of the falling edge of the pulse. This is called a "Read Slot." Figure 5.21 shows typical Read Slots performed by the BASIC Stamp. See the OWOUT command for information on Write Slots.

The demo program uses a Dallas Semiconductor DS1820 Digital Thermometer device connected as follows. Note that the 4.7 kΩ pull-up resistor is required for proper operation.

Figure 5.22: DS1820 Circuit. NOTE: The 4.7 kΩ resistor is required for proper operation.

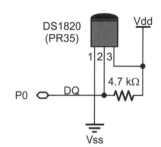

NOTE: This example program can be used with the BS2p, BS2pe and BS2px by changing the $STAMP directive accordingly.

Demo Program (OWIN_OWOUT.bsp)

```
' OWIN_OWOUT.bsp
' This program demonstrates interfacing to a Dallas Semiconductor DS1822
' 1-Wire Digital Thermometer chip using the BS2p's 1-Wire commands. Connect
' the BS2p, BS2pe, or BS2px to the DS1822 as shown in the diagram in the
' OWIN or OWOUT command description. This program uses a simplified
' approach that ignores the fractional portion of the temperature.

' {$STAMP BS2p}
' {$PBASIC 2.5}

DQ              PIN     0               ' 1-Wire buss pin

RdROM           CON     $33             ' read serial number
MatchROM        CON     $55             ' match SN -- for multiple devices
SkipROM         CON     $CC             ' ignore SN -- use for one device
CvrtTmp         CON     $44             ' start temperature conversion
RdSP            CON     $BE             ' read DS1822 scratch pad

tempIn          VAR     Word            ' raw temperature
sign            VAR     tempIn.BIT11    ' 1 = negative temperature
tLo             VAR     tempIn.BYTE0
tHi             VAR     tempIn.BYTE1
tSign           VAR     Bit             ' saved sign bit
tempC           VAR     Word            ' final Celsius temp
tempF           VAR     Word            ' final Fahrenheit temp


Main:
  DO
    GOSUB Get_Temperature               ' read temperature from DS1822
    DEBUG HOME,                         ' display
          "DS1822", CR,
          "------", CR,
```

```
          SDEC tempC, " C ", CR,
          SDEC tempF, " F "
     PAUSE 1000
  LOOP
  END

Get_Temperature:
  OWOUT DQ, 1, [SkipROM, CvrtTmp]        ' send convert temperature command
  DO                                      ' wait on conversion
    PAUSE 25                              ' small loop pad
    OWIN DQ, 4, [tempIn]                  ' check status (bit transfer)
  LOOP UNTIL (tempIn)                     ' 1 when complete
  OWOUT DQ, 1, [SkipROM, RdSP]           ' read DS1822 scratch pad
  OWIN  DQ, 2, [tLo, tHi]                 ' get raw temp data
  tSign = sign                            ' save sign bit
  tempC = tempIn >> 4                     ' round to whole degrees
  tempC.BYTE1 = $FF * tSign               ' correct twos complement bits
  tempF = (ABS tempC) * 9 / 5            ' start F conversion
  IF (tSign) THEN                         ' finish F conversion
    tempF = 32 - tempF                    ' C was negative
  ELSE
    tempF = tempF + 32                    ' C was positive
  ENDIF
  RETURN
```

OWOUT

OWOUT *Pin, Mode,* [*OutputData*]

Function

Send data to a device using the 1-Wire protocol.

- **Pin** is a variable/constant/expression (0 – 15) that specifies which I/O pin to use. 1-Wire devices require only one I/O pin (called DQ) to communicate. This I/O pin will be toggled between output and input mode during the OWOUT command and will be set to input mode by the end of the OWOUT command.

- **Mode** is a variable/constant/expression (0 – 15) indicating the mode of data transfer. The *Mode* argument controls placement of reset pulses (and detection of presence pulses) as well as byte vs. bit input and normal vs. high speed. See explanation below.

- **OutputData** is a list of variables and modifiers that tells OWOUT how to format outgoing data. OWOUT can transmit individual or repeating bytes, convert values into decimal, hexadecimal or binary text representations, or transmit strings of bytes from variable arrays. These actions can be combined in any order in the *OutputData* list.

Quick Facts

Table 5.68: OWOUT Quick Facts.

	BS2p, BS2pe, and BS2px
Transmission Rate	Approximately 20 kbits/sec (low speed, not including reset pulse)
Special Notes	The DQ pin (specified by *Pin*) must have a 4.7 KΩ pull-up resistor. The BS2pe is not capable of high-speed transfers.
Related Command	OWIN

Explanation

The 1-Wire protocol is a form of asynchronous serial communication developed by Dallas Semiconductor. It only requires one I/O pin and that pin can be shared between multiple 1-Wire devices. The OWOUT command allows the BASIC Stamp to send data to a 1-Wire device.

A SIMPLE OWOUT EXAMPLE.

The following is an example of the OWOUT command:

```
OWOUT  0, 1, [$4E]
```

This code will transmit a "reset" pulse to a 1-Wire device (connected to I/O pin 0) and then will detect the device's "presence" pulse and then transmit one byte (the value $4E).

The *Mode* argument is used to control placement of reset pulses (and detection of presence pulses) and to designate byte vs. bit input and normal vs. high speed. Figure 5.23 shows the meaning of each of the 4 bits of *Mode*. Table 5.69 shows just some of the 16 possible values and their effect.

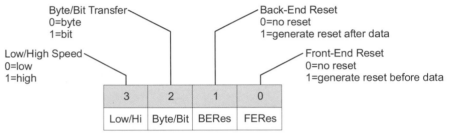

Figure 5.23: *MODE* Format.

Mode	Effect
0	No Reset, Byte mode, Low speed
1	Reset before data, Byte mode, Low speed
2	Reset after data, Byte mode, Low speed
3	Reset before and after data, Byte mode, Low speed
4	No Reset, Bit mode, Low speed
5	Reset before data, Bit mode, Low speed
8	No Reset, Byte mode, High speed
9	Reset before data, Byte mode, High speed

Table 5.69: OWOUT Mode Values.

NOTE: The BS2pe is not capable of high-speed transfers.

The proper value for *Mode* depends on the 1-Wire device and the portion of the communication you're working on. Please consult the data sheet for the device in question to determine the correct value for *Mode*. In many cases, however, when using the OWOUT command, *Mode* should be set for a Front-End Reset (to initialize the transaction). This may vary due to device and application requirements, however.

When using the Bit (rather than Byte) mode of data transfer, all variables in the *OutputData* argument will only transmit one bit. For example, the following code could be used to send two bits using this mode:

```
bitOne   VAR     Bit
bitTwo   VAR     Bit

bitOne = 0
bitTwo = 1
OWOUT 0, 5, [bitOne, bitTwo]
```

In the code above, we chose the value "5" for *Mode*. This sets Bit transfer and Front-End Reset modes. Also, we could have chosen to make the *bitOne* and *bitTwo* variables each a byte in size, but the BASIC Stamp would still only use the their lowest bit (BIT0) as the value to transmit in the OWOUT command (due to the *Mode* we chose).

SENDING AND FORMATTING DATA.

The OWOUT command's *OutputData* argument is similar to the DEBUG and SEROUT command's *OutputData* argument. This means data can be sent as literal text, ASCII character values, repetitive values, decimal, hexadecimal and binary translations and string data as in the examples below. (Assume a 1-wire device is used and that it transmits the string, "Value: 3A:101" every time it receives a Front-End Reset pulse).

```
value   VAR     Byte
value = 65

OWOUT 0, 1, [value]                      ' send "A"
OWOUT 0, 1, [REP value\5]                ' send "AAAAA"
OWOUT 0, 1, [DEC value]                  ' send "6" and "5"
OWOUT 0, 1, [HEX value]                  ' send "4" and "1"
OWOUT 0, 1, [BIN value]                  ' send "1000001"
```

Table 5.70 and Table 5.71 list all the special formatters and conversion formatters available to the OWOUT command. See the DEBUG and SEROUT commands for additional information and examples of their use.

Table 5.70: OWOUT Special Formatters.

Special Formatter	Action
?	Displays "symbol = x' + carriage return; where x is a number. Default format is decimal, but may be combined with conversion formatters (ex: BIN ? x to display "x = binary_number").
ASC ?	Displays "symbol = 'x'" + carriage return; where x is an ASCII character.
STR *ByteArray* {\L}	Send character string from an array. The optional \L argument can be used to limit the output to L characters, otherwise, characters will be sent up to the first byte equal to 0 or the end of RAM space is reached.
REP *Byte* \L	Send a string consisting of *Byte* repeated L times (ex: REP "X"\10 sends "XXXXXXXXXX").

Conversion Formatter	Type of Number	Notes
DEC{1..5}	Decimal, optionally fixed to 1 – 5 digits	1
SDEC{1..5}	Signed decimal, optionally fixed to 1 – 5 digits	1,2
HEX{1..4}	Hexadecimal, optionally fixed to 1 – 4 digits	1,3
SHEX{1..4}	Signed hexadecimal, optionally fixed to 1 – 4 digits	1,2
IHEX{1..4}	Indicated hexadecimal, optionally fixed to 1 – 4 digits ($ prefix)	1
ISHEX{1..4}	Signed, indicated hexadecimal, optionally fixed to 1 – 4 digits ($ prefix)	1,2
BIN{1..16}	Binary, optionally fixed to 1 – 16 digits	1
SBIN{1..16}	Signed binary, optionally fixed to 1 – 16 digits	1,2
IBIN{1..16}	Indicated binary, optionally fixed to 1 – 16 digits (% prefix)	1
ISBIN{1..16}	Signed, indicated binary, optionally fixed to 1 – 16 digits (% prefix)	1,2

Table 5.71: OWOUT Conversion Formatters.

1 Fixed-digit formatters like DEC4 will pad the number with leading 0s if necessary; ex: DEC4 65 sends 0065. If a number is larger than the specified number of digits, the leading digits will be dropped; ex: DEC4 56422 sends 6422.
2 Signed modifiers work under two's complement rules.
3 The HEX modifier can be used for BCD to Decimal Conversion. See "Hex to BCD Conversion" on page 97.

The 1-Wire protocol has a well-defined standard for transaction sequences. Every transaction sequence consists of four parts: 1) Initialization, 2) ROM Function Command, 3) Memory Function Command, and 4) Transaction/Data. Additionally, the ROM Function Command and Memory Function Command are always 8 bits wide (1 byte in size) and is sent least-significant-bit (LSB) first.

The Initialization part consists of a reset pulse (generated by the master) and will be followed by a presence pulse (generated by all slave devices). Figure 5.24 details the reset pulse generated by the BASIC Stamp and a typical presence pulse generated by a 1-Wire slave, in response.

Figure 5.24: OWOUT Reset and Presence Pulse.

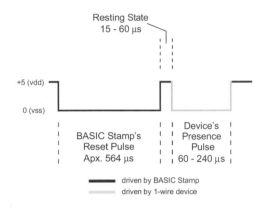

This reset pulse is controlled by the lowest two bits of the *Mode* argument in the OWOUT command. It can be made to appear before the ROM Function Command (ex: *Mode* = 1), after the Transaction/Data portion (ex: *Mode* = 2), before and after the entire transaction (ex: *Mode* = 3) or not at all (ex: *Mode* = 0). See the section on *Mode*, above, for more information.

Following the Initialization part is the ROM Function Command. The ROM Function Command is used to address the desired 1-Wire device. Table 5.72 shows common ROM Function Commands. If only a single 1-wire device is connected, the Skip ROM command may be used to address it. If more than one 1-wire device is attached, the BASIC Stamp will ultimately have to address them individually using the Match ROM command.

Table 5.72: OWOUT ROM Function Commands.

Command	Value (in Hex)	Action
Read ROM	$33	Reads the 64-bit ID of the 1-Wire device. This command can only be used if there is a single 1-Wire device on the line.
Match ROM	$55	This command, followed by a 64-bit ID, allows the BASIC Stamp to address a specific 1-Wire device.
Skip ROM	$CC	Address a 1-Wire device without its 64-bit ID. This command can only be used if there is a single 1-wire device on the line.
Search ROM	$F0	Reads the 64-bit IDs of all the 1-Wire devices on the line. A process of elimination is used to distinguish each unique device.

The third part, the Memory Function Command, allows the BASIC Stamp to address specific memory locations, or features, of the 1-wire device.

Refer to the 1-Wire device's data sheet for a list of the available Memory Function Commands.

Finally, the Transaction/Data section is used to read or write data to the 1-Wire device. The OWOUT command will write data at this point in the transaction. A write is accomplished by generating a low-pulse of a varying width to indicate a 0 or a 1. This is called a "Write Slot" and must be at least 60 µs wide. Figure 5.25 shows typical Write Slots performed by the BASIC Stamp. See the OWIN command for information on Read Slots.

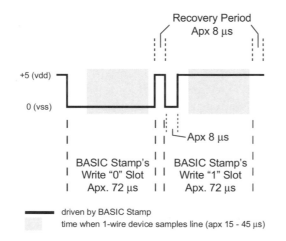

Figure 5.25: Example Write Slots.

The demo program uses a Dallas Semiconductor DS1820 Digital Thermometer device connected as follows. Note that the 4.7 kΩ pull-up resistor is required for proper operation.

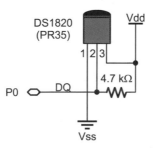

Figure 5.26: DS1820 Circuit. NOTE: The 4.7 kΩ resistor is required for proper operation.

🔲🔲🔲
ᵖ ᵖᵉ ᵖˣ

Demo Program (OWIN_OWOUT.bsp)

NOTE: This example program can be used with the BS2p, BS2pe, and BS2px by changing the $STAMP directive accordingly.

```
' OWIN_OWOUT.bsp
' This program demonstrates interfacing to a Dallas Semiconductor DS1822
' 1-Wire Digital Thermometer chip using the BS2p's 1-Wire commands. Connect
' the BS2p, BS2pe or BS2px to the DS1822 as shown in the diagram in the
' OWIN or OWOUT command description. This program uses a simplified
' approach that ignores the fractional portion of the temperature.

' {$STAMP BS2p}
' {$PBASIC 2.5}

DQ              PIN    0              ' 1-Wire buss pin

RdROM           CON    $33            ' read serial number
MatchROM        CON    $55            ' match SN -- for multiple devices
SkipROM         CON    $CC            ' ignore SN -- use for one device
CvrtTmp         CON    $44            ' start temperature conversion
RdSP            CON    $BE            ' read DS1822 scratch pad

tempIn          VAR    Word           ' raw temperature
sign            VAR    tempIn.BIT11   ' 1 = negative temperature
tLo             VAR    tempIn.BYTE0
tHi             VAR    tempIn.BYTE1
tSign           VAR    Bit            ' saved sign bit
tempC           VAR    Word           ' final Celsius temp
tempF           VAR    Word           ' final Fahrenheit temp


Main:
  DO
    GOSUB Get_Temperature             ' read temperature from DS1822
    DEBUG HOME,                       ' display
          "DS1822", CR,
          "------", CR,
          SDEC tempC, " C ", CR,
          SDEC tempF, " F "
    PAUSE 1000
  LOOP
  END

Get_Temperature:
  OWOUT DQ, 1, [SkipROM, CvrtTmp]     ' send convert temperatrue command
  DO                                  ' wait on conversion
    PAUSE 25                          ' small loop pad
    OWIN DQ, 4, [tempIn]              ' check status (bit transfer)
  LOOP UNTIL (tempIn)                 ' 1 when complete
  OWOUT DQ, 1, [SkipROM, RdSP]        ' read DS1822 scratch pad
  OWIN  DQ, 2, [tLo, tHi]             ' get raw temp data
  tSign = sign                        ' save sign bit
  tempC = tempIn >> 4                 ' round to whole degrees
  tempC.BYTE1 = $FF * tSign           ' correct twos complement bits
```

```
tempF = (ABS tempC) * 9 / 5        ' start F conversion
IF (tSign) THEN                    ' finish F conversion
  tempF = 32 - tempF               ' C was negative
ELSE
  tempF = tempF + 32               ' C was positive
ENDIF
RETURN
```

PAUSE

BS1	BS2	BS2e	BS2sx	BS2p	BS2pe	BS2px

PAUSE *Duration*

Function

NOTE: Expressions are not allowed as arguments on the BS1.

Pause the program (do nothing) for the specified *Duration*.

- **Duration** is a variable/constant/expression (0 – 65535) that specifies the duration of the pause. The unit of time for *Duration* is 1 millisecond.

Explanation

PAUSE delays the execution of the next program instruction for the specified number of milliseconds. For example:

```
Flash:
  LOW 0
  PAUSE 100
  HIGH 0
  PAUSE 100
  GOTO Flash
```

This code causes pin 0 to go low for 100 ms, then high for 100 ms. The delays produced by PAUSE are as accurate as the ceramic-resonator time base (on the BASIC Stamp modules), ±1 percent. When you use PAUSE in timing-critical applications, keep in mind the relatively low speed of the PBASIC interpreter. This is the time required for the BASIC Stamp to read and interpret an instruction stored in the EEPROM.

Demo Program (PAUSE.bs2)

NOTE: This example program can be used with the BS1 and all BS2 models by changing the $STAMP directive accordingly.

```
' PAUSE.bs2
' This program demonstrates the PAUSE command's time delays. Once a second,
' the program will put the message "Paused..." on the screen.
' {$STAMP BS2}

Main:
  DEBUG "Paused...", CR
  PAUSE 1000
  GOTO Main
```

POLLIN

POLLIN *Pin, State*

Function

Specify a polled-input pin and active state.

- *Pin* is a variable/constant/expression (0 – 15) that specifies the I/O pin to use. This I/O pin will be set to input mode.

- *State* is a variable/constant/expression (0 – 1) that specifies whether to poll the I/O pin for a low (0) or a high (1) level.

Quick Facts

Table 5.73: POLLIN Quick Facts.

	BS2p, BS2pe, and BS2px
Available actions in response to reaching the desired *State*	1) Nothing, 2) Set polled-output pins to a specified state, 3) Run another program (in a specified program-slot), 4) Wait (pause program execution) until desired *State* is reached, 5) Any combination of 2, 3 and 4, above.
Special notes	• The polled-input pins are monitored (polled) in-between each command within the PBASIC code. • On the BS2p40, polled-input pins can be defined on both Main I/O and Auxiliary I/O pins. These are all active regardless of which group the program happens to be using at the time of a polling event.
Useful SPRAM locations	Locations 128 – 135 hold polled interrupt status. See Table 5.77 in the POLLMODE command section for more information.
Related commands	POLLMODE, POLLOUT, POLLRUN and POLLWAIT

Explanation

The POLLIN command is used to specify an input pin to monitor, or "poll", in-between instructions during the rest of the PBASIC program. The BASIC Stamp will then perform some activity (in-between instructions) when the specified *State* is detected. The activity performed depends on the POLLMODE, POLLOUT and POLLRUN commands.

The "polling" commands allow the BASIC Stamp to respond to certain I/O pin events at a faster rate than what is normally possible through manual PBASIC programming. The term "poll" comes from the fact that the BASIC Stamp module's interpreter periodically checks the state of the designated polled-input pins. It "polls" these pins after the end of each PBASIC command and before it reads the next PBASIC command from the user program; giving the appearance that it is polling "in the background". This feature should not be confused with the concept of interrupts, as the BASIC Stamp *does not support true interrupts*.

The following is an example of the POLLIN command:

A SIMPLE POLLIN EXAMPLE.

```
POLLIN 0, 0
POLLMODE 2
```

The POLLIN command in the above code will cause the BASIC Stamp to set I/O pin 0 to an input mode and get ready to poll it for a low (0) state. The BASIC Stamp will not actually start polling until it is set to the appropriate mode, however. The second line, POLLMODE, initiates the polling process (see the POLLMODE description for more information). From then on, as the BASIC Stamp executes the rest of the program, it will check for a low level (logic 0) on I/O pin 0, in-between instructions.

In the code above, no obvious action will be noticed since we didn't tell the BASIC Stamp what to do when it detects a change on the I/O pin. One possible action the BASIC Stamp can be instructed to take is to change the state of an output, called a polled-output. Take a look at the next example:

SETTING ONE OF THE POSSIBLE ACTIONS: POLLED-OUTPUTS

```
POLLIN 0, 0
POLLOUT 1, 1
POLLMODE 2

Main:
  DEBUG "Looping...", CR
  GOTO Main
```

In this example, in addition to an endless loop, we've added another polling command called POLLOUT (see the POLLOUT description for more information). Our POLLOUT command tells the BASIC Stamp to set I/O pin 1 to an output mode and set it high (1) when it detects the desired poll state. The poll state is the low (0) level on I/O pin 0 that POLLIN told it to look for. If the polled-input pin is high, it will set polled-output pin 0 to low (0), instead.

Once the program reaches the endless loop, at *Main*, it will continuously print "Looping..." on the PC screen. In between reading the DEBUG command and the GOTO command (and vice versa) it will check polled-input pin 0 and set polled-output pin 1 accordingly. In this case, when I/O pin 0 is set low, the BASIC Stamp will set I/O pin 1 high. When I/O pin 0 is set low, the BASIC Stamp will set I/O pin 1 high. It will continue to perform this operation, in-between each command in the loop, endlessly.

THE BASIC STAMP "REMEMBERS" THE POLLING CONFIGURATION FOR THE DURATION OF THE PBASIC PROGRAM.

It's important to note that, in this example, only the DEBUG and GOTO commands are being executed over and over again. The first three lines of code are only run once, yet their effects are "remembered" by the BASIC Stamp throughout the rest of the program.

FOR COMPARISON: ACHIEVING THE SAME EFFECTS WITHOUT THE POLLING COMMANDS.

If the polling commands were not used, the program would have to look like the one below in order to achieve the same effect.

```
INPUT 0
OUTPUT 1

Main:
  OUT1 = ~IN0
  DEBUG "Looping...", CR
  OUT1 = ~IN0
  GOTO Main
```

In this example, we create the inverse relationship of input pin 0 and output pin 1 manually, in-between the DEBUG and GOTO lines. Though the effects are the same as when using the polling commands, this program actually takes a little longer to run and consumes 7 additional bytes of program (EEPROM) space. Clearly, using the polling commands is more efficient.

USING MULTIPLE POLLED-INPUT AND POLLED-OUTPUT PINS.

You can have as many polled-input and polled-output pins as you have available. If multiple polled-input pins are defined, any one of them can trigger changes on the polled-output pins that are also defined. For example:

```
POLLIN 0, 0
POLLIN 1, 0
POLLOUT 2, 1
POLLOUT 3, 1
POLLMODE 2

Main:
  DEBUG "Looping...", CR
  GOTO Main
```

This code sets I/O pins 0 and 1 to polled-input pins (looking for a low (0) state) and sets I/O pins 2 and 3 to polled-output pins (with a high-active

POLLIN – BASIC Stamp Command Reference

state). If either I/O pin 0 or 1 goes low, the BASIC Stamp will set I/O pins 2 and 3 high. This works similar to a logical OR operation. The truth table below shows all the possible states of these two polled-input pins and the corresponding states the BASIC Stamp will set the polled-output pins to.

Polled-Inputs		Polled-Outputs	
0	1	2	3
0	0	0	0
0	1	1	1
1	0	1	1
1	1	1	1

Table 5.74: Polled-Inputs / Polled-Outputs Truth Table.

Normally, any polled-output pins reflect the state changes continuously, as described above. The POLLMODE command supports another feature, however, where the polled-output pins will latch the active state; they will change only once (when the poll state is reached) and stay in the new state until the PBASIC program tells it to change again. See the POLLMODE description for more information.

POLLED-OUTPUTS CAN BE "LATCHED" ALSO.

Other possible actions in response to polled-input states are: 1) Running another program (in a specified program slot), 2) Waiting (pausing program execution with or without low-power mode) until the poll state is reached, or 3) Any combination of the above-mentioned actions.

Demo Program (POLL.bsp)

```
' POLL.bsp
' This program demonstrates POLLIN, POLLOUT, and the use of the POLLMODE
' instruction.  Connect active-low inputs to pins 0, 1, 2, and 3.  Then
' connect an LED to pin 7. The program will print "." to the Debug
' window until one of the alarm buttons are pressed.  This will cause
' the termination of the main loop.  At this point the program will
' save the latched bits, clear them (and the polling process), then
' report the input(s) that triggered the alarm.

' {$STAMP BS2p}
' {$PBASIC 2.5}


FDoor          PIN    0
BDoor          PIN    1
Patio          PIN    2
Rst            PIN    3
AlarmLed       PIN    7

alarms         VAR    Byte            ' alarm bits
```

NOTE: This example program can be used with the BS2p, BS2pe, and BS2px by changing the $STAMP directive accordingly.

```
idx             VAR     Nib                     ' loop control


Setup:
  POLLIN FDoor, 0                               ' define alarm inputs
  POLLIN BDoor, 0
  POLLIN Patio, 0
  POLLOUT AlarmLed, 1                           ' alarm indicator
  POLLMODE 10                                   ' activate latched polling
  DEBUG CLS,
        "Alarms Activated", CR

Main:
  DO
    DEBUG "."                                   ' foreground activity
    PAUSE 50
  LOOP UNTIL (AlarmLed = 1)                     ' loop until LED is on
  GET 128, alarms                               ' get alarm bits
  POLLMODE 0                                    ' deactivate polling

Report:
  DEBUG CLS,                                    ' alarms report
        "Front Door : ", CR,
        "Back Door  : ", CR,
        "Patio      : ", CR

  FOR idx = 0 TO 2                              ' scan alarm bits
    DEBUG CRSRXY, 13, idx                       ' move cursor
    IF (alarms.LOWBIT(idx)) THEN                ' report each bit status
      DEBUG "Alarm", CR
    ELSE
      DEBUG "-", CR
    ENDIF
  NEXT
  DEBUG CR, "Press RESET to clear..."
  DO : LOOP UNTIL (Rst = 0)                     ' wait until Rst pressed
  GOTO Setup
  END
```

POLLMODE | BS1 | BS2 | BS2e | BS2sx | **BS2p** | **BS2pe** | **BS2px** |

POLLMODE *Mode*

Function

Specify a polled command mode.

- *Mode* is a variable/constant/expression (0 – 15) that indicates the mode in which to process the polled command configuration.

Quick Facts

Table 5.75: POLLMODE Quick Facts.

	BS2p, BS2pe, and BS2px
Special Notes	• Polled-output pins will either change states continuously, just once or not at all, depending on the POLLMODE command. • A poll-mode of 2 or 4 is required for a POLLWAIT command to work. • If both polled-outputs and polled-run are active, the polled-output event will occur before the polled-run event.
Useful SPRAM Locations	Locations 128 – 135 hold polled interrupt status. See Table 5.77 for more information.
Related Commands	POLLIN, POLLOUT, POLLRUN and POLLWAIT

Explanation

The POLLMODE command is used to specify the mode in which polling events and activities are processed. This activity will occur in-between instructions during the rest of the PBASIC program.

The "polling" commands allow the BASIC Stamp to respond to certain I/O pin events at a faster rate than what is normally possible through manual PBASIC programming. The term "poll" comes from the fact that the BASIC Stamp's interpreter periodically checks the state of the designated polled-input pins. It "polls" these pins after the end of each PBASIC command and before it reads the next PBASIC command from the user program; giving the appearance that it is polling "in the background". This feature should not be confused with the concept of interrupts, as the BASIC Stamp *does not support true interrupts*.

The POLLMODE command sets one of 15 possible modes for the polling commands. It is used mainly before and/or after any POLLIN, POLLOUT or POLLRUN commands to disable and enable the polling features as desired. Table 5.76 shows the mode values and their effect.

Mode	Effect
0	Deactivate polling, clear polled-input and output configuration.
1	Deactivate polling, save polled-input and output configuration.
2	Activate polling with polled-output action (and polled-wait) only.
3[1]	Activate polling with polled-run action only.
4[2]	Activate polling with polled-output/polled-wait and polled-run actions.
5[3]	Clear polled-input configuration.
6[3]	Clear polled-output configuration.
7[3]	Clear polled-input and output configuration.
8 – 15	Same at 0 – 7 except polled-output states are latched.

Table 5.76: POLLMODE *Mode* Values.

[1] After the polled-run action occurs, the mode switches to 1 (deactivated, saved)
[2] After the polled-run action occurs, the mode switches to 2 (activated, outputs)
[3] These modes do not override the previous mode. Also, the output state of polled-outputs does not change as a result of these modes.

The polled-run modes, 3 and 4, are unique. As soon as the polled-run action occurs, the mode switches to 1 (deactivated, saved) or 2 (activated, outputs), respectively. This is so that the BASIC Stamp doesn't continuously go to the start of the designated program slot while the polled-inputs are in the desired poll state. Without this "one shot" feature, your program would appear to lock-up as long as the polled-inputs are in the designated state.

The clear configuration modes, 5, 6 and 7, are also unique. These modes do not override the previous mode. For example, if polled-inputs, polled-outputs and a polled-run configuration was set and the mode was set to 4 (activated, outputs and run) and later the program issued a POLLMODE 6 command, the polled-output configuration would be cleared but the mode would switch back to 4… still allowing the run action. This also means if, later still, the program issues a POLLOUT command, this polled-output would take effect immediately (since the mode is still 4). Also note that these modes do not change the output state of previously defined polled-output pins.

The POLLMODE command determines what action, if any, will occur in response to a polled-input event. This command works in conjunction with the POLLIN, POLLOUT and POLLRUN commands. The following is an example of the POLLMODE command:

A SIMPLE POLLMODE EXAMPLE.

```
POLLIN 0, 0
POLLOUT 1, 1
POLLMODE 2

Main:
  DEBUG "Looping...", CR
  GOTO Main
```

In this example, the first two lines configure I/O pin 0 as a polled-input (looking for a low state) and I/O pin 1 as a polled-output (going high if I/O pin 0 goes low, and vice versa). The third line, POLLMODE, initiates the polling process and configures polled-outputs to be active. From then on, as the BASIC Stamp executes the rest of the program, it will check for a low level (logic 0) on I/O pin 0, in-between instructions and will set I/O pin 1 accordingly.

If, in the above example, the poll mode was set to 1 (which means deactivate polling but save configuration) I/O pins 0 and 1 would still be defined the same way, and I/O pin 1 would still be set to output mode, but no polling would take place during the rest of the program.

Here's another example that demonstrates mode 1 (deactivate but save configuration).

```
POLLIN 0, 0
POLLOUT 1, 1
POLLMODE 2

DEBUG "Polling configured.", CR

Main:
  POLLMODE 1
  DEBUG "No polling allowed here...", CR
  PAUSE 1000
  POLLMODE 2

Poll_Now:
  DEBUG "Polling now...", CR
  GOTO Poll_Now
```

In this case, polling is configured and activated before "Polling configured" is printed on the screen. Once we reach the *Main* routine, however, polling is disabled (via the POLLMODE 1 command) and no polling occurs during the printing of "No polling allowed here..." or during the 1 second pause afterward. Finally, polling is activated again, and since the configuration was saved (because of mode 1, before) the polling activity acts just like it did initially for the remainder of the program. The ability to temporarily disable polling, without changing the configuration, can be a powerful feature for certain "critical" parts of a program.

The following example contains two programs. The first should be downloaded into program slot 0 and the second into program slot 1.

```
' Pgm #1 (Slot 0) -------------

POLLIN 0, 0
POLLOUT 1, 1
POLLRUN 1
POLLMODE 4

Main:
  DEBUG "Running Program 1", CR
  GOTO Main

' Pgm #2 (Slot 1) -------------

Main:
  DEBUG "Running Program 2", CR
  GOTO Main
```

In this example (containing two programs; one is slot 0 and the other in slot 1) program 1 (slot 0) will configure polled-input pin 0 to detect a low state and polled-output 1 to go high in response. Program 1 also configures a polled-run activity (see the POLLRUN description for more information) to run the program in slot 1. The POLLMODE setting activates the polled-output and the polled-run. Then, program 1 continuously prints "Running Program 1" on the PC screen.

Once I/O pin 0 goes low, however, the BASIC Stamp will set I/O pin 1 high, then execution will be switched to the program in slot 1 (program 2). Program 2 will continuously print "Running Program 2" on the screen. From this point forward, I/O pin 1 will continue to be set low and high in response to changes occurring on I/O pin 0, but the polled-run activity is disabled and the BASIC Stamp endlessly runs the code in program 2's *Main* routine.

The highest locations of Scratch Pad RAM contain run-time information about polled interrupts. See Table 5.77 below.

Table 5.77: Special Purpose Scratch Pad RAM Locations.

Location	BS2p and BS2pe
127	Bits 0-3, Active program slot #. Bits 4-7, program slot for READ and WRITE operations.
128	Polled input trigger status of Main I/O pins 0-7 (0 = not triggered, 1 = triggered).
129	Polled input trigger status of Main I/O pins 8-15 (0 = not triggered, 1 = triggered).
130	Polled input trigger status of Auxiliary I/O pins 0-7 (0 = not triggered, 1 = triggered).
131	Polled input trigger status of Auxiliary I/O pins 8-15 (0 = not triggered, 1 = triggered).
132	Bits 0-3: Polled-interrupt mode, set by POLLMODE
133	Bits 0-2: Polled-interrupt "run" slot, set by POLLRUN.
134	Bit 0: Active I/O group; 0 = Main I/O, 1 = Auxiliary I/O.
135	Bit 0: Polled-output status (set by POLLMODE); 0 = disabled, 1= enabled. Bit 1: Polled-input status; 0 = none defined, 1 = at least one defined. Bit 2: Polled-run status (set by POLLMODE); 0 = disabled, 1 = enabled. Bit 3: Polled-output latch status; 0 = real-time mode, 1 = latch mode. Bit 4: Polled-input state; 0 = no trigger, 1 = triggered. Bit 5: Polled-output latch state; 0 = nothing latched, 1 = signal latched. Bit 6: Poll-wait state; 0 = No Event, 1 = Event Occurred. (Cleared by POLLMODE only). Bit 7: Polling status; 0 = not active, 1 = active.

Demo Program (POLL.bsp)

NOTE: This example program can be used with the BS2p, BS2pe, and BS2px by changing the $STAMP directive accordingly.

```
' POLL.bsp
' This program demonstrates POLLIN, POLLOUT, and the use of the POLLMODE
' instruction.  Connect active-low inputs to pins 0, 1, 2, and 3.  Then
' connect an LED to pin 7. The program will print "." to the Debug
' window until one of the alarm buttons are pressed.  This will cause
' the termination of the main loop.  At this point the program will
' save the latched bits, clear them (and the polling process), then
' report the input(s) that triggered the alarm.

' {$STAMP BS2p}
' {$PBASIC 2.5}


FDoor          PIN      0
BDoor          PIN      1
Patio          PIN      2
Rst            PIN      3
AlarmLed       PIN      7

alarms         VAR      Byte          ' alarm bits
idx            VAR      Nib           ' loop control
```

```
Setup:
  POLLIN FDoor, 0                     ' define alarm inputs
  POLLIN BDoor, 0
  POLLIN Patio, 0
  POLLOUT AlarmLed, 1                 ' alarm indicator
  POLLMODE 10                         ' activate latched polling
  DEBUG CLS,
        "Alarms Activated", CR

Main:
  DO
    DEBUG "."                         ' foreground activity
    PAUSE 50
  LOOP UNTIL (AlarmLed = 1)           ' loop until LED is on
  GET 128, alarms                     ' get alarm bits
  POLLMODE 0                          ' deactivate polling

Report:
  DEBUG CLS,                          ' alarms report
        "Front Door : ", CR,
        "Back Door  : ", CR,
        "Patio      : ", CR

  FOR idx = 0 TO 2                    ' scan alarm bits
    DEBUG CRSRXY, 13, idx             ' move cursor
    IF (alarms.LOWBIT(idx)) THEN      ' report each bit status
      DEBUG "Alarm", CR
    ELSE
      DEBUG "-", CR
    ENDIF
  NEXT
  DEBUG CR, "Press RESET to clear..."
  DO : LOOP UNTIL (Rst = 0)           ' wait until Rst pressed
  GOTO Setup
  END
```

POLLOUT

| BS1 | BS2 | BS2e | BS2sx | **BS2p** | **BS2pe** | **BS2px** |

POLLOUT *Pin, State*

Function

Specify a polled-output pin and active state.

- **Pin** is a variable/constant/expression (0 – 15) that specifies the I/O pin to use. This I/O pin will be set to output mode.

- **State** is a variable/constant/expression (0 – 1) that specifies whether to set the I/O pin low (0) or high (1) when a polled-input pin changes to its poll state.

Quick Facts

Table 5.78: POLLOUT Quick Facts.

	BS2p, BS2pe, and BS2px
Special Notes	• The POLLOUT command will immediately change the I/O pin to an output mode and set its level opposite to that of *State*, regardless of the polled-input states or the polled mode. • Polled-output pins will either change states continuously, just once or not at all, depending on the POLLMODE command. • On the BS2p40, polled-output pins can be defined on both main I/O and auxiliary I/O pins. These are all active regardless of which group the program happens to be using at the time of a polling event. • If both polled-outputs and polled-run are active, the polled-output event will occur before the polled-run event.
Useful SPRAM Locations	Locations 128 – 135 hold polled interrupt status. See Table 5.77 in the POLLMODE command section for more information.
Related Commands	POLLMODE, POLLIN, POLLRUN and POLLWAIT

Explanation

The POLLOUT command is used to specify an output pin that changes states in response to changes on any of the defined polled-input pins. This activity will occur in-between instructions during the rest of the PBASIC program.

The "polling" commands allow the BASIC Stamp to respond to certain I/O pin events at a faster rate than what is normally possible through manual PBASIC programming. The term "poll" comes from the fact that the BASIC Stamp's interpreter periodically checks the state of the designated polled-input pins. It "polls" these pins after the end of each PBASIC command and before it reads the next PBASIC command from the user program; giving the appearance that it is polling "in the background".

This feature should not be confused with the concept of interrupts, as the BASIC Stamp *does not support true interrupts*.

The POLLOUT command achieves one of three possible actions in response to a polled-input event. This command works in conjunction with the POLLIN and POLLMODE commands. The following is an example of the POLLOUT command:

A SIMPLE POLLOUT EXAMPLE.

```
POLLIN 0, 0
POLLOUT 1, 1
POLLMODE 2

Main:
  DEBUG "Looping...", CR
  GOTO Main
```

In this example, the POLLOUT command tells the BASIC Stamp to set I/O pin 1 to an output mode and set it high (1) when it detects the desired poll state. The poll state is the low (0) level on I/O pin 0 that POLLIN told it to look for. If the polled-input pin is high, the BASIC Stamp will set polled-output pin 1 to low (0), instead. The BASIC Stamp will not actually start polling until it is set to the appropriate mode, however. The third line, POLLMODE, initiates the polling process (see the POLLMODE description for more information). From then on, as the BASIC Stamp executes the rest of the program, it will check for a low level (logic 0) on I/O pin 0, in-between instructions.

Once the program reaches the endless loop, it will continuously print "Looping…" on the PC screen. In between reading the DEBUG command and the GOTO command (and vice versa) it will check polled-input pin 0 and set polled-output pin 1 accordingly. In this case, when I/O pin 0 is set high, the BASIC Stamp will set I/O pin 1 low. When I/O pin 0 is set low, the BASIC Stamp will set I/O pin 1 high. It will continue to perform this operation, in-between each command in the loop, endlessly.

It's important to note that in this example only the DEBUG and GOTO commands are being executed over and over again. The first three lines of code are only run once, yet their effects are "remembered" by the BASIC Stamp throughout the rest of the program.

THE BASIC STAMP "REMEMBERS" THE POLLING CONFIGURATION FOR THE DURATION OF THE PBASIC PROGRAM.

If the polling commands were not used, the program would have to look like the one below in order to achieve the same effect.

FOR COMPARISON: ACHIEVING THE SAME EFFECTS WITHOUT THE POLLING COMMANDS.

```
INPUT 0
OUTPUT 1

Main:
  OUT1 = ~IN0
  DEBUG "Looping...", CR
  OUT1 = ~IN0
  GOTO Main
```

In this example, we create the inverse relationship of input pin 0 and output pin 1 manually, in-between the DEBUG and GOTO lines. Though the effects are the same as when using the polling commands, this program actually takes a little longer to run and consumes 7 additional bytes of program (EEPROM) space. Clearly, using the polling commands is more efficient.

USING MULTIPLE POLLED-INPUT AND POLLED-OUTPUT PINS.

You can have as many polled-input and polled-output pins as you have available. If multiple polled-output pins are defined, all of them change in response to changes on the polled-input pins. For example:

```
POLLIN 0, 0
POLLOUT 1, 0
POLLOUT 2, 1
POLLOUT 3, 1
POLLMODE 2

Main:
  DEBUG "Looping...", CR
  GOTO Main
```

This code sets up I/O pin 0 as a polled-input pin (looking for a low (0) state) and sets I/O pins 1, 2 and 3 to polled-output pins. Polled-output pin 1 is set to a low-active state and pins 2 and 3 are set to a high-active state. If I/O pin 0 goes low, the BASIC Stamp will set I/O pin 1 low and I/O pins 2 and 3 high. The table below shows the two possible states of the polled-input pin and the corresponding states the BASIC Stamp will set the polled-output pins to.

Table 5.79: POLLOUT Truth Table.

Polled-Input	Polled-Outputs		
0	1	2	3
1	1	0	0
0	0	1	1

POLLED-OUTPUTS CAN BE "LATCHED" ALSO.

Normally, any polled-output pins reflect the state changes continuously, as described above. The POLLMODE command supports another feature, however, where the polled-output pins will latch the active state; they will change only once (when the poll state is reached) and stay in the new state until the PBASIC program tells it to change again. See the POLLMODE description for more information.

A clever use of the "latched" feature is to set a polled input on the same pin as a polled output. This leaves the pin in an input state, and the "latched" state of that input pin will be saved in the pin's output latch bit (which is otherwise not used because the pin was last set to input mode). This gives us the advantage of having a run-time readable bit that indicates whether the input pin changed state while we were busy. For example, suppose an application needed to respond in some way if an input pin goes high, but it doesn't need to respond immediately, and the other tasks should not be interrupted. In essence, we need a way to know if the pin has gone high since the last time we checked it. Look at this example:

A CLEVER TRICK WITH POLLOUT AND THE "LATCHED" FEATURE.

```
alarm           VAR     OUT0
idx             VAR     Byte

Setup:
  POLLOUT 0, 1
  POLLIN 0, 0
  POLLMODE 10

Work:
  FOR idx = 1 TO 25
    DEBUG "Working...", CR
  NEXT
  IF (Alarm = 0) THEN Work

Respond:
  DEBUG CR, "Hey, the Alarm was tripped!", CR
  PAUSE 1000
  POLLMODE 10
  GOTO Work
```

Here, we set I/O pin 0 to a polled-output, then immediately set it to a polled-input. Then we set the polled-mode to latch the polled-outputs. Afterwards, the program performs some work, and once in a while, checks the state of OUT0 (named *Alarm* in the program). If *Alarm* is 0, I/O pin 0 was never seen to go high. If, however, *Alarm* is 1, I/O pin 0 must have gone high while the program was doing other work, and now it can respond in the proper manner. This even works if the input pin had gone high and then low again before we check it (as long as it was high at some point in between the instructions in our *Work* routine).

It is important to note that during the time between the POLLOUT and POLLIN commands, I/O pin 0 will be set to an output direction. This can cause a temporary short within the circuitry connected to I/O pin 0, so it is vital that a large enough series resistor (perhaps 100 ohms or greater) be inserted on that pin to protect the external device and the BASIC Stamp.

Demo Program (POLL.bsp)

NOTE: This example program can be used with the BS2p, BS2pe, and BS2px by changing the $STAMP directive accordingly.

```
' POLL.bsp
' This program demonstrates POLLIN, POLLOUT, and the use of the POLLMODE
' instruction.  Connect active-low inputs to pins 0, 1, 2, and 3.  Then
' connect an LED to pin 7. The program will print "." to the Debug
' window until one of the alarm buttons are pressed.  This will cause
' the termination of the main loop.  At this point the program will
' save the latched bits, clear them (and the polling process), then
' report the input(s) that triggered the alarm.

' {$STAMP BS2p}
' {$PBASIC 2.5}


FDoor          PIN      0
BDoor          PIN      1
Patio          PIN      2
Rst            PIN      3
AlarmLed       PIN      7

alarms         VAR      Byte          ' alarm bits
idx            VAR      Nib           ' loop control


Setup:
  POLLIN FDoor, 0                     ' define alarm inputs
  POLLIN BDoor, 0
  POLLIN Patio, 0
  POLLOUT AlarmLed, 1                 ' alarm indicator
  POLLMODE 10                         ' activate latched polling
  DEBUG CLS,
        "Alarms Activated", CR

Main:
  DO
    DEBUG "."                         ' foreground activity
    PAUSE 50
  LOOP UNTIL (AlarmLed = 1)           ' loop until LED is on
  GET 128, alarms                     ' get alarm bits
  POLLMODE 0                          ' deactivate polling

Report:
  DEBUG CLS,                          ' alarms report
```

```
        "Front Door : ", CR,
        "Back Door  : ", CR,
        "Patio      : ", CR

FOR idx = 0 TO 2                    ' scan alarm bits
  DEBUG CRSRXY, 13, idx            ' move cursor
  IF (alarms.LOWBIT(idx)) THEN     ' report each bit status
    DEBUG "Alarm", CR
  ELSE
    DEBUG "-", CR
  ENDIF
NEXT
DEBUG CR, "Press RESET to clear..."
DO : LOOP UNTIL (Rst = 0)          ' wait until Rst pressed
GOTO Setup
END
```

POLLRUN

BS1	BS2	BS2e	BS2sx	BS2p	BS2pe	BS2px

POLLRUN *ProgramSlot*

Function

Specify a program to run upon a polled-input event.

- **ProgramSlot** is a variable/constant/expression (0 – 7) that specifies the program slot to run when a polled-input event occurs.

Quick Facts

	BS2p, BS2pe, and BS2px
Default *ProgramSlot*	The default polled-run slot is 0. If no POLLRUN command is given and a poll mode of 3 or 4 is set, the program in slot 0 will run in response to a polled-input event.
Special Notes	• If both polled-outputs and polled-run are active, the polled-output event will occur before the polled-run event.
Useful SPRAM locations	Locations 128 – 135 hold polled interrupt status. See Table 5.77 in the POLLMODE command section for more information.
Related commands	POLLMODE, POLLIN, POLLOUT, POLLWAIT and RUN

Explanation

The POLLRUN command is used to specify a program slot to run in response to a polled event. This activity can occur in between any two instructions within the rest of the PBASIC program.

The "polling" commands allow the BASIC Stamp to respond to certain I/O pin events at a faster rate than what is normally possible through manual PBASIC programming. The term "poll" comes from the fact that the BASIC Stamp's interpreter periodically checks the state of the designated polled-input pins. It "polls" these pins after the end of each PBASIC command and before it reads the next PBASIC command from the user program; giving the appearance that it is polling "in the background". This feature should not be confused with the concept of interrupts, as the BASIC Stamp *does not support true interrupts*.

The following is a simple example of the POLLRUN command.

```
POLLIN 0, 0
POLLRUN 1
POLLMODE 3

Main:
  DEBUG "Waiting in Program Slot 0...", CR
  GOTO Main
```

The first line of the above code will set up I/O pin 0 as a polled-input pin looking for a low (0) state. The second line, POLLRUN, tells the BASIC Stamp that when I/O pin 0 goes low, it should switch execution over to the program residing in program slot 1. The third line, POLLMODE, activates the polled-run configuration.

Once the BASIC Stamp reaches the *Main* routine, it will continuously print "Waiting in Program Slot 0..." on the PC screen. In between reading the DEBUG and GOTO commands, however, the BASIC Stamp will poll I/O pin 0 and check for a high or low state. If the state of pin 0 is high, it will do nothing and continue as normal. If the state of pin 0 is low, it will switch execution over to the program in slot 1 (the second program is not shown in this example). The switch to another program slot works exactly like with the RUN command; the designated program is run and the BASIC Stamp does not "return" to the previous program (similar to a GOTO command).

Note that in order for the polled-run activity to occur, the poll mode must be set to either 3 or 4 (the two modes that activate polled-run). Also note, that the polled-run modes, 3 and 4, are unique. As soon as the polled-run action occurs, the mode switches to 1 (deactivated, saved) or 2 (activated, outputs), respectively. This is so that the BASIC Stamp doesn't continuously go to the start of the designated program slot while the polled-inputs are in the desired poll state. Without this "one shot" feature, your program would appear to lock-up as long as the polled-inputs are in the designated state.

After the program switch takes place, the *ProgramSlot* value is maintained. Any future change to poll mode 3 or 4, without another POLLRUN command, will result in the previously defined program slot being used.

Demo Program (POLLRUN0.bsp)

```
' POLLRUN0.bsp
' This program demonstrates the POLLRUN command.  It is intended to be
' downloaded to program slot 0, and the program called POLLRUN1.bsp
' should be downloaded to program slot 1.  I/O pin 0 is set to watch for
' a low signal.  Once the Main routine starts running, the program
' continuously prints it's program slot number to the screen.  If I/O
' pin 0 goes low, the program in program slot 1 (which should be
' POLLRUN1.bsp) is run.

' {$STAMP BS2p, POLLRUN1.BSP}
' {$PBASIC 2.5}

pgmSlot          VAR      Byte

Setup:
  POLLIN  0, 0                          ' polled-input, look for 0
  POLLRUN 1                             ' run slot 1 on polled activation
  POLLMODE 3                            ' enable polling

Main:
  GET 127, pgmSlot
  DEBUG "Running Program #", DEC pgmSlot.LOWNIB, CR
  GOTO Main
  END
```

Demo Program (POLLRUN1.bsp)

```
' POLLRUN1.bsp
' This program demonstrates the POLLRUN command.  It is intended to be
' downloaded to program slot 1, and the program called POLLRUN0.bsp
' should be downloaded to program slot 0.  This program is run when
' program 0 detects a low on I/O pin 0 via the polled commands.

' {$STAMP BS2p}
' {$PBASIC 2.5}

pgmSlot          VAR      Byte

Main:
  GET 127, pgmSlot
  DEBUG "Running Program #", DEC pgmSlot.LOWNIB, CR
  GOTO Main
  END
```

POLLWAIT | BS1 | BS2 | BS2e | BS2sx | **BS2p** | **BS2pe** | **BS2px**

POLLWAIT *Duration*

Function

Pause program execution, in a low-power mode, in units of *Duration* until any polled-input pin reaches the desired poll state.

- **Duration** is a variable/constant/expression (0 – 8) that specifies the duration of the low-power state. The duration is (2^*Duration*) * 18 ms. Table 5.82 on page 336 indicates the low-power length for any given *Duration*. Using 8 as the *Duration* is a special case; the BS2p, BS2pe, and BS2px will not go into low-power mode and will respond quicker to polled-inputs.

Quick Facts

Table 5.81: POLLWAIT Quick Facts.

	BS2p	**BS2pe**	**BS2px**
Current draw during POLLWAIT	350 µA	36 µA	450 µA
Response Time with Duration set to 8	Less than 160 µs	Less than 250 µs	Less than 100 µs
Accuracy of NAP	–50 to 100% (±10% @ 75°F with stable power supply)		
Special Notes	• Poll mode must be 2 or 4 and at least one polled-input must be set to activate POLLWAIT (POLLWAIT will be ignored otherwise). • If both polled-wait and polled-run are active, the polled-run event will occur immediately after the polled-wait detects an event.		
Useful SPRAM Locations	Locations 128 – 135 hold polled interrupt status. See Table 5.77 in the POLLMODE command section for more information.		
Related Commands	POLLMODE, POLLIN, POLLOUT, POLLRUN, END, NAP and SLEEP		

Explanation

The POLLWAIT command is used to pause program execution and go into a low-power state until any polled-input pin reaches the desired poll state.

The "polling" commands allow the BASIC Stamp to respond to certain I/O pin events at a faster rate than what is normally possible through manual PBASIC programming. The term "poll" comes from the fact that the BASIC Stamp's interpreter periodically checks the state of the designated polled-input pins. It "polls" these pins after the end of each PBASIC command and before it reads the next PBASIC command from the user program; giving the appearance that it is polling "in the background". This feature should not be confused with the concept of interrupts, as the BASIC Stamp *does not support true interrupts*.

The POLLWAIT command is unique among the polling commands in that it actually causes execution to halt, until a polled-input pin event occurs. The *Duration* argument is similar to that of the NAP command; using the values 0 to 7 specifies the duration of the low-power period. After the low-power period is over, the BASIC Stamp polls the polled-input pins and determines if any meet the desired poll state. If no polled-input is in the desired state (as set by POLLIN command) the BASIC Stamp goes back into low-power mode, again, for the same duration as before. If any polled-input is in the desired state, however, the BASIC Stamp will continue execution with the next line of code.

A *Duration* of 8 makes the BASIC Stamp pause execution in normal running mode (not low-power mode) until a polled-input event occurs. The response time is indicated in Table 5.81 on page 335. Since the response time is so fast, this feature can be used to synchronize a portion of PBASIC code to an incoming pulse.

Duration	Length of Low-Power Mode
0	18 ms
1	36 ms
2	72 ms
3	144 ms
4	288 ms
5	576 ms
6	1152 ms (1.152 seconds)
7	2304 ms (2.304 seconds)
8	No power-down

Table 5.82: *Duration* values and associated low-power modes.

The following is a simple example of the POLLWAIT command.

A SIMPLE POLLWAIT EXAMPLE.

```
POLLIN 0, 0
POLLMODE 2

Main:
  POLLWAIT 2
  TOGGLE 1
  GOTO Main
```

In this example, the POLLIN command sets I/O pin 0 to be a polled-input pin looking for a low (0) state. The *Main* routine immediately runs a POLLWAIT command and specifies a *Duration* of 2 (which results in a low-power state of 72 ms). This means that every 72 ms, the BASIC Stamp wakes-up and checks I/O pin 0 for a low. If I/O pin 0 is high, it goes back to sleep for another 72 ms. If I/O pin 0 is low, it runs the next line of code, which toggles the state of I/O pin 1. Then the loop starts all over again. Note: Due to the nature of low-power mode, I/O pin 1 may toggle between high and low (at 72 ms intervals in this case) even if I/O pin 0 stays high. This is an artifact of the "reset" condition in the interpreter chip that occurs when the chip wakes up from a low-power state. Upon this "reset" condition, all the I/O pins are switched to inputs for approximately 18 ms. It is the switching to inputs that will cause I/O pin 1 to appear to toggle. See the NAP or SLEEP commands for more information.

If low-power mode is not required, change the POLLWAIT command in the example above to "POLLWAIT 8" instead. This will have the effect of keeping the BASIC Stamp in normal running mode (i.e.: no low-power glitches) and will also cause the TOGGLE command to execute in a much shorter amount of time after a polled-input event occurs.

Demo Program (POLLWAIT.bsp)

NOTE: This example program can be used with the BS2p, BS2pe, and BS2px by changing the $STAMP directive accordingly.

```
' POLLWAIT.bsp
' This program demonstrates the POLLWAIT command.  I/O pin 0 is set to
' watch for a low signal.  Once the Main routine starts running, the
' POLLWAIT command causes the program to halt until the polled event
' happens (I/O pin is low) then it prints a message on the PC screen.
' It will do nothing until I/O pin is low.

' {$STAMP BS2p}
' {$PBASIC 2.5}


Setup:
  POLLIN 0, 0                          ' polled-input, look for 0
  POLLMODE 2                           ' enable polling

Main:
  POLLWAIT 8                           ' Wait for polled event
  DEBUG "I/O pin 0 is LOW!", CR        ' Print message
  GOTO Main
  END
```

POT

POT *Pin, Scale, Variable*

(See RCTIME)

Function

Read a 5 kΩ to 50 kΩ potentiometer, thermistor, photocell, or other variable resistance.

- **Pin** is a variable/constant (0 – 7) that specifies the I/O pin to use. This pin will be set to output mode initially, then to input mode.

- **Scale** is a variable/constant (0 – 255) used to scale the command's internal 16-bit result. See explanation below for steps to finding the scale value to use for your circuit.

- **Variable** is a variable (usually a byte) where the final result of the reading will be stored. Internally, the POT command calculates a 16-bit value, which is scaled down to an 8-bit value.

Explanation

POT reads a variable resistance and returns a value (0 – 255) representing the amount of time it took to discharge the capacitor through the resistance. *Pin* must be connected to one side of the variable resistance, whose other side is connected through a capacitor to ground, as shown in Figure 5.27.

Figure 5.27: Example Variable Resistance Circuit.

PO

5 kΩ to 50 kΩ variable resistance

0.1 uF

Vss

HOW POT REALLY WORKS.

POT works by first setting the specified I/O pin to an output and setting its state high. This step places +5 volts on one side of the capacitor (see Figure 5.27) and ground (0 volts) on the other side, which charges the capacitor. POT waits for 10 ms and then sets the I/O pin to an input mode and starts its timer. Initially the I/O pin will see a high (1) that will eventually drop to a low (0) when the capacitor discharges past the 1.4-volt threshold. The timer stops once the low is seen. The value of the variable resistor affects the time it takes to discharge the capacitor from 5 volts to approximately 1.4 volts.

The 16-bit reading is multiplied by (*Scale*/256), so a scale value of 128 would reduce the range by approximately 50%, a scale of 64 would reduce to 25%, and so on. The amount by which the internal value must be scaled varies with the size of the resistor being used.

Finding the best Scale value:
1. Build the circuit shown in Figure 5.27 and plug the BS1 into the PC.
2. In the BASIC Stamp editor select *Pot Scaling* from the *Run* menu. A special calibration window appears, allowing you to find the best value.
3. The window asks for the number of the I/O pin to which the variable resistor is connected. Select the appropriate pin (0-7) from the drop-down.
4. The editor downloads a short program to the BS1 (this overwrites any program already stored in the BS1).
5. The window will now show the Scale Factor. Adjust the resistor until the smallest number is shown for scale (assuming you can adjust the resistor, as with a potentiometer).
6. Once you've found the smallest number for scale, you're done. This number should be used for the Scale in the POT command.
7. Optionally, you can verify the scale number found above by selecting the POT Value checkbox (so it's checked). This locks the scale and causes the BS1 to read the resistor continuously. The window displays the value. If the scale is good, you should be able to adjust the resistor, achieving a 0–255 reading for the value (or as close as possible). To change the scale value and repeat this step, deselect the POT Value checkbox. Continue this process until you find the best scale.

Demo Program (POT.bs1)

```
' POT.bs1
' This program demonstrates the use of the POT command.  Connect one side
' of a 5-50K potentiometer to P0.  To the other side of the potentiometer
' connect a 0.1 uF capacitor, and then connect the other side of the
' capacitor to Vss (ground).  Before running demo program,
' use the Run | POT Scaling dialog to determine the best Scale factor.
```

```
' {$STAMP BS1}
' {$PBASIC 1.0}

SYMBOL   PotPin        = 0          ' pot connected to P0
SYMBOL   Scale         = 111        ' scale value for test circuit

SYMBOL   level         = B2         ' storage of pot "level"

Main:
  POT PotPin, Scale, level         ' read pot level
  DEBUG CLS, "Level = ", #level     ' display
  PAUSE 50                          ' short delay
  GOTO Main                         ' repeat forever
  END
```

PULSIN

| BS1 | BS2 | BS2e | BS2sx | BS2p | BS2pe | BS2px |

PULSIN *Pin, State, Variable*

Function

Measure the width of a pulse on *Pin* described by *State* and store the result in *Variable*.

- **Pin** is a variable/constant/expression (0 – 15) that specifies the I/O pin to use. This pin will be set to input mode.

- **State** is a variable/constant/expression (0 – 1) that specifies whether the pulse to be measured is low (0) or high (1). A low pulse begins with a 1-to-0 transition and a high pulse begins with a 0-to-1 transition.

- **Variable** is a variable (usually a word) in which the measured pulse duration will be stored. The unit of time for *Variable* is described in Table 5.83.

Quick Facts

Table 5.83: PULSIN Quick Facts.

	BS1	BS2	BS2e	BS2sx	BS2p	BS2pe	BS2px
Units in Variable	10 µs	2 µs	2 µs	0.8 µs	0.8 µs	2 µs	0.81 µs
Maximum Pulse Width	655.35 ms	131.07 ms	131.07 ms	52.428 ms	52.428 ms	123.6 ms	53.08 ms
Related Commands	PULSOUT and COUNT						

Explanation

PULSIN is like a fast stopwatch that is triggered by a change in state (0 or 1) on the specified pin. The entire width of the specified pulse (high or low) is measured, in units shown in Table 5.83, and stored in *Variable*.

Many analog properties (voltage, resistance, capacitance, frequency, duty cycle) can be measured in terms of pulse durations. This makes PULSIN a valuable form of analog-to-digital conversion.

SPECIFICS OF PULSIN'S OPERATION.

PULSIN will wait, for the desired pulse, for up to the maximum pulse width it can measure, shown in Table 5.83. If it sees the desired pulse, it measures the time until the end of the pulse and stores the result in *Variable*. If it never sees the start of the pulse, or the pulse is too long (greater than the Maximum Pulse Width shown in Table 5.83) PULSIN "times out" and store 0 in *Variable*. This operation keeps your program from locking-up should the desired pulse never occur.

Regardless of the size of *Variable*, PULSIN internally uses a 16-bit timer. Unless the pulse widths are known to be short enough to fit in an 8-bit result, it is recommended to use a word-sized variable. Not doing so may result in strange and misleading results as the BASIC Stamp will only store the lower 8-bits into a byte variable.

HOW THE RESULT IS REPORTED.

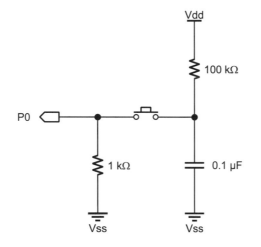

Vdd

100 kΩ

P0

1 kΩ

0.1 µF

Vss

Vss

Figure 5.28: R/C Pulse Generator.

Demo Program (PULSIN.bs1)

```
' PULSIN.bs1
' This program uses PULSIN to measure a pulse generated by discharging a
' 0.1 uF capacitor through a 1k resistor. Pressing the switch generates
' the pulse, which should ideally be approximately 120 us (12 PULSIN units
' of 10 us) long. Variations in component values may produce results that
' are up to 10 units off from this value. For more information on
' calculating resistor-capacitor timing, see the RCTIME command.

' {$STAMP BS1}
' {$PBASIC 1.0}

SYMBOL  Pulse       = 7            ' pulse input pin

SYMBOL  time        = W1           ' pulse width (10 uS units)
```

```
Main:
  PULSIN Pulse, 1, time                  ' measure positive pulse
  IF time = 0 THEN Main                  ' if 0, try again
  DEBUG CLS, time                        '   else display result
  GOTO Main
  END
```

Demo Program (PULSIN.bs2)

All 2

NOTE: This example program can be used with all BS2 models. This program uses conditional compilation techniques; see Chapter 3 for more information.

```
' PULSIN.bs2
' This program uses PULSIN to measure a pulse generated by discharging a
' 0.1 uF capacitor through a 1K resistor. Pressing the switch generates
' the pulse, which should ideally be approximately 120 us (60 PULSIN units
' of 2 us) long (for BS2 and BS2e). Variations in component values may
' produce results that are up to 10 units off from this value.  For more
' information on calculating resistor-capacitor timing, see the RCTIME
' command.

' {$STAMP BS2}
' {$PBASIC 2.5}

Pulse           PIN     7                ' pulse input pin

#SELECT $STAMP
  #CASE BS2, BS2E, BS2PE
    Scale       CON     $200             ' 2.0 us per unit
  #CASE BS2SX, BS2P
    Scale       CON     $0CC             ' 0.8 us per unit
  #CASE BS2PX
    Scale       CON     $0CF             ' 0.81 us per unit

#ENDSELECT

time            VAR     Word

Main:
  PULSIN Pulse, 1, time                  ' measure positive pulse
  IF (time > 0) THEN                     ' if not 0
    DEBUG HOME,
          DEC time, " units ", CLREOL    ' display raw input
    time = time */ Scale                 ' adjust for Stamp
    DEBUG CR,
          DEC time, " us  "              ' display microseconds
  ELSE
    DEBUG CLS, "Out of Range"            ' else error message
  ENDIF
  PAUSE 200
  GOTO Main
  END
```

PULSOUT

| BS1 | BS2 | BS2e | BS2sx | BS2p | BS2pe | BS2px |

PULSOUT *Pin, Duration*

Function

Generate a pulse on *Pin* with a width of *Duration*.

- **Pin** is a variable/constant/expression (0 – 15) that specifies the I/O pin to use. This pin will be set to output mode.

- **Duration** is a variable/constant/expression (0 – 65535) that specifies the duration of the pulse. The unit of time for *Duration* is described in Table 5.84.

NOTE: Expressions are not allowed as arguments on the BS1. The range of the *Pin* argument on the BS1 is 0 – 7.

Quick Facts

Table 5.84: PULSOUT Quick Facts.

	BS1	BS2	BS2e	BS2sx	BS2p	BS2pe	BS2px
***Duration* units**	10 µs	2 µs	2 µs	0.8 µs	0.8 µs	2 µs	0.8 µs
Maximum Pulse Width	655.35 ms	131.07 ms	131.07 ms	52.428 ms	52.428 ms	131.07 ms	52.428 ms
Related Command	PULSIN						

Explanation

PULSOUT sets *Pin* to output mode, inverts the state of that pin; waits for the specified *Duration*; then inverts the state of the pin again; returning the bit to its original state. The unit of *Duration* is described in Table 5.84. The following example will generate a 100 µs pulse on I/O pin 7 (of the BS2):

```
PULSOUT 7, 50                           ' generate 100 us pulse on P7
```

CONTROLLING THE POLARITY OF THE PULSE.

The polarity of the pulse depends on the state of the pin before the command executes. In the example above, if pin 7 was low, PULSOUT would produce a positive (high) pulse. If the pin was high, PULSOUT would produce a negative (low) pulse.

WATCH OUT FOR UNDESIRABLE PULSE GLITCHES.

If the pin is an input, the output state bit, OUT7 (PIN7 on the BS1) won't necessarily match the state of the pin. What happens then? For example: pin 7 is an input (DIR7 = 0) and pulled high by a resistor as shown in Figure 5.29a. Suppose that pin 7 is low when we execute the instruction:

```
PULSOUT 7, 5                            ' generate pulse on P7
```

Figure 5.29b shows the sequence of events on that pin. Initially, pin 7 is high. Its output driver is turned off (because it is in input mode), so the 10 kΩ resistor sets the state on the pin. When PULSOUT executes, it turns on the output driver, allowing OUT7 (PIN7 on the BS1) to control the pin.

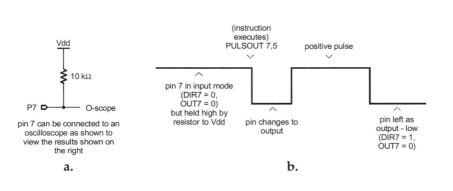

Figure 5.29: Example Pulse Diagram.

Since OUT7 (PIN7 on the BS1) is low, the pin goes low. After a few microseconds of preparation, PULSOUT inverts the state of the pin; from low to high. It leaves the pin in that state for the specified time (10µs if using a BS2) and then inverts it again, leaving the pin in its original state.

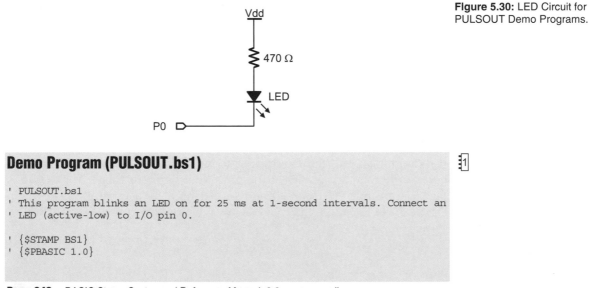

Figure 5.30: LED Circuit for PULSOUT Demo Programs.

Demo Program (PULSOUT.bs1)

```
' PULSOUT.bs1
' This program blinks an LED on for 25 ms at 1-second intervals. Connect an
' LED (active-low) to I/O pin 0.

' {$STAMP BS1}
' {$PBASIC 1.0}
```

```
Setup:
  HIGH 0                              ' make P0 high (LED off)

Main:
  PULSOUT 0, 2500                     ' flash LED for 25 mS
  PAUSE 1000                          ' one second delay
  GOTO Main
  END
```

All 2
Demo Program (PULSOUT.bs2)

NOTE: This example program can be used with all BS2 models. This program uses conditional compilation techniques; see Chapter 3 for more information.

```
' PULSOUT.bs2
' This program blinks an LED on for 25 ms at 1-second intervals. Connect an
' LED (active-low) to I/O pin 0.

' {$STAMP BS2}
' {$PBASIC 2.5}

#SELECT $STAMP
  #CASE BS2, BS2E, BS2PE
    Scale       CON     500           ' to ms for 2 us per unit
  #CASE BS2SX, BS2P, BS2PX
    Scale       CON     1250          ' to ms for 0.8 us per unit
#ENDSELECT

Flash           CON     25 * Scale    ' 25 milliseconds


Setup:
  HIGH 0                              ' make P0 high (LED off)

Main:
  PULSOUT 0, Flash                    ' flash LED
  PAUSE 1000                          ' one second delay
  GOTO Main
  END
```

PUT

BS1	BS2	BS2e	BS2sx	BS2p	BS2pe	BS2px

PUT *Location*, **{ WORD }** *Value* **{ , { WORD }** *Value...* **}**

NOTE: The optional arguments require PBASIC 2.5.

Function

Write one or more values to the Scratch Pad RAM (SPRAM), starting at *Location*.

- **Location** is a variable/constant/expression (0 – 62 for BS2e and BS2sx, and 0 – 126 for BS2p, BS2pe, and BS2px) that specifies the SPRAM location to write to.

- **Value** is a variable/constant/expression (0 – 255, or 0 – 65535 if using the optional WORD modifier) to store in the SPRAM.

Quick Facts

Table 5.85: PUT Quick Facts.

NOTE: When the WORD modifier is used, the low byte of the value is written to *Location*, the high byte to *Location* + 1.

	BS2e and BS2sx	BS2p, BS2pe, and BS2px
Scratch Pad RAM Size and Organization	64 bytes (0 – 63). Organized as bytes only.	136 bytes (0 – 135). Organized as bytes only.
General Purpose Locations	0 - 62	0 – 126
Special Use Location	Location 63: Active program slot number (read only).	Location 127: READ/WRITE slot and Active Program slot (read only). Locations 128-135: Polled Interrupt status (read only).
Related Commands	GET	GET and STORE, and SPSTR formatter.
PBASIC 2.5 Syntax Options	Multiple sequential variables may be written to the Scratch Pad RAM. The optional WORD modifier may be specified to store 16-bit values.	

Explanation

The PUT command writes value into the specified Scratch Pad RAM (SPRAM) location. All values in the general-purpose locations can be written to from within any of the 8 program slots.

USES FOR SCRATCH PAD RAM.

SPRAM is useful for passing data to programs in other program slots and for additional workspace. It is different than regular RAM in that symbol names cannot be assigned directly to locations and each location is always configured as a byte only. The following code will write the value 100 to location 25, read it back out with GET, and display it:

```
temp     VAR     byte

PUT 25, 100                              ' put low byte
GET 25, temp                             ' read byte value
DEBUG DEC temp                           ' display byte value
```

When using the $PBASIC 2.5 directive, multiple sequential values may be stored to SPRAM, starting at *Location*, and the WORD modifier may be specified to store 16-bit values.

```
' {$PBASIC 2.5}

temp     VAR     Word

PUT 25, Word 2125                        ' write word value
GET 25, Word temp                        ' read word value
DEBUG DEC temp                           ' display 2125
```

Most Scratch Pad RAM locations are available for general use. The highest locations have a special, read-only purpose; see the GET command for more information.

SCRATCH PAD RAM LOCATIONS AND THEIR PURPOSE.

Demo Program (GET_PUT1.bsx)

NOTE: This is written for the BS2sx but can be used with the BS2e, BS2p, BS2pe and BS2px also. This program uses conditional compilation techniques; see Chapter 3 for more information.

```
' GET_PUT1.bsx
' This example demonstrates the use of the GET and PUT commands.  First,
' slot location is read using GET to display the currently running program
' number.  Then a set of values are written (PUT) into locations 0 TO 9.
' Afterwards, program number 1 is RUN.  This program is a BS2SX project
' consisting of GET_PUT1.BSX and GET_PUT2.BSX, but will run on the BS2e,
' BS2p, BS2pe, and BS2px without modification.

' {$STAMP BS2sx, GET_PUT2.BSX}
' {$PBASIC 2.5}

#SELECT $STAMP
  #CASE BS2
    #ERROR "BS2e or greater required."
  #CASE BS2E, BS2SX
    Slot        CON      63
  #CASE BS2P, BS2PE, BS2PX
    Slot        CON      127
#ENDSELECT

value           VAR      Byte
idx             VAR      Byte


Setup:
  GET Slot, value
```

```
    DEBUG "Program Slot #", DEC value.NIB0, CR

Main:
  FOR idx = 0 TO 9
    value = (idx + 3) * 8
    PUT idx, value
    DEBUG "  Writing: ", DEC2 value, " to location: ", DEC2 idx, CR
  NEXT
  DEBUG CR
  RUN 1
  END
```

NOTE: This is written for the BS2sx but can be used with the BS2e, BS2p, BS2pe, and BS2px also. This program uses conditional compilation techniques; see Chapter 3 for more information.

Demo Program (GET_PUT2.bsx)

```
' GET_PUT2.bsx
' This example demonstrates the use of the GET and PUT commands.  First,
' the Slot location is read using GET to display the currently running
' program number.  Then a set of values are read (GET) from locations
' 0 to 9 and displayed on the screen for verification.  This program is a
' BS2SX project consisting of GET_PUT1.BSX and GET_PUT2.BSX, but will run
' on the BS2e, BS2p, BS2pe, and BS2px without modification.

' {$STAMP BS2sx}
' {$PBASIC 2.5}

#SELECT $STAMP
  #CASE BS2
    #ERROR "BS2e or greater required."
  #CASE BS2E, BS2SX
    Slot        CON     63
  #CASE BS2P, BS2PE, BS2PX
    Slot        CON     127
#ENDSELECT

value           VAR     Byte
idx             VAR     Byte


Setup:
  GET Slot, value
  DEBUG "Program Slot #", DEC value.NIB0, CR

Main:
  FOR idx = 0 TO 9
    GET idx, value
    DEBUG "  Reading: ", DEC2 value, " from location: ", DEC2 idx, CR
  NEXT
  END
```

PWM

BS1	BS2	BS2e	BS2sx	BS2p	BS2pe	BS2px

 PWM *Pin, Duty, Cycles*

Function

Convert a digital value to analog output via pulse-width modulation.

- ***Pin*** is a variable/constant/expression (0 – 15) that specifies the I/O pin to use. This pin will be set to output mode initially then set to input mode when the command finishes.

- ***Duty*** is a variable/constant/expression (0 - 255) that specifies the analog output level (0 to 5V).

- ***Cycles*** is a variable/constant/expression (0 - 255) that specifies the duration of the PWM signal.

Quick Facts

Table 5.86: PWM Quick Facts

	BS1	BS2	BS2e	BS2sx	BS2p	BS2pe	BS2px
Units in *Cycles*	5 ms	1 ms	1 ms	0.4 ms	0.65 ms	1.62 ms	0.4 ms
Average Voltage Equation	Average Voltage = (Duty / 255) * 5 volts						
Required ChargeTime (*Cycles*) Equation	Charge time = 5 * R * C						
Special Notes	*Pin* is set to output initially, and set to input at end						
Related Commands	none	FREQOUT and DTMFOUT					

Explanation

Pulse-width modulation (PWM) allows the BASIC Stamp (a purely digital device) to generate an analog voltage. The basic idea is this: If you make a pin output high, the voltage at that pin will be close to 5 V. Output low is close to 0 V. What if you switched the pin rapidly between high and low so that it was high half the time and low half the time? The average voltage over time would be halfway between 0 and 5 V (2.5 V). PWM emits a burst of 1s and 0s whose ratio is proportional to the duty value you specify, making the average voltage over time somewhere between 0 and 5 V.

DETERMINING AVERAGE VOLTAGE FOR A PARTICULAR DUTY CYCLE.

The proportion of 1s to 0s in PWM is called the duty cycle. The duty cycle controls the analog voltage in a very direct way; the higher the duty cycle the higher the voltage. In the case of the BASIC Stamp, the duty cycle can range from 0 to 255. Duty is literally the proportion of 1s to 0s output by the PWM command. To determine the proportional PWM output voltage, use this formula: $(Duty/255) * 5V$. For example, if $Duty$ is 100, $(100/255) * 5V = 1.96V$; PWM outputs a train of pulses whose average voltage is 1.96V.

In order to convert PWM into an analog voltage we have to filter out the pulses and store the average voltage. The resistor/capacitor combination in Figure 5.31 will do the job. The capacitor will hold the voltage set by PWM even after the instruction has finished. How long it will hold the voltage depends on how much current is drawn from it by external circuitry, and the internal leakage of the capacitor. In order to hold the voltage relatively steady, a program must periodically repeat the PWM instruction to give the capacitor a fresh charge. FILTERING THE PWM SIGNAL.

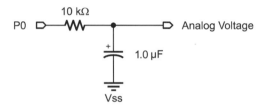

Figure 5.31: Example PWM Filter Circuit.

Just as it takes time to discharge a capacitor, it also takes time to charge it in the first place. The PWM command lets you specify the charging time in terms of PWM cycles. The period of each cycle is shown in Table 5.86. So, on the BS2, to charge a capacitor for 5ms, you would specify 5 cycles in the PWM instruction. DETERMINING THE APPROPRIATE CYCLE TIME FOR YOUR CIRCUIT.

How do you determine how long to charge a capacitor? Use this rule-of-thumb formula: Charge time = 5 * R * C. For instance, Figure 5.31 uses a 10 kΩ (10×10^3 ohm) resistor and a 1 µF (1×10^{-6} F) capacitor:

Charge time = $5 * 10 \times 10^3 * 1 \times 10^{-6} = 50 \times 10^{-3}$ seconds, or 50 ms.

Since, on the BS2, each cycle is approximately a millisecond, it would take at least 50 cycles to charge the capacitor.   Assuming the circuit is connected to pin 0, here's the complete PWM instruction:

```
PWM 0, 100, 50                    ' charge to 1.96 V
```

After outputting the PWM pulses, the BASIC Stamp leaves the pin in input mode (0 in the corresponding bit of DIRS). In input mode, the pin's output driver is effectively disconnected. If it were not, the steady output state of the pin would change the voltage on the capacitor and undo the voltage setting established by PWM. Keep in mind that leakage currents of up to 1 µA can flow into or out of this "disconnected" pin. Over time, these small currents will cause the voltage on the capacitor to drift. The same applies for leakage current from an op-amp's input, as well as the capacitor's own internal leakage. Executing PWM occasionally will reset the capacitor voltage to the intended value.

PWM charges the capacitor; the load presented by your circuit discharges it. How long the charge lasts (and therefore how often your program should repeat the PWM command to refresh the charge) depends on how much current the circuit draws, and how stable the voltage must be. You may need to buffer PWM output with a simple op-amp follower if your load or stability requirements are more than the passive circuit of Figure 5.31 can handle.

HOW PULSE-WIDTH-MODULATION IS GENERATED.

The term "PWM" applies only loosely to the action of the BASIC Stamp's PWM command. Most systems that output PWM do so by splitting a fixed period of time into an on time (1) and an off time (0). Suppose the interval is 1 ms and the duty cycle is 100 / 255. Conventional PWM would turn the output on for 0.39 ms and off for 0.61 ms, repeating this process each millisecond. The main advantage of this kind of PWM is its predictability; you know the exact frequency of the pulses (in this case, 1 kHz), and their widths are controlled by the duty cycle.

BASIC Stamp's PWM does not work this way. It outputs a rapid sequence of on/off pulses, as short as 1.6 µs in duration, whose overall proportion over the course of a full PWM cycle of approximately a millisecond is equal to the duty cycle. This has the advantage of very quickly zeroing in on the desired output voltage, but it does not produce the neat, orderly pulses that you might expect. All BS2 models also use this high-speed PWM to generate pseudo-sine wave tones with the DTMFOUT and FREQOUT instructions.

Demo Program (PWM.bs1)

```
' PWM.BS1
' Connect a voltmeter (such as a digital multimeter set to its voltage
' range) to the output of the circuit shown in the figure for the PWM
' command (in the manual).  Run the program and observe the readings on
' the meter. They should come very close to 1.96V, then decrease slightly
```

```
' as the capacitor discharges. Try varying the interval between PWM bursts
' (by changing the PAUSE value) and the number of PWM cycles to see their
' effect.

' {$STAMP BS1}
' {$PBASIC 1.0}


Main:
  PWM 0, 100, 10                    ' PWM at 100/255 duty (~50 ms)
  PAUSE 1000                        ' wait one second
  GOTO Main
  END
```

Demo Program (PWM.bs2)

```
' PWM.bs2
' Connect a voltmeter (such as a digital multimeter set to its voltage
' range) to the output of the circuit shown in the figure for the PWM
' command (in the manual).  Run the program and observe the readings on
' the meter. They should come very close to 1.96V, then decrease slightly
' as the capacitor discharges. Try varying the interval between PWM bursts
' (by changing the PAUSE value) and the number of PWM cycles to see their
' effect.

' {$STAMP BS2}
' {$PBASIC 2.5}

#SELECT $STAMP
  #CASE BS2, BS2E
    CycAdj        CON       $100      ' x 1.0, cycle adjustment (for ms)
  #CASE BS2SX
    CycAdj        CON       $280      ' x 2.5
  #CASE BS2P
    CycAdj        CON       $187      ' x 1.53
  #CASE BS2PE
    CycAdj        CON       $09E      ' x 0.62
  #CASE BS2PX
    CycAdj        CON       $280      ' x 2.5
#ENDSELECT

Cycles          CON       50

Main:
  PWM 0, 100, (Cycles */ CycAdj)      ' PWM at 100/255 duty (~50 ms)
  PAUSE 1000                          ' wait one second
  GOTO Main
  END
```

All 2

NOTE: This example program can be used with all BS2 models. This program uses conditional compilation techniques; see Chapter 3 for more information.

RANDOM

BS1	BS2	BS2e	BS2sx	BS2p	BS2pe	BS2px

RANDOM *Variable*

Function

Generate a pseudo-random number.

- **Variable** is a variable (usually a word) whose bits will be scrambled to produce a random number. *Variable* acts as RANDOM's input and its result output. Each pass through RANDOM stores the next number, in the pseudorandom sequence, in *Variable*.

Explanation

RANDOM generates pseudo-random numbers ranging from 0 to 65535. They're called "pseudo-random" because they appear random, but are generated by a logic operation that uses the initial value in *Variable* to "tap" into a sequence of 65535 essentially random numbers. If the same initial value, called the "seed", is always used, then the same sequence of numbers is generated. The following example demonstrates this:

```
SYMBOL   result        = W1

Main:
  result = 11000
  RANDOM result
  DEBUG result
  GOTO Main
```

-- or --

```
result         VAR    Word

Main:
  result = 11000
  RANDOM result
  DEBUG DEC ? result
  GOTO Main
```

In this example, the same number would appear on the screen over and over again. This is because the same seed value was used each time; specifically, the first line of the loop sets *result* to 11,000. The RANDOM command really needs a different seed value each time. Moving the "result =" line out of the loop will solve this problem, as in:

```
SYMBOL  result          = W1

Setup:
  result = 11000

Main:
  RANDOM result
  DEBUG result
  GOTO Main
```

-- or --

```
result          VAR     Word

Setup:
  result = 11000

Main:
  RANDOM result
  DEBUG DEC ? result
  GOTO Main
```

Here, *result* is only initialized once, before the loop. Each time through the loop, the previous value of *result*, generated by RANDOM, is used as the next seed value. This generates a more desirable set of pseudorandom numbers.

In applications requiring more apparent randomness, it's necessary to "seed" RANDOM with a more random value every time. For instance, in the demo program below, RANDOM is executed continuously (using the previous resulting number as the next seed value) while the program waits for the user to press a button. Since the user can't control the timing of button presses very accurately, the results approach true randomness.

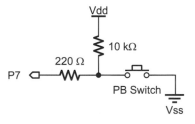

Figure 5.32: RANDOM Button Circuit.

Demo Program (RANDOM.bs1)

```
' RANDOM.bs1
' Connect a button to I/O pin 7 as shown in the figure in the RANDOM
' command description and run this program. This program uses RANDOM to
' simulate a coin toss. After 100 trials, it reports the total number of
' heads and tails thrown.

' {$STAMP BS1}
' {$PBASIC 1.0}

SYMBOL  Btn             = 7                     ' button input

SYMBOL  flip            = W0                    ' a random number
SYMBOL  coin            = BIT0                  ' a bit from random number
SYMBOL  trials          = B2                    ' number of flips
SYMBOL  heads           = B3                    ' throws that come up heads
SYMBOL  tails           = B4                    ' throws that come up tails
SYMBOL  btnWrk          = B5                    ' workspace for BUTTON

Start:
  DEBUG CLS, "Press the button to toss coin.", CR

Main:
  FOR trials = 1 TO 100                         ' flip coin 100 times

Hold:
    RANDOM flip                                 ' randomize while waiting
    BUTTON Btn, 0, 250, 100, btnWrk, 0, Hold    ' wait for button press
    BRANCH coin, (Head,.Tail)                   ' 0 = heads, 1 = tails

Head:
    DEBUG CR, "Heads!"
    heads = heads + 1                           ' increment heads counter
    GOTO Next_Toss

Tail:
    DEBUG CR, "Tails..."
    tails = tails + 1                           ' increment heads counter

Next_Toss:
  NEXT

  DEBUG CR, CR, "Heads: ", #heads, CR, "Tails: ", #tails
  END
```

Demo Program (RANDOM.bs2)

NOTE: This example program can be used with all BS2 models by changing the $STAMP directive accordingly.

```
' RANDOM.BS2
' Connect a button to I/O pin 7 as shown in the figure in the RANDOM
' command description and run this program. This program uses RANDOM to
' simulate a coin toss. After 100 trials, it reports the total number of
```

```
' heads and tails thrown.

' {$STAMP BS2}
' {$PBASIC 2.5}

Btn             PIN     7                       ' button input

flip            VAR     Word                    ' a random number
coin            VAR     flip.BIT0               ' Bit0 of the random number
trials          VAR     Byte                    ' number of flips
heads           VAR     Byte                    ' throws that come up heads
tails           VAR     Byte                    ' throws that come up tails
btnWrk          VAR     Byte                    ' workspace for BUTTON


Start:
  DEBUG CLS, "Press button to start"

Main:
  FOR trials = 1 TO 100                         ' flip coin 100 times

Hold:
    RANDOM flip                                 ' randomize while waiting
    BUTTON Btin, 0, 250, 100, btnWrk, 0, Hold   ' wait for button press
    IF (coin = 0) THEN                          ' 0 = heads, 1 = tails
      DEBUG CR, "Heads!"
      heads = heads + 1                         ' increment heads counter
    ELSE
      DEBUG CR, "Tails..."
      tails = tails + 1                         ' increment tails counter
    ENDIF
  NEXT

Done:
  DEBUG CR, CR, "Heads: ", DEC heads, " Tails: ", DEC tails
  END
```

RCTIME

| BS1 | BS2 | BS2e | BS2sx | BS2p | BS2pe | BS2px |

⌂1 **(See POT)**

All 2 **RCTIME** *Pin, State, Variable*

Function

Measure time while *Pin* remains in *State*; usually to measure the charge/discharge time of resistor/capacitor (RC) circuit.

- **Pin** is a variable/constant/expression (0 – 15) that specifies the I/O pin to use. This pin will be placed into input mode.

- **State** is a variable/constant/expression (0 - 1) that specifies the desired state to measure. Once *Pin* is not in *State*, the command ends and stores the result in *Variable*.

- **Variable** is a variable (usually a word) in which the time measurement will be stored. The unit of time for *Variable* is described in Table 5.87.

Quick Facts

Table 5.87: RCTIME Quick Facts.

	BS2	BS2e	BS2sx	BS2p	BS2pe	BS2px
Units in *Variable*	2 µs	2 µs	0.8 µs	0.75 µs	2 µs	0.75 µs
Maximum Pulse Width	131.07 ms	131.07 ms	52.428 ms	49.151 ms	131.07 ms	49.151 ms

Explanation

RCTIME can be used to measure the charge or discharge time of a resistor/capacitor circuit. This allows you to measure resistance or capacitance; use R or C sensors such as thermistors or capacitive humidity sensors or respond to user input through a potentiometer. In a broader sense, RCTIME can also serve as a fast, precise stopwatch for events of very short duration.

HOW RCTIME'S TIMER WORKS.

When RCTIME executes, it makes *Pin* an input, then starts a counter (who's unit of time is shown in Table 5.87). It stops this counter as soon as the specified pin is no longer in *State* (0 or 1). If pin is not in *State* when the instruction executes, RCTIME will return 1 in *Variable*, since the instruction requires one timing cycle to discover this fact. If pin remains in *State* longer than 65535 timing cycles RCTIME returns 0.

RCTIME – BASIC Stamp Command Reference

Figure 5.33 shows suitable RC circuits for use with RCTIME. The circuit in Figure 5.33a is preferred, because the BASIC Stamp's logic threshold is approximately 1.4 volts. This means that the voltage seen by the pin will start at 5V then fall to 1.4V (a span of 3.6V) before RCTIME stops. With the circuit of Figure 5.33b, the voltage will start at 0V and rise to 1.4V (spanning only 1.4V) before RCTIME stops. For the same combination of R and C, the circuit shown in Figure 5.33a will yield a higher count, and therefore more resolution than Figure 5.33b.

SUITABLE RCTIME CIRCUITS.

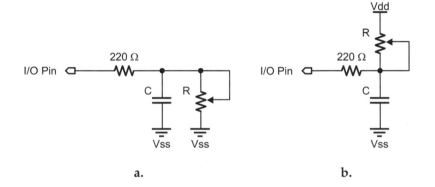

Figure 5.33: Example RC Circuits. Use **a** (left) with *State* = 1. Use **b** (right) with *State* = 0.

Before RCTIME executes, the capacitor must be put into the state specified in the RCTIME instruction. For example, with Figure 5.33a, the capacitor must be charged until the top plate is at 5V, then a State value of 1 will be used to monitor the discharge of the capacitor through the variable resistance.

DON'T FORGET TO DISCHARGE THE CAPACITOR BEFORE EXECUTING RCTIME.

Here's a typical sequence of instructions for Figure 5.33a (assuming I/O pin 7 is used):

```
result  VAR     Word

HIGH 7                                  ' charge the cap
PAUSE 1                                 '   for 1 ms
RCTIME 7, 1, result                     ' measure RC discharge time
DEBUG DEC ? result                      ' display result
```

Using RCTIME is very straightforward, except for one detail: For a given R and C, what value will RCTIME return? It's easy to figure, based on a value called the RC time constant, or tau (τ) for short. Tau represents the time required for a given RC combination to charge or discharge by 63

PREDICTING THE RETURNED VALUE.

percent of the total change in voltage that they will undergo. More importantly, the value τ is used in the generalized RC timing calculation. Tau's formula is just R multiplied by C:

$$\tau = R \times C$$

CALCULATING CHARGE AND DISCHARGE TIME.

The general RC timing formula uses τ to tell us the time required for an RC circuit to change from one voltage to another:

$$\text{time} = -\tau * (\ln (V_{final} / V_{initial}))$$

In this formula ln is the natural logarithm; it's a key on most scientific calculators. Let's do some math. Assume we're interested in a 10 k resistor and 0.1 µF cap. Calculate τ:

$$\tau = (10 \times 10^3) \times (0.1 \times 10^{-6}) = 1 \times 10^{-3}$$

The RC time constant is 1×10^{-3} or 1 millisecond. Now calculate the time required for this RC circuit to go from 5V to 1.4V (as in Figure 5.33a):

$$\text{time} = -1 \times 10^{-3} \times (\ln(1.4v / 5.0v)) = 1.273 \times 10^{-3}$$

THE RC TIME EQUATION.

On the BS2, the unit of time is 2µs (See Table 5.87), that time (1.273×10^{-3}) works out to 636 units. With a 10 kΩ resistor and 0.1 µF cap, RCTIME would return a value of approximately 635. Since $V_{initial}$ and V_{final} doesn't change, we can use a simplified rule of thumb to *estimate* RCTIME results for circuits like Figure 5.33a:

RCTIME units = 635 x R (in kΩ) x C (in µF)

DETERMINING HOW LONG TO CHARGE OR DISCHARGE THE CAPACITOR BEFORE EXECUTING RCTIME.

Another handy rule of thumb can help you calculate how long to charge/discharge the capacitor before RCTIME. In the example above that's the purpose of the HIGH and PAUSE commands. A given RC charges or discharges 98 percent of the way in 5 time constants (5 x R x C). In Figure 5.33, the charge/discharge current passes through the 220 Ω series resistor and the capacitor. So if the capacitor were 0.1 µF, the minimum charge/discharge time should be:

Charge time = $5 \times 220 \times (0.1 \times 10^{-6}) = 110 \times 10^{-6}$

So it takes only 110 μs for the cap to charge/discharge, meaning that the 1 ms charge/discharge time of the example is plenty.

A final note about Figure 5.33: You may be wondering why the 220 Ω resistor is necessary at all. Consider what would happen if resistor R in Figure 5.33a were a pot, and were adjusted to 0 Ω. When the I/O pin went high to charge the cap, it would see a short direct to ground. The 220 Ω series resistor would limit the short circuit current to 5V/220 Ω = 23 mA and protect the BASIC Stamp from damage. (Actual current would be quite a bit less due to internal resistance of the pin's output driver, but you get the idea.)

NOTES ABOUT 220 Ω RESISTOR IN THE RC CIRCUITS.

Demo Program (RCTIME1.bs2)

All 2

```
' RCTIME1.BS2
' This program shows the standard use of the RCTIME instruction measuring
' an RC charge/discharge time. Use the circuit in the RCTIME description
' (in the manual) with R = 10K pot and C = 0.1 uF. Connect the circuit to
' pin 7 and run the program.  Adjust the pot and watch the value shown on
' the Debug screen change.

' {$STAMP BS2}
' {$PBASIC 2.5}

RC              PIN    7

result          VAR    Word


Main:
  DO
    HIGH RC                        ' charge the cap
    PAUSE 1                        '   for 1 ms
    RCTIME RC, 1, result           ' measure RC discharge time
    DEBUG HOME, DEC result         ' display value
    PAUSE 50
  LOOP
  END
```

NOTE: This example program can be used with all BS2 models by changing the $STAMP directive accordingly.

Figure 5.34: Relay Circuit for Demo Program RCTIME2.bs2.

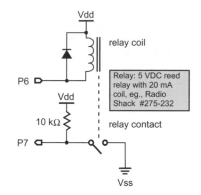

NOTE: This example program can be used with all BS2 models. This program uses conditional compilation techniques; see Chapter 3 for more information.

All 2

Demo Program (RCTIME2.bs2)

```
' RCTIME2.BS2
' This program illustrates the use of RCTIME as a fast stopwatch. The
' program energizes a relay coil, then measures how long it takes for the
' relay contacts to close.  The circuit for this program can be found in
' the manual. Note that RCTIME doesn't start timing instantly -- as with
' all PBASIC instructions, it must be fetched from program EEPROM before
' it can execute.

' {$STAMP BS2}
' {$PBASIC 2.5}

Coil            PIN     6
RC              PIN     7

#SELECT $STAMP
  #CASE BS2, BS2E, BS2PE
    Adjust      CON     $200            ' x 2 us per unit
  #CASE BS2SX
    Adjust      CON     $0CC            ' x 0.8 us per unit
  #CASE BS2P, BS2PX
    Adjust      CON     $0C0            ' x 0.75 us per unit
#ENDSELECT

result          VAR     Word

Main:
  DO
    LOW Coil                            ' energize relay coil
    RCTIME RC, 1, result                ' measure time to contact closure
    result = result */ Adjust           ' adjust for device
    DEBUG "Time to close: ",
```

```
        DEC Result, CR
   HIGH Coil                       ' release relay
   PAUSE 1000                      ' wait one second
LOOP
END
```

READ

BS1	BS2	BS2e	BS2sx	BS2p	BS2pe	BS2px

NOTE: Optional arguments require PBASIC 2.5.

READ *Location, Variable*

READ *Location,* **{ WORD }** *Variable* **{, { WORD }** *Variable...* **}**

NOTE: Expressions are not allowed as arguments on the BS1.

Function

Read the value at *Location* in EEPROM and store the result in *Variable*.

- *Location* is a variable/constant/expression (0 – 255 on BS1, 0 – 2047 on all BS2 models) that specifies the EEPROM address to read from.

- *Variable* is a variable (usually a byte, or word when the optional WORD modifier is used) in which to store the value.

Quick Facts

Table 5.88: READ Quick Facts.

	BS1	BS2, BS2e, BS2sx	BS2p, BS2pe, BS2px
Range of EEPROM Locations	0 to 255	0 to 2047	0 to 2047 (see notes below)
Special Notes	n/a	READ only works with current program slot on BS2e and BS2sx.	READ works with any program slot as set by the STORE command.
Related Commands	WRITE and EEPROM	WRITE and DATA	WRITE, DATA and STORE
PBASIC 2.5 Syntax Options	n/a	Multiple sequential variables may be read from the Scratch Pad RAM, and the optional WORD modifier may be specified to retrieve 16-bit values.	

Explanation

The EEPROM is used for both program storage (which builds downward from address 255 on BS1, 2047 on all BS2 models) and data storage (which builds upward from address 0). The READ instruction retrieves a value from any EEPROM address and stores that value in *Variable*. When the optional WORD modifier is used, the low byte of *Variable* is read from *Location*, the high byte of *Variable* from *Location + 1*. Any location within the EEPROM can be read (including your PBASIC program's tokens) at run-time. This feature is mainly used to retrieve long-term data from EEPROM; data stored in EEPROM is not lost when the power is removed.

The following READ command retrieves the value at location 100 and stores it into the variable called *result*:

A SIMPLE READ COMMAND.

```
SYMBOL   result  = B2

READ 100, result
```

☐1

--or--

```
result  VAR     Byte

READ 100, result
```

All 2

The EEPROM is organized as a sequential set of byte-sized memory locations. The READ command normally only retrieves byte-sized values from EEPROM. This does not mean that you can't read word-sized values, however. A word consists of two bytes, called a low-byte and a high-byte. With PBASIC 1.0 or 2.0, if you want to read a word-sized value, you'll need to use two READ commands and a word-sized variable.

READING WORD VALUES VS. BYTE VALUES.

```
SYMBOL   result  = W0
SYMBOL   resltLo = B0
SYMBOL   resltHi = B1

EEPROM  (101, 4)

READ 0, resltLo                 'read low byte
READ 1, resltHi                 'read high byte
DEBUG #result
```

☐1

--or--

```
result  VAR     Word

DATA    Word 1125

READ 0, result.LOWBYTE          'read low byte
READ 1, result.HIGHBYTE         'read high byte
```

All 2
NOTE: this method is required only if using PBASIC 2.0. See section below for PBASIC 2.5 method.

On all BS2 models, by using the $PBASIC 2.5 directive, you can use a single READ command with the WORD modifier. For example,

All 2

```
' {$PBASIC 2.5}

result    VAR     Word

DATA      Word 1125

READ 0, Word result
DEBUG DEC ? result
```

This code uses the EEPROM or DATA directive to write the low-byte and high-byte of the number 1125 into locations 0 and 1 during download. The BS1 code the uses two READ commands to read each of the bytes out of EEPROM and reconstructs them into a single word-sized variable.

PBASIC 2.5 uses READ's optional WORD modifier to read both bytes from EEPROM and into a word-sized variable. Both programs then display the value on the screen.

When using PBASIC 2.5, a single READ command can retrieve multiple bytes and words from sequential EEPROM locations. For example:

All 2

```
' {$PBASIC 2.5}

temp     VAR     Byte
temp2    VAR     Word

READ 25, temp, Word temp2    ' retrieve byte from location 25
                             ' and word from locations 26 and 27
DEBUG DEC temp, CR           ' display value of temp, carriage return
DEBUG DEC temp2              ' display value of temp2
```

SPECIAL NOTES FOR EEPROM USAGE.

Note that the EEPROM and DATA directives store data in the EEPROM before the program runs, however, the WRITE command can be used to store data while the program is running. Additionally, the EEPROM locations can be read an unlimited number of times, but EEPROM locations can be worn out by excessive writes. See the WRITE command for more information.

When using the READ and WRITE commands, take care to ensure that your program doesn't overwrite itself. On the BS1, location 255 holds the address of the last instruction in your program. Therefore, your program can use any space below the address given in location 255. For example, if location 255 holds the value 100, then your program can use locations 0–99 for data. You can read location 255 at run-time or simply view the

Memory Map of the program before you download it. On all BS2 models you will need to view the Memory Map of the program before you download it, to determine the last EEPROM location used. See the "Memory Map Function" section in Chapter 3.

On the BS2p, BS2pe, and BS2px, the READ and WRITE commands can affect locations in any program slot as set by the STORE command. See the STORE command for more information.

Demo Program (READ.bs1)

```
' READ.bs1
' This program reads a string of data stored in EEPROM. The EEPROM data is
' downloaded to the BS1 at compile-time and remains there (even with the
' power off) until overwritten. Put ASCII characters into EEPROM, followed
' by 0, which will serve as the end-of-message marker.  For programs with
' multiple strings, use the Memory Map window to find the starting character
' address.

' {$STAMP BS1}
' {$PBASIC 1.0}

SYMBOL  strAddr       = B2
SYMBOL  char          = B3

Msg1:
  EEPROM ("BS1", 13, "EEPROM Storage!", 0)


Main:
  strAddr = 0                          ' set to start of message
  GOSUB String_Out
  END

String_Out:
  READ strAddr, char                   ' read byte from EEPROM
  strAddr = strAddr + 1                ' point to next character
  IF char = 0 THEN StrOut_Exit         ' if 0, exit routine
  DEBUG #@char                         ' otherwise print char
  GOTO String_Out                      ' get next character

StrOut_Exit:
  RETURN
```

All 2 ## Demo Program (READ.bs2)

NOTE: This example program can be used with all BS2 models by changing the $STAMP directive accordingly.

```
' READ.bs2
' This program reads a string of data stored in EEPROM. The EEPROM data is
' downloaded to the BS2 at compile-time and remains there (even with the
' power off) until overwritten. Put ASCII characters into EEPROM, followed
' by 0, which will serve as the end-of-message marker.

' {$STAMP BS2}
' {$PBASIC 2.5}

strAddr         VAR     Word
char            VAR     Byte

Msg1            DATA    "BS2", CR, "EEPROM Storage!", 0


Main:
  strAddr = Msg1                        ' set to start of message
  GOSUB String_Out
  END

String_Out:
  DO
    READ strAddr, char                  ' read byte from EEPROM
    strAddr = strAddr + 1               ' point to next character
    IF (char = 0) THEN EXIT             ' if 0, exit routine
    DEBUG char                          ' otherwise print char
  LOOP
  RETURN
```

RETURN

1 All 2 **RETURN**

BS1	BS2	BS2e	BS2sx	BS2p	BS2pe	BS2px

Function

Return from a subroutine, assuming there was a previous GOSUB executed.

Quick Facts

Table 5.89: RETURN Quick Facts.

	BS1	BS2 Models
Related Commands	GOSUB	GOSUB and ON
Maximum Number of RETURNS per Program	Unlimited. However, the number of GOSUBs are limited. See GOSUB for more information.	

Explanation

1

NOTE: On the BS1, a RETURN without a GOSUB will return the program to the last GOSUB (or will end the program if no GOSUB was executed).

RETURN sends the program back to the address (instruction) immediately following the most recent GOSUB. If RETURN is executed without a prior GOSUB, the BASIC Stamp will return to the first executable line of the program; usually resulting in a logical bug in the code. See the GOSUB command for more information.

The example below will start out by GOSUB'ing to the section of code beginning with the label *Hello*. It will print "Hello, my friend!" on the screen then RETURN to the line after the GOSUB... which prints "How are you?" and ENDs.

```
Main:
  GOSUB Hello
  DEBUG "How are you?"
  END

Hello:
  DEBUG "Hello, my friend!", CR
  RETURN
```

WATCH OUT FOR SUBROUTINES THAT YOUR PROGRAM CAN "FALL INTO."

There's another interesting lesson here; what would happen if we removed the END command from this example? Since the BASIC Stamp reads the code from left to right / top to bottom (like the English language) once it had returned to and run the "How are you?" line, it would naturally "fall into" the *Hello* routine again. Additionally, at the end of the *Hello* routine, it would see the RETURN again (although it didn't GOSUB to that routine this time) and because there wasn't a previous place to return to, the BASIC Stamp will start the entire program over again. This would cause an endless loop. The important thing to remember here is to always make sure your program doesn't allow itself to "fall into" a subroutine.

Demo Program (RETURN.bs2)

NOTE: This example program can be used with the BS1 and all BS2 models by changing the $STAMP directive accordingly.

```
' RETURN.BS2
' This program demonstrates a potential bug caused by allowing a program to
' "fall into" a subroutine.  The program was intended to indicate that it
' is "Starting...", then "Executing Subroutine,", then "Returned..." from
' the subroutine and stop.  Since we left out the END command (indicated in
' the comments), the program then falls into the subroutine, displays
' "Executing..." again and then RETURNs to the start of the program and
' runs continuously in an endless loop.

' {$STAMP BS2}


Reset:
  DEBUG "Starting Program", CR        ' show start-up

Main:
  PAUSE 1000
  GOSUB Demo_Sub                      ' call the subroutine
  PAUSE 1000
  DEBUG "Returned from Subroutine", CR ' show that we're back
  PAUSE 1000

                                      ' <-- Forgot to put END here

Demo_Sub:
  DEBUG "  Executing Subroutine", CR  ' show subroutine activity
  RETURN
```

REVERSE

| BS1 | BS2 | BS2e | BS2sx | BS2p | BS2pe | BS2px |

 REVERSE *Pin*

Function

Reverse the data direction of the specified pin.

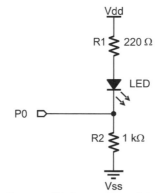
NOTE: Expressions are not allowed as arguments on the BS1. The range of the *Pin* argument on the BS1 is 0 – 7.

- *Pin* is a variable/constant/expression (0 – 15) that specifies the I/O pin to use. This pin will be placed into the mode opposite its current input/output mode.

Quick Facts

Table 5.90: REVERSE Quick Facts.

	BS1 and all BS2 models
Related Commands	INPUT and OUTPUT

Explanation

REVERSE is a convenient way to switch the I/O direction of a pin. If the pin is an input, REVERSE makes it an output; if it's an output, REVERSE makes it an input.

Remember that "input" really has two meanings: (1) Setting a pin to input makes it possible to check the state (1 or 0) of external circuitry connected to that pin. The current state is in the corresponding bit of the INS register (PINS on the BS1). (2) Setting a pin to input also disconnects the output driver, the corresponding bit of OUTS (PINS on the BS1).

The demo program below illustrates this second fact with a two-tone LED blinker.

Figure 5.35: LED Circuit for Demo Programs.

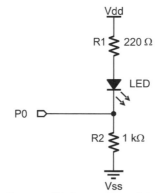

Demo Program (REVERSE.bs1)

```
' REVERSE.bs1
' Connect the circuit shown in the REVERSE command description to I/O pin
' 0 and run this program.  The LED will alternate between two states, dim
' and bright. The BASIC Stamp is using the REVERSE command to toggling I/O
' pin 0 between input and output states. When pin 0 is an input, current
' flows through R1, through the LED, through R2 to ground. Pin 0 is
' effectively disconnected and doesn't play a part in the circuit. The
' total resistance encountered by current flowing through the LED is R1 +
' R2 = 1220 ohms. When pin 0 is reversed to an output, current flows
' through R1, through the LED, and into pin 0 to ground (because of the 0
' written to PIN0). The total resistance encountered by current flowing
' through the LED is R1,220 ohms. With only 20% of the resistance, the LED
' glows brighter.

' {$STAMP BS1}
' {$PBASIC 1.0}


Setup:
  PIN0 = 0                           ' Put a low in the pin 0
                                     '  output driver

Main:
  PAUSE 250                          ' 1/4th second pause
  REVERSE 0                          ' reverse pin 0 I/O direction
  GOTO Main                          ' do forever
```

Demo Program (REVERSE.bs2)

NOTE: This example program can be used with all BS2 models by changing the $STAMP directive accordingly.

```
' REVERSE.bs2
' Connect the circuit shown in the REVERSE command description to I/O pin
' 0 and run this program.  The LED will alternate between two states, dim
' and bright. The BASIC Stamp is using the REVERSE command to toggling I/O
' pin 0 between input and output states. When pin 0 is an input, current
' flows through R1, through the LED, through R2 to ground. Pin 0 is
' effectively disconnected and doesn't play a part in the circuit. The
' total resistance encountered by current flowing through the LED is R1 +
' R2 = 1220 ohms. When pin 0 is reversed to an output, current flows
' through R1, through the LED, and into pin 0 to ground (because of the 0
' written to OUT0). The total resistance encountered by current flowing
' through the LED is R1,220 ohms. With only 20% of the resistance, the LED
' glows brighter.

' {$STAMP BS2}
' {$PBASIC 2.5}


Setup:
  OUT0 = 0                           ' Put a low in the pin 0
                                     '  output driver
```

```
Main:
  PAUSE 250                          ' 1/4th second pause
  REVERSE 0                          ' reverse pin 0 I/O direction
  GOTO Main                          ' do forever
```

RUN

BS1	BS2	BS2e	BS2sx	BS2p	BS2pe	BS2px

RUN *ProgramSlot*

Function

Switches execution to another BASIC Stamp program (in a different program slot).

- **ProgramSlot** is a variable/constant/expression (0 – 7) that specifies the program slot to run.

Quick Facts

Table 5.91: RUN Quick Facts.

	BS2e	BS2sx	BS2p	BS2pe	BS2px
Time Delay to Switch Between Program Slots	770 µs	300 µs	250 µs	736 µs	195 µs
Related Commands	n/a		POLLRUN		
Special Notes	RUN is similar to a GOTO… you can not "return" from a RUN				

Explanation

The BS2e, BS2sx, BS2p, BS2pe and BS2px have a total of 16 k bytes of code space. This code space is organized into eight slots of 2 k bytes each. The BS2pe has 32 k of EEPROM but only the first 16 k (eight slots) can be sued for programs. Up to eight different programs can be downloaded to the BASIC Stamp (one program per code slot). When the BASIC Stamp powers up, or is reset, the program in slot 0 is executed.

The RUN command allows you to activate another program and causes the BASIC Stamp to stay in the newly activated program until it receives another RUN command, or until a power-down or reset condition occurs. The RUN command is similar to a GOTO command in that it allows you to "goto" another program. Normally a master-type program will be used in program slot 0 (since slot 0 runs first) and will control initial execution of the other programs.

A SIMPLE EXAMPLE OF RUN.

Look at the following example (there are two programs here, make sure to download them into program slots 0 and 1, respectively. See the Compiler Directives section of Chapter 3 for more information):

```
' Download this program to Slot 0

DEBUG "Hello "
RUN 1

' Download this program to Slot 1

DEBUG "World!"
PAUSE 1000
RUN 0
```

The above two programs (assuming they have been downloaded into program slots 0 and 1, respectively) will display "Hello World!" on the screen. Program 0 is the first to run and it displays "Hello ", then issues a RUN 1 command. The BASIC Stamp then starts execution of program 1, from its first line of code, which causes "World!" to be displayed. Program 1 then pauses for 1 second and the runs program 0 again.

The I/O pins retain their current state (directions and output latches) and all RAM and SPRAM locations retain their current data during a transition between programs with the RUN command. If sharing data between programs within RAM, make sure to keep similar variable declarations (defined in the same order) in all programs so that the variables align themselves on the proper word, byte, nibble and bit boundaries across programs. The following programs illustrate what happens with mismatched variable declarations:

WHAT HAPPENS TO I/O PINS AND RAM WHEN USING RUN?

```
' Download this program to Slot 0
cats      VAR      Byte
dogs      VAR      Byte

Setup:
  cats = 3
  dogs = 1
  DEBUG ? cats
  DEBUG ? dogs
  RUN 1

' Download this program to Slot 1
cats      VAR      Byte
dogs      VAR      Byte
fleas     VAR      Word

Main:
  DEBUG ? cats
  DEBUG ? dogs
  DEBUG ? fleas
  END
```

When the Slot 1 program runs you may be surprised to see that cats and dogs are now zero and fleas are up to 259! – even though we didn't explicitly define them. What happened? The key to remember is that variable names are simply pointers to RAM addresses, and the PBASIC compiler assigns variable names to RAM in descending order by size. This means that in the Slot 1 program, fleas was assigned to RAM locations 0 and 1 which are holding the values 3 and 1 respectively. Since words are stored low-byte first, the value 259 for fleas makes sense $(3 + (1 * 256))$.

There may be occasions when you need to preserve the RAM space in a program slot before calling on another slot that has different variable requirements. You can use the following subroutines to save your RAM space to the SPRAM and restore it on returning from the other program slot.

```
Save_RAM:
  PUT 0, B0                        ' move RAM 0 value to SP
  FOR B0 = 1 TO 25                 ' loop through other RAM bytes
    PUT B0, B0(B0)                 ' move RAM value to SP location
  NEXT
  RETURN

Restore_RAM:
  FOR B0 = 1 TO 25                 ' loop through RAM
    GET B0, B0(B0)                 ' retrieve RAM value from SP
  NEXT
  GET 0, B0                        ' retrieve RAM 0 value from SP
  RETURN
```

While the use of internal variable names is usually discouraged, these subroutines demonstrate a valid opportunity for their use, as well as the ability to take advantage of the BASIC Stamp's unique memory architecture.

The Save_RAM routine starts by saving the first byte of RAM (internal name: B0) to location 0 in the SPRAM. This is done so that B0 can be used as a loop index for the other locations. The FOR...NEXT loop provides control of that index. The following line is probably the most difficult to comprehend, but works due to the nature of the BASIC Stamp module's RAM organization

```
PUT B0, B0(B0)                     ' move RAM value to SP location
```

In the BASIC Stamp, the variable RAM is implicitly considered an array. What this line is doing, then, is moving the value in each RAM address (B0(1), B0(2), B0(3), ...) to the SPRAM address that corresponds with its byte index. The process is simply reversed to retrieve the RAM variable space.

Any *ProgramSlot* specified above 7 will wrap around and result in running one of the 8 programs (RUN 8 will run program 0, RUN 9 will run program 1, etc).

Review the Advanced Compilation Techniques section beginning on page 68 for more information on downloading multiple programs.

Demo Program (RUN1.bsx)

NOTE: This example program was written for the BS2sx but can be used with the BS2e, BS2p, BS2pe, and BS2px. This program uses conditional compilation techniques; see Chapter 3 for more information.

```
' RUN1.bsx
' This example demonstrates the use of the RUN command.  First, the SPRAM
' location that holds the current slot is read using the GET command to
' display the currently running program number.  Then a set of values
' (based on the program number) are displayed on the screen.  Afterwards,
' program number 1 is run. This program is a BS2sx project consisting of
' RUN1.BSX and RUN2.BSX, but will run on all multi-slot BASIC Stamp models.

' {$STAMP BS2sx, RUN2.BSX}
' {$PBASIC 2.5}

#SELECT $STAMP                         ' set SPRAM of slot number
  #CASE BS2
    #ERROR "Multi-slot BASIC Stamp required."
  #CASE BS2E, BS2SX
    Slot        CON     63
  #CASE BS2P, BS2PE, BS2PX
    Slot        CON     127
#ENDSELECT

slotNum       VAR     Nib             ' current slot
idx           VAR     Nib             ' loop counter
value         VAR     Byte            ' value from EEPROM

EEtable       DATA    100, 40, 80, 32, 90
              DATA    200, 65, 23, 77, 91


Setup:
  GET Slot, slotNum                   ' read current slot
  DEBUG "Program #", DEC slotNum, CR  ' display

Main:
```

```
FOR idx = 0 TO 4                          ' read/display table values
  READ (slotNum * 5) + idx, value
  DEBUG DEC3 value, " "
NEXT
DEBUG CR
PAUSE 1000

RUN 1                                     ' run Slot 1 pgm
```

Demo Program (RUN2.bsx)

```
' RUN2.bsx
' This example demonstrates the use of the RUN command.  First, the SPRAM
' location that holds the current slot is read using the GET command to
' display the currently running program number.  Then a set of values
' (based on the program number) are displayed on the screen.  Afterwards,
' program number 0 is run. This program is a BS2sx project consisting of
' RUN1.BSX and RUN2.BSX, but will run on all multi-slot BASIC Stamp models.

' {$STAMP BS2sx}
' {$PBASIC 2.5}

#SELECT $STAMP                            ' set SPRAM of slot number
  #CASE BS2
    #ERROR "Multi-slot BASIC Stamp required."
  #CASE BS2E, BS2SX
    Slot         CON      63
  #CASE BS2P, BS2PE, BS2PX
    Slot         CON      127
#ENDSELECT

slotNum         VAR      Nib              ' current slot
idx             VAR      Nib              ' loop counter
value           VAR      Byte             ' value from EEPROM

EEtable         DATA     100, 40, 80, 32, 90
                DATA     200, 65, 23, 77, 91


Setup:
  GET Slot, slotNum                       ' read current slot
  DEBUG  "Program #", DEC slotNum, CR     ' display

Main:
  FOR idx = 0 TO 4                        ' read/display table values
    READ (slotNum * 5) + idx, value
    DEBUG DEC3 value, " "
  NEXT
  DEBUG CR
  PAUSE 1000

  RUN 0                                   ' back to Slot 0 pgm
```

SELECT…CASE

BS1	BS2	BS2e	BS2sx	BS2p	BS2pe	BS2px

SELECT *Expression*

  CASE *Condition(s)*

    Statement(s)

  { **CASE** *Condition(s)*

    Statement(s)… }

  { **CASE ELSE**

    Statement(s) }

ENDSELECT

All 2

NOTE: SELECT…CASE requires
PBASIC 2.5.

Function

Evaluate *Expression* and conditionally execute a code block based on comparison to *Condition(s)* then continue execution with line following ENDSELECT.

- **Expression** is a variable, a constant, or an expression.

- **Condition** is a statement that, when comapred to *Expression*, can be evaluated as True or False. The *Condition* can be a very simple or very complex relationship, as described below. Multiple conditions within the same CASE can be separated by commas (,).

- **Statement** is any valid PBASIC instruction.

Quick Facts

Table 5.92: SELECT…CASE Quick Facts.

	All BS2 Models
Comparison Operators	=, <>, >, <, >=, <=
Conditional Logic Operators	Not allowed, however multiple conditions can be separated by commas (,) which act like a logical OR operator.
Format of Condition	Comparison *Value* where *Value* can by any of variable, constant or expression
Parentheses	Allowed to specify order of execution within expressions.
Maximum Nested SELECT Statements	16
Maximum CASEs per SELECT	16
Related Commands	IF…THEN, ON, and BRANCH

Explanation

SELECT...CASE is an advanced decision-making structure that is often used to replace compound IF...THEN...ELSE structures. SELECT...CASE statements are good for performing one of many possible actions depending on the value of a single expression.

Upon reaching a SELECT...CASE statement, the BASIC Stamp will evaluate *Expression* once and then compare it to the *Condition(s)* of each CASE until it finds a "case" that evaluates to True, or it runs out of cases to compare to. As soon as a True case is found, the BASIC Stamp executes that CASE's *Statement(s)* and then continues execution on the program line following ENDSELECT.

To understand how SELECT...CASE statements work, it helps to review how IF...THEN statements behave. The condition argument of IF...THEN takes the form:

> *Value1 Comparison Value2*

and *Value1* is "compared" to *Value2* using the *Comparison* operator.

In SELECT...CASE statements, the *Value1* component is always *Expression* and so the format of *Condition(s)* is simplified to:

> { *Comparison* } *Value*

Comparison is optional and can be any of the comparison operators shown in Table 5.93. If *Comparison* is not specified, it is an implied Equal (=) operator. *Value* can be a variable, constant or expression.

Comparison Operator Symbol	Definition
=	Equal
<>	Not Equal
>	Greater Than
<	Less Than
>=	Greater Than or Equal To
<=	Less Than or Equal To

Table 5.93: Comparison Operators for SELECT...CASE.

Condition(s) also has a special, additional format that can be used to indicate a range of sequential values:

Value1 TO *Value2*

This indicates a range of Value1 to Value2, inclusive. For example, *20* TO *23* means 20, 21, 22 and 23. Similarly, *"A"* TO *"F"* means all the characters in the range "A" through "F".

Finally, multiple conditions can be included in a single CASE by separating them with commas (,). For example,

```
CASE  20, 25 TO 30, >100
```

will evaluate to True if the *Expression* (from the SELECT statement) is equal to 20, or is in the range 25 through 30, or is greater than 100.

An example will help clarify this function.

```
'{$PBASIC 2.5}

guess    VAR    WORD

DEBUG "Guess my favorite number: "          ' prompt user

DO
  DEBUGIN DEC Guess                         ' get answer

  SELECT guess
    CASE < 100                              ' less than 100?
      DEBUG CR, "Not even close. Higher."
    CASE > 140                              ' greater than 140?
      DEBUG CR, "Too high."
    CASE 100 TO 120, 126 TO 140             ' 100-120 or 126-140?
      DEBUG CR, "Getting closer..."
    CASE 123                                ' 123? Got it!
      DEBUG CR, "That's it!  123!"
      DEBUG CR, "Good Guessing!"
      STOP
    CASE 121 TO 125                         ' close to 123?
      DEBUG CR, "You're so close!"
  ENDSELECT

  DEBUG CR, "Try again: "                   ' encourage another try
LOOP
```

This program will ask the user to guess a number, store that value in *guess* and check the results in the SELECT statement. If *guess* is less than 100, the first CASE is true and BASIC Stamp will display "Not even close.

Higher." then continues after the ENDSELECT, displaying "Try again: " on the screen and giving the user another guess. If *guess* is greater than 140, the second CASE is true, "Too high." will be displayed followed by "Try again: ", etc. If the user guesses 123, they are congratulated and the program stops.

You may have noticed a potential error in the code: both of the last two CASEs are true if *guess* is 123. So why didn't the second CASE execute? The answer is because only the first "true" case is executed and any further cases are ignored. If we had swapped the order of the last two cases, we'd have a bug in the program and the user would never find out that 123 was the correct number because "CASE 123" would never have been evaluated. It's not recommend to write code this way; "CASE 121 TO 122, 124 TO 125" or even "CASE 121, 122, 124, 125" would have been more clear and would prevent potential bugs like this one.

Many situations call for special handling of a few cases and every other case is handled another way. There is a special form of CASE to handle this as well, called CASE ELSE. In our example above, we could have replaced "CASE 121 TO 125" with "CASE ELSE" and it would behave exactly the same. CASE ELSE is a way to ensure that every possible *Expression* value is handled by a case; it's like saying, "If none of the previous cases were true, run this case." For a SELECT...CASE statement to work properly, it must have no more than one CASE ELSE statement, and that CASE ELSE statement must be the very last CASE.

The *Condition(s)* have a format similar to that of the IF...THEN commands except, in SELECT...CASE statements, *Expression* is always implied as the first part of the condition.

Demo Program (SELECT-CASE.bs2)

All 2

```
' SELECT-CASE.bs2
' This program generates a series of 16-bit random numbers and tests each
' to determine odd or even, and where it falls in the possible range:
' lower third, middle third, or upper third.  The program is useful for
' testing various seed values for RANDOM.

' {$STAMP BS2}
' {$PBASIC 2.5}
```

NOTE: This example program can be used with all BS2 models by changing the $STAMP directive accordingly.

```
test            VAR     Byte            ' counter for tests
sample          VAR     Word            ' random number to be tested
odd             VAR     Byte            ' odd throws
even            VAR     Byte            ' even throws
isLo            VAR     Byte            ' sample in lower third
isMid           VAR     Byte            '          in middle thrid
isHi            VAR     Byte            '          in upper third


Main:
  sample = 11000                        ' initialize seed
  FOR test = 1 TO 100                   ' "throw" 100 times
    RANDOM sample                       ' randomize

    IF (sample.BIT0) THEN               ' check odd/even bit
      odd = odd + 1                     ' increment odd count
    ELSE
      even = even + 1                   ' increment even count
    ENDIF

    SELECT sample
      CASE <= 21845                     ' test lower third
        isLo = isLo + 1

      CASE 21846 TO 43691               ' test middle third
        isMid = isMid + 1

      CASE ELSE                         ' otherwise upper third
        isHi = isHi + 1
    ENDSELECT
  NEXT

Show_Results:
  DEBUG CLS,
        "Odd Throws.... ", DEC odd, "%", CR,
        "Even Throws... ", DEC even, "%", CR,
        "Low.......... ", DEC isLo, "%", CR,
        "Mid.......... ", DEC isMid, "%", CR,
        "High.......... ", DEC isHi, "%", CR
  END
```

SERIN	BS1	BS2	BS2e	BS2sx	BS2p	BS2pe	BS2px

`1`
SERIN *Rpin, Baudmode,* { (*Qualifier*), } { # } *InputData*

`All 2`
SERIN *Rpin* { *Fpin* }, *Baudmode,* { *Plabel,* } { *Timeout, Tlabel,* } [*InputData*]

Function

Receive asynchronous serial data (e.g., RS-232 data).

`1`
NOTE: Expressions are not allowed as arguments on the BS1. The range of the *Rpin* argument on the BS1 is 0 – 7.

- **Rpin** is a variable/constant/expression (0 – 16) that specifies the I/O pin through which the serial data will be received. This pin will be set to input mode. On all BS2 models, if Rpin is set to 16, the BASIC Stamp uses the dedicated serial-input pin (SIN, physical pin 2), which is normally used by the Stamp Editor during the download process.

- **Fpin** is an optional variable/constant/expression (0 – 15) that specifies the I/O pin to indicate flow control status on. This pin will be set to output mode.

- **Baudmode** is variable/constant/expression (0 – 7 on the BS1, 0 – 65535 on all BS2 models) that specifies serial timing and configuration.

- **Qualifier** is an optional variable/constant (0 – 255) indicating data that must be received before execution can continue. Multiple qualifiers can be indicated with commas separating them.

- **Plabel** is an optional label indicating where the program should go in the event of a parity error. This argument should only be provided if *Baudmode* indicates 7 bits, and even parity.

- **Timeout** is an optional variable/constant/expression (0 – 65535) that tells SERIN how long to wait for incoming data. If data does not arrive in time, the program will jump to the address specified by *Tlabel*.

- **Tlabel** is an optional label that must be provided along with *Timeout*, indicating where the program should go in the event that data does not arrive within the period specified by *Timeout*.

`1`
NOTE: The BS1's *InputData* argument can only be a list of variables and the optional decimal modifier (#).

- **InputData** is list of variables and formatters that tells SERIN what to do with incoming data. SERIN can store data in a variable or array, interpret numeric text (decimal, binary, or hex) and store the corresponding value in a variable, wait for a fixed or variable sequence of bytes, or ignore a specified number of bytes. These actions can be combined in any order in the *InputData* list.

Quick Facts

	BS1	BS2	BS2e	BS2sx	BS2p	BS2pe	BS2px
Units in *Timeout*	n/a	1 ms	1 ms	0.4 ms	0.4 ms	1 ms	0.4 ms
Baud range	300, 600, 1200, and 2400 only	243 to 50K	243 to 50K	608 to 115.2K	608 to 115.2K	243 to 50K	972 to 115.2K
Baud limit with flow control	n/a	19.2K	19.2K	19.2K	19.2K	19.2K	19.2K
Limit to qualifiers	Unlimited	6 (in WAIT formatter)					
I/O pins available	0 - 7	0 – 15	0 - 15	0 – 15	0 – 15 (in current I/O block)	0 – 15 (in current I/O block)	0 – 15 (in current I/O block)
Other serial port pins	n/a	SIN pin (physical pin 2) when *Rpin* = 16					
Related Command	SEROUT	SEROUT and DEBUGIN					

Table 5.94: SERIN Quick Facts.

Explanation

One of the most popular forms of communication between electronic devices is serial communication. There are two major types of serial communication; asynchronous and synchronous. The SERIN and SEROUT commands are used to receive and send asynchronous serial data. See the SHIFTIN and SHIFTOUT command for information on the synchronous method.

SERIAL COMMUNICATION BACKGROUND.

SERIN can wait for, filter and convert incoming data in powerful ways. SERIN deserves some lengthy discussion, below, since all this power brings some complexity.

The term asynchronous means "no clock." More specifically, "asynchronous serial communication" means data is transmitted and received without the use of a separate "clock" wire. Data can be sent using as little as two wires; one for data and one for ground. The PC's serial ports (also called COM ports or RS-232 ports) use asynchronous serial communication. Note: the other kind of serial communication, synchronous, uses at least three wires; one for clock, one for data and one for ground.

PHYSICAL AND ELECTRICAL DETAILS.

RS-232 is the electrical specification for the signals that PC serial ports use. Unlike normal logic, where 5 volts is a logic 1 and 0 volts is logic 0, RS-232 uses -12 volts for logic 1 and +12 volts for logic 0. This specification allows communication over longer wire lengths without amplification.

Most circuits that work with RS-232 use a line driver/receiver. This component does two things: (1) it converts the ±12 volts of RS-232 to TTL-compatible 0 to 5-volt levels and (2) it inverts the relationship of the voltage levels, so that 5 volts = logic 1 and 0 volts = logic 0.

USING THE BUILT-IN SERIAL PORT ON ALL BS2 MODELS.

All BS2 models have a line receiver on its SIN pin (*Rpin* = 16). See the "Introduction to the BASIC Stamp" chapter. The SIN pin goes to a PC's serial data-out pin on the DB9 connector built into BASIC Stamp development boards. The connector is wired to allow both programming and run-time serial communication (unless you are using the BASIC Stamp 2 Carrier Board (#27120) which is designed for programming only). For the built-in serial port set the *Rpin* argument to 16 in the SERIN command.

All BASIC Stamp models (including the BS1) can also receive RS-232 data through any of their I/O pins (*Rpin* = 0 – 7 for BS1, *Rpin* = 0 – 15 on all BS2 models). The I/O pins don't need a line receiver, just a 22 kΩ resistor. The resistor limits current into the I/O pins' built-in clamping diodes, which keep input voltages within a safe range. See Figure 5.36.

Figure 5.36: Serial Port Diagram Showing Correct Connections to a BASIC Stamp's I/O pin. NOTE: The 22 kΩ resistor is not required if connecting to the SIN pin.

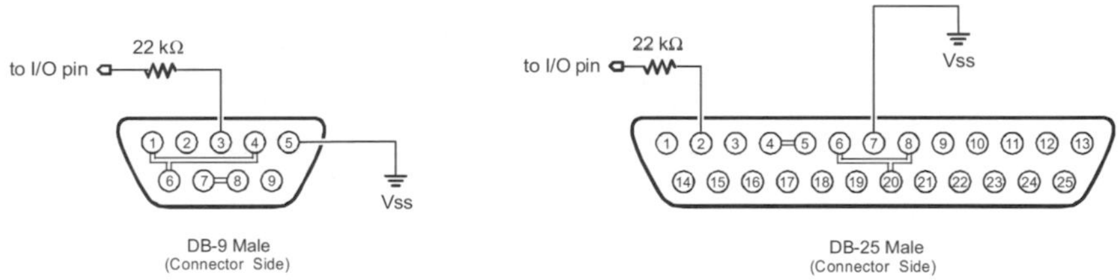

to I/O pin 22 kΩ

DB-9 Male
(Connector Side)

to I/O pin 22 kΩ

Vss

DB-25 Male
(Connector Side)

Function	DB9	DB25
Data Carrier Detect (DCD)	1	8
Receive Data (RD)	2	3
Transmit Data (TD)	3	2
Data Terminal Ready (DTR)	4	20
Signal Ground (SG)	5	7
Data Set Ready (DSR)	6	6
Request to Send (RTS)	7	4
Clear to Send (CTS)	8	5

NOTE: The connections shown with double-lines are normally not necessary. They indicate optional connections to disable hardware handshaking (DTR-DSR-DCD and RTS-CTS). This is only necessary if you are using software or hardware that expects hardware handshaking.

Figure 5.36 shows the pinouts of the two styles of PC serial ports and how to connect them to the BASIC Stamp's I/O pin (the 22 kΩ resistor is not needed if connecting to the SIN pin). Though not normally needed, the figure also shows loop back connections that defeat hardware handshaking used by some PC software. Note that PC serial ports are always male connectors. The 25-pin style of serial port (called a DB25) looks similar to a printer (parallel) port except that it is male, whereas a parallel port is female.

Asynchronous serial communication relies on precise timing. Both the sender and receiver must be set for identical timing, usually expressed in bits per second (bps) called baud.

SERIAL TIMING AND MODE (BAUDMODE).

On all BASIC Stamp models, SERIN requires a value called *Baudmode* that tells it the important characteristics of the incoming serial data; the bit period, number of data and parity bits, and polarity.

On the BS1, serial communication is limited to: no-parity, 8-data bits and 1-stop bit at one of four different speeds: 300, 600, 1200 or 2400 baud. Table 5.95 indicates the *Baudmode* value or symbols to use when selecting the desired mode.

Baudmode Value	Symbol	Baud Rate	Polarity
0	T2400	2400	TRUE
1	T1200	1200	TRUE
2	T600	600	TRUE
3	T300	300	TRUE
4	N2400	2400	INVERTED
5	N1200	1200	INVERTED
6	N600	600	INVERTED
7	N300	300	INVERTED

Table 5.95: BS1 Baudmode Values.

On all BS2 models, serial communication is very flexible. The *Baudmode* argument for SERIN accepts a 16-bit value that determines its characteristics: 1-stop bit, 8-data bits/no-parity or 7-data bits/even-parity and virtually any speed from as low as 300 baud to greater than 100K baud (depending on the BASIC Stamp). Table 5.96 shows how *Baudmode* is calculated, while Table 5.97, Table 5.98, and Table 5.99 show common baud modes for standard serial baud rates.

Table 5.96: *Baudmode* calculation for all BS2 models. Add the results of steps 1, 2 and 3 to determine the proper value for the *Baudmode* argument.

Step 1: Determine the bit period (bits 0 – 11).	BS2, BS2e and BS2pe: = INT(1,000,000 / baud rate) – 20 BS2sx and BS2p: = INT(2,500,000 / baud rate) – 20 BS2px: = INT(4,000,000 / baud rate) – 20 Note: INT means 'convert to integer;' drop the numbers to the right of the decimal point.
Step 2: Set data bits and parity (bit 13).	8-bit/no-parity = 0 7-bit/even-parity = 8192
Step 3: Select polarity (bit 14).	True (noninverted) = 0 Inverted = 16384

Table 5.97: BS2, BS2e, and BS2pe common baud rates and corresponding *Baudmodes*.

Baud Rate	8-bit no-parity inverted	8-bit no-parity true	7-bit even-parity inverted	7-bit even-parity true
300	19697	3313	27889	11505
600	18030	1646	26222	9838
1200	17197	813	25389	9005
2400	16780	396	24972	8588
4800*	16572	188	24764	8380
9600*	16468	84	24660	8276

*The BS2, BS2e and BS2pe may have trouble synchronizing with the incoming serial stream at this rate and higher due to the lack of a hardware input buffer. Use only simple variables and no formatters to try to solve this problem.

Table 5.98: BS2sx and BS2p common baud rates and corresponding *Baudmodes*.

Baud Rate	8-bit no-parity inverted	8-bit no-parity true	7-bit even-parity inverted	7-bit even-parity true
1200	18447	2063	26639	10255
2400	17405	1021	25597	9213
4800*	16884	500	25076	8692
9600*	16624	240	24816	8432

*The BS2sx and BS2p may have trouble synchronizing with the incoming serial stream at this rate and higher due to the lack of a hardware input buffer. Use only simple variables and no formatters to try to solve this problem.

Table 5.99: BS2px common baud rates and corresponding *Baudmodes*.

Baud Rate	8-bit no-parity inverted	8-bit no-parity true	7-bit even-parity inverted	7-bit even-parity true
1200	19697	3313	27889	11505
2400	18030	1646	26222	9838
4800	17197	813	25389	9005
9600	16780	396	24792	8588

CHOOSING THE PROPER BAUD MODE.

If you're communicating with existing software or hardware, its speed(s) and mode(s) will determine your choice of baud rate and mode. In general, 7-bit/even-parity (7E) mode is used for text, and 8-bit/no-parity (8N) for byte-oriented data. Note: the most common mode is 8-bit/no-parity, even when the data transmitted is just text. Most devices that use a 7-bit data mode do so in order to take advantage of the parity feature. Parity can detect some communication errors, but to use it you lose one data bit. This means that incoming data bytes transferred in 7E (even-parity) mode can only represent values from 0 to 127, rather than the 0 to 255 of 8N (no-parity) mode.

Usually a device requires only 1 stop bit per byte. Occasionally, however, you may find a device that requires 2 or more stop bits. Since a stop bit is really just a delay between transmitted bytes (leaving the line in a resting state) the BASIC Stamp can receive transmissions with multiple stop bits per byte without any trouble. In fact, sometimes it is desirable to have multiple stop bits (see the "SERIN Troubleshooting" section, below, for more information).

The example below will receive a single byte through I/O pin 1 at 2400 baud, 8N1, inverted:

A SIMPLE FORM OF SERIN.

```
SYMBOL   serData = B2

SERIN 1, N2400, serData
```

--or--

```
serData VAR     Byte

SERIN 1, 16780, [serData]
```

Note: This is written with the BS2's *Baudmode* value. Be sure to adjust the value for your BASIC Stamp model.

Here, SERIN will wait for and receive a single byte of data through pin 1 and store it in the variable *serData*. If the BASIC Stamp were connected to a PC running a terminal program (set to the same baud rate) and the user pressed the "A" key on the keyboard, after the SERIN command executed, the variable *serData* would contain 65, the ASCII code for the letter "A" (see the ASCII character chart in Appendix A).

What would happen if, using the example above, the user pressed the "1" key? The result would be that *serData* would contain the value 49 (the ASCII code for the character "1"). This is a critical point to remember: every time you press a character on the keyboard, the computer receives the ASCII value of that character. It is up to the receiving side (in serial communication) to interpret the values as necessary. In this case, perhaps we actually wanted *serData* to end up with the value 1, rather than the ASCII code 49.

A SIMPLE NUMERIC CONVERSION; ASCII TEXT TO DECIMAL.

The SERIN command provides a formatter, called the decimal formatter, which will interpret this for us. Look at the following code:

```
SYMBOL   serData = B2

SERIN 1, N2400, #serData
-- or --

serData VAR     Byte

SERIN 1, 16780, [DEC serData]
```

Note: This is written with the BS2's *Baudmode* value. Be sure to adjust the value for your BASIC Stamp.

Notice the decimal formatter in the SERIN command. It is the "#" (for the BS1) or "DEC" (for all BS2 models) that appears just to the left of the *serData* variable. This tells SERIN to convert incoming text representing decimal numbers into true-decimal form and store the result in *serData*. If the user running the terminal software pressed the "1", "2" and then "3" keys followed by a space or other non-numeric text, the value 123 will be stored in *serData*. Afterwards, the program can perform any numeric operation on the number just like with any other number. Without the decimal formatter, however, you would have been forced to receive each character ("1", "2" and "3") separately, and then would still have to do some manual conversion to arrive at the number 123 (one hundred twenty three) before you can do the desired calculations on it.

DECIMAL FORMATTER SPECIFICS.

The decimal formatter is designed to seek out text that represents decimal numbers. The characters that represent decimal numbers are the characters "0" through "9". Once the SERIN command is asked to use the decimal formatter for a particular variable, it monitors the incoming serial data, looking for the first decimal character. Once it finds the first decimal character, it will continue looking for more (accumulating the entire multi-digit number) until is finds a non-decimal numeric character. Keep in mind that it will not finish until it finds at least one decimal character followed by at least one non-decimal character.

To further illustrate this, consider the following examples (assuming we're using the same code example as above):

1) **Serial input:** ABC
   Result: The BASIC Stamp halts at the SERIN command, continuously waiting for decimal text.

2) **Serial input:** 123 (with no characters following it)
Result: The BASIC Stamp halts at the SERIN command. It recognizes the characters "1", "2" and "3" as the number one hundred twenty three, but since no characters follow the "3", it waits continuously, since there's no way to tell whether 123 is the entire number or not.

3) **Serial input:** 123 (followed by a space character)
Result: Similar to example 2, above, except once the space character is received, the BASIC Stamp knows the entire number is 123, and stores this value in *serData*. The SERIN command then ends, allowing the next line of code, if any, to run.

4) **Serial input:** 123A
Result: Same as example 3, above. The "A" character, just like the space character, is the first non-decimal text after the number 123, indicating to the BASIC Stamp that it has received the entire number.

5) **Serial input:** ABCD123EFGH
Result: Similar to examples 3 and 4 above. The characters "ABCD" are ignored (since they're not decimal text), the characters "123" are evaluated to be the number 123 and the following character, "E", indicates to the BASIC Stamp that it has received the entire number.

For examples of all formatters and how they process incoming data, see Appendix C.

Of course, as with all numbers in the BASIC Stamp, the final result is limited to 16 bits (up to the number 65535). If a number larger than this is received by the decimal formatter, the end result will look strange because the result rolled-over the maximum 16-bit value.

WATCH OUT FOR ROLLOVER ERRORS.

The BS1 is limited to the decimal formatter shown above, however all the BS2 models have many more conversion formatters available for the SERIN command. If not using a BS1, see the "Additional Conversion Formatters" section below for more information.

USING SERIN TO WAIT FOR SPECIFIC
DATA BEFORE PROCESSING.

The SERIN command can also be configured to wait for specified data before it retrieves any additional input. For example, suppose a device that is attached to the BASIC Stamp is known to send many different sequences of data, but the only data you desire happens to appear right after the unique characters, "XYZ". The BS1 has optional *Qualifier* arguments for this purpose. On all BS2 models, a special formatter called WAIT can be used for this.

```
SYMBOL   serData = B2

SERIN 1, N2400, ("XYZ"), #serData
```

-- or --

This is written with the BS2's *Baudmode* value. Be sure to adjust the value for your BASIC Stamp.

```
serData VAR     Byte

SERIN 1, 16780, [WAIT("XYZ"), DEC serData]
```

The above code waits for the characters "X", "Y" and "Z" to be received, in that order, and then it looks for a decimal number to follow. If the device in this example were to send the characters "XYZ100" followed by a carriage return or some other non-decimal numeric character, the *serData* variable would end up with the number 100 after the SERIN line finishes. If the device sent some data other than "XYZ" followed by a number, the BASIC Stamp would continue to wait at the SERIN command.

The BS1 will accept an unlimited number of *Qualifiers*. All BS2 models will only accept up to six bytes (characters) in the WAIT formatter.

USING ASCII CODES AND CASE
SENSITIVITY.

Keep in mind that when we type "XYZ" into the SERIN command, the BASIC Stamp actually uses the ASCII codes for each of those characters for its tasks. We could also have typed: 88, 89, 90 in place of "XYZ" and the code would run the same way since 88 is the ASCII code for the "X" character, 89 is the ASCII code for the "Y" character, and so on. Also note, serial communication with the BASIC Stamp is case sensitive. If the device mentioned above sent, "xYZ" or "xyZ", or some other combination of lower and upper-case characters, the BASIC Stamp would have ignored it because we told it to look for "XYZ" (all capital letters).

The BS1's SERIN command is limited to above-mentioned features. If you are not using a BS1, please continue reading about the additional features below.

The decimal formatter is only one of a whole family of conversion formatters available with SERIN on all the BS2 models. See Table 5.100 for a list of available conversion formatters. All of the conversion formatters work similar to the decimal formatter (as described in the "Decimal Formatter Specifics" section, above). The formatters receive bytes of data, waiting for the first byte that falls within the range of characters they accept (e.g., "0" or "1" for binary, "0" to "9" for decimal, "0" to "9" and "A" to "F" for hex, and "-" for signed variations of any type). Once they receive a numeric character, they keep accepting input until a non-numeric character arrives or (in the case of the fixed length formatters) the maximum specified number of digits arrives.

ADDITIONAL CONVERSION FORMATTERS.

All 2

Table 5.100: Conversion Formatters for all BS2 models.

Conversion Formatter	Type of Number	Numeric Characters Accepted	Notes
DEC{1..5}	Decimal, optionally limited to 1 – 5 digits	0 through 9	1
SDEC{1..5}	Signed decimal, optionally limited to 1 – 5 digits	-, 0 through 9	1,2
HEX{1..4}	Hexadecimal, optionally limited to 1 – 4 digits	0 through 9, A through F	1,3,5
SHEX{1..4}	Signed hexadecimal, optionally limited to 1 – 4 digits	-, 0 through 9, A through F	1,2,3
IHEX{1..4}	Indicated hexadecimal, optionally limited to 1 – 4 digits	$, 0 through 9, A through F	1,3,4
ISHEX{1..4}	Signed, indicated hexadecimal, optionally limited to 1 – 4 digits	-, $, 0 through 9, A through F	1,2,3,4
BIN{1..16}	Binary, optionally limited to 1 – 16 digits	0, 1	1
SBIN{1..16}	Signed binary, optionally limited to 1 – 16 digits	-, 0, 1	1,2
IBIN{1..16}	Indicated binary, optionally limited to 1 – 16 digits	%, 0, 1	1,4
ISBIN{1..16}	Signed, indicated binary, optionally limited to 1 – 16 digits	-, %, 0, 1	1,2,4
NUM	Generic numeric input (decimal, hexadecimal or binary); hexadecimal or binary number must be indicated	$, %, 0 through 9, A through F	1, 3, 4
SNUM	Similar to NUM with value treated as signed with range -32768 to +32767	-, $, %, 0 through 9, A through F	1,2,3,4

1 All numeric conversions will continue to accept new data until receiving either the specified number of digits (ex: three digits for DEC3) or a non-numeric character.

2 To be recognized as part of a number, the minus sign (-) must immediately precede a numeric character. The minus sign character occurring in non-numeric text is ignored and any character (including a space) between a minus and a number causes the minus to be ignored.

3 The hexadecimal formatters are not case-sensitive; "a" through "f" means the same as "A" through "F".

4 Indicated hexadecimal and binary formatters ignore all characters, even valid numerics, until they receive the appropriate prefix ($ for hexadecimal, % for binary). The indicated formatters can differentiate between text and hexadecimal (ex: ABC would be interpreted by HEX as a number but IHEX would ignore it unless expressed as $ABC). Likewise, the binary version can distinguish the decimal number 10 from the binary number %10. A prefix occurring in non-numeric text is ignored, and any character (including a space) between a prefix and a number causes the prefix to be ignored. Indicated, signed formatters require that the minus sign come before the prefix, as in -$1B45.

5 The HEX modifier can be used for Decimal to BCD Conversion. See "Hex to BCD Conversion" on page 97.

For examples of all conversion formatters and how they process incoming data, see Appendix C.

SERIN - BASIC Stamp Command Reference

While very effective at filtering and converting input text, the formatters aren't completely foolproof. As mentioned before, many conversion formatters will keep accepting text until the first non-numeric text arrives, even if the resulting value exceeds the size of the variable. After SERIN, a byte variable will contain the lowest 8 bits of the value entered and a word would contain the lowest 16 bits. You can control this to some degree by using a formatter that specifies the number of digits, such as DEC2, which would accept values only in the range of 0 to 99.

ONCE AGAIN, PAY ATTENTION TO POTENTIAL ROLLOVER ERRORS.

All BS2 models also have special formatters for handling a string of characters, a sequence of characters and undesirable characters. See Table 5.101 for a list of these special formatters. Also, see Appendix C for example serial inputs and the result of using these formatters.

Special Formatter	Action
STR ByteArray \L {\E}	Input a character string of length L into an array. If specified, an end character E causes the string input to end before reaching length L. Remaining bytes are filled with 0s (zeros).
WAIT (Value)	Wait for a sequence of bytes specified by value. Value can be numbers separated by commas or quoted text (ex: 65, 66, 67 or "ABC"). The WAIT formatter is limited to a maximum of six characters.
WAITSTR ByteArray {\L}	Wait for a sequence of bytes matching a string stored in an array variable, optionally limited to L characters. If the optional L argument is left off, the end of the array-string must be marked by a byte containing a zero (0).
SKIP Length	Ignore Length bytes of characters.

Table 5.101: SERIN Special Formatters for all BS2 Models.

There is an additional special formatter for the BS2p, BS2pe, and BS2px, shown below.

Special Formatter	Action
SPSTR L	Input a character string of L bytes (up to 126) into Scratch Pad RAM, starting at location 0. Use GET to retrieve the characters.

Table 5.102: Additional SERIN Special Formatter for the BS2p, BS2pe, and BS2px.

The string formatter is useful for receiving a string of characters into a byte array variable. A string of characters is a set of characters that are arranged or accessed in a certain order. The characters "ABC" could be stored in a string with the "A" first, followed by the "B" and then followed by the "C." A byte array is a similar concept to a string; it contains data that is arranged in a certain order. Each of the elements in an array is the same size. The string "ABC" could be stored in a byte array containing

THE STR (STRING) FORMATTER.

three bytes (elements). See the "Defining Arrays" section in Chapter 4 for more information on arrays.

Here is an example that receives nine bytes through I/O pin 1 at 9600 bps, N81/inverted and stores them in a 10-byte array:

```
serStr          VAR     Byte(10)        ' make 10-byte array

serStr(9) = 0                           ' put 0 in last byte of array
SERIN 1, 16468, [STR serStr\9]          ' get nine bytes
DEBUG STR serStr                        ' display
```

Why store only 9 bytes in a 10-byte array? We want to reserve space for the 0 byte that many BASIC Stamp string-handling routines regard as an end-of-string marker. This becomes important when dealing with variable-length arrays. For example, the STR formatter (see Table 5.101) can accept an additional parameter telling it to end the string when a particular byte is received, or when the specified length is reached, whichever comes first. An example:

```
serStr          VAR     Byte(10)        ' make 10-byte array

serStr(9) = 0                           ' put 0 in last byte of array
SERIN 1, 16468, [STR serStr\9\"*"]      ' stop at "*" or nine bytes
DEBUG STR serStr                        ' display
```

If the serial input were "hello*" DEBUG would display "hello" since it collects bytes up to (but not including) the end character. It fills the unused bytes up to the specified length with 0s. DEBUG's normal STR formatter understands a 0 to mean end-of-string. However, if you use DEBUG's fixed-length string modifier, STR *ByteArray*\L, you will inadvertently clear the DEBUG screen. The fixed-length specification forces DEBUG to read and process the 0s at the end of the string, and 0 is equivalent to DEBUG's CLS (clear-screen) control character! Be alert for the consequences of mixing fixed- and variable-length string operations.

MATCHING A SEQUENCE OF CHARACTERS WITH WAIT.

As shown before, SERIN can compare incoming data with a predefined sequence of bytes using the WAIT formatter. The simplest form waits for a sequence of up to six bytes specified as part of the *InputData* list, like so:

```
SERIN 1, 16468, [WAIT("SESAME")]
DEBUG "Password accepted."
```

SERIN will wait for that word, and the program will not continue until it is received. Since WAIT is looking for an exact match for a sequence of bytes, it is case-sensitive—"sesame" or "SESAmE" or any other variation from "SESAME" would be ignored.

SERIN can also wait for a sequence that matches a string stored in an array variable with the WAITSTR formatter. In the example below, we'll capture a string with STR then have WAITSTR look for an exact match:

```
serStr          VAR     Byte(10)        ' make 10-byte array

serStr(9) = 0                           ' put 0 in last byte of array
SERIN 1, 16468, [STR serStr\9\"!"]      ' get the string
DEBUG "Waiting for:", STR serStr, CR
SERIN 1, 16468, [WAITSTR serStr]        ' wait for match
DEBUG "Password accepted."
```

You can also use WAITSTR with fixed-length strings as in the following example:

```
serStr          VAR     Byte(4)         ' make 4-byte array

DEBUG "Enter 4-character password"
SERIN 1, 16468, [STR serStr\4]          ' get the string
DEBUG "Waiting for:", STR serStr\4, CR
SERIN 1, 16468, [WAITSTR serStr\4]      ' wait for match
DEBUG "Password accepted."
```

SERIN's *InputData* can be structured as a sophisticated list of actions to perform on the incoming data. This allows you to process incoming data in powerful ways. For example, suppose you have a serial stream that contains "pos: xxxx yyyy" (where xxxx and yyyy are 4-digit numbers) and you want to capture just the decimal y value. The following code would do the trick:

```
yOffset         VAR     Word

SERIN 1, 16468, [WAIT("pos: "), SKIP 4, DEC4 yOffset]
DEBUG ? yOffset
```

The items of the *InputData* list work together to locate the label "pos: ", skip over the four-byte x data, then convert and capture the decimal y data. This sequence assumes that the x data is always four digits long; if its length varies, the following code would be more appropriate:

```
yOffset         VAR     Word

SERIN 1, 16468, [WAIT("pos: "), DEC yOffset, DEC4 yOffset]
DEBUG ? yOffset
```

The unwanted x data is stored in yOffset then replaced by the desired y data. This is a sneaky way to filter out a number of any size without using an extra variable. With a little creativity, you can combine the *InputData* modifiers to filter and extract almost any data.

USING PARITY AND HANDLING PARITY ERRORS.

Parity is a simple error-checking feature. When a serial sender is set for even parity (the mode the BASIC Stamp supports) it counts the number of 1s in an outgoing byte and uses the parity bit to make that number even. For instance, if it is sending the 7-bit value: %0011010, it sets the parity bit to 1 in order to make an even number of 1s (four).

The receiver also counts the data bits to calculate what the parity bit should be. If it matches the parity bit received, the serial receiver assumes that the data was received correctly. Of course, this is not necessarily true, since two incorrectly received bits could make parity seem correct when the data was wrong, or the parity bit itself could be bad when the rest of the data was OK.

Many systems that work exclusively with text use (or can be set for) 7-bit/even-parity mode. Table 5.97 and Table 5.98 show appropriate *Baudmode* settings for different BASIC Stamp models. For example, with the BS2, to receive one data byte through pin 1 at 9600 baud, 7E, inverted:

```
serData VAR     Byte

SERIN 1, 24660, [serData]
```

That instruction will work, but it doesn't tell the BS2 what to do in the event of a parity error. Here's an improved version that uses the optional *Plabel* argument:

```
serData VAR     Byte

Main:
  SERIN 1, 24660, Bad_Data, [serData]
  DEBUG ? serData
  STOP

Bad_Data:
  DEBUG "Parity error."
  STOP
```

If the parity matches, the program continues at the DEBUG instruction after SERIN. If the parity doesn't match, the program goes to the label

SERIN - BASIC Stamp Command Reference

Bad_Data. Note that a parity error takes precedence over other *InputData* specifications (as soon as an error is detected, SERIN aborts and goes to the *Plabel* routine).

In all the examples above, the only way to end the SERIN instruction (other than RESET or power-off) is to give SERIN the serial data it wants. If no serial data arrives, the program is stuck. However, you can tell the BASIC Stamp to abort SERIN if it doesn't receive a byte within a specified number of milliseconds. For instance, to receive a decimal number through pin 1 at 9600 baud, 8N, inverted and abort SERIN after 2 seconds (2000 ms) of inactivity on the serial input:

USING THE SERIAL TIME-OUT FEATURE.

```
result          VAR     Word

Main:
  SERIN 1, 16468, 2000, No_Data, [DEC result]
  DEBUG CLS, ? result
  STOP

No_Data:
  DEBUG CLS, "Timeout error"
  STOP
```

All 2

If no data arrives within 2 seconds, the program aborts SERIN and continues at the label *No_Data*. Note that on multi-byte input, the timeout timer is reset after the receipt of any valid data byte; with long timeout values this factor could have an adverse affect on program operation if data packets are transmitted with gaps between individual data bytes. Finally, be cautious when using very short timeout values. Without external flow control, very short timeout values may cause the program to branch to the Tlabel address unnecessarily.

Here's a very important concept: this timeout feature is not picky about the kind of data SERIN receives; if any serial data is received, it prevents the timeout. In the example above, SERIN wants a decimal number. But even if SERIN received letters "ABCD..." at intervals of less than two seconds, it would never abort.

REMEMBER: *TIMEOUT* DOES NOT CARE WHAT KIND OF DATA IS RECEIVED, ONLY THAT DATA IS RECEIVED OR NOT!

You can combine parity and serial timeouts. Here is an example for the BS2 designed to receive a decimal number through pin 1 at 9600 baud, 7E, inverted with a 10-second timeout:

COMBINING PARITY AND TIME-OUT.

```
' {$PBASIC 2.5}

result          VAR     Word

Main:
  DO
     SERIN 1, 24660, Bad_Data, 10000, No_Data, [DEC result]
     DEBUG CLS, ? result
  LOOP

Bad_Data:
  DEBUG CLS, "Parity error"
  GOTO Main

No_Data:
  DEBUG CLS, "Timeout error"
  GOTO Main
```

CONTROLLING DATA FLOW.

When you design an application that requires serial communication between BASIC Stamp modules, you have to work within these limitations:

- When the BASIC Stamp is sending or receiving data, it can't execute other instructions.
- When the BASIC Stamp is executing other instructions, it can't send or receive data. *The BASIC Stamp does not have a serial buffer* as there is in PCs. At most serial rates, the BASIC Stamp cannot receive data via SERIN, process it, and execute another SERIN in time to catch the next chunk of data, unless there are significant pauses between data transmissions.

These limitations can sometimes be addressed by using flow control; the *Fpin* option for SERIN and SEROUT (at baud rates of up to the limitation shown in Table 5.94). Through *Fpin*, SERIN can tell a BASIC Stamp sender when it is ready to receive data. (For that matter, *Fpin* flow control follows the rules of other serial handshaking schemes, but most computers other than the BASIC Stamp cannot start and stop serial transmission on a byte-by-byte basis. That's why this discussion is limited to communication between BASIC Stamp modules.)

Here's an example using flow control on the BS2 (data through I/O pin 1, flow control through I/O pin 0, 9600 baud, N8, noninverted):

```
serData         VAR     Byte

SERIN 1\0, 84, [serData]
```

When SERIN executes, I/O pin 1 (*Rpin*) is made an input in preparation for incoming data, and I/O pin 0 (*Fpin*) is made output low, to signal "go" to the sender. After SERIN finishes receiving, I/O pin 0 goes high to tell the sender to stop. If an inverted *BaudMode* had been specified, the *Fpin's* responses would have been reversed. Here's the relationship of serial polarity to *Fpin* states.

	Ready to Receive ("Go")	Not Ready to Receive ("Stop")
Inverted	Fpin is High (1)	Fpin is Low (0)
Non-inverted	Fpin is Low (0)	Fpin is High (1)

Table 5.103: Flow control pin states in relation to polarity (inverted or non-inverted) for all BS2 models.

See the demo program, below, for a flow control example using two BS2s. In the demo program example, without flow control, the sender would transmit the whole word "Hello!" in about 6 ms. The receiver would catch the first byte at most; by the time it got back from the first 1-second PAUSE, the rest of the data would be long gone. With flow control, communication is flawless since the sender waits for the receiver to catch up.

In Figure 5.37, I/O pin 0, *Fpin*, is pulled to ground through a 10k resistor. This is to ensure that the sender sees a stop signal (0 for inverted communications) when the receiver is being programmed.

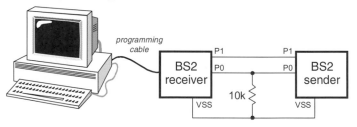

Figure 5.37: Flow-Control Example Circuit.

Serial communication, because of its complexity, can be very difficult to work with at times. Please follow these guidelines when developing a project using the SERIN and SEROUT commands:

SERIN TROUBLESHOOTING.

1. Always build your project in steps.
   a. Start with small, manageable pieces of code, that deals with serial communication) and test them, one at a time.

      b. Add more and more small pieces, testing them each time, as you go.

      c. Never write a large portion of code that works with serial communication without testing its smallest workable pieces first.

2. Pay attention to timing.

      a. Be very careful to calculate and overestimate the amount of time operations should take within the BASIC Stamp. Misunderstanding the timing constraints is the source of most problems with code that communicate serially.

      b. If the serial communication in your project is bi-directional, the above statement is even more critical.

3. Pay attention to wiring.

      a. Take extra time to study and verify serial communication wiring diagrams. A mistake in wiring can cause strange problems in communication, or no communication at all. Make sure to connect the ground pins (Vss) between the devices that are communicating serially.

4. Verify port setting on the PC and in the SERIN/SEROUT commands.

      a. Unmatched settings on the sender and receiver side will cause garbled data transfers or no data transfers. If the data you receive is unreadable, it is most likely a baud rate setting error.

5. If receiving data from another device that is not a BASIC Stamp, try to use baud rates of 4800 and below.

      a. Because of additional overhead in the BASIC Stamp, and the fact that the BASIC Stamp has no hardware receive buffer for serial communication, received data may sometimes be missed or garbled. If this occurs, try lowering the baud rate (if possible), adding extra stop bits, and not using formatters in the SERIN command. Using simple variables (not arrays) and no formatters will increase the chance that the BASIC Stamp can receive the data properly.

6. Be sure to study the effects of SERIN formatters.

      a. Some formatters have specific requirements that may cause problems in received data. For example, the DEC formatter requires a non-decimal-numeric character to follow the received number before it will allow the BASIC

Stamp to continue. See Appendix C for example input data and the effects on formatters.

Demo Program (SERIN.bs1)

```
' SERIN.bs1
' This program waits for the characters "A", "B", "C", and "D" to arrive
' at the serial input (inverted, 2400 baud, N81), followed by a number,
' then a carriage-return or some other non-number character.  The number is
' then displayed in the Debug window.

' {$STAMP BS1}
' {$PBASIC 1.0}

SYMBOL  SIn         = 0
SYMBOL  Baud        = N2400

SYMBOL  result      = W1


Main:
  SERIN SIn, Baud, ("ABCD"), #result
  DEBUG #result, CR
  GOTO Main
  END
```

Demo Program (SERIN_SEROUT1.bs2)

```
' SERIN_SEROUT1.bs2
' Using two BS2-IC's, connect the circuit shown in the SERIN command
' description and run this program on the BASIC Stamp designated as the
' Sender. This program demonstrates the use of Flow Control (FPin).
' Without flow control, the sender would transmit the whole word "Hello!"
' in about 1.5 ms. The receiver would catch the first byte at most; by the
' time it got back from the first 1-second PAUSE, the rest of the data
' would be long gone. With flow control, communication is flawless since
' the sender waits for the receiver to catch up.

' {$STAMP BS2}
' {$PBASIC 2.5}

SO              PIN     1               ' serial output
FC              PIN     0               ' flow control pin

#SELECT $STAMP
  #CASE BS2, BS2E, BS2PE
    T1200       CON     813
    T2400       CON     396
    T9600       CON     84
    T19K2       CON     32
```

NOTE: This example program was written for the BS2 but it can be used with the BS2e, BS2sx, BS2p, BS2pe, and BS2px. This program uses conditional compilation techniques; see Chapter 3 for more information.

```
    T38K4       CON     6
#CASE BS2SX, BS2P
    T1200       CON     2063
    T2400       CON     1021
    T9600       CON     240
    T19K2       CON     110
    T38K4       CON     45
#CASE BS2PX
    T1200       CON     3313
    T2400       CON     1646
    T9600       CON     396
    T19K2       CON     188
    T38K4       CON     84
#ENDSELECT

Inverted        CON     $4000
Open            CON     $8000
Baud            CON     T38K4 + Inverted


Main:
  DO
    SEROUT SO\FC, Baud, ["Hello!", CR]    ' send the greeting
    PAUSE 2500                            ' wait 2.5 seconds
  LOOP                                    ' repeat forever
  END
```

Demo Program (SERIN_SEROUT2.bs2)

NOTE: This example program was written for the BS2 but it can be used with the BS2e, BS2sx, BS2p, BS2pe, and BS2px. This program uses conditional compilation techniques; see Chapter 3 for more information.

```
' SERIN_SEROUT2.bs2
' Using two BS2-IC's, connect the circuit shown in the SERIN command
' description and run this program on the BASIC Stamp designated as the
' Receiver.  This program demonstrates the use of Flow Control (FPin).
' Without flow control, the sender would transmit the whole word "Hello!"
' in about 1.5 ms. The receiver would catch the first byte at most; by the
' time it got back from the first 1-second PAUSE, the rest of the data
' would be long gone. With flow control, communication is flawless since
' the sender waits for the receiver to catch up.

' {$STAMP BS2}
' {$PBASIC 2.5}

SI              PIN     0               ' serial input
FC              PIN     1               ' flow control pin

#SELECT $STAMP
  #CASE BS2, BS2E, BS2PE
    T1200       CON     813
    T2400       CON     396
    T9600       CON     84
    T19K2       CON     32
    T38K4       CON     6
```

```
    #CASE BS2SX, BS2P
      T1200        CON      2063
      T2400        CON      1021
      T9600        CON      240
      T19K2        CON      110
      T38K4        CON      45
    #CASE BS2PX
      T1200        CON      3313
      T2400        CON      1646
      T9600        CON      396
      T19K2        CON      188
      T38K4        CON      84
    #ENDSELECT

    Inverted       CON      $4000
    Open           CON      $8000
    Baud           CON      T38K4 + Inverted

    letter         VAR      Byte


    Main:
      DO
        SERIN SI\FC, Baud, [letter]      ' receive one byte
        DEBUG letter                     ' display on screen
        PAUSE 1000                       ' wait one second
      LOOP                               ' repeat forever
      END
```

SEROUT

BS1	BS2	BS2e	BS2sx	BS2p	BS2pe	BS2px

1 **SEROUT** *Tpin, Baudmode, ({#} OutputData)*

All 2 **SEROUT** *Tpin { \Fpin }, Baudmode, { Pace, } { Timeout, Tlabel, } [OutputData]*

Function

Transmit asynchronous serial data (e.g., RS-232 data).

1
NOTE: Expressions are not allowed as arguments on the BS1. The range of the Rp*in* argument on the BS1 is 0 – 7.

- **Tpin** is a variable/constant/expression (0 – 16) that specifies the I/O pin through which the serial data will be transmitted. This pin will be set to output mode. On all BS2 models, if Tpin is set to 16, the BASIC Stamp uses the dedicated serial-output pin (SOUT, physical pin 1), which is normally used by the Stamp Editor during the download process.

- **Fpin** is an optional variable/constant/expression (0 – 15) that specifies the I/O pin to monitor for flow control status. This pin will be set to input mode. NOTE: Fpin must be specified to use the optional *Timeout* and *Tlabel* arguments in the SEROUT command.

- **Baudmode** is variable/constant/expression (0 – 7 on the BS1, 0 – 65535 on all BS2 models) that specifies serial timing and configuration.

- **Pace** is an optional variable/constant/expression (0 – 65535) that determines the length of the pause between transmitted bytes. NOTE: Pace cannot be used simultaneously with *Timeout* and *Fpin*.

- **Timeout** is an optional variable/constant/expression (0 – 65535) that tells SEROUT how long to wait for *Fpin* permission to send. If permission does not arrive in time, the program will jump to the address specified by *Tlabel*. NOTE: Fpin must be specified to use the optional *Timeout* and *Tlabel* arguments in the SEROUT command.

- **Tlabel** is an optional label that must be provided along with *Timeout*. Tlabel indicates where the program should go in the event that permission to send data is not granted within the period specified by *Timeout*.

1
NOTE: The BS1's *OutputData* argument can only be a list of variables and the optional decimal modifier (#).

- **OutputData** is list of variables, constants, expressions and formatters that tells SEROUT how to format outgoing data. SEROUT can transmit individual or repeating bytes, convert values into decimal, hex or binary text representations, or transmit strings of bytes from variable arrays. These actions can be combined in any order in the *OutputData* list.

Quick Facts

	BS1	BS2, BS2e	BS2sx	BS2p	BS2pe	BS2px
Units in *Pace*	n/a	1 ms	1 ms	1 ms	1 ms	1 ms
Units in *Timeout*	n/a	1 ms	0.4 ms	0.4 ms	1 ms	0.4 ms
Baud range	300, 600, 1200, and 2400 only	243 to 50K	608 to 115.2K	608 to 115.2K	243 to 50K	972 to 115.2K
Baud limit with flow control	n/a	19.2K	19.2K	19.2K	19.2K	19.2K
I/O Pins Available	0 - 7	0 – 15	0 - 15	0 – 15 (in current I/O block)	0 – 15 (in current I/O block)	0 – 15 (in current I/O block)
Other serial port pins	n/a	SOUT pin (physical pin 1) when *Tpin* = 16				
Special cases	n/a	*Fpin* must be specified to use *Timeout* and *Tlabel*. *Pace* cannot be specified at the same time as *Timeout*.				
Related Commands	SERIN	SERIN and DEBUG				

Table 5.104: SEROUT Quick Facts.

Explanation

One of the most popular forms of communication between electronic devices is serial communication. There are two major types of serial communication; asynchronous and synchronous. The SERIN and SEROUT commands are used to receive and send asynchronous serial data. See the SHIFTIN and SHIFTOUT command for information on the synchronous method.

SERIAL COMMUNICATION BACKGROUND.

The following information is supplemental to what is discussed in the SERIN command section. Please read through the SERIN command section for additional information.

All BS2 models have a line driver on its SOUT pin (*Tpin* = 16). The SOUT pin goes to a PC's serial data-in pin on the DB9 connector built into BASIC Stamp development boards. The connector is wired to allow both programming and run-time serial communication (unless you are using the BASIC Stamp 2 Carrier Board (#27120) which is only designed for programming). For the built-in serial port set the *Tpin* argument to 16 in the SEROUT command.

USING THE BUILT-IN SERIAL PORT FOUND ON ALL BS2 MODELS.

All 2

All BASIC Stamp models (including the BS1) can also transmit RS-232 data through any of their I/O pins (*Tpin* = 0 – 7 for BS1, *Tpin* = 0 – 15 on all other BASIC Stamp models). The I/O pins only provide a 0 to +5 volt swing (outside of RS-232 specs) and may need to be connected through a line driver for proper operation with all serial ports. Most serial ports are able to recognize a 0 to +5 volt swing, however. See Figure 5.38 for sample wiring.

Figure 5.38: Serial port diagram showing correct connections to a BASIC Stamp's I/O pin.

NOTE: A line driver may have to be used between the I/O pin and the receiving serial port to ensure proper communication.

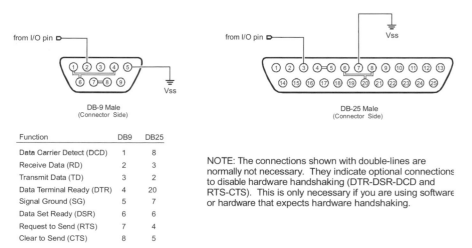

DB-9 Male
(Connector Side)

DB-25 Male
(Connector Side)

Function	DB9	DB25
Data Carrier Detect (DCD)	1	8
Receive Data (RD)	2	3
Transmit Data (TD)	3	2
Data Terminal Ready (DTR)	4	20
Signal Ground (SG)	5	7
Data Set Ready (DSR)	6	6
Request to Send (RTS)	7	4
Clear to Send (CTS)	8	5

NOTE: The connections shown with double-lines are normally not necessary. They indicate optional connections to disable hardware handshaking (DTR-DSR-DCD and RTS-CTS). This is only necessary if you are using software or hardware that expects hardware handshaking.

Figure 5.38 shows the pinouts of the two styles of PC serial ports and how to connect them to the BASIC Stamp's I/O pin. Though not normally needed, the figure also shows loop back connections that defeat hardware handshaking used by some PC software. Note that PC serial ports are always male connectors. The 25-pin style of serial port (called a DB25) looks similar to a printer (parallel) port except that it is male, whereas a parallel port is female.

SERIAL TIMING AND MODE (BAUDMODE).

Asynchronous serial communication relies on precise timing. Both the sender and receiver must be set for identical timing, usually expressed in bits per second (bps) called baud.

SEROUT requires a value called *Baudmode* that tells it the important characteristics of the outgoing serial data; the bit period, number of data and parity bits, and polarity.

On the BS1, serial communication is limited to: no-parity, 8-data bits and 1-stop bit at one of four different speeds: 300, 600, 1200 or 2400 baud. Table 5.105 indicates the Baudmode value or symbols to use when selecting the desired mode.

Baudmode Value	Symbol	Baud Rate	Polarity and Output Mode
0	T2400	2400	TRUE (always driven)
1	T1200	1200	TRUE (always driven)
2	T600	600	TRUE (always driven)
3	T300	300	TRUE (always driven)
4	N2400	2400	INVERTED (always driven)
5	N1200	1200	INVERTED (always driven)
6	N600	600	INVERTED (always driven)
7	N300	300	INVERTED (always driven)
8	OT2400	2400	TRUE (open drain, driven high)
9	OT1200	1200	TRUE (open drain, driven high)
10	OT600	600	TRUE (open drain, driven high)
11	OT300	300	TRUE (open drain, driven high)
12	ON2400	2400	INVERTED (open source, driven low)
13	ON1200	1200	INVERTED (open source, driven low)
14	ON600	600	INVERTED (open source, driven low)
15	ON300	300	INVERTED (open source, driven low)

Table 5.105: BS1 *Baudmode* Values.

On all BS2 models, serial communication is very flexible. The *Baudmode* argument for SEROUT accepts a 16-bit value that determines its characteristics: 1-stop bit, 8-data bits/no-parity or 7-data bits/even-parity and virtually any speed from as low as 300 baud to greater than 100K baud (depending on the BASIC Stamp model). Table 5.106 shows how *Baudmode* is calculated, while Table 5.107, Table 5.108, and Table 5.109 show common baud modes for standard serial baud rates.

Step 1: Determine the bit period (bits 0 – 11)	BS2, BS2e and BS2pe: $= INT(1,000,000 / baud\ rate) - 20$ BS2sx and BS2p: $= INT(2,500,000 / baud\ rate) - 20$ BS2px: $= INT(4,000,000 / baud\ rate) - 20$ Note: INT means 'convert to integer;' drop the numbers to the right of the decimal point.
Step 2: Set data bits and parity (bit 13)	8-bit/no-parity = 0 7-bit/even-parity = 8192
Step 3: Select polarity (bit 14)	True (noninverted) = 0 Inverted = 16384
Step 4: Select driven or open output (bit 15)	Driven = 0 Open = 32768

Table 5.106: *Baudmode* calculation for all BS2 models. Add the results of steps 1, 2, 3 and 4 to determine the proper value for the *Baudmode* argument.

Table 5.107: BS2, BS2e and BS2pe common baud rates and corresponding *Baudmodes*.

Baud Rate	8-bit no-parity inverted	8-bit no-parity true	7-bit even-parity inverted	7-bit even-parity true
300	19697	3313	27889	11505
600	18030	1646	26222	9838
1200	17197	813	25389	9005
2400	16780	396	24972	8588
4800	16572	188	24764	8380
9600	16468	84	24660	8276

NOTE: For "open" baudmodes used in networking, add 32768 to the values from the table above. If the dedicated serial port (*Tpin*=16) is used, the data is inverted and driven regardless of the baudmode setting.

Table 5.108: BS2sx and BS2p common baud rates and corresponding *Baudmodes*.

Baud Rate	8-bit no-parity inverted	8-bit no-parity true	7-bit even-parity inverted	7-bit even-parity true
1200	18447	2063	26639	10255
2400	17405	1021	25597	9213
4800	16884	500	25076	8692
9600	16624	240	24816	8432

NOTE: For "open" baudmodes used in networking, add 32768 to the values from the table above. If the dedicated serial port (*Tpin*=16) is used, the data is inverted and driven regardless of the baudmode setting.

Table 5.109: BS2px common baud rates and corresponding *Baudmodes*.

Baud Rate	8-bit no-parity inverted	8-bit no-parity true	7-bit even-parity inverted	7-bit even-parity true
1200	19697	3313	27889	11505
2400	18030	1646	26222	9838
4800	17197	813	25389	9005
9600	16780	396	24792	8588

CHOOSING THE PROPER BAUD MODE.

If you're communicating with existing software or hardware, its speed(s) and mode(s) will determine your choice of baud rate and mode. See the SERIN command description for more information.

A SIMPLE FORM OF SEROUT.

The example below will transmit a single byte through I/O pin 1 at 2400 baud, 8N1, inverted:

```
SEROUT 1, N2400, (65)
```

--or--

```
SEROUT 1, 16780, [65]
```

This is written with the BS2's *Baudmode* value. Be sure to adjust the value for your BASIC Stamp model.

Here, SEROUT will transmit a byte equal to 65 (the ASCII value of the character "A") through pin 1. If the BASIC Stamp were connected to a PC running a terminal program (set to the same baud rate) the character "A" would appear on the screen (see the ASCII character chart in Appendix A).

What if you really wanted the value 65 to appear on the screen? If you remember from the discussion in the SERIN command, "It is up to the receiving side (in serial communication) to interpret the values..." In this case, the PC is interpreting the byte-sized value to be the ASCII code for the character "A". Unless you're also writing the software for the PC, you can't change how the PC interprets the incoming serial data, so to solve this problem, the data needs to be translated before it is sent.

A SIMPLE NUMERIC CONVERSION; DECIMAL TO ASCII NUMERIC TEXT.

The SEROUT command provides a formatter, called the decimal formatter, which will translate the value 65 to two ASCII codes for the characters "6" and "5" and then transmit them. Look at the following code:

```
SEROUT 1, N2400, (#65)
```

--or--

```
SEROUT 1, 16780, [DEC 65]
```

This is written with the BS2's *Baudmode* value. Be sure to adjust the value for your BASIC Stamp model.

Notice the decimal formatter in the SEROUT command. It is the "#" (for the BS1) or "DEC" (for all BS2 models) that appears just to the left of the number 65. This tells SEROUT to convert the number into separate ASCII characters which represent the value in decimal form. If the value 65 in the code were changed to 123, the SEROUT command would send three bytes (49, 50 and 51) corresponding to the characters "1", "2" and "3".

All BS2 models have many more conversion formatters available for the SEROUT command. See the "Additional Conversion Formatters" section below for more information.

The SEROUT command sends quoted text exactly as it appears in the *OutputData* list:

```
SEROUT 1, N2400, ("Hello" CR)
SEROUT 1, N2400, ("Num = ", #100)
```

--or--

All 2

```
SEROUT 1, 16780, ["Hello", CR]
SEROUT 1, 16780, ["Num = ", DEC 100]
```

This is written with the BS2's *Baudmode* value. Be sure to adjust the value for your BASIC Stamp model.

The above code will display "HELLO" on one line and "Num = 100" on the next line. Notice that you can combine data to output in one SEROUT command, separated by commas. In the example above, we could have written it as one line of code, with "HELLO", CR, "Num = ", DEC 100 in the *OutputData* list.

The BS1's SEROUT command is limited to above-mentioned features. If you are not using a BS1, please continue reading about the additional features below.

USING SEROUT'S *PACE* ARGUMENT TO INSERT DELAYS BETWEEN TRANSMITTED BYTES.

All 2

NOTE: The rest of the code examples for this section are written for the BS2, using the BS2's *Baudmode* and *Timeout* values. Be sure to adjust the value for your BASIC Stamp model.

The SEROUT command can also be configured to pause between transmitted bytes. This is the purpose of the optional *Pace* argument. For example (9600 baud N8, inverted):

```
SEROUT 1, 16780, 1000, ["Slowly..."]
```

Here, the BASIC Stamp transmits "Slowly..." with a 1 second delay between each character. See Table 5.104 for units of the *Pace* argument. One good reason to use the *Pace* feature is to support devices that require more than one stop bit. Normally, the BASIC Stamp sends data as fast as it can (with a minimum of 1 stop bit between bytes). Since a stop bit is really just a resting state in the line (no data transmitted), using the *Pace* option will effectively add multiple stop bits. Since the requirement for 2 or more stop bits (on some devices) is really just a "minimum" requirement, the receiving side should receive this data correctly.

USING ASCII CODES.

Keep in mind that when we type something like "XYZ" into the SEROUT command, the BASIC Stamp actually uses the ASCII codes for each of those characters for its tasks. We could also typed: 88, 89, 90 in place of "XYZ" and the program would run the same way since 88 is the ASCII code for the "X" character, 89 is the ASCII code for the "Y" character, and so on.

ADDITIONAL CONVERSION FORMATTERS.

The decimal formatter is only one of a whole family of conversion formatters available with SERIN on all BS2 models. See Table 5.110 for a list of available conversion formatters. All of the conversion formatters work similar to the decimal formatter. The formatters translate the value into separate bytes of data until the entire number is translated or until the indicated number of digits (in the case of the fixed length formatters) is translated.

All BS2 models also have special formatters for outputting a string of characters, and repeated characters. See Table 5.111 for a list of these special formatters.

All 2

Conversion Formatter	Type of Number	Notes
DEC{1..5}	Decimal, optionally fixed to 1 – 5 digits	1
SDEC{1..5}	Signed decimal, optionally fixed to 1 – 5 digits	1,2
HEX{1..4}	Hexadecimal, optionally fixed to 1 – 4 digits	1,3
SHEX{1..4}	Signed hexadecimal, optionally fixed to 1 – 4 digits	1,2
IHEX{1..4}	Indicated hexadecimal, optionally fixed to 1 – 4 digits ($ prefix)	1
ISHEX{1..4}	Signed, indicated hexadecimal, optionally fixed to 1 – 4 digits ($ prefix)	1,2
BIN{1..16}	Binary, optionally fixed to 1 – 16 digits	1
SBIN{1..16}	Signed binary, optionally fixed to 1 – 16 digits	1,2
IBIN{1..16}	Indicated binary, optionally fixed to 1 – 16 digits (% prefix)	1
ISBIN{1..16}	Signed, indicated binary, optionally fixed to 1 – 16 digits (% prefix)	1,2

Table 5.110: Conversion Formatters for all BS2 models.

1 Fixed-digit formatters like DEC4 will pad the number with leading 0s if necessary; ex: DEC4 65 sends 0065. If a number is larger than the specified number of digits, the leading digits will be dropped; ex: DEC4 56422 sends 6422.
2 Signed modifiers work under two's complement rules.
3 The HEX modifier can be used for BCD to Decimal Conversion. See "Hex to BCD Conversion" on page 97.

Special Formatter	Action
?	Displays "symbol = x' + carriage return; where x is a number. Default format is decimal, but may be combined with conversion formatters (ex: BIN ? x to display "x = binary_number").
ASC ?	Displays "symbol = 'x'" + carriage return; where x is an ASCII character.
STR ByteArray {\L}	Send character string from an array. The optional \L argument can be used to limit the output to L characters, otherwise, characters will be sent up to the first byte equal to 0 or the end of RAM space is reached.
REP Byte \L	Send a string consisting of Byte repeated L times (ex: REP "X"\10 sends "XXXXXXXXXX").

Table 5.111: Special Formatters for all BS2 models.

The string formatter is useful for transmitting a string of characters from a byte array variable. A string of characters is a set of characters that are arranged or accessed in a certain order. The characters "ABC" could be stored in a string with the "A" first, followed by the "B" and then followed by the "C." A byte array is a similar concept to a string; it contains data that is arranged in a certain order. Each of the elements in an array is the

THE STR (STRING) FORMATTER.

same size. The string "ABC" could be stored in a byte array containing three bytes (elements). See the "Defining Arrays" section in Chapter 4 for more information on arrays.

Here is an example that transmits five bytes (from a byte array) through I/O pin 1 at 9600 bps, N81/inverted:

```
serStr          VAR     Byte(5)          ' create 5-byte array

Main:
  serStr(0) = "H"                        ' fill array
  serStr(1) = "E"
  serStr(2) = "L"
  serStr(3) = "L"
  serStr(4) = "O"
  SEROUT 1, 16468, [STR serStr\5]        ' transmit
```

Note that we use the optional \L argument of STR. If we didn't specify this, the BASIC Stamp would try to keep sending characters until it found a byte equal to 0. Since we didn't specify a last byte of 0 in the array, we chose to tell it explicitly to only send 5 characters.

USING PARITY AND HANDLING PARITY ERRORS.

Parity is a simple error-checking feature. When the SEROUT command's *Baudmode* is set for even parity it counts the number of 1s in the outgoing byte and uses the parity bit to make that number even. For instance, if it is sending the 7-bit value: %0011010, it sets the parity bit to 1 in order to make an even number of 1s (four).

The receiver also counts the data bits to calculate what the parity bit should be. If it matches the parity bit received, the serial receiver assumes that the data was received correctly. Of course, this is not necessarily true, since two incorrectly received bits could make parity seem correct when the data was wrong, or the parity bit itself could be bad when the rest of the data was OK. Parity errors are only detected on the receiver side. Generally, the receiver determines how to handle the error. In a more robust application, the receiver and transmitter might be set up such that the receiver can request a re-send of data that was received with a parity error.

CONTROLLING DATA FLOW.

When you design an application that requires serial communication between BASIC Stamp modules, you have to work within these limitations:

- When the BASIC Stamp is sending or receiving data, it can't execute other instructions.
- When the BASIC Stamp is executing other instructions, it can't send or receive data. *The BASIC Stamp does not have a serial buffer* as there is in PCs. At most serial rates, the BASIC Stamp cannot receive data via SERIN, process it, and execute another SERIN in time to catch the next chunk of data, unless there are significant pauses between data transmissions.

These limitations can sometimes be addressed by using flow control; the *Fpin* option for SERIN and SEROUT (at baud rates of up to the limitation shown in Table 5.94). Through *Fpin*, SERIN can tell a BASIC Stamp sender when it is ready to receive data and SEROUT (on the sender) will wait for permission to send. (For that matter, *Fpin* flow control follows the rules of other serial handshaking schemes, but most computers other than the BASIC Stamp cannot start and stop serial transmission on a byte-by-byte basis. That's why this discussion is limited to communication between BASIC Stamp modules.)

Here's an example using flow control on the BS2 (data through I/O pin 1, flow control through I/O pin 0, 9600 baud, N8, noninverted):

```
SerData    VAR    BYTE
SEROUT  1\0, 84, [SerData]
```

When SEROUT executes, I/O pin 1 (*Tpin*) is made an output, and I/O pin 0 (*Fpin*) is made an input, to wait for the "go" signal from the receiver. Here's the relationship of serial polarity to *Fpin* states.

	Ready to Receive ("Go")	Not Ready to Receive ("Stop")
Inverted	Fpin is High (1)	Fpin is Low (0)
Non-inverted	Fpin is Low (0)	Fpin is High (1)

Table 5.112: Flow control pin states in relation to polarity (inverted or non-inverted) for all BS2 models.

See the demo program, below, for a flow control example using two BS2s. In the demo program example, without flow control, the sender would transmit the whole word "Hello!" in about 6 ms. The receiver would catch the first byte at most; by the time it got back from the first 1-second PAUSE, the rest of the data would be long gone. With flow control, communication is flawless since the sender waits for the receiver to catch up.

In Figure 5.39 below, I/O pin 0, *Fpin*, is pulled to ground through a 10k resistor. This is to ensure that the sender sees a stop signal (0 for inverted communications) when the receiver is being programmed.

USING THE SERIAL TIME-OUT FEATURE.

In the flow control examples above, the only way the SEROUT instruction will end (other than RESET or power-off) is if the receiver allows it to send the entire *OutputData* list. If *Fpin* permission never occurs, the program is stuck. However, you can tell the BASIC Stamp to abort SEROUT if it doesn't receive *Fpin* permission within a specified time period. For instance, to transmit a decimal number through pin 1 at 9600 baud, 8N, inverted and abort SEROUT after 2 seconds (2000 ms) if no *Fpin* permission arrives on I/O pin 0:

```
SEROUT 1\0, 16468, 2000, No_Permission, [DEC 150]
STOP

No_Permission:
  DEBUG "Timeout error", CR
```

If no *Fpin* permission arrives within 2 seconds, the program aborts SEROUT and continues at the label *No_Permission*.

Figure 5.39: Flow-Control Example Circuit.

Host PC (for Debug)

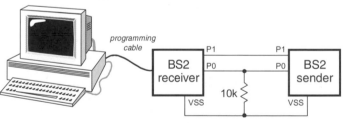

USING OPEN BAUDMODES FOR NETWORKING BASIC STAMPS.

The SEROUT command supports open-drain and open-source output, which makes it possible to network multiple BASIC Stamp modules on a single pair of wires. These "open baudmodes" only actively drive the *Tpin* in one state (for the other state, they simply disconnect the pin; setting it to an input mode). If two BASIC Stamp modules in a network had their SEROUT lines connected together (while a third device listened on that line) and the BASIC Stamp modules were using always-driven baudmodes, they could simultaneously output two opposite states (i.e.: +5 volts and ground). This would create a short circuit. The heavy current flow would likely damage the I/O pins or the BASIC Stamp modules themselves. Since the open baudmodes only drive in one state and float in the other, there's no chance of this kind of short.

The polarity selected for SEROUT determines which state is driven and which is open as in Table 5.113.

	State (0)	State (1)	Resistor Pulled to
Inverted	Open	Driven	Gnd (Vss)
Non-inverted	Driven	Open	+5V (Vdd)

Table 5.113: Open Baudmode States for all BS2 models.

Since open baudmodes only drive to one state, they need a resistor to pull the networked line into the other state, as shown in Table 5.113 and in Figure 5.40 and Figure 5.41.

Open baudmodes allow the BASIC Stamp to share a line, but it is up to your program to resolve other networking issues such as who talks when and how to detect, prevent and fix data errors.

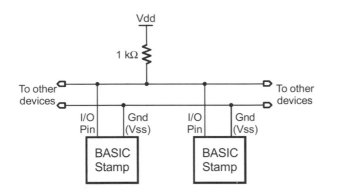

Figure 5.40: SEROUT Open-Drain Circuit. This circuit is for use with the Open, Non-inverted baudmode.

Figure 5.41: SEROUT Open-Source Circuit. This circuit is for use with the Open, Inverted baudmode.

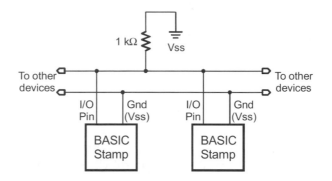

SEROUT TROUBLESHOOTING.

Serial communication, because of its complexity, can be very difficult to work with at times. Please follow these guidelines (and those in the "SERIN Troubleshooting" section of the SERIN command description) when developing a project using the SERIN and SEROUT commands:

1. Always build your project in steps.
   a. Start with small, manageable pieces of code, that deals with serial communication) and test them, one at a time.
   b. Add more and more small pieces, testing them each time, as you go.
   c. Never write a large portion of code that works with serial communication without testing its smallest workable pieces first.
2. Pay attention to timing.
   a. Be very careful to calculate and overestimate the amount of time operations should take within the BASIC Stamp. Misunderstanding the timing constraints is the source of most problems with code that communicate serially.
   b. If the serial communication in your project is bi-directional, the above statement is even more critical.
3. Pay attention to wiring.
   a. Take extra time to study and verify serial communication wiring diagrams. A mistake in wiring can cause strange problems in communication, or no communication at all. Make sure to connect the ground pins (Vss) between the devices that are communicating serially.
4. Verify port setting on the PC and in the SERIN/SEROUT commands.

a. Unmatched settings on the sender and receiver side will cause garbled data transfers or no data transfers. If the data you receive is unreadable, it is most likely a baud rate setting error.

5. If data transmitted to the Stamp Editor's Debug Terminal is garbled, verify the output format.

a. A common mistake is to send data with SEROUT in ASCII format. For example, SEROUT 16, 84, [0] instead of SEROUT 16, 84, [DEC 0]. The first example will send a byte equal to 0 to the PC, resulting in the Debug Terminal clearing the screen (since 0 is the control character for a clear-screen action).

Demo Program (SEROUT.bs1)

```
' SEROUT.bs1
' This program transmits the string "ABCD" followed by a number and a
' carriage-return at 2400 baud, inverted, N81 format.

' {$STAMP BS1}
' {$PBASIC 1.0}

SYMBOL    SOut          = 1
SYMBOL    Baud          = N2400

SYMBOL    value         = W1


Setup:
  value = 1

Main:
  SEROUT SOut, Baud, ("ABCD", #value)
  value = value + 1
  PAUSE 250
  GOTO Main
  END
```

Demo Program (SERIN_SEROUT1.bs2)

```
' SERIN_SEROUT1.bs2
' Using two BS2-IC's, connect the circuit shown in the SERIN command
' description and run this program on the BASIC Stamp designated as the
' Sender. This program demonstrates the use of Flow Control (FPin).
' Without flow control, the sender would transmit the whole word "Hello!"
' in about 1.5 ms. The receiver would catch the first byte at most; by the
' time it got back from the first 1-second PAUSE, the rest of the data
```

NOTE: This example program was written for BS2's but it can be used with the BS2e, BS2sx, BS2p, BS2pe, and BS2px. This program uses conditional compilation techniques; see Chapter 3 for more information.

```
' would be long gone. With flow control, communication is flawless since
' the sender waits for the receiver to catch up.

' {$STAMP BS2}
' {$PBASIC 2.5}

SO              PIN     1               ' serial output
FC              PIN     0               ' flow control pin

#SELECT $STAMP
  #CASE BS2, BS2E, BS2PE
    T1200       CON     813
    T2400       CON     396
    T9600       CON     84
    T19K2       CON     32
    T38K4       CON     6
  #CASE BS2SX, BS2P
    T1200       CON     2063
    T2400       CON .   1021
    T9600       CON     240
    T19K2       CON     110
    T38K4       CON     45
  #CASE BS2PX
    T1200       CON     3313
    T2400       CON     1646
    T9600       CON     396
    T19K2       CON     188
    T38K4       CON     84
#ENDSELECT


Inverted        CON     $4000
Open            CON     $8000
Baud            CON     T38K4 + Inverted


Main:
  DO
    SEROUT SO\FC, Baud, ["Hello!", CR]  ' send the greeting
    PAUSE 2500                          ' wait 2.5 seconds
  LOOP                                  ' repeat forever.
  END
```

[All 2] Demo Program (SERIN_SEROUT2.bs2)

NOTE: This example program was written for BS2's but it can be used with the BS2e, BS2sx, BS2p, BS2pe, and BS2px . This program uses conditional compilation techniques; see Chapter 3 for more information.

```
' SERIN_SEROUT2.bs2
' Using two BS2-IC's, connect the circuit shown in the SERIN command
' description and run this program on the BASIC Stamp designated as the
' Receiver.  This program demonstrates the use of Flow Control (FPin).
' Without flow control, the sender would transmit the whole word "Hello!"
' in about 1.5 ms. The receiver would catch the first byte at most; by the
' time it got back from the first 1-second PAUSE, the rest of the data
' would be long gone. With flow control, communication is flawless since
```

```
' the sender waits for the receiver to catch up.

' {$STAMP BS2}
' {$PBASIC 2.5}

SI              PIN    0                ' serial input
FC              PIN    1                ' flow control pin

#SELECT $STAMP
  #CASE BS2, BS2E, BS2PE
    T1200       CON    813
    T2400       CON    396
    T9600       CON    84
    T19K2       CON    32
    T38K4       CON    6
  #CASE BS2SX, BS2P
    T1200       CON    2063
    T2400       CON    1021
    T9600       CON    240
    T19K2       CON    110
    T38K4       CON    45
  #CASE BS2PX
    T1200       CON    3313
    T2400       CON    1646
    T9600       CON    396
    T19K2       CON    188
    T38K4       CON    84
#ENDSELECT

Inverted        CON    $4000
Open            CON    $8000
Baud            CON    T38K4 + Inverted

letter          VAR    Byte


Main:
  DO
    SERIN SI\FC, Baud, [letter]        ' recieve one byte
    DEBUG letter                       ' display on screen
    PAUSE 1000                         ' wait one second
  LOOP                                 ' repeat forever
  END
```

SHIFTIN

| BS1 | **BS2** | **BS2e** | **BS2sx** | **BS2p** | **BS2pe** | **BS2px** |

 SHIFTIN *Dpin, Cpin, Mode,* [*Variable* { *\Bits* } {, *Variable* { *\Bits* }...}]

Function

Shift data in from a synchronous serial device.

- *Dpin* is a variable/constant/expression (0 – 15) that specifies the I/O pin that will be connected to the synchronous serial device's data output. This pin will be set to input mode.

- *Cpin* is a variable/constant/expression (0 – 15) that specifies the I/O pin that will be connected to the synchronous serial device's clock input. This pin will be set to output mode.

- *Mode* is a variable/constant/expression (0 – 3), or one of four predefined symbols, that tells SHIFTIN the order in which data bits are to be arranged and the relationship of clock pulses to valid data. See Table 5.115 for value and symbol definitions.

- *Variable* is a variable in which incoming data bits will be stored.

- *Bits* is an optional variable/constant/expression (1 – 16) specifying how many bits are to be input by SHIFTIN. If no *Bits* argument is given, SHIFTIN defaults to 8 bits.

Quick Facts

Table 5.114: SHIFTIN Quick Facts.

	BS2/BS2e	BS2sx/BS2p	BS2pe	BS2px
Timing of T_h and t_l	14 µs / 46 µs	5.6 µs / 18 µs	14 µs / 46 µs	3.6 µs / 11.8 µs
Transmission Rate	~16 kbits/sec.	~42 kbits/sec.	~16 kbits/sec.	~ 65 kbits/sec.
Related Command	SHIFTOUT			

Explanation

SHIFTIN and SHIFTOUT provide an easy method of acquiring data from synchronous serial devices. Synchronous serial differs from asynchronous serial (like SERIN and SEROUT) in that the timing of data bits (on a data line) is specified in relationship to clock pulses (on a clock line). Data bits may be valid after the rising or falling edge of the clock line. This kind of serial protocol is called Synchronous Peripheral Interface (SPI) and is commonly used by controller peripherals like ADCs, DACs, clocks, memory devices, etc.

At their heart, synchronous-serial devices are essentially shift-registers; trains of flip-flops that pass data bits along in a bucket brigade fashion to a single data output pin. Another bit is output each time the appropriate edge (rising or falling, depending on the device) appears on the clock line.

The SHIFTIN instruction first causes the clock pin to output low and the data pin to switch to input mode. Then, SHIFTIN either reads the data pin and generates a clock pulse (PRE mode) or generates a clock pulse then reads the data pin (POST mode). SHIFTIN continues to generate clock pulses and read the data pin for as many data bits as are required.

SHIFTIN OPERATION.

Making SHIFTIN work with a particular device is a matter of matching the mode and number of bits to that device's protocol. Most manufacturers use a timing diagram to illustrate the relationship of clock and data. Items to look for include: 1) which bit of the data arrives first; most significant bit (MSB) or least significant bit (LSB) and 2) is the first data bit ready before the first clock pulse (PRE) or after the first clock pulse (POST). Table 5.115 shows the values and symbols available for *Mode*, and Figure 5.42 shows SHIFTIN's timing.

Symbol	Value	Meaning
MSBPRE	0	Data is msb-first; sample bits before clock pulse
LSBPRE	1	Data is lsb-first; sample bits before clock pulse
MSBPOST	2	Data is msb-first; sample bits after clock pulse
LSBPOST	3	Data is lsb-first; sample bits after clock pulse

Table 5.115: SHIFTIN *Mode* Values and Symbols.

(Msb is most-significant bit; the highest or leftmost bit of a nibble, byte, or word. Lsb is the least-significant bit; the lowest or rightmost bit of a nibble, byte, or word.)

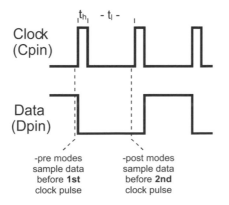

Figure 5.42: SHIFTIN Timing Diagram. Refer to the SHIFTIN Quick Facts table for timing information on t_h (t high) and t_l (t low).

A SIMPLE SHIFTIN EXAMPLE.

Here is a simple example:

```
result          VAR     Byte

SHIFTIN 0, 1, MSBPRE, [result]
```

Here, the SHIFTIN command will read I/O pin 0 (*Dpin*) and will generate a clock signal on I/O 1 (*Cpin*). The data that arrives on *Dpin* depends on the device connected to it. Let's say, for example, that a shift register is connected and has a value of $AF (10101111) waiting to be sent. Additionally, let's assume that the shift register sends out the most significant bit first, and the first bit is on *Dpin* before the first clock pulse (MSBPRE). The SHIFTIN command above will generate eight clock pulses and sample the data pin (*Dpin*) eight times. Afterward, the *result* variable will contain the value $AF.

CONTROLLING THE NUMBER OF BITS RECEIVED.

By default, SHIFTIN acquires eight bits, but you can set it to shift any number of bits from 1 to 16 with the *Bits* argument. For example:

```
result          VAR     Byte

SHIFTIN 0, 1, MSBPRE, [result\4]
```

Will only input the first 4 bits. In the example discussed above, the *result* variable will be left with %1010.

Some devices return more than 16 bits. For example, most 8-bit shift registers can be daisy-chained together to form any multiple of 8 bits; 16, 24, 32, 40... To solve this, you can use a single SHIFTIN instruction with multiple variables. Each variable can be assigned a particular number of bits with the *Bits* argument. As in:

```
resultLo        VAR     Word
resultHi        VAR     Nib

SHIFTIN 0, 1, MSBPRE, [resultHi\4, resultLo\16]
```

The above code will first shift in four bits into *resultHi* and then 16 bits into *resultLo*. The two variables together make up a 20 bit value.

Demo Program (SHIFTIN.bs2)

```
' SHIFTIN.bs2
' This program uses the SHIFTIN instruction to interface with the ADC0831
' 8-bit analog-to-digital converter from National Semiconductor.

' {$STAMP BS2}
' {$PBASIC 2.5}

CS              PIN    0                ' chip select
AData           PIN    1                ' data pin
Clk             PIN    2                ' clock pin

adcRes          VAR    Byte             ' ADC result

Setup:
  HIGH CS                               ' deselect ADC

' In the loop below, just three lines of code are required to read the
' ADC0831. The SHIFTIN command does most of the work.  The mode argument in
' the SHIFTIN command specifies MSB or LSB-first and whether to sample data
' before or after the clock. In this case, we chose MSB-first, post-clock.
' The ADC0831 precedes its data output with a dummy bit, which we take care
' of by specifying 9 bits of data instead of 8.

Main:
  DO
    LOW CS                              ' activate the ADC0831
    SHIFTIN AData, Clk, MSBPOST, [adcRes\9]   ' shift in the data
    HIGH CS                            ' deactivate ADC0831
    DEBUG ? adcRes                     ' show conversion result
    PAUSE 1000                         ' wait one second
  LOOP                                  ' repeat
  END
```

All 2

NOTE: This example program can be used with all BS2 models by changing the $STAMP directive accordingly.

SHIFTOUT	BS1	BS2	BS2e	BS2sx	BS2p	BS2pe	BS2px

 SHIFTOUT *Dpin, Cpin, Mode,* **[** *OutputData* **{** *\Bits* **}** { *,OutputData* **{** *\Bits* **}...}**]

Function

Shift data out to a synchronous serial device.

- **Dpin** is a variable/constant/expression (0 – 15) that specifies the I/O pin that will be connected to the synchronous serial device's data input. This pin will be set to output mode.

- **Cpin** is a variable/constant/expression (0 – 15) that specifies the I/O pin that will be connected to the synchronous serial device's clock input. This pin will be set to output mode.

- **Mode** is a variable/constant/expression (0 – 1), or one of two predefined symbols, that tells SHIFTOUT the order in which data bits are to be arranged. See Table 5.117 for value and symbol definitions.

- **OutputData** is a variable/constant/expression containing the data to be sent.

- **Bits** is an optional variable/constant/expression (1 – 16) specifying how many bits are to be output by SHIFTOUT. When the *Bits* argument is given, the BASIC Stamp transmits the rightmost number of bits specifed, regardless of the *Mode*. If no *Bits* argument is given, SHIFTOUT defaults to 8 bits.

Quick Facts

Table 5.116: SHIFTOUT Quick Facts.

	BS2, BS2e	BS2sx, BS2p	BS2pe	BS2px
Timing of t$_h$ and t$_l$,	14 µs / 46 µs	5.6 µs / 18 µs	14 µs / 46 µs	3.6 µs / 11.8 µs
Timing of t$_a$ and t$_b$	15 µs / 30 µs	6.3 µs / 12.5 µs	15 µs / 30 µs	4 µs / 7.8 µs
Transmission Rate	~16 kbits/sec.	~42 kbits/sec.	~16 kbits/sec.	~65 kbits/sec.
Related Command	SHIFTOUT			

Explanation

SHIFTIN and SHIFTOUT provide an easy method of acquiring data from synchronous serial devices. Synchronous serial differs from asynchronous serial (like SERIN and SEROUT) in that the timing of data bits (on a data line) is specified in relationship to clock pulses (on a clock line). Data bits may be valid after the rising or falling edge of the clock line. This kind of serial protocol is commonly called Synchronous Peripheral Interface (SPI) and is used by controller peripherals like ADCs, DACs, clocks, memory devices, etc.

At their heart, synchronous-serial devices are essentially shift-registers; trains of flip-flops that receive data bits in a bucket brigade fashion from a single data input pin. Another bit is input each time the appropriate edge (rising or falling, depending on the device) appears on the clock line.

The SHIFTOUT instruction first causes the clock pin to output low and the data pin to switch to output mode. Then, SHIFTOUT sets the data pin to the next bit state to be output and generates a clock pulse. SHIFTOUT continues to generate clock pulses and places the next data bit on the data pin for as many data bits as are required for transmission.

SHIFTOUT OPERATION.

Making SHIFTOUT work with a particular device is a matter of matching the mode and number of bits to that device's protocol. Most manufacturers use a timing diagram to illustrate the relationship of clock and data. One of the most important items to look for is which bit of the data should be transmitted first; most significant bit (MSB) or least significant bit (LSB). Table 5.117 shows the values and symbols available for *Mode* and Figure 5.43 shows SHIFTOUT's timing.

Symbol	Value	Meaning
LSBFIRST	0	Data is shifted out lsb-first
MSBFIRST	1	Data is shifted out msb-first

Table 5.117: SHIFTOUT Mode Values and Symbols.

(Msb is most-significant bit; the highest or leftmost bit of a nibble, byte, or word. Lsb is the least-significant bit; the lowest or rightmost bit of a nibble, byte, or word.)

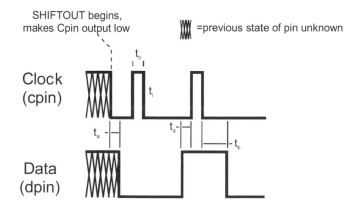

Figure 5.43: SHIFTOUT Timing Diagram. Refer to the SHIFTOUT Quick Facts table for timing information on t_h, t_i, t_a and t_b.

Here is a simple example:

```
SHIFTOUT 0, 1, MSBFIRST, [250]
```

Here, the SHIFTOUT command will write to I/O pin 0 (*Dpin*) and will generate a clock signal on I/O pin 1 (*Cpin*). The SHIFTOUT command will generate eight clock pulses while writing each bit (of the 8-bit value 250) onto the data pin (*Dpin*). In this case, it will start with the most significant bit first as indicated by the *Mode* value of MSBFIRST.

By default, SHIFTOUT transmits eight bits, but you can set it to shift any number of bits from 1 to 16 with the *Bits* argument. For example:

```
SHIFTOUT 0, 1, MSBFIRST, [250\4]
```

Will output only the lowest (rightmost) four bits (%1010 in this case). But what if you want to output the leftmost bits of a given value? By adding the right-shift operator (>>) to the code you can adjust the output as required:

```
SHIFTOUT 0, 1, MSBFIRST, [(250 >> 2)\6]
```

will output the upper six bits (%111110 in this case).

Some devices require more than 16 bits. To solve this, you can use a single SHIFTOUT command with multiple values. Each value can be assigned a particular number of bits with the *Bits* argument. As in:

```
SHIFTOUT 0, 1, MSBFIRST, [250\4, 1045\16]
```

The above code will first shift out four bits of the number 250 (%1010) and then 16 bits of the number 1045 (%0000010000010101). The two values together make up a 20 bit value.

In the examples above, specific numbers were entered as the data to transmit, but, of course, the SHIFTOUT command will accept variables and expressions for the *OutputData* and even for the *Bits* argument.

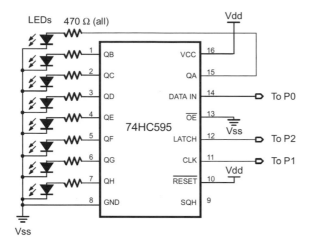

Demo Program (SHIFTOUT.bs2)

```
' SHIFTOUT.bs2
' This program uses the SHIFTOUT command to interface to the 74HC595 shift
' register as an 8-bit output port.  The '595 requires a minimum of three
' inputs: data, clock, and latch. See the figure in the SHIFTOUT command
' description in the manual for wiring information. SHIFTOUT automatically
' handles the data and clock, pulsing the clock to shift data bits into the
' '595. An extra step (pulsing the latch input) is required to move the
' shifted bits in parallel onto the '595's output pins. Note: this code
' does not control the output-enable or reset lines of the '595. This means
' that before the BASIC Stamp first sends, the '595's output latches are
' turned on and may contain random data. In critical applications, you
' should hold output-enable high (disabled) until the BASIC Stamp can take
' control.

' {$STAMP BS2}
' {$PBASIC 2.5}

Dpin            PIN     0               ' data pin to 74HC595
Clk             PIN     1               ' shift clock to 74HC595
Latch           PIN     2               ' latch 74HC595 outputs

counter         VAR     Byte

Setup:
  LOW Latch                             ' initialize latch output

' This loop moves the 8-bit value 'counter' onto the output lines of the
' '595, pauses, then increments counter and repeats.  The data is shifted
```

NOTE: This example program can be used with all BS2 models by changing the $STAMP directive accordingly.

```
' msb first so that the msb appears on pin QH and the lsb on QA. Changing
' MSBFIRST to LSBFIRST causes the data to appear backwards on the outputs.

Main:
  DO
    SHIFTOUT Dpin, Clk, MSBFIRST, [counter]     ' send the bits
    PULSOUT Latch, 1                            ' transfer to outputs
    PAUSE 100                                   ' Wait 0.1 seconds
    counter = counter + 1                       ' increment counter
  LOOP
  END
```

SLEEP

| BS1 | BS2 | BS2e | BS2sx | BS2p | BS2pe | BS2px |

SLEEP *Duration*

Function

Put the BASIC Stamp into low-power mode for a specified time.

NOTE: Expressions are not allowed as arguments on the BS1.

- **Duration** is a variable/constant/expression (1 – 65535) that specifies the duration of sleep. The unit of time for *Duration* is 1 second, though the BASIC Stamp rounds up to the nearest multiple of 2.3 seconds.

Quick Facts

Table 5.118: SLEEP Quick Facts.

NOTE: Current measurements are based on 5-volt power, no extra loads and 75° F ambient temperature.

	BS1	BS2	BS2e	BS2sx	BS2p	BS2pe	BS2px
Current Draw during Run	1 mA	3 mA	25 mA	60 mA	40 mA	15 mA	55 mA
Current Draw during SLEEP	25 µA	50 µA	200 µA	500 µA	350 µA	36 µA	450 µA
Related Commands	END and NAP				END, NAP and POLLWAIT		
Accuracy of SLEEP	±1% @ 75°F with stable power supply						

Explanation

SLEEP allows the BASIC Stamp to turn itself off, then turn back on after a programmed period of time. The length of SLEEP can range from 2.3 seconds to slightly over 18 hours. Power consumption is reduced to the amount described in Table 5.118, assuming no loads are being driven. The resolution of the SLEEP instruction is 2.304 seconds. SLEEP rounds the specified number of seconds up to the nearest multiple of 2.304. For example, SLEEP 1 causes 2.304 seconds of sleep, while SLEEP 10 causes 11.52 seconds (5 x 2.304) of sleep.

Pins retain their previous I/O directions during SLEEP. However, outputs are interrupted every 2.3 seconds during SLEEP due to the way the chip keeps time. The alarm clock that wakes the BASIC Stamp up is called the watchdog timer. The watchdog is a resistor/capacitor oscillator built into the interpreter chip. During SLEEP, the chip periodically wakes up and adjusts a counter to determine how long it has been asleep. If it isn't time to wake up, the chip "hits the snooze bar" and goes back to sleep.

To ensure accuracy of SLEEP intervals, the BASIC Stamp periodically compares the watchdog timer to the more-accurate resonator time base. It calculates a correction factor that it uses during SLEEP. As a result, longer SLEEP intervals are accurate to approximately ±1 percent.

If your application is driving loads (sourcing or sinking current through output-high or output-low pins) during SLEEP, current will be interrupted for about 18 ms (60 μs on the BS2pe) when the BASIC Stamp wakes up every 2.3 seconds. The reason is that the watchdog-timer reset that awakens the BASIC Stamp also causes all of the pins to switch to input mode for approximately 18 ms. When the interpreter firmware regains control of the processor, it restores the I/O directions dictated by your program.

If you plan to use END, NAP, POLLWAIT or SLEEP in your programs, make sure that your loads can tolerate these periodic power outages. The simplest solution is often to connect resistors high or low (to +5V or ground) as appropriate to ensure a continuing supply of current during the reset glitch. The demo program demonstrates the effects of this glitch.

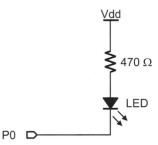

Figure 5.45: SLEEP Example LED Circuit.

Demo Program (SLEEP.bs2)

```
' SLEEP.bs2
' This program lights an LED and then goes to sleep. Connect an LED to pin
' 0 as shown in the description of SLEEP in the manual and run the program.
' The LED will turn on, then the BASIC Stamp will go to sleep. During
' sleep,the LED will remain on, but will blink at intervals of
' approximately 2.3 seconds due to the watchdog timeout and reset.

' {$STAMP BS2}

Setup:
  LOW 0                                    ' turn LED on
```

NOTE: This example program is written for the BS2, but it also can be used with the BS1 and all other BS2 models by changing the $STAMP directive accordingly.

```
Snooze:
  SLEEP 10                              ' sleep for 10 seconds
  GOTO Snooze
  END
```

SOUND

BS1	BS2	BS2e	BS2sx	BS2p	BS2pe	BS2px

SOUND *Pin, (Note, Duration { , Note, Duration...})*
(See FREQOUT)

Function
Generate square-wave tones for a specified period.

- **Pin** is a variable/constant (0 – 7) that specifies the I/O pin to use. This pin will be set to output mode.

- **Note** is a variable/constant (0 – 255) specifying the type and frequency of the tone. 1 – 127 are ascending tones and 128 – 255 are ascending white noises ranging from buzzing (128) to hissing (255).

- **Duration** is a variable/constant (1 - 255) specifying the amount of time to generate the tone(s). The unit of time for *Duration* is 12 ms.

Quick Facts

Table 5.119: SOUND Quick Facts.

	BS1
Units in *Duration*	12 ms
Available Sounds	256
Frequency Range	94.8 Hz to 10,550 Hz

Explanation
SOUND generates one of 256 square-wave frequencies on an I/O pin. The output pin should be connected as shown in Figure 5.46.

The tones produced by SOUND can vary in frequency from 94.8 Hz (1) to 10,550 Hz (127). If you need to determine the frequency corresponding to a given note value, or need to find the note value that will give you best approximation for a given frequency, use the equations below.

$$\text{Note} = 127 - (\,((1/\text{Frequency})\text{-}0.000095)/0.000083\,)$$

--and--

$$\text{Frequency} = (\,1/(0.000095 + ((127\text{–Note})*0.000083)\,)$$

In the above equations, Frequency is in Hertz (Hz).

Driving an Audio Amplifier

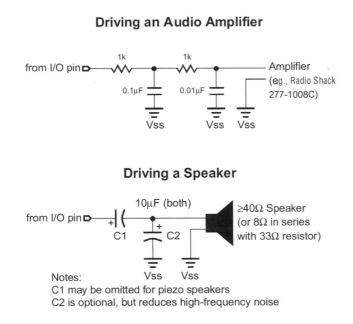

Figure 5.46: Example RC filter circuits for driving an audio amplifier (*top*) or a speaker(*bottom*).

Driving a Speaker

Notes:
C1 may be omitted for piezo speakers
C2 is optional, but reduces high-frequency noise

Demo Program (SOUND.bs1)

```
' SOUND.bs1
' This program generates a constant tone 25 followed by an ascending tones.
' Both the tones have the same duration.

' {$STAMP BS1}
' {$PBASIC 1.0}

SYMBOL  tone          = B2


Main:
  FOR tone = 0 TO 255
    SOUND 0, (25, 10, tone, 10)
  NEXT
  END
```

STOP

[All 2] **STOP**

BS1	BS2	BS2e	BS2sx	BS2p	BS2pe	BS2px

Function

Stop program execution.

Quick Facts

Table 5.120: STOP Quick Facts.

	All BS2 Models
Related Command	END

Explanation

STOP prevents the BASIC Stamp from executing any further instructions until it is reset. The following actions will reset the BASIC Stamp:

1. Pressing and releasing the RESET button on the development board.
2. Driving the RES pin low then letting it float (high).
3. Downloading a new program
4. Disconnecting then reconnecting the power.

STOP differs from END in two respects:

1. Stop does not put the BASIC Stamp into low-power mode. The BASIC Stamp draws just as much current as if it were actively running program instructions.
2. The output glitch that occurs after a program has "ended" does not occur after a program has "stopped."

[All 2] ### Demo Program (STOP.bs2)

NOTE: This example program can be used with all BS2 models by changing the $STAMP directive accordingly.

```
' STOP.bs2
' This program is similar to SLEEP.BS2 except that the LED will not blink
' since the BASIC Stamp does not go into low power mode.  Use the circuit
' shown in the description of the SLEEP command for this example.

' {$STAMP BS2}
' {$PBASIC 2.5}


Main:
  LOW 0                             ' turn LED on
  STOP                              ' stop program
```

STORE

| BS1 | BS2 | BS2e | BS2sx | **BS2p** | **BS2pe** | **BS2px** |

STORE *ProgramSlot*

Function

Designate a program slot for the READ/WRITE instructions to operate upon.

- *ProgramSlot* is a variable/constant/expression (0 – 7 on BS2p and BS2px, 0-15 on BS2pe) that specifies the program slot to use for READ and WRITE instructions.

Quick Facts

Table 5.121: STORE Quick Facts.

	BS2p and BS2px	BS2pe
Program Slot Range	0 —7	0 —15
Related Commands	READ and WRITE	

Explanation

STORE tells the BS2p, BS2pe, and BS2px which program slot to use when a READ or WRITE instruction is executed. The STORE command only affects the READ and WRITE instructions.

The STORE command allows a program to access all EEPROM locations that exist on the BS2p, BS2pe, and BS2px regardless of which program is running. The READ and WRITE commands can only access locations 0 to 2047 within a single program slot. The STORE command switches the program slot that the READ and WRITE commands operate on.

The default program slot that the READ and WRITE instructions operate on is that of the currently running program. The STORE command can be used to temporarily change this, to any program slot. The change will remain in effect until another STORE command is issued, or until another program slot is executed.

Demo Program (STORE0.bsp)

```
' STORE0.bsp
' This program demonstrates the STORE command and how it affects the READ
' and WRITE commands.  This program "STORE0.BSP" is intended to be down-
' loaded into program slot 0.  It is meant to work with STORE1.BSP and
' STORE2.BSP.  Each program is very similar (they display the current
' Program Slot and READ/WRITE Slot numbers and the values contained in the
' first five EEPROM locations.  Each program slot will have different data
' due to different DATA commands in each of the programs downloaded.

' {$STAMP BS2p, STORE1.BSP, STORE2.BSP}
' {$PBASIC 2.5}

#IF ($STAMP < BS2P) #THEN
  #ERROR "This program requires BS2p, BS2pe, or BS2px."
#ENDIF

idx             VAR     Word            ' index
value           VAR     Byte

LocalData       DATA    @0, 1, 2, 3, 4, 5


Main:
  GOSUB Show_Slot_Info                  ' show slot info/data
  PAUSE 2000
  STORE 1                               ' point READ/WRITE to Slot 1
  GOSUB Show_Slot_Info
  PAUSE 2000
  RUN 1                                 ' run program in Slot 1
  END

Show_Slot_Info:
  GET 127, value
  DEBUG CR, "Pgm Slot: ", DEC value.NIB0,
        CR, "R/W Slot: ", DEC value.NIB1,
        CR, CR

  FOR idx = 0 TO 4
    READ idx, value
    DEBUG "Location: ", DEC idx, TAB,
          "Value: ", DEC3 value, CR
  NEXT
  RETURN
```

NOTE: This example program can be used with the BS2p, BS2pe, and BS2px. This program uses conditional compilation techniques; see Chapter 3 for more information.

Demo Program (STORE1.bsp)

NOTE: This example program can be used with the BS2p, BS2pe, and BS2px by changing the $STAMP directive accordingly.

```
' STORE1.bsp

' {$STAMP BS2p}
' {$PBASIC 2.5}

idx             VAR     Word            ' index
value           VAR     Byte

LocalData       DATA    @0, 6, 7, 8, 9, 10


Main:
  GOSUB Show_Slot_Info                  ' show slot info/data
  PAUSE 2000
  STORE 0                               ' point READ/WRITE to Slot 0
  GOSUB Show_Slot_Info
  PAUSE 2000
  RUN 2                                 ' run program in Slot 2
  END

Show_Slot_Info:
  GET 127, value
  DEBUG CR, "Pgm Slot: ", DEC value.NIB0,
        CR, "R/W Slot: ", DEC value.NIB1,
        CR, CR

  FOR idx = 0 TO 4
    READ idx, value
    DEBUG "Location: ", DEC idx, TAB,
          "Value: ", DEC3 value, CR
  NEXT
  RETURN
```

Demo Program (STORE2.bsp)

NOTE: This example program can be used with the BS2p, BS2pe, and BS2px by changing the $STAMP directive accordingly.

```
' STORE2.bsp

' {$STAMP BS2p}
' {$PBASIC 2.5}

idx             VAR     Word            ' index
value           VAR     Byte

LocalData       DATA    @0, 11, 12, 13, 14, 15


Main:
  GOSUB Show_Slot_Info                  ' show slot info/data
  PAUSE 2000
  STORE 0                               ' point READ/WRITE to Slot 0
```

```
  GOSUB Show_Slot_Info
  END

Show_Slot_Info:
  GET 127, value
  DEBUG CR, "Pgm Slot: ", DEC value.NIB0,
        CR, "R/W Slot: ", DEC value.NIB1,
        CR, CR

  FOR idx = 0 TO 4
    READ idx, value
    DEBUG "Location: ", DEC idx, TAB,
          "Value: ", DEC3 value, CR
  NEXT
  RETURN
```

The next Demo program, STOREALL.bsp, is not related to the previous
three programs. STOREALL.bsp demonstrates the use of the STORE
command to treat contiguous program slots as one block of memory (14
kBytes on the BS2p and BS2px, 30 kBytes on the BS2pe). This illustrates
one of the most powerful uses of the STORE command.

Demo Program (STOREALL.bsp)

```
' STOREALL.bsp
' This program demonstrates the STORE command and how it can be used to
' "flatten" the EEPROM space for applications requiring a lot of storage.
' This program writes to EEPROM locations within program slots 1 though 7
' on the BS2p and BS2px, and 1 through 15 on the BS2pe, thus, has access to
' 14- or 30-kBytes of space.

' {$STAMP BS2p}
' {$PBASIC 2.5}

#SELECT $STAMP
  #CASE BS2, BS2E, BS2SX
    #ERROR "This program requires BS2p, BS2pe, or BS2px."
  #CASE BS2P, BS2PX
    HiSlot      CON     7
  #CASE BS2PE
    HiSlot      CON     15
#ENDSELECT

LoSlot          CON     1                       ' first slot for "flat" EE
MemSize         CON     HiSlot - LoSlot + 1 * 2048

eeAddr          VAR     Word                    ' address pointer
value           VAR     Word                    ' cell value
slot            VAR     Byte                    ' current R/W slot
```

```
Main:
  DEBUG "Flat Memory", CR,
        "--------------------", CR,
        "First Slot..... ", DEC LoSlot, CR,
        "Last Slot...... ", DEC HiSlot, CR,
        "Flat EE Size... ", DEC MemSize, CR, CR

  PAUSE 2000
  DEBUG "Writing to flat Memory...", CR
  PAUSE 1000
  FOR eeAddr = 0 TO (MemSize - 1) STEP 128    ' step through "flat" EE
    value = eeAddr * 2                         ' generate value
    GOSUB Write_Word                           ' write it
    GET 127, slot                              ' get R/W slot
    DEBUG "--> Location: ", DEC5 eeAddr, "   ", ' show "flat" address
          "Value: ", DEC5 value, "   ",        ' show value
          "(", DEC slot.NIB1, ")", CR          ' show slot
  NEXT
  DEBUG CR

  DEBUG "Reading from flat Memory...", CR
  PAUSE 1000
  FOR eeAddr = 0 TO (MemSize - 1) STEP 128
    GOSUB Read_Word                            ' read value from EE
    GET 127, slot                              ' get W/R slot
    DEBUG "<-- Location: ", DEC5 eeAddr, "   ",
          "Value: ", DEC5 value, "   ",
          "(", DEC slot.NIB1, ") "
    IF (value <> (2 * eeAddr)) THEN            ' verify location
      DEBUG "- Error"
    ENDIF
    DEBUG CR
  NEXT
  END

Write_Word:
' NOTE: only use even-byte eeAddr with this routine
  STORE (eeAddr >> 11) + LoSlot                ' set slot
  WRITE eeAddr, Word value                     ' write value
  RETURN

Read_Word:
' NOTE: only use even-byte eeAddr with this routine
  STORE (eeAddr >> 11) + LoSlot                ' set slot
  READ eeAddr, Word value                      ' read value
  RETURN
```

TOGGLE

BS1	BS2	BS2e	BS2sx	BS2p	BS2pe	BS2px

TOGGLE *Pin*

Function

Invert the state of an output pin.

- **Pin** is a variable/constant/expression (0 – 15) that specifies which I/O pin to switch logic state. This pin will be placed into output mode.

NOTE: Expressions are not allowed as arguments on the BS1. The range of the *Pin* argument on the BS1 is 0 – 7.

Quick Facts

Table 5.122: TOGGLE Quick Facts.

	BS1	All BS2 Models
Affected Register	PINS	OUTS
Related Commands	HIGH and LOW	

Explanation

TOGGLE sets a pin to output mode and inverts the output state of the pin, changing 0 to 1 and 1 to 0.

In some situations TOGGLE may appear to have no effect on a pin's state. For example, suppose pin 2 is in input mode and pulled to +5V by a 10k resistor. Then the following code executes:

```
DIR2 = 0          ' make P2 an input
PIN2 = 0          ' make P2 output driver low
DEBUG PIN2        ' show P2 state (1 due to pull-up)
TOGGLE 2          ' toggle P2
DEBUG PIN2        ' show P2 state (1 again)
```

- or -

```
DIR2 = 0          ' make P2 an input
OUT2 = 0          ' make P2 output driver low
DEBUG ? IN2       ' show P2 state (1 due to pull-up)
TOGGLE 2          ' toggle P2
DEBUG ? IN2       ' show P2 state (1 again)
```

The state of pin 2 doesn't change; it's high (due to the resistor) before TOGGLE, and it's high (due to the pin being output high) afterward. The point is that TOGGLE works on the OUTS register (PINS on the BS1), which may not match the pin's state when the pin is initially an input. To guarantee that the state actually changes, regardless of the initial input or output mode, do this:

```
PIN2 = PIN2                       ' make output driver match input
TOGGLE 2                          ' then toggle
```
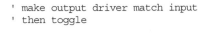

- or -

```
OUT2 = IN2                        ' make output driver match input
TOGGLE 2                          ' then toggle
```

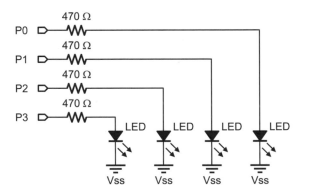

Figure 5.47: Example LED Circuit for TOGGLE Demo Programs.

Demo Program (TOGGLE.bs1)

```
' TOGGLE.bs1
' Connect LEDs to pins 0 through 3 as shown in the TOGGLE command descrip-
' tion in the manual and run this program. The TOGGLE command will treat
' you to a light show. You may also run the demo without LEDs. The Debug
' window will show you the states of pins 0 through 3.

' {$STAMP BS1}
' {$PBASIC 1.0}

SYMBOL  thePin      = B0              ' pin 0 - 3

Setup:
  DIRS = %1111                        ' make LEDs output, low

Main:
  FOR thePin = 0 TO 3                 ' loop through pins
    TOGGLE thePin                     ' toggle current pin
    DEBUG CLS, %PINS                  ' show on Debug
    PAUSE 100                         ' short delay
  NEXT
  GOTO Main                           ' repeat forever
  END
```

[All 2] ## Demo Program (TOGGLE.bs2)

NOTE: This example program can be used with all BS2 models by changing the $STAMP directive accordingly.

```
' TOGGLE.bs2
' Connect LEDs to pins 0 through 3 as shown in the TOGGLE command descrip-
' tion in the manual and run this program. The TOGGLE command will treat
' you to a light show. You may also run the demo without LEDs. The Debug
' window will show you the states of pins 0 through 3.

' {$STAMP BS2}
' {$PBASIC 2.5}

thePin          VAR    Nib              ' pin 0 - 3


Setup:
  DIRA = %1111                          ' make LEDs output, low

Main:
  DO
    FOR thePin = 0 TO 3                 ' loop through pins
      TOGGLE thePin                     ' toggle current pin
      DEBUG HOME, BIN4 OUTA             ' show on Debug
      PAUSE 250                         ' short delay
    NEXT
  LOOP                                  ' repeat forever
  END
```

WRITE	BS1	BS2	BS2e	BS2sx	BS2p	BS2pe	BS2px

WRITE *Location, Value*
WRITE *Location,* { **WORD** } *Value* {, { **WORD** } *Value...* }

Function

Write *Value* into *Location* in EEPROM.

- ***Location*** is a variable/constant/expression (0 – 255 on BS1, 0 – 2047 on all BS2 models) that specifies the EEPROM address to write to.

- ***Value*** is a variable/constant/expression (0 – 255, or 0 – 65535 if using the optional WORD modifier) to store in the EEPROM.

Quick Facts

Table 5.123: WRITE Quick Facts.

	BS1	BS2	BS2e and BS2sx	BS2p, BS2pe, BS2px
Range of EEPROM Locations	0 to 255	0 to 2047	0 to 2047	0 to 2047 (see notes below)
Maximum Number of Writes per Location	10 million	10 million	100,000	100,000
Special Notes	n/a	n/a	WRITE only works with current program slot on BS2e and BS2sx.	WRITE works with any program slot as set by the STORE command.
Related Commands	READ and EEPROM	READ and DATA	READ and DATA	READ, DATA, and STORE
PBASIC 2.5 Syntax Options	n/a	Multiple sequential variables may be written to the Scratch Pad RAM, and the optional WORD modifier may be specified to store 16-bit values.		

Explanation

The EEPROM is used for both program storage (which builds downward from address 255 on BS1, 2047 on all BS2 models) and data storage (which builds upward from address 0). The WRITE instruction stores a value to any EEPROM address. Any location within the EEPROM can be written to (including your PBASIC program's locations) at run-time. This feature is mainly used to store long-term data to EEPROM; data stored in EEPROM is not lost when the power is removed.

WRITE – BASIC Stamp Command Reference

The following WRITE command stores the value 245 at location 100:

A SIMPLE WRITE COMMAND.

```
WRITE 100, 245
```

--or--

```
WRITE 100, 245
```

The EEPROM is organized as a sequential set of byte-sized memory locations. The WRITE command normally only stores byte-sized values into EEPROM. This does not mean that you can't write word-sized values, however. A word consists of two bytes, called a low-byte and a high-byte. If you wanted to write a word-sized value, you'll need to use two WRITE commands and a word-sized value or variable. For example,

WRITING WORD VALUES VS. BYTE VALUES.

```
SYMBOL   value   = W0
SYMBOL   valLo   = B0
SYMBOL   valHi   = b1

value = 1125

WRITE 0, valLo                  ' write low byte
WRITE 1, valHi                  ' write high byte
```

- or -

```
value   VAR   Word

value   = 1125

WRITE 0, value.LOWBYTE          ' write low byte
WRITE 1, value.HIGHBYTE         ' write high byte
```

NOTE: this method is required only if using PBASIC 2.0. See section below for PBASIC 2.5 method.

When this program runs, the two WRITE commands will store the low-byte and high-byte of the number 1125 into EEPROM.

On all BS2 models, with PBASIC 2.5 you can use a single WRITE command with the WORD modifier to write a 16-bit value. The low-byte of the value will be written to *Location*, the high byte will be written to *Location* + 1.

```
All 2   ' {$PBASIC 2.5}

        value   VAR     Word

        value = 1125

        WRITE 0, Word value              ' write two bytes
```

When using PBASIC 2.5, a single WRITE command can write multiple bytes and words to sequential EEPROM locations. For example:

```
All 2   ' {$PBASIC 2.5}

        value   VAR     Byte
        value2  VAR     Word

        value  = 18
        value2 = 1125

        WRITE 25, value, Word value2     ' write byte to location 25
                                         ' and word to locations 26 and 27
```

SPECIAL NOTES FOR EEPROM USAGE.

EEPROM differs from RAM, the memory in which variables are stored, in several respects:

1. Writing to EEPROM takes more time than storing a value in a variable. Depending on many factors, it may take several milliseconds for the EEPROM to complete a write. RAM storage is nearly instantaneous.
2. The EEPROM can only accept a finite number of write cycles per location before it wears out. Table 5.123 indicates the guaranteed number of writes before failure. If a program frequently writes to the same EEPROM location, it makes sense to estimate how long it might take to exceed the guaranteed maximum. For example, on the BS2, at one write per second (86,400 writes/day) it would take nearly 116 days of continuous operation to exceed 10 million.
3. The primary function of the EEPROM is to store programs (data is stored in leftover space). If data overwrites a portion of your program, the program will most likely crash.

Check the program's memory map to determine what portion of memory your program occupies and make sure that EEPROM writes cannot stray into this area. You may also use the DATA directive on all BS2 models to set aside EEPROM space.

On the BS1, location 255 holds the address of the last instruction in your program. Therefore, your program can use any space below the address given in location 255. For example, if location 255 holds the value 100, then your program can use locations 0–99 for data. You can read location 255 at run-time or simply view the Memory Map of the program before you download it. On all BS2 models, you will need to view the Memory Map of the program before you download it to determine the last EEPROM location used. See the Memory Map section of Chapter 3.

On the BS2p, BS2pe, and BS2px, the READ and WRITE commands can affect locations in any program slot as set by the STORE command. See the STORE command for more information.

Demo Program (WRITE.bs1)

```
' WRITE.bs1
' This program writes a few bytes to EEPROM and then reads them back out
' and displays them in the Debug window.

' {$STAMP BS1}
' {$PBASIC 1.0}

SYMBOL  addr           = B2        ' address
SYMBOL  value          = B3        ' value


Main:
  WRITE 0, 100                     ' write some data to locations 0 - 3
  WRITE 1, 200
  WRITE 2, 45
  WRITE 3, 28

Read_EE:
  FOR addr = 0 TO 3
    READ addr, value               ' read value from address
    DEBUG #addr, ": ", #value, CR  ' display address and value
  NEXT
  END
```

Demo Program (WRITE.bs2)

NOTE: This example program can be used with all BS2 models by changing the $STAMP directive accordingly.

```
' WRITE.bs2
' This program writes some data to EEPROM and then reads them back out
' and displays the data in the Debug window.

' {$STAMP BS2}
' {$PBASIC 2.5}

idx              VAR    Byte              ' loop control
value            VAR    Word(3)           ' value(s)


Main:
  WRITE 0, 100                            ' single byte
  WRITE 1, Word 1250                      ' single word
  WRITE 3, 45, 90, Word 725               ' multi-value write

Read_EE:
  FOR idx = 0 TO 6                        ' show raw bytes in EE
    READ idx, value
    DEBUG DEC1 idx, " : ", DEC value, CR
  NEXT
  DEBUG CR

  ' read values as stored

  READ 0, value
  DEBUG DEC value, CR
  READ 1, Word value
  DEBUG DEC value, CR
  READ 3, value(0), value(1), Word value(2)
  FOR idx = 0 TO 2
    DEBUG DEC value(idx), CR
  NEXT
  END
```

XOUT

| BS1 | BS2 | BS2e | BS2sx | BS2p | BS2pe | BS2px |

All 2 **XOUT** *Mpin, Zpin,* [*House \Command* { *\Cycles*} {, *House \Command* { *\Cycles* }...}]

Function

Send an X-10 power-line control command (through the appropriate power-line interface).

- **Mpin** is a variable/constant/expression (0 – 15) that specifies the I/O pin to output X-10 signals (modulation) to the power-line interface device. This pin will be set to output mode.

- **Zpin** is a variable/constant/expression (0 – 15) that specifies the I/O pin that inputs the zero-crossing signal from the power-line interface device. This pin will be set to input mode.

- **House** is a variable/constant/expression (0 – 15) that specifies the X-10 house code (values 0 - 15 representing letters A through P).

- **Command** is a variable/constant/expression (0 – 31) that specifies the command to send. Values 0 – 15 correspond to unit codes 1 – 16. Other commands are shown in Table 5.125.

- **Cycles** is an optional variable/constant/expression (1 – 255) specifying the number of times to transmit a given key or command. If no *Cycles* argument is used, XOUT defaults to two. The *Cycles* argument should be used only with the DIM and BRIGHT command codes

Quick Facts

Table 5.124: XOUT Quick Facts.

	All BS2 Models
Compatible Power-line Interfaces	PL-513 and TW-523
Special Notes	The XOUT command will stop the BASIC Stamp program until it is able to send the transmission. If there is no AC power to the power-line interface, the BASIC Stamp program will halt forever.

Explanation

XOUT lets you control appliances via signals sent through household AC wiring to X-10 modules. The appliances plugged into these modules can be switched on or off; lights may also be dimmed. Each module is assigned a house code and unit code by setting dials or switches on the module. To talk to a particular module, XOUT sends the appropriate house code and unit code. The module with the corresponding code listens for its house code again followed by a command (on, off, dim, or bright).

X-10 signals are digital codes imposed on a 120 kHz carrier that is transmitted during zero crossings of the AC line. To send X-10 commands, a controller must synchronize to the AC line frequency with 50 µs precision, and transmit an 11-bit code sequence representing the command.

X-10 PROTOCOL DETAILS.

XOUT interfaces to the AC power-line through an approved interface device such as a PL-513 or TW-523, available from X-10 dealers. The hookup requires a length of four-conductor phone cable and a standard modular phone-base connector (6P4C type). Connections are shown in Figure 5.48.

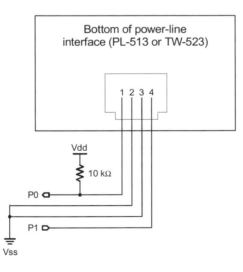

Figure 5.48: XOUT Power-Line Interface Circuit.

Table 5.125 lists the XOUT command codes and their functions:

Table 5.125: XOUT Commands and Their Function.

Command	Value	Function
UNITON	%10010	Turn on the currently selected unit.
UNITOFF	%11010	Turn off the currently selected unit.
UNITSONf	%11100	Turn off all modules in this house code.
LIGHTSON	%10100	Turn on all lamp modules in this house code.
DIM	%11110	Reduce brightness of currently selected lamp.
BRIGHT	%10110	Increase brightness of currently selected lamp.

Note: In most applications, it's not necessary to know the code for a given X-10 instruction. Just use the command constant (UnitOn, Dim, etc.) instead. But knowing the codes leads to some interesting possibilities. For example, XORing a UnitOn command with the value %1000 turns it into a UnitOff command, and vice-versa. This makes it possible to write the equivalent of an X-10 "toggle" instruction.

A SIMPLE XOUT EXAMPLE: TURNING AN APPLIANCE ON.

Here is an example of the XOUT instruction:

```
Mpin            PIN     0               ' modulation pin
Zpin            PIN     1               ' zero-cross input

HouseA          CON     0               ' House code A = 0
Unit1           CON     0               ' Unit code 1 = 0

XOUT Mpin, Zpin, [HouseA\Unit1]         ' get Unit1's attention
XOUT Mpin, Zpin, [HouseA\UNITON]        ' turn it on
```

COMBINING MULTIPLE COMMANDS.

You can combine those two XOUT instructions into one like so:

```
XOUT  Mpin, Zpin, [HouseA\Unit1\2, HouseA\UNITON]          ' Unit 1 on.
```

Note that to complete the attention-getting code HouseA\Unit1 we tacked on the normally optional cycles entry \2 to complete the command before beginning the next one. Always specify two cycles in multiple commands unless you're adjusting the brightness of a lamp module.

DIMMING LIGHTS.

Here is an example of a lamp-dimming instruction:

```
Mpin            PIN     0               ' modulation pin
Zpin            PIN     1               ' zero-cross input

HouseA          CON     0               ' House code A = 0
Unit1           CON     0               ' Unit code 1 = 0

XOUT Mpin, Zpin, [HouseA\Unit1]         ' get Unit1's attention
XOUT Mpin, Zpin, [HouseA\UNITOFF\2]     ' turn it off
XOUT Mpin, Zpin, [HouseA\DIM\10]        ' dim half way
```

The dim/bright commands support 19 brightness levels. Lamp modules may also be turned on and off using the standard UnitOn and UnitOff commands. In the example instruction above, we dimmed the lamp by first turning it completely off, then sending 10 cycles of the Dim command. This may seem odd, but it follows the peculiar logic of the X-10 system.

Demo Program (X10.bs2)

All 2

```
' XOUT.BS2
' This program--really two program fragments--demonstrates the syntax and
' use of the XOUT command. XOUT works like pressing the buttons on an X-10
' control box; first you press one of 16 keys to identify the unit you want
' to control, then you press the key for the action you want that unit to
' take (turn ON, OFF, Bright, or Dim). There are also two group-action
' keys, Lights ON and All OFF. Lights ON turns all lamp modules on without
' affecting appliance modules. All OFF turns off all modules, both lamp and
' appliance types.  Connect the BASIC Stamp to a power-line interface as
' shown in the XOUT command description in the manual.

' {$STAMP BS2}
' {$PBASIC 2.5}

Mpin            PIN     0           ' modulation pin
Zpin            PIN     1           ' zero-cross input

HouseA          CON     0           ' House code A = 0
Unit1           CON     0           ' Unit code 1 = 0
Unit2           CON     1           ' Unit code 2 = 1

' This first example turns a standard (appliance or non-dimmer lamp) module
' ON, then OFF. Note that once the Unit code is sent, it need not be
' repeated
' --subsequent instructions are understood to be addressed to that unit.

Main:
  XOUT Mpin, Zpin, [HouseA\Unit1\2]    ' select Unit1 (appliance module)
  XOUT Mpin, Zpin, [HouseA\UNITON]     ' turn it on

  PAUSE 1000                           ' wait one second

  XOUT Mpin, Zpin, [HouseA\UNITOFF]    ' then turn it off

' The next example talks to a lamp module using the dimmer feature. Dimmers
' go from full ON to dimmed OFF in 19 steps. Because dimming is relative to
' the current state of the lamp, the only guaranteed way to set a
' predefined brightness level is to turn the dimmer fully OFF, then ON,
' then dim to the desired level.

  XOUT Mpin, Zpin, [HouseA\Unit2\2]    ' select Unit2 (lamp module)
```

NOTE: This example program can be used with all BS2 models by changing the $STAMP directive accordingly.

```
' This example shows the use of the optional Cycles argument.  Here we DIM
' for 10 cycles.

  XOUT Mpin, Zpin, [HouseA\UNITOFF\2, HouseA\DIM\10]
  STOP
```

ASCII Chart (first 128 characters)

Dec	Hex	Char	Name / Function	Dec	Hex	Char	Dec	Hex	Char	Dec	Hex	Char
0	00	NUL	Null	32	20	space	64	40	@	96	60	`
1	01	SOH	Start Of Heading	33	21	!	65	41	A	97	61	a
2	02	STX	Start Of Text	34	22	"	66	42	B	98	62	b
3	03	ETX	End Of Text	35	23	#	67	43	C	99	63	c
4	04	EOT	End Of Transmit	36	24	$	68	44	D	100	64	d
5	05	ENQ	Enquiry	37	25	%	69	45	E	101	65	e
6	06	ACK	Acknowledge	38	26	&	70	46	F	102	66	f
7	07	BEL	Bell	39	27	'	71	47	G	103	67	g
8	08	BS	Backspace	40	28	(	72	48	H	104	68	h
9	09	HT	Horizontal Tab	41	29	)	73	49	I	105	69	i
10	0A	LF	Line Feed	42	2A	*	74	4A	J	106	6A	j
11	0B	VT	Vertical Tab	43	2B	+	75	4B	K	107	6B	k
12	0C	FF	Form Feed	44	2C	,	76	4C	L	108	6C	l
13	0D	CR	Carriage Return	45	2D	-	77	4D	M	109	6D	m
14	0E	SO	Shift Out	46	2E	.	78	4E	N	110	6E	n
15	0F	SI	Shift In	47	2F	/	79	4F	O	111	6F	o
16	10	DLE	Data Line Escape	48	30	0	80	50	P	112	70	p
17	11	DC1	Device Control 1	49	31	1	81	51	Q	113	71	q
18	12	DC2	Device Control 2	50	32	2	82	52	R	114	72	r
19	13	DC3	Device Control 3	51	33	3	83	53	S	115	73	s
20	14	DC4	Device Control 4	52	34	4	84	54	T	116	74	t
21	15	NAK	Non Acknowledge	53	35	5	85	55	U	117	75	u
22	16	SYN	Synchronous Idle	54	36	6	86	56	V	118	76	v
23	17	ETB	End Transmit Block	55	37	7	87	57	W	119	77	w
24	18	CAN	Cancel	56	38	8	88	58	X	120	78	x
25	19	EM	End Of Medium	57	39	9	89	59	Y	121	79	y
26	1A	SUB	Substitute	58	3A	:	90	5A	Z	122	7A	z
27	1B	ESC	Escape	59	3B	;	91	5B	[	123	7B	{
28	1C	FS	File Separator	60	3C	<	92	5C	\	124	7C		
29	1D	GS	Group Separator	61	3D	=	93	5D	]	125	7D	}
30	1E	RS	Record Separator	62	3E	>	94	5E	^	126	7E	~
31	1F	US	Unit Separator	63	3F	?	95	5F	_	127	7F	delete

Note that the control codes (lowest 32 ASCII characters) have no standardized screen symbols. The characters listed for them are just names used in referring to these codes. For example, to move the cursor to the beginning of the next line of a printer or terminal often requires sending line feed and carriage return codes. This common pair is referred to as "LF/CR."

ASCII Chart

Reserved Words

This appendix contains complete listings of the reserved words for PBASIC 1.0, PBASIC 2.0, and PBASIC 2.5, current with the BASIC Stamp Editor v2.1.

The reserved word lists have been organized into 4 tables, because it varies with each BASIC Stamp model and version of PBASIC. Table B.1 shows the reserved words for the BASIC Stamp 1, using the required PBASIC 1.0.

Table B.1: BS1 Reserved Words.

BS1				
AND	GOSUB	N2400	PIN0..PIN7	SOUND
B0..B13	GOTO	NAP	PINS	STEP
BIT0..BIT15	HIGH	NEXT	PORT	SYMBOL
BRANCH	IF	ON300	POT	T300
BSAVE	INPUT	ON600	PULSIN	T600
BUTTON	LET	ON1200	PULSOUT	T1200
CLS	LOOKDOWN	ON2400	PWM	T2400
CR	LOOKUP	OR	RANDOM	THEN
DEBUG	LOW	OT300	READ	TO
DIR0..DIR7	MAX	OT600	RETURN	TOGGLE
DIRS	MIN	OT1200	REVERSE	W0..W6
EEPROM	N300	OT2400	SERIN	WRITE
END	N600	OUTPUT	SEROUT	
FOR	N1200	PAUSE	SLEEP	

Table B.2 on the following page lists the reserved words common to all BS2 models, including those for PBASIC 2.0 and PBASIC 2.5. Words listed that are only reserved when using PBASIC 2.5 are marked with ([2.5]).

All BS2 Models			
#CASE$^{2.5}$	CRSRX$^{2.5}$	INC	PULSIN
#DEFINE$^{2.5}$	CRSRXY$^{2.5}$	IND	PULSOUT
#ELSE$^{2.5}$	CRSRY$^{2.5}$	INH	PWM
#ENDIF$^{2.5}$	DATA	INL	RANDOM
#ENDSELECT$^{2.5}$	DCD	INPUT	RCTIME
#ERROR$^{2.5}$	DEBUG	INS	READ
#IF$^{2.5}$	DEBUGIN$^{2.5}$	ISBIN	REP
#SELECT$^{2.5}$	DEC	ISBIN1...ISBIN16	RETURN
#THEN$^{2.5}$	DEC1...DEC5	ISHEX	REV
$PBASIC	DIG	ISHEX1...ISHEX4	REVERSE
$PORT	DIM	LF$^{2.5}$	SBIN
$STAMP	DIR0...DIR15	LIGHTSON	SBIN1...SBIN16
ABS	DIRA	LOOKDOWN	SDEC
AND	DIRB	LOOKUP	SDEC1...SDEC5
ASC	DIRC	LOOP$^{2.5}$	SELECT$^{2.5}$
ATN	DIRD	LOW	SERIN
B0...B25	DIRH	LOWBIT	SEROUT
BELL	DIRL	LOWBYTE	SHEX
BIN	DIRS	LOWNIB	SHEX1...SHEX4
BIN1...BIN16	DO$^{2.5}$	LSBFIRST	SHIFTIN
BIT	DTMFOUT	LSBPOST	SHIFTOUT
BIT0...BIT15	ELSE$^{2.5}$	LSBPRE	SIN
BKSP	ELSEIF$^{2.5}$	MAX	SKIP
BRANCH	END	MIN	SLEEP
BRIGHT	ENDIF$^{2.5}$	MSBFIRST	SNUM
BS1	ENDSELECT$^{2.5}$	MSBPOST	SQR
BS2	EXIT$^{2.5}$	MSBPRE	STEP
BS2E	FOR	NAP	STOP
BS2P	FREQOUT	NCD	STR
BS2PE	GOSUB	NEXT	TAB
BS2SX	GOTO	NIB	THEN
BUTTON	HEX	NIB0...NIB3	TO
BYTE	HEX1...HEX4	NOT	TOGGLE
BYTE0	HIGH	NUM	UNITOFF
BYTE1	HIGHBIT	ON$^{2.5}$	UNITON
CASE$^{2.5}$	HIGHBYTE	OR	UNITSOFF
CLRDN$^{2.5}$	HIGHNIB	OUT0...OUT15	UNTIL$^{2.5}$
CLREOL$^{2.5}$	HOME	OUTA	VAR
CLS	HYP	OUTB	W0...W12
CON	IBIN	OUTC	WAIT
COS	IBIN1...IBIN16	OUTD	WAITSTR
COUNT	IF	OUTH	WHILE$^{2.5}$
CR	IHEX	OUTL	WORD
CRSRDN$^{2.5}$	IHEX1...IHEX4	OUPUT	WRITE
CRSRLF$^{2.5}$	IN0...IN15	OUTS	XOR
CRSRRT$^{2.5}$	INA	PAUSE	XOUT
CRSRUP$^{2.5}$	INB	PIN$^{2.5}$	

Table B.2 Reserved Words common to all BS2 Models.

NOTE: This list includes reserved words for both PBASIC 2.0 and PBASIC 2.5. Words indicated with the symbol ($^{2.5}$) are only reserved if used with PBASIC 2.5.

There are some reserved words unique to specific BS2 models.

The BS2e and BS2sx have all the reserved words shown in Table B.2, plus those shown in Table B.3. These additional words are reserved in both PBASIC 2.0 and PBASIC 2.5.

Table B.3: Additional Reserved Words for the BS2e and BS2sx.

BS2e and BS2sx		
GET	PUT	RUN

The BS2p and BS2pe have all the reserved words shown in Table B.2, plus those shown in Table B.4. These additional words are reserved in both PBASIC 2.0 and PBASIC 2.5.

Table B.4: Additional Reserved Words for the BS2p and BS2pe.

BS2p and BS2pe			
AUXIO	LCDCMD	OWOUT	POLLWAIT
GET	LCDIN	POLLIN	PUT
I2CIN	LCDOUT	POLLMODE	RUN
I2COUT	MAINIO	POLLOUT	SPSTR
IOTERM	OWIN	POLLRUN	STORE

The BS2px has all the reserved words shown in Table B.2, plus those shown in Table B.5. These additional words are reserved in both PBASIC 2.0 and PBASIC 2.5.

Table B.5: Additional Reserved Words for the BS2px.

BS2px			
AUXIO	IOTERM	POLLIN	RUN
COMPARE	LCDCMD	POLLMODE	SCHMITT
CONFIGPIN	LCDIN	POLLOUT	SPSTR
DIRECTION	LCDOUT	POLLRUN	STORE
GET	MAINIO	POLLWAIT	THRESHOLD
I2CIN	OWIN	PULLUP	
I2COUT	OWOUT	PUT	

Reserved Words

Conversion Formatters

This appendix lists the Conversion Formatters available for the commands DEBUGIN, I2CIN, LCDIN, OWIN and SERIN and demonstrates, through various input/output data examples, exactly what will be received when using these formatters.

The following tables show data examples (characters received) across the top and formatters across the left side, with the results of that combination shown in the target cell.

For example, with the following code:

```
Value      VAR     WORD

DEBUGIN SDEC Value
```

the Decimal Formatters table shows us that if the characters -123 (followed by a carriage return) are received, the SDEC formatter will translate that to the word-sized decimal number -123 and will store that value into the *Value* variable.

NOTE: In all tables below, values in target cells represent the number base of the formatter (decimal for DEC, hexadecimal for HEX, etc) except where noted. Additionally, "--" means no valid data (or not enough valid data) was received so the command will halt forever unless additional data is received or SERIN's *Timeout* argument is used.

Table C.1: Decimal Formatters.

Decimal Formatters	Characters Received						
	⊗	123	123⊗	-123⊗	⊗123⊗	12345⊗	65536⊗	255255⊗
DEC	--	--	123	123	123	12345	0	58647
DEC1	--	1	1	1	1	1	6	2
DEC2	--	12	12	12	12	12	65	25
DEC3	--	123	123	123	123	123	655	255
DEC4	--	--	123	123	123	1234	6553	2552
DEC5	--	--	123	123	123	12345	0	25525
SDEC	--	--	123	-123	123	12345	0	-6889
SDEC1	--	1	1	-1	1	1	6	2
SDEC2	--	12	12	-12	12	12	65	25
SDEC3	--	123	123	-123	123	123	655	255
SDEC4	--	--	123	-123	123	1234	6553	2552

⊗ Means any non-decimal-numeric characters such as letters, spaces, minus signs, carriage returns, control characters, etc. (Decimal numerics are: 0,1,2,3,4,5,6,7,8 and 9).

Conversion Formatters

Hexadecimal Formatters	Characters Received							
	⊗	1F	1F⊗	-1F⊗	⊗1F⊗	15AF⊗	10000⊗	3E517⊗
HEX	--	--	1F	1F	1F	15AF	0	E517
HEX1	--	1	1	1	1	1	1	3
HEX2	--	1F	1F	1F	1F	15	10	3E
HEX3	--	--	1F	1F	1F	15A	100	3E5
HEX4	--	--	1F	1F	1F	15AF	1000	3E51
SHEX	--	--	1F	-1F	1F	15AF	0	-1AE9
SHEX1	--	1	1	-1	1	1	1	3
SHEX2	--	1F	1F	-1F	1F	15	10	3E
SHEX3	--	--	1F	-1F	1F	15A	100	3E5

Table C.2: Hexadecimal Formatters.

NOTE: The HEX formatters are not case sensitive. For example, 1F is the same as 1f.

⊗ Means any non-hexadecimal-numeric characters such as letters (greater than F), spaces, minus signs, carriage returns, control characters, etc. (Hexadecimal numerics are: 0,1,2,3,4,5,6,7,8,9,A,B,C,D,E,F).

Additional Hexadecimal Formatters	Characters Received							
	⊗	1F	1F⊗	$1F	$1F⊗	-$1F⊗	⊗$1F⊗	$15AF⊗
IHEX	--	--	--	--	1F	1F	1F	15AF
IHEX1	--	--	--	1	1	1	1	1
IHEX2	--	--	--	1F	1F	1F	1F	15
IHEX3	--	--	--	--	1F	1F	1F	15A
IHEX4	--	--	--	--	1F	1F	1F	15AF
ISHEX	--	--	--	--	1F	-1F	1F	15AF
ISHEX1	--	--	--	1	1	-1	1	1
ISHEX2	--	--	--	1F	1F	-1F	1F	15
ISHEX3	--	--	--	--	1F	-1F	1F	15A
ISHEX4	--	--	--	--	1F	-1F	1F	15AF

Table C.3: Additional Hexadecimal Formatters.

NOTE: The HEX formatters are not case sensitive. For example, 1F is the same as 1f.

⊗ Means any non-hexadecimal-numeric characters such as letters (greater than F), spaces, minus signs, carriage returns, control characters, etc. (Hexadecimal numerics are: 0,1,2,3,4,5,6,7,8,9,A,B,C,D,E,F).

Binary Formatters	Characters Received						
	⊗	11	11⊗	-11⊗	⊗11⊗	101⊗	3E517⊗
BIN	--	--	11	11	11	101	1
BIN1	--	1	1	1	1	1	1
BIN2	--	11	11	11	11	10	1
BIN3 – BIN16	--	--	11	11	11	101	1
SBIN	--	--	11	-11	11	101	1
SBIN1	--	1	1	-1	1	1	1
SBIN2	--	11	11	-11	11	10	1

Table C.4: Binary Formatters.

⊗ Means any non-binary-numeric characters such as letters, spaces, minus signs, carriage returns, control characters, etc. (Binary numerics are: 0 and 1).

Table C.5: Additional Binary Formatters.

Additional Binary Formatters	Characters Received							
	⊗	11	11⊗	%11	%11⊗	-%11⊗	⊗%11⊗	%101⊗
IBIN	--	--	--	--	11	11	11	101
IBIN1	--	--	--	1	1	1	1	1
IBIN2	--	--	--	11	11	11	11	10
IBIN3 – IBIN16	--	--	--	--	11	11	11	101
ISBIN	--	--	--	--	11	-11	11	101
ISBIN1	--	--	--	1	1	-1	1	1
ISBIN2	--	--	--	11	11	-11	11	10
ISBIN3 – ISBIN16	--	--	--	--	11	-11	11	101

⊗ Means any non-binary-numeric characters such as letters, spaces, minus signs, carriage returns, control characters, etc. (Binary numerics are: 0 and 1).

Table C.6: NUM and SNUM with Decimal Data.

General (Dec. Data)	Characters Received							
	⊗	123	123⊗	-123⊗	⊗123⊗	12345⊗	65536⊗	255255⊗
NUM	--	--	123	123	123	12345	0	58647

⊗ Means any non-decimal-numeric characters such as letters, spaces, minus signs, carriage returns, control characters, etc. (Decimal numerics are: 0,1,2,3,4,5,6,7,8 and 9).

Table C.7: NUM and SNUM with Hexadecimal Data.

General (Hex. Data)	Characters Received							
	⊗	1F	1F⊗	$1F	$1F⊗	-$1F⊗	⊗$1F⊗	$15AF⊗
NUM	--	1*	1*	--	1F	1F	1F	15AF

NOTE: Hexadecimal data is not case sensitive. For example, 1F is the same as 1f.

⊗ Means any non-hexadecimal-numeric characters such as letters (greater than F), spaces, minus signs, carriage returns, control characters, etc. (Hexadecimal numerics are: 0,1,2,3,4,5,6,7,8,9,A,B,C,D,E,F).

* Invalid data; treated as decimal number *one* because no $ preceded it and non-decimal digit followed it.

Table C.8: NUM and SNUM with Binary Data.

General (Bin. Data)	Characters Received							
	⊗	11	11⊗	%11	%11⊗	-%11⊗	⊗%11⊗	%101⊗
NUM	--	--	11*	--	11	11	11	101

⊗ Means any non-binary-numeric characters such as letters, spaces, minus signs, carriage returns, control characters, etc. (Binary numerics are: 0 and 1).

* Invalid data; treated as decimal number *eleven* because no % preceded it.

Conversion Formatters

BASIC Stamp 1 Schematic (Rev B)

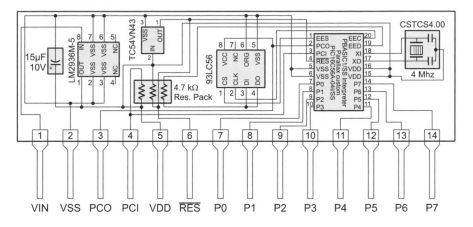

Notes:

The 15µF, 10V capacitor may be a 10-22µF, 6.3-16V tantalum capacitor.

The 93LC56 EEPROM may be a 93LC56A, 93LC66 or 93LC66A.

The 4 MHz resonator is not polarity sensitive and the middle pin can be connected to either VDD or VSS.

The PBASIC/SS Interpreter chip may be a commercial PIC16C56A-04/SS or an industrial PIC16C56A-04I/SS

BASIC Stamp 2 Schematic (Rev G)

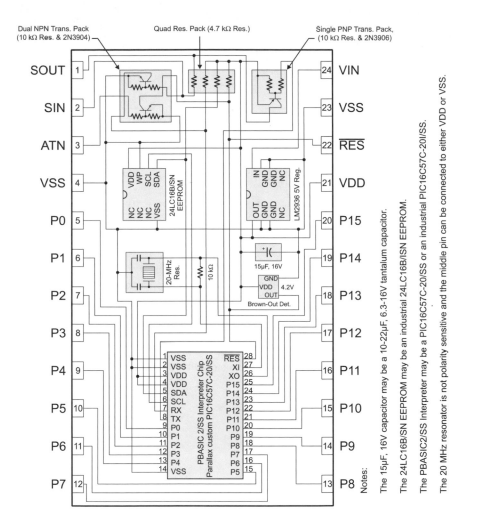

Dual NPN Trans. Pack
(10 kΩ Res. & 2N3904)

Quad Res. Pack (4.7 kΩ Res.)

Single PNP Trans. Pack,
(10 kΩ Res. & 2N3906)

The 15µF, 16V capacitor may be a 10-22µF, 6.3-16V tantalum capacitor.

The 24LC16B/SN EEPROM may be an industrial 24LC16B/ISN EEPROM.

The PBASIC2/SS Interpreter may be a PIC16C57C-20/SS or an industrial PIC16C57C-20I/SS.

The 20 MHz resonator is not polarity sensitive and the middle pin can be connected to either VDD or VSS.

Notes:

BASIC Stamp 2e Schematic (Rev B)

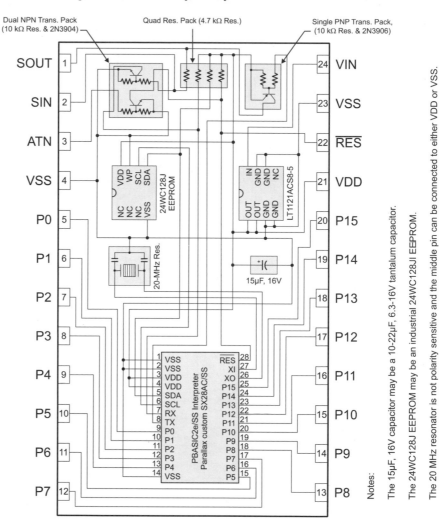

Dual NPN Trans. Pack
(10 kΩ Res. & 2N3904)

Quad Res. Pack (4.7 kΩ Res.)

Single PNP Trans. Pack,
(10 kΩ Res. & 2N3906)

Notes:

The 15µF, 16V capacitor may be a 10-22µF, 6.3-16V tantalum capacitor.

The 24WC128J EEPROM may be an industrial 24WC128JI EEPROM.

The 20 MHz resonator is not polarity sensitive and the middle pin can be connected to either VDD or VSS.

BASIC Stamp Schematics

BASIC Stamp 2sx Schematic (Rev E)

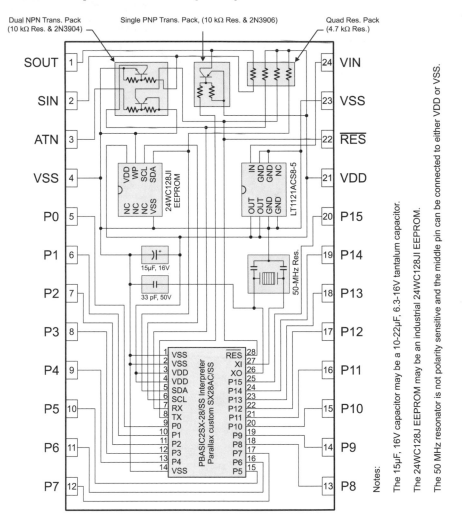

Dual NPN Trans. Pack (10 kΩ Res. & 2N3904)

Single PNP Trans. Pack, (10 kΩ Res. & 2N3906)

Quad Res. Pack (4.7 kΩ Res.)

Notes:

The 15µF, 16V capacitor may be a 10-22µF, 6.3-16V tantalum capacitor.

The 24WC128J EEPROM may be an industrial 24WC128JI EEPROM.

The 50 MHz resonator is not polarity sensitive and the middle pin can be connected to either VDD or VSS.

BASIC Stamp 2p24 Schematic (Rev C)

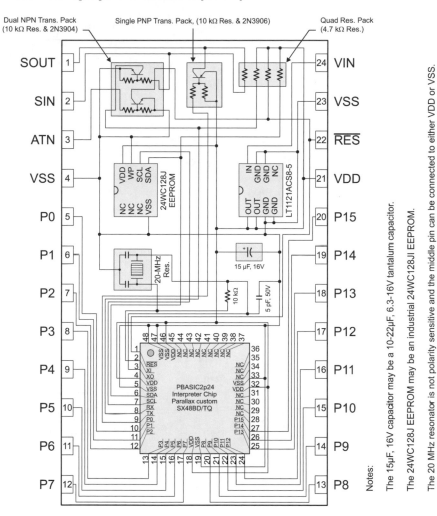

Dual NPN Trans. Pack (10 kΩ Res. & 2N3904)

Single PNP Trans. Pack, (10 kΩ Res. & 2N3906)

Quad Res. Pack (4.7 kΩ Res.)

Notes:

The 15µF, 16V capacitor may be a 10-22µF, 6.3-16V tantalum capacitor.

The 24WC128J EEPROM may be an industrial 24WC128JI EEPROM.

The 20 MHz resonator is not polarity sensitive and the middle pin can be connected to either VDD or VSS.

BASIC Stamp Schematics

BASIC Stamp 2p40 Schematic (Rev B)

Notes:

The 15µF, 16V capacitor may be a 10-22µF, 6.3-16V tantalum capacitor.

The 24WC128J EEPROM may be an industrial 24WC128JI EEPROM.

The 20 MHz resonator is not polarity sensitive and the middle pin can be connected to either VDD or VSS.

PC to BS2p40-IC Connection

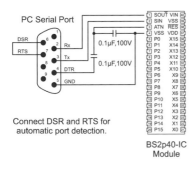

PC Serial Port

Connect DSR and RTS for automatic port detection.

BS2p40-IC Module

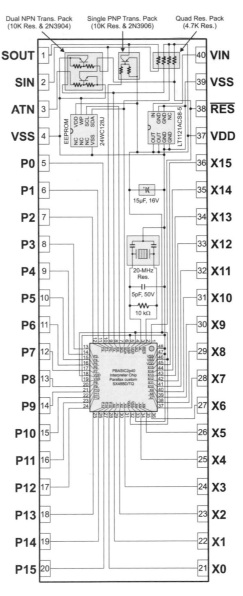

Dual NPN Trans. Pack (10K Res. & 2N3904)
Single PNP Trans. Pack (10K Res. & 2N3906)
Quad Res. Pack (4.7K Res.)

SOUT	1	40	VIN
SIN	2	39	VSS
ATN	3	38	RES
VSS	4	37	VDD
P0	5	36	X15
P1	6	35	X14
P2	7	34	X13
P3	8	33	X12
P4	9	32	X11
P5	10	31	X10
P6	11	30	X9
P7	12	29	X8
P8	13	28	X7
P9	14	27	X6
P10	15	26	X5
P11	16	25	X4
P12	17	24	X3
P13	18	23	X2
P14	19	22	X1
P15	20	21	X0

15µF, 16V

20-MHz Res.

5pF, 50V

10 kΩ

BASIC Stamp 2pe Schematic (Rev B)

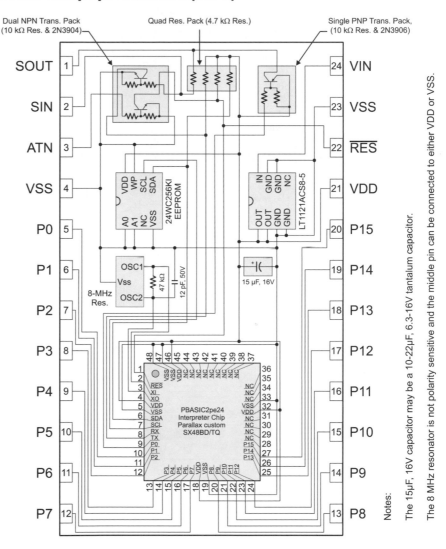

Dual NPN Trans. Pack
(10 kΩ Res. & 2N3904)

Quad Res. Pack (4.7 kΩ Res.)

Single PNP Trans. Pack,
(10 kΩ Res. & 2N3906)

Notes:

The 15µF, 16V capacitor may be a 10-22µF, 6.3-16V tantalum capacitor.

The 8 MHz resonator is not polarity sensitive and the middle pin can be connected to either VDD or VSS.

BASIC Stamp Schematics

BASIC Stamp 2px Schematic (Rev A)

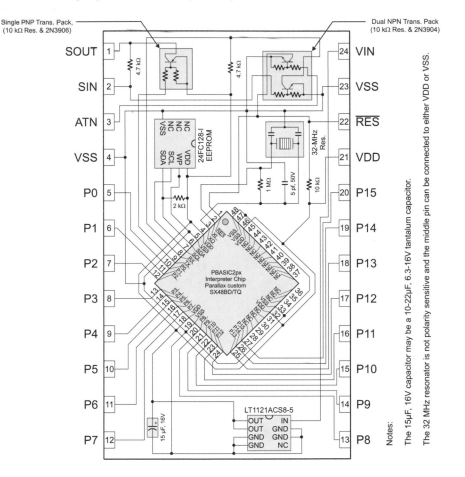

Index

Index

Index

Index

Index

— S —

Index

Index

and Identify Function, 48